The United Nations and the Principles of International Law

Essays in memory of Michael Akehurst

Since the fall of communism and the appearance of a new world order, it is hoped that the United Nations will become the principal organisation for the regulation of relations between states as well as for the settlement of conflict. The recent crisis over Iraq and the continuing bloodshed in the former Yugoslavia have ensured a higher profile for the United Nations, but have at the same time placed great pressure on the UN to resolve conflict and organise relations between states in a manner acceptable to the international community.

The essays collected in this volume re-examine the Declaration of Principles of International Law Governing Friendly Relations between States. The Declaration embodies the fundamental values of the international system and is the nearest thing that states have to an international constitution. The great changes in the international system since 1989 hold out the prospect for the reinvigoration of the Charter, perhaps for a new system of international legal relations, and make the reconsideration of the Declaration in these essays particularly timely.

This collection, produced in conjunction with the International Law Group, should prove particularly useful to both undergraduate and postgraduate students of international law, since the essays provide comprehensive coverage of the fundamental principles of contemporary international law by leading scholars in the field.

Vaughan Lowe is a Fellow of Corpus Christi College, Cambridge.
Colin Warbrick is a Senior Lecturer in the Law Department, Durham University.

The United Nations and the Principles of International Law

Essays in memory of Michael Akehurst

Edited by Vaughan Lowe and Colin Warbrick

ROUTLEDGE

London and New York

First published 1994
by Routledge
11 New Fetter Lane, London EC4P 4EE

Reprinted 1999

Simultaneously published in the USA and Canada
by Routledge
29 West 35th Street, New York, NY 10001

Routledge is an imprint of the Taylor & Francis Group

Typeset in Times by Intype, London

Printed and bound in Great Britain by
T.J.I. Digital, Padstow, Cornwall

Printed on acid-free paper

British Library Cataloguing in Publication Data
A catalogue record for this book is available from the British Library

Library of Congress Cataloging in Publication Data

ISBN 0–415–08441–5

Contents

Contributors vii
Foreword ix

1 **The significance of the Friendly Relations Declaration** 1
Sir Ian Sinclair

2 **The principle of non-use of force** 33
Christine Gray

3 **The principle of peaceful settlement of disputes** 49
J. G. Merrills

4 **The principle of non-intervention: use of force** 66
Vaughan Lowe

5 **The principle of non-intervention: human rights** 85
Dominic McGoldrick

6 **The principle of co-operation: the environment** 120
Alan E. Boyle

7 **The principle of co-operation: terrorism** 137
David Freestone

8 **The principle of co-operation: United Nations peacekeeping** 160
Alan James

9 **The principle of self-determination** 175
Patrick Thornberry

10 **The principle of sovereign equality** 204
Colin Warbrick

11 **The principle of good faith** 230
Gillian White

Appendix: Declaration on Principles of International Law concerning Friendly Relations and Co-operation among States in accordance with the Charter of the United Nations 256

Index 264

Contributors

Alan Boyle is Senior Lecturer in Law in Queen Mary and Westfield College in the University of London.

David Freestone is Professor of International Law in the University of Hull.

Christine Gray is a Lecturer in the University of Oxford and fellow of St Hilda's College, Oxford.

Alan James is Research Professor of International Relations in the University of Keele.

Vaughan Lowe is a Lecturer in the University of Cambridge and Fellow and Director of Studies in Law in Corpus Christi College, Cambridge.

Dominic McGoldrick is a Lecturer in the University of Liverpool.

John Merrills is Professor of International Law in the University of Sheffield.

Sir Ian Sinclair is a barrister and member of the Institute of International Law and a former Legal Adviser to the Foreign and Commonwealth Office.

Patrick Thornberry is Senior Lecturer in Law in the University of Keele.

Colin Warbrick is Senior Lecturer in Law in the University of Durham

Gillian White is Professor Emeritus of International Law in the University of Manchester.

Foreword

Michael Akehurst (1940–89)

Michael Akehurst was one of the most gifted international lawyers of his generation. His textbook, *A Modern Introduction to International Law*, which has been translated into Spanish, Portuguese and Japanese, remains one of the most succinct and readable introductions to the subject, and was designed to appeal to an audience much wider than that of professional lawyers. The need to bridge the gap between legal theory and the less tidy world of practical politics informed all of Michael's writings, and perhaps owes something to the days which he spent early in his career with UNRWA in Beirut. None the less, he was a lawyer of consummate technical skill. His book on *The Law Governing Employment in International Organisations* (1967) remains a standard work of reference, and his many articles in the *British Yearbook of International Law* include some of the finest analyses of topics as diverse as jurisdiction, the nature of customary international law, and reprisals.

As a person, Michael could be difficult, especially for his colleagues. He did not suffer fools gladly, and had more of a gift for trenchancy than diplomacy in his language. But as a teacher he showed endless patience in the supervision of his students. A private, and in some ways a lonely man, his life came to a tragically premature end. But he leaves behind him a body of work which will be a permanent testimony to his outstanding abilities, and a degree of affection and admiration which, sadly, he would probably not have expected. This volume of essays is a tribute to his memory, offered as a mark of respect by some of those who benefited most directly from their acquaintance with this man of exceptional talent.

1 The significance of the Friendly Relations Declaration

Sir Ian Sinclair

Michael Akehurst, to whose memory this volume of essays is dedicated, devoted several substantial articles to the problem of the sources of international law, and particularly the role of custom. One need only mention in this context his stimulating articles on 'Custom as a source of international law' and 'The hierarchy of the sources of international law'.[1] It is therefore particularly appropriate that the focus of this series of articles by some of his former friends and colleagues should be on what has popularly come to be known as the Friendly Relations Declaration,[2] an instrument which, although adopted by the United Nations General Assembly well over twenty years ago, has had a continuing impact and influence on the subsequent development of international law.

First let me preface my remarks by making a declaration of interest. I served as legal counsellor to the United Kingdom Mission to the United Nations in New York between the years 1964 and 1967, and indeed as United Kingdom representative to successive sessions of the Special Committee on Friendly Relations between 1964 and 1970 (omitting only the 1969 session). Thus, I was intimately involved in all stages of the elaboration of the Friendly Relations Declaration. In the present context, this has both advantages and disadvantages. The advantages stem primarily from the insight which this experience gives me as to the object and purpose sought to be achieved through the adoption of the Friendly Relations Declaration. The disadvantages stem from the consideration that this direct involvement in the formulation of the Declaration may blind me to the broader perspective from which the Declaration should be viewed. Whatever may be the balance of advantage and disadvantage, I must in any event acknowledge that, for me, it is a challenging, if occasionally chastening, experience to attempt a reassessment today of the significance of an instrument adopted as long ago as 1970.

One of the most heartening features of such a reassessment must be that it is now possible to analyse the content of the Declaration without having to take too closely into account the deep ideological divisions between West and East which were such a feature of the 1960s. It is, however, necessary to bear in mind the general international situation during the period in which the Declaration was being negotiated, since that provides the essential background against which the content of the Declaration must be assessed. In the late 1950s and early 1960s, an initiative was taken by Soviet and other Eastern European international lawyers to place on the agenda of selected non-governmental international organisations (notably, the International Law Association) items concerning the legal aspects of 'peaceful coexistence', a concept which bore the hallmarks of the Soviet ideology of the time.[3] The debates on the legal aspects of 'peaceful coexistence' within the framework of the International Law Association were confused and contradictory. The proponents of the notion that an attempt should be made to codify the legal principles of 'peaceful coexistence' did not exactly help their cause by producing varying lists of assorted legal principles expressed at such a level of abstraction and generality as to be open to criticism, if not indeed to ridicule. Many Western international lawyers were highly sceptical of the value of this initiative, viewing with particular suspicion what they saw as the propaganda origins of the enterprise. On the other hand, many international lawyers from the Third World were attracted by the idea of seeking to articulate a 'new' international law which, in their view, it was necessary for the international community to construct in the wake of the advent of large numbers of newly independent states resulting from the process of decolonisation.

Matters took a new and more constructive turn when the issue surfaced in the Sixth (Legal) Committee of the UN General Assembly in 1960/1 in the context of a general debate on future work in the progressive development and codification of international law. At this time, the Sixth Committee was practically moribund. The only regular item of substance on its agenda was the annual Report of the International Law Commission, a subordinate body of distinguished legal experts elected in their personal capacity (and therefore independent of governments) to prepare proposals for the progressive development and codification of international law. The Commission was active enough in all conscience; it had by this time seen its proposals for the progressive development and codification of the law of the sea converted into the four Geneva conventions of 1958, and it was about to see (in 1961 and 1963 respectively) its draft articles on diplomatic law transformed into the Vienna Convention on Diplomatic Relations and the Vienna Convention on Consular Relations. The Commission also had much in the way of unfinished business arising out of its long-term programme of work. By way of contrast, the Sixth Committee itself was seriously underemployed; and the arrival in its midst of the representatives of a number of newly independent states admitted to the United Nations in 1960 meant that there was growing support for exploring new methods of promoting the progressive development and codification of international law.

The resumed general debate in the Sixth Committee in 1962 served to crystallise opinion. There gradually emerged the beginnings of a consensus among delegations that a detailed study could be undertaken, within the framework of the General Assembly itself, of certain selected principles of international law embodied in the UN Charter, described as 'the principles of international law concerning friendly relations and co-operation among States in accordance with the Charter'. Seven of these principles were selected for study, notably:

1 the principle that States shall refrain in their international relations from the threat or use of force against the territorial integrity or political independence of any State, or in any other manner inconsistent with the purpose of the United Nations;
2 the principle that States shall settle their international disputes by peaceful means in such a manner that international peace and security and justice are not endangered;
3 the duty not to intervene in matters within the domestic jurisdiction of any State, in accordance with the Charter;
4 the duty of States to co-operate with one another in accordance with the Charter;
5 the principle of equal rights and self-determination of peoples;
6 the principle of sovereign equality of States;
7 the principle that States shall fulfil in good faith the obligations assumed by them in accordance with the Charter.[4]

It has been correctly pointed out that the agreement recorded in General Assembly Resolution 1815(XVII) to describe the legal principles in this way 'constituted a milestone in the further development of the entire action'.[5] As I have indicated elsewhere:

> In the first place, the cumbersome title chosen for the seven principles thus identified reflected a desire on the part of the Sixth Committee to move from propaganda to substance. It was no longer sufficient to designate certain ambiguous and contradictory principles as principles of 'peaceful coexistence' and to claim that these represented the 'new' international law. In the second place, the title eventually selected for the item, and indeed the wording of the seven principles chosen for study, derived in very large measure from the language of Article 2 of the Charter. The study was accordingly to be a study of seven *Charter* principles. It was not to be a study at large, which would quickly lose itself in abstractions and generalities. It was rather to be an attempt to distil, from the practice of States and of the United Nations and other international organisations, whether universal or regional, the legal content of these seven principles built into the Charter system.[6]

Paragraph 3 of General Assembly Resolution 1815(XVII) in addition decided to place an item entitled 'Consideration of principles of international law concerning friendly relations and co-operation among States in accordance with the Charter of the United Nations' on the provisional agenda of its eighteenth (1963) session, in order to study four of the principles. This debate duly took place, and it resulted in the adoption of General Assembly Resolution 1966(XVIII) of 16 December 1963, which decided '*inter alia*' to establish an intersessional Special Committee on Principles of International Law concerning Friendly Relations and Co-operation among States which was instructed to 'draw up a report containing, for the purpose of the progressive development and codification of the four principles[7] so as to secure their more effective application, the conclusions of its study and its recommendations'. The president of the General Assembly duly appointed, on the basis of the principle of equitable geographical distribution and the requirement that the principal legal systems of the world should be represented, twenty-seven member states to serve on the Special Committee which met in Mexico City between 27 August and 2 October 1964.

It is unnecessary to give here a blow-by-blow account of the deliberations of the six successive intersessional meetings of the Special Committee (reconstituted in 1965 by the addition of four other member States) held in Mexico City (1964), New York (1966), Geneva (1967), New York (1968 and 1969) and Geneva (1970). The mandate of the Special Committee was enlarged in 1965 to include consideration of the three remaining principles,[8] the Special Committee being then requested 'to submit a comprehensive report on the seven principles . . . including its conclusions and recommendations, with a view to enabling the General Assembly to adopt a declaration containing an enunciation of these principles'.[9] Interested outside observers have published accounts of the first (Mexico City) session of the Special Committee in 1964.[10] Others have written on the deliberations of the second (New York) session of the Special Committee in 1966.[11] Others again, during the late 1960s, wrote about the more general aspects of this special exercise in the field of progressive development and codification of international law.[12]

Perhaps of greater significance in this context than these relatively ephemeral accounts of the early stages of the 'Friendly Relations exercise' (to give it its colloquial title) are the more considered analyses produced after the adoption of the Declaration by a number of international lawyers, several of whom had participated in the work by the Special Committee. These naturally reflect the views of their authors. Pride of place among these analyses must be given to the comprehensive course of lectures delivered by Professor Arangio-Ruiz (who had been the Italian representative at all sessions of the Special Committee) to the Hague Academy of International Law in 1973.[13] Milan Sahovic (who had been the Yugoslav representative at all sessions of the Special Committee) also delivered a course of lectures to the Hague Academy in 1973 on the same topic,[14] having previously edited a book embodying a series of studies by Yugoslav jurists on the seven principles.[15] Rosenstock (one of the United States' participants in the work of the Special Committee) produced his own analysis in 1971;[16] and the present author published his views in an article published in 1975 (though internal evidence shows that it was prepared in 1971/2).[17]

These varying analyses by some of the participants in the Friendly Relations exercise reveal a wide spread of views as to the significance of the Friendly Relations Declaration. The most critical and sceptical commentator is undoubtedly Arangio-Ruiz. He distrusts intensely the procedures by which the Special Committee sought to achieve consensus texts on each of the seven principles. He forthrightly condemns the emphasis which the Special Committee put on the formulation of norms of conduct for states without attempting to reinforce the institutions of the United Nations called upon in practice to assess the extent to which states have adhered to these norms in particular cases. He is equally critical of the failure of the Special Committee to resolve points of disagreement among its members, and to disguise these points of disagreement by formulating general texts capable of a variety of interpretations in order to paper over the differences. His pronounced scepticism as to the value of the Friendly Relations Declaration is perhaps best illustrated by the following citation:

> Reverting to the Declaration as a whole, the vagueness of its formulations, the scarcity of progressive content, and the lack of an adequate co-ordination between conflicting or partially conflicting principles, do not seem to recommend it as the rich and reliable source of legal policies (or *de lege ferenda* policies *tout court*) one should have expected to emerge from about seven years of a work aimed at setting a *landmark* in the progressive development and codification of international law.[18]

Indeed, Arangio-Ruiz expresses the belief that the Declaration would be invoked in the future primarily for propaganda purposes:

> Under such circumstances, the declaration seems bound to remain, at least for some time, little more than an object of re-citation on the part of the same organ from which it emanates, and a relatively organic assembly of materials of lego-diplomatic jousting among States within and without the United Nations.[19]

In stark contrast to this splenetic view of the significance of the Declaration are the laudatory observations of Sahovic. In his introduction to the book entitled *Principles of International Law concerning Friendly Relations and Co-operation*, Sahovic writes:

> We should only add that the results of the progressive development and codification of the seven selected legal principles of coexistence,

> adopted within the framework of the Declaration . . . should be viewed as an outstanding contribution to the strengthening of international legality. Its significance may only grow as time goes on and as international law becomes more and more efficient as a comprehensive system of legal rules governing the relations between States and the life of the international community as a whole.[20]

In similar vein is the very positive assessment made by Sahovic in his course of lectures at The Hague in 1972:

> Approvée à l'unanimité après une activité intense de tous les membres de l'organisation mondiale, la Declaration et l'expérience des travaux de la Sixième Commission et du Comité speciale sont dignes d'être traités comme un des plus grands succès dans la voie du développement progressif et de la codification du droit international après la deuxième guerre mondiale.[21]

Between these extremes of disapprobation and approbation are situated the views of other participants in the Friendly Relations exercise. Rosenstock echoes some of the criticisms voiced by Arangio-Ruiz:

> The text of the Declaration on Friendly Relations is incomplete if viewed as a blueprint for world order. Too many issues are not covered: too many of those that are covered are dealt with in a vague manner. Moreover, there is room for debate as to the nature of the binding force of the Declaration among States. Finally, the text is largely oriented toward the preservation and protection of state sovereignty rather than the development of new norms and new mechanisms more suited to the increasingly interdependent world of today and the future. It speaks of international co-operation but fails to deal meaningfully with such matters as increasing the mechanisms of the United Nations for peacekeeping and the peaceful settlement of disputes.[22]

But these criticisms of some of the imperfections of the Declaration are counterbalanced by Rosenstock's more positive remarks:

> In spite of these *caveats*, the text represents a very substantial contribution to clarification of the key concepts of international law involved – so much so that a significant number of States pointed to the provisions in the course of a recent debate in the United Nations as an example of the type of evolution which at this stage better served the needs of the international community than a formal Charter review.[23]

The assessment made by the present author in 1975 of the significance of the Declaration is similarly ambivalent. He characterises the Declaration as representing 'an endeavour to state, in terms which command the general consent of the overwhelming majority of States members of the international community, the essential legal content of seven fundamental principles embodied in the Charter of the United Nations.'[24] This assessment points to the shortcomings of the Declaration and seeks to explain them:

> [The Declaration] represents on many points . . . an accommodation between conflicting and strongly-held views, between the exigencies of the *lex lata* and the pressures for recognition of an emerging *lex ferenda* and, above all, between the antinomies of stability and change. As such, it has all the imperfections which a document of this nature might be expected to have. . . . It is also true that there are *lacunae* in the Declaration and that it embodies many inelegancies and inconsistencies of wording and some quite deliberate ambiguities.[25]

While admitting that the Declaration is considerably less than perfect, he none the less maintains that, given the polarities of position adopted by different delegations, given the fact that any abstract formulation of the legal content of the principles was bound to have repercussions on existing international tensions and disputes, given the opposed interpretations of Charter provisions and given the conflicting interests, 'the fact that it was possible eventually to achieve such a large area of agreement on the legal content of the seven principles (however imperfectly expressed) is a tribute to the tenacity displayed in pursuing the original objective'.[26]

More generally, he is cautious as to the future significance of the Declaration:

> The Declaration nevertheless has a certain real value and significance. It is not intended to be, and it is not, *jus cogens*; but it does set certain standards of international conduct against which the activities of States may in future be judged. Here of course is the crux of the matter. It is the extent to which the Declaration will be observed which will determine its true value. . . . Its significance for the future remains to be seen; but there can be little doubt that it represents a strenuous effort to find as much common ground as possible between states representing the various regional and ideological groups within the United Nations on a whole series of sorely contested issues of international law.[27]

Many other publicists have focused their attention on the Friendly Relations Declaration, principally in the context of discussing the role of law-declaring resolutions of the General Assembly as a potential source of customary international law. Some have been highly critical of particular formulations in the Declaration. For example, Fitzmaurice, in his luminous and elegiac report to the centenary session of the Institut de Droit International in 1973, focuses his attention on the principle of self-determination as articulated in the Declaration. He regards the notion of a legal 'right' of self-determination as a 'nonsense', posing the question whether an as yet juridically non-existent entity (a 'people') can be the possessor of a legal right.[28] More significantly, he draws attention to the penultimate (safeguard) clause in the statement of the principle of self-determination, commenting:

> It is hardly necessary to point out the extreme circularity and latent discriminatoriness of [this paragraph], and the virtual impossibility of applying it, since it assumes the existence of the very circumstances that would be in issue if a concrete case arose, and hardly contains a word or a phrase that could not plausibly be given more than one meaning.[29]

On the more general issue, Fitzmaurice clearly favours the 'classical' method of codification involving the preparation of proposals by the International Law Commission, their submission to governments for comment, their revision in the light of comments received, and the forwarding of the finished product to the General Assembly, followed by their reference, where appropriate, to a diplomatic conference as the basic text for consideration and conclusion in the form of a codification convention.[30] But he denies any legislative or quasi-legislative effect to General Assembly resolutions as such, although acknowledging that: 'they are capable, like many other things, of *contributing* to the formation of rules of *lex communis*, and can in that sense constitute material influencing the content of the law, but not creating it.'[31]

Fitzmaurice has evident sympathy with the view propounded by Falk that, if international society is to function effectively, it requires a limited legislative authority, at minimum, to translate an overwhelming consensus among states into rules of order and norms of obligation despite the opposition of one or more sovereign states.[32] Indeed, this serves as the keynote for his imaginative (but cumbersome) scheme for the establishment of a 'Consortium of jurists', operating within the framework of a standing 'College of the United Nations' designed to impart legislative authority to selected General Assembly resolutions of a law-declaring or law-generating character.[33]

Jimènez de Arechaga takes a more positive view of the value of the Friendly Relations Declaration, considering it as declaratory of existing rules of international law:

> This Resolution does not purport to amend the Charter, but to clarify the basic legal principles contained in Article 2.
>
> Adopted in these terms and without a dissenting vote, it constitutes an authoritative expression of the views held by the totality of the parties to the Charter as to these basic principles and certain corollaries resulting from them. In the light of these circumstances, it seems difficult to deny the legal weight and authority of the Declaration both as a resolution recognising what the Members themselves believe

constitute existing rules of customary law and as an interpretation of the Charter by the subsequent agreement and the subsequent practice of all its members.[34]

Schachter focuses his attention on the general issue of law-declaring resolutions and takes a slightly more forward position than Fitzmaurice:

> Few issues of international law have aroused as much controversy as that engendered by resolutions and declarations of the General Assembly which appear to express principles and rules of law. . . . It is of course true that such resolutions are not a formal source of law within the explicit categories of Article 38(1) of the Statute of the ICJ. It is also clear that under the United Nations Charter the General Assembly does not have the legal power to make law or to adopt binding decisions except for certain organizational matters. . . . .Yet few would deny that General Assembly resolutions have had a formative influence in the development of international law in matters of considerable importance to national states.[35]

At a slightly later stage, Schachter develops his view as to the legal character and significance of law-declaring resolutions which he describes as being neither in form nor intent recommendatory; and he points to the fact that, as early as its first session in 1946, the General Assembly had adopted the Nuremberg principles and declared genocide to be a crime under international law without any question being raised as to its power to do so. More generally, he takes the view that such resolutions can be treated as *evidence* for the propositions of law which they may embody:

> It still remains important to clarify the legal force of the declaration or determination of law. Much of the debate has focused on the choice between two polar categories: 'binding' and 'hortatory' (i.e. without legal force *et al.*). That categorization, however clear it may appear, seems much less appropriate than treating the law-declaring resolutions as evidence for the asserted proposition of law. This would be compatible with the basic principle that such resolutions are not binding in the sense that treaties or judicial judgments are legally binding on the parties. However, it recognises that interpretations and declarations of law by the Assembly are official expressions by the governments concerned and consequently are relevant and entitled to be given weight in determinations of the law in question. By characterising them as 'evidentiary' we invite an assessment of the pertinent data. We would assess the degree and character of support in the United Nations and the relation, if any, of the asserted rule to an underlying Charter or customary law principle. Moreover, relevant State practice and *opinio juris* manifested outside of the United Nations would be considered.[36]

As to the Friendly Relations Declaration in particular, Schachter takes a view which is practically indistinguishable from that of Jimènez de Arechaga:

> The law-declaring resolutions that construed and 'concretized' the principles of the Charter – whether as general rules or in regard to particular cases – may be regarded as authentic interpretation by the parties of their existing treaty obligations. To the extent that they were interpretation, and agreed by all the Member States, they fitted comfortably into an established source of law. A prominent example cited by governments and lawyers is the [Friendly Relations Declaration] adopted by consensus . . . in 1970.[37]

By way of contrast, Virally denies that the Friendly Relations Declaration can be considered an authentic interpretation of the Charter principles which it seeks to elaborate:

> Fréquemment, des résolutions se rattachent expressément au texte d'un traité, notammement de la charte constitutive de l'organisation, et ont pour objet d'énoncer les conséquences juridiques qui en découlent. Leur propos est donc de donner une interprétation autorisée du traité considéré. Ce fut le cas, par example de la résolution 2625. . . .
>
> Une telle interprétation ne peut être considérée comme authentique, au sens propre de la terme, comme le serait un accord interprétatif d'un traité, conclu entre toutes les parties. Elle n'en présente pas moins une grande autorité, surtout si elle a été approuvée à une trés large majorité ou par consensus (*a fortiori* si elle est unanime). Les Etats membres qui l'ont acceptée pourraient difficilement la contester par la suite sans manquer à la bonne foi. Et cela reste vrai même si la résolution en question, sous couleur d'interprétation, développe et compléte les dispositions auxquelles elle se réfère, ce qui est habituellement le cas.[38]

Virally distinguishes the Friendly Relations Declaration from other declarations of principles adopted by the General Assembly on new subjects such as outer space and the legal regime of the deep sea-bed. The latter type of declaration he regards as an important step in a difficult negotiation leading to a treaty, the declaration itself recording general agreement on the essential principles to be taken into account in the treaty negotiations. [39]

Thirlway takes a very reserved and cautious attitude towards the legal effect of law-declaring or potentially law-making resolutions of the General Assembly. He starts from the basic (and relatively non-controversial) premise that the requirements for the formation of a rule of customary law are (a) a general practice of states accepted as law and (b) the *opinio juris*. He is strongly critical of the view advanced by Asamoah[40] and Cheng[41] that resolutions of the General Assembly may by themselves constitute state practice. But he acknowledges that they may, particularly if adopted by unanimity or consensus, reflect the *opinio juris* of states:

> There would appear to be no objection of theory to the assertion that a General Assembly resolution may be evidence of the *opinio juris* with regard to a practice of which there is, apart from the resolution itself, adequate evidence of usage. It is in this way, and probably only in this way, that weight can be attached to the resolution itself, rather than to the multiple consents involved in its adoption by States; if a resolution stating or declaring the state of the law on a given subject is adopted by a sufficient majority to be regarded as sufficiently representative, and provided the majority does not exclude the States most directly concerned, then it will probably be impossible to challenge the authority of the rules so stated on the ground that the *opinio juris* is lacking or unproved. This however presupposes a sufficient body of State practice for the usage element of the alleged custom to be established without reference to the resolution.[42]

It is in the context of lack or insufficiency of state practice that Thirlway attacks the view that the Declaration of Legal Principles governing the Activities of State in the Exploration and Use of Outer Space, adopted by the General Assembly in 1963, constitutes a codification of the legal rules governing the matter.[43]

A number of commentators have drawn attention in recent years to the enormous variety and range of potentially norm-creating provisions contained in instruments which cannot be characterised, strictly speaking, as international agreements creative of enforceable rights and duties. This is the whole problem of so-called 'soft' law. Baxter, in one of his last contributions to the science of international law, concentrated on this phenomenon. He examines, *inter alia*, treaty provisions amounting to no more than *pacta de contrahendo*, and international 'arrangements' which have not been treated by the parties as amounting to international agreements in the strict sense, such as the Helsinki Final Act, the Stockholm Declaration (of 1972) on the Human Environment, and various 'codes of conduct' or voluntary guidelines adopted within the framework of international organisations. He concludes:

> What I have said about the instruments to which States subscribe – treaties, declarations, statements of policy, final acts, resolutions of international organisations, and other forms of expression of agreement – will, I hope, have persuaded the reader that it is excessively simplistic to divide written norms into those that are binding and those that are not. Provisions of treaties may create little or no obligations, although inserted in a form of instrument which presumptively creates rights and duties, while, on the other hand, instruments of lesser dignity may influence or control the conduct of States and individuals

> to a certain degree, even though their norms are not technically binding.[44]

In discussing resolutions of the General Assembly, Baxter (rightly) mentions those General Assembly resolutions 'which serve as way-stations on the road to the conclusion of a treaty', such as the Universal Declaration of Human Rights and the Declaration of Legal Principles governing the Activities of States in the Exploration and Use of Outer Space, but he makes no specific reference to the Friendly Relations Declaration.[45] However, referring to norms of 'soft' law in general, he concludes, *inter alia*:

> The norm will establish the legal framework within which the dispute about its application may be resolved. It will establish presumptions, indicate the prevailing trend of opinion, provide a guiding principle which may have a certain inherent appeal for the parties, and channel negotiation and settlement into legal and orderly paths.[46]

Sir Robert Jennings is another who is somewhat troubled by the incoherence of some of the modern trends and techniques utilised in the formulation of norms of conduct, and the legal uncertainty created thereby. He is particularly concerned about the consequences of this incoherence for the constituent elements of customary law, and, in particular, the *opinio juris*:

> But the difficulty today is now the embarrassingly rich and varied range of evidence of *opinio juris*, not only in the digests of so-called State practice, but also in the almost daily spate of material, more or less with legal content, emanating from one more or less authoritive body or another; and, of course, the fact that this great flood of material is likely to show dispute and contention about what the *opinio juris* should be. How is one to distil an *opinio juris* from a welter of ostensibly authoritative but mutually incompatible positions?[47]

Sir Robert hesitates to answer his own question. He does not think it appropriate to try to force these new trends and techniques into one or other of the sources of international law identified in Article 38 of the International Court of Justice Statute. He simply concludes with the tentative suggestion:

> So perhaps the time has come to recognize that what we still quaintly call custom includes some custom certainly, but also many other kinds of law, of which neither the method of the making of it, nor yet the tests of its validity, have anything much to do with custom.[48]

More controversially, he poses the following issue:

> Perhaps it is time to face squarely the fact that the orthodox tests of custom – practice and *opinio juris* – are often not only inadequate but

> even irrelevant for the identification of much new law today. And the reason is not far to seek: much of this new law is not custom at all, and does not even resemble custom. It is recent, it is innovatory, it involves topical policy decisions, and it is often the focus of contention. Anything less like custom in the ordinary meaning of that term it would be difficult to imagine.[49]

The passages cited from these contributions by Baxter and Jennings do, of course, raise issues going far beyond the scope of this article, and it is simply not possible to address those issues in any depth. The concerns voiced are none the less relevant to an assessment of the legal effect of General Assembly declarations in general, and of the Friendly Relations Declaration in particular, and of the interaction between the content of such declarations and the constituent elements of customary law.

It would be discourteous in the extreme if no reference were made in this article to the views of Michael Akehurst on the relationship between General Assembly declarations articulating, or purporting to articulate, existing or emerging norms of general international law, on the one hand, and the constituent elements of customary law, on the other hand. Akehurst espouses a broad (some might argue overly broad) view of what is meant by state practice in the context of the formation of custom: 'It is submitted that State practice covers any act or statement by a State from which views can be inferred about international law'.[50]

Thirlway had earlier maintained, in the context of his analysis of General Assembly resolutions, that a distinction had to be drawn between 'the mere assertion *in abstracto* of the existence of a legal right or legal rule' (this *not* being, in his view, an act of state practice contributing to the formation of custom) and a statement made in the context of a specific dispute or potential dispute forming part of 'an accumulation of acts which are material or concrete in the sense that they are intended to have an immediate effect on the legal relationships of the State concerned'.[51] Thirlway had used this distinction to maintain that an assertion by a state representative *in abstracto* could not be constitutive of custom, but only confirmatory of it. Akehurst rejects this distinction as being unrealistic, and indeed goes further:

> An assertion that something ought to be the law is obviously not evidence that it is the law; indeed it may even be interpreted as evidence that it is not the law. Of course there is a danger that States may dress up claims for changes in the law as statements of existing law. But it is always open to other States to dispute such statements if they disagree with them. The making of such statements, coupled with the failure of other States to challenge them, may often be regarded as creating a new rule of customary law; the fact that the State making the statement knew that the statement did not reflect

> pre-existing law does not necessarily prevent the statement from giving rise to a new rule of customary law.[52]

Akehurst goes on to draw attention to the self-evident proposition that assertions made *in abstracto* concerning the content of existing law are sometimes found in resolutions passed by the representatives of states at meetings of international organisations, and that such resolutions are authority for the content of customary law only if they claim to be declaratory of existing law. He acknowledges that there is a problem of distinguishing, in the case of statements concerning the content of customary law *in abstracto*, between assertions of *lex lata* and *lex ferenda*, and he does not seek to disguise the problems which arise whenever one seeks to infer rules of customary law from state practice – how frequent, long, widespread and consistent must the practice be? What if different states accept differing rules of customary law? What is meant by *opinio juris*? But he still regards assertions about the content of customary law made by states *in abstracto* as constituting state practice.[53]

Blaine Sloan takes an even more forward position on the legal effect of law-declaring resolutions of the General Assembly. In an important and comprehensive article on General Assembly resolutions published in 1987,[54] he unreservedly adopts the position that 'General Assembly resolutions which are collective pronouncements of States must be considered a part of State practice';[55] but he later qualifies this proposition by acknowledging that 'it is still a further question whether a resolution or series of resolutions may in themselves be sufficient to constitute the state practice or usage necessary to satisfy the material element of customary international law.'[56] He argues that both the element of state practice and the element of *opinio juris* may be present in the same resolution:

> In the case of the General Assembly, the element of *opinio juris* may predominate in declaratory resolutions, while the element of practice may be more evident in resolutions dealing with specific incidents. Both elements may, however, be present in either type of resolution.[57]

Blaine Sloan goes much further than other publicists in suggesting that General Assembly resolutions may be on the way to becoming a new source of international law: 'It is the submission of this article that while an assumption of present legislative capacity may be over optimistic, the processes towards establishing a legislative function are more fully advanced than is generally recognized'.[58] This visionary approach is likely to remain no more than visionary. This is not to deny the influence or impact of General Assembly recommendations, particularly those of a law-declaring or law-developing nature, but it is to question a truly legislative rule for the General Assembly in the absence of Charter amendment, which, on this point, is extremely unlikely to be forthcoming, as even Blaine Sloan admits.[59] He takes the view that General Assembly declarations can somehow be distinguished from resolutions, but reaches a conclusion which does not differ all that much from the conclusion reached by other commentators:

> Where, however, there is an intent to declare law, whether customary, general principles or instant, spontaneous or new law, and the resolution is adopted by a unanimous or nearly unanimous vote or by genuine consensus, there is a presumption that the rules and principles embodied in the declaration are law. This presumption could only be overcome by evidence of substantial conflicting practice supported by an *opinio juris* contrary to that stated or implied in the resolution. If the declaration is adopted by a majority vote its evidentiary value is to be weighed in the light of all relevant factors. It would in any event be part of the material sources of customary law and would constitute an expression of *opinio juris*, or a lack of *opinio juris* for conflicting norms, of those States voting for the resolution.[60]

Many (including the present author) would of course query the proposition that a General Assembly declaration may be a material source of international law, while not denying that a state's vote in favour of such a declaration may constitute an expression of *opinio juris* as regards the norms articulated in that declaration. In this context, the present author would not regard an abstention as equivalent to a positive favourable vote.

This brief, and far from exhaustive, survey of doctrinal opinion on the significance of General Assembly declarations purporting to articulate principles of general international law demonstrates the varying opinions which can be, and are, held, as to the significance of such instruments. A much more comprehensive account of the differing views held is to be found in the three detailed reports prepared recently by Kryzysztof Skubiszewski for the Institut de Droit International on 'Resolutions of the General Assembly' having a normative function or objective.[61] The work of the Institut on this topic reveals continuing uncertainty about the status and legal effect of General Assembly declarations formulating general rules of international law *in abstracto*. This is reflected in the fact that the final resolution of the Institut does not specifically endorse or approve the conclusions of the Commission appointed to study the topic, although these conclusions are attached to the resolution. The conclusions themselves are expressed in suitably cautious and balanced terms. Conclusion 1 reaffirms the basic constitutional position under the UN Charter whereby the powers of the General Assembly are in principle limited to the making of non-binding recommendations:

> Although the Charter of the United Nations does not confer on the General Assembly the power to enact rules binding on States in their relations *inter se*, the Assembly may make recommendations

> contributing to the progressive development of international law, its consolidation and codification. This may be accomplished through a variety of resolutions.

Conclusion 3 seeks to categorise various types of resolutions:

> The recommendations referred to in Conclusion 1 include resolutions of the following types:
> (a) resolutions expressly formulating or reiterating general and abstract rules of conduct for States;
> (b) resolutions dealing with specific situations but assuming, expressly or impliedly, a general and abstract rule of conduct for States;
> (c) resolutions addressed to specific States, but assuming that the rule of conduct required of the State specifically named would be required of all States.
>
> Some of these resolutions constitute a restatement of the existing law (Conclusion 4), while others contribute to crystallising or generating new law (Conclusion 5). Other resolutions set forth standards relevant to the application or interpretation of law.
>
> Various provisions of a single resolution may have different functions.

It is worth interjecting here that the Friendly Relations Declaration clearly falls within category (a) of Conclusion 3, although the last sentence of Conclusion 3 is also applicable to the Friendly Relations Declaration which, on its face, embodies many formulations which are undoubtedly expressions of *lex lata*, alongside some formulations in the nature of *lex ferenda*.

Conclusions 4 and 5 distinguish between 'law-declaring' and 'law-developing' resolutions. Conclusion 4 states:

> A law-declaring resolution purports to state an existing rule of law. In particular, it may be a means for the determination or interpretation of international law, it may constitute evidence of international custom, or it may set forth general principles of law.

The Friendly Relations Declaration should almost certainly be characterised as a 'law-declaring' resolution as opposed to a 'law-developing' resolution, even if it can be seen to embody some elements put forward *de lege ferenda*. The fact that it is designated as a 'declaration' does not alter its legal character in terms of this analysis, since Conclusion 12 states:

> The legal status of resolutions designated as declarations is not different from that of other resolutions. Yet this particular form may emphasize the importance of the norms enunciated.

Conclusion 13, which can also be regarded as relevant to an assessment of the Friendly Relations Declaration, states:

> A law-declaring resolution, adopted without negative vote or abstention, creates a presumption that the resolution contains a correct statement of law. That presumption is subject to rebuttal.

Conclusions 19–21, under the rubric 'Particular problems of law-declaring resolutions', touch upon the evidentiary value of such resolutions. Conclusion 19 asserts that a law-declaring resolution:

> may serve as a supplementary means for the determination of a rule of international law, particularly where evidence of State practice or of *opinio juris* is not otherwise readily available.

Conclusion 20 postulates that a law-declaring resolution:

> may constitute evidence of customary law or of one of its ingredients (custom-creating practice, *opinio juris*), in particular when that has been the intention of the States in adopting the resolution or when the procedures applied have led to the elaboration of a statement of law.

Conclusion 21 simply states laconically that 'evidence supplied by a resolution is rebuttable'.

Further light is shed on the function and legal effect of law-declaring resolutions of the General Assembly, and particularly of the Friendly Relations Declaration, in the preliminary reports of Skubiszewski (rapporteur for the topic within the Institut). One of his most penetrating observations is the following:

> The nature of the rules embodied in a declaration should be distinguished from the nature of the act itself. The inclusion of rules into a recommendatory resolution (whether termed 'declaration' or not) does not automatically signify that they are equally recommendatory. The rules can already be part of international law. . . . The practice of the Assembly knows of several declarations which already recite well-established principles or other rules of international law.[62]

In this context, however, Skubiszewski has some cautionary observations to make about resolutions which certainly incorporate statements of law but which may also embody other elements, referring *inter alia* to the Friendly Relations Declaration (General Assembly Resolution 2625(xxv)):

> But there are resolutions in which elements of law are mixed with declarations of intention or recommendations, and political motives additionally blur the picture. . . . Resolution 2625 (xxv) recites and develops several principles of international law, and yet, according to

> some official statements, it contains 'guidelines' or 'markers and guidelines which might have a significant influence on the conduct of States'; the resolution is 'a code of good conduct' and 'a source of inspiration.' All this may be true on the plane of politics, but such statements are harmful, for they throw some doubt on the otherwise unquestionable legal status of the principles involved.[63]

All this points to the importance of analysing carefully the content of any resolution before determining whether any of the rules embodied in it (and, if so, which) are truly of a law-declaring character. In this context, the terminology utilised in the resolution will be highly relevant.

Skubiszewski's preliminary reports also discuss the much-debated question whether the act of voting in favour of a law-declaring resolution constitutes state practice constitutive of custom. It is clear that a significant majority of the Commission rejects this notion, some however being prepared to concede that it might constitute some *evidence* of state practice: 'The preponderant majority of the Commission reject the view that resolutions of the General Assembly can or do constitute State practice'.[64]

Skubiszewski himself gives an explanation for this reticence to accept that a positive vote in favour of a law-declaring resolution may constitute an act of state practice:

> When a State votes in favour of a resolution, it remains to be seen whether its conduct will conform to the resolution. The casting of a favourable vote is not *per se* conclusive of practice. Equally, when a state has voted against a resolution, its attitude cannot be regarded as automatically amounting to a protest whereby that State prevents, so far as it is concerned, the birth of a practice or, if the practice is already in existence, its relevance for that State's legal position. For the State may reject the resolution because of reasons which need not be connected with its custom-creating influence. In other words, the State may otherwise follow a course of action that would not be contrary to the pattern of behaviour laid down in the resolution, though there is a different cause which prompts it to vote against the specific resolution.[65]

The present author has made virtually the same point in the context of the law of treaties. Referring to the hint given by the International Court of Justice in its *Namibia* advisory opinion that adoption of an article at the Vienna Conference on the Law of Treaties without a dissenting vote may serve to establish that the rule embodied in that article is declaratory of customary law,[66] he observed:

> Certainly, the converse proposition does not hold good, if only for the reason that States represented at a codification conference may vote against a provision which is clearly declaratory of existing customary law for wholly unrelated reasons. A good example is afforded by

> Article 6 of the Convention providing that 'every State possesses capacity to conclude treaties'. This is unquestionably expressive of a customary rule. Yet Article 6 was finally adopted by the Vienna Conference by a divided vote of eighty-eight to five, with ten abstentions, the reason being that a controversial second paragraph dealing with the capacity of States members of a federal union to conclude treaties subject to certain conditions had previously been deleted.[67]

However, even if the act of voting in favour of a law-declaring resolution of the General Assembly is not to be taken as state practice *per se*, can it be said to reflect the *opinio juris* of the state concerned? Here again, views within the Commission were sharply divided, though most members seemed to envisage that a General Assembly law-declaring or even law-developing resolution can play a creative role in the emergence of custom. Skubiszewski takes what would seem to be a fairly traditional position on this aspect:

> A resolution can help to establish the *opinio juris* and, depending on circumstances, it can even be the decisive element in proving it. The transformation of practice into a legal rule operates through the conduct of States whereby they accept the legal nature of the rule engendered in their practice. This acceptance can find expression in an Assembly resolution. Besides having an exclusively declaratory function, i.e. stating an acceptance already in existence, the resolution can play a more creative role with regard to the *opinio juris*. In particular, when the acceptance of the rule as law is still doubtful, the resolution may contribute to the consolidation of the rule and remove the doubts. The *opinio juris* (as the composite element of custom) cannot precede custom-creating practice; by definition, it follows practice, or at least some part of it. The *opinio juris* results from State practice but, in the final stage of the process leading to the birth of customary law, it is also part of State practice. For the transformation of practice into a legal rule or rules operates through the conduct of States consisting in claiming a right and submitting to it as matter of obligation. In other words, the resolution is not a substitute for practice accompanied by *opinio juris*.[68]

This passage reflects the long-held view that the primary element in the formation of custom (i.e. the *material* element) is the accumulation of state acts asserting or repudiating claims with respect to concrete situations – what Thirlway refers to as acts 'which are material or concrete in the sense that they are intended to have an immediate effect on the legal relationships of the State concerned'.[69] This primary element has to be accompanied by the *opinio juris* (i.e. the *subjective* or *psychological* element). The *locus classicus* for this view of the matter is the statement by the International Court of Justice in the *North Sea Continental Shelf* case:

> Not only must the acts concerned amount to a settled practice, but they must also be such, or be carried out in such a way, as to be evidence of a belief that this practice is rendered obligatory by the existence of a rule of law requiring it. The need for such a belief, i.e., the existence of a subjective element, is implicit in the very notion of the *opinio juris sive necessitatis*. The States concerned must therefore feel that they are conforming to what amounts to a legal obligation.[70]

The logical difficulty to which this definition of the *opinio juris* gives rise is well-known: how can such a belief accompany the earliest acts constitutive of the practice, unless an unfounded belief is sufficient? Various solutions have been suggested. Indeed, some commentators, including Haggenmacher, have gone so far as to propose the abandonment of the *opinio juris* entirely as a required element in the formation of custom and base it exclusively upon the accumulation of practice of an appropriate kind.[71]

All this is by way of preliminary to a brief analysis of the legal effect attributed to the Friendly Relations Declaration in the judgment of the ICJ on the merits of the case of *Nicaragua* v. *United States*. The analysis will be brief since later essays in this volume will also touch upon this aspect.[72] It is, however, necessary to explain how the Court was moved to pray in aid the Friendly Relations Declaration as an element in its decision. The Vandenberg reservation to the United States' acceptance of the optional clause (generally referred to in the judgment as 'the multilateral treaty reservation') excluded from the jurisdiction of the Court: 'disputes arising under a multilateral treaty unless (1) all parties to the treaty affected by the decision are also parties to the case before the Court, or (2) the United States of America specially agrees to jurisdiction'. After protracted consideration, the Court eventually held, in its judgment on the merits, that, in the proceedings instituted by Nicaragua, El Salvador, a state party to the United Nations Charter and to the Charter of the Organization of American States, was a state which would be 'affected' by the Court's decision so that the Court was, by virtue of the multilateral treaty reservation, not permitted to entertain Nicaraguan claims asserting that the United States had violated Articles 2(4) of the UN Charter and Articles 18, 20 and 21 of the OAS Charter.[73] But Nicaragua had, in the alternative, pleaded that, by its actions, the United States had violated parallel norms of customary international law, and the Court had already, in its 1984 judgment on jurisdiction and admissibility, indicated that it could not dismiss the claims of Nicaragua under principles of customary and general international law, simply because such principles had been enshrined in the texts of conventions relied upon by Nicaragua:

The fact that the above-mentioned principles, recognised as such, have been codified or embodied in multilateral conventions does not mean that they cease to exist and to apply as principles of customary law, even as regards countries that are parties to such conventions. Principles such as those of the non-use of force, non-intervention, respect for the independence and territorial integrity of States, and the freedom of navigation, continue to be binding as part of customary international law, despite the operation of provisions of conventional law in which they have been incorporated.[74]

In its 1986 judgment on the merits, the Court confirmed, and elaborated upon, this view of the matter. It first of all determined that the rules of customary law capable of being invoked in the case did not have a content exactly identical with that of the treaty rules which could not be applied by virtue of the multilateral treaty reservation. But it went on to observe that, even if a treaty norm and a customary norm relevant to the dispute before it were to have exactly the same content, this would not be a reason for the Court to take the view that the operation of the treaty process must necessarily deprive the customary norm of its separate applicability:[75] 'It will therefore be clear that customary international law continues to exist and to apply, separately from international treaty law, even where the two categories of law have an identical content'.[76] The logic of this conclusion is, in principle, difficult to fault. But, in the particular case, and taking into account the admitted applicability of the multilateral treaty reservation to bar Nicaragua's claims asserting violations of the Charter and the OAS Charter, it was to lead the Court into uncharted waters and to expose it to criticism from several quarters: for the Court was thus obliged to determine the content of the customary law rules relating to the non-use of force and non-intervention without reference to the primary sources of law binding the parties to the dispute – namely, the two Charters.

In approaching this task, the Court acknowledged that it had to direct its attention to the actual practice and *opinio juris* of states. There then follows a curious passage in the Court's judgment:

In this respect the Court must not lose sight of the Charter of the United Nations and that of the OAS, notwithstanding the operation of the multilateral treaty reservation. Although the Court has no jurisdiction to determine whether the conduct of the United States constitutes a breach of those conventions, it can and must take them into account in ascertaining the content of the customary international law which the United States is also alleged to have infringed.[77]

Judge Jennings in his dissenting opinion, refers to this passage in the Court's judgment and continues:

This use of treaty provisions as 'evidence' of custom, takes the form

> of an interpretation of the treaty text. Yet the Court itself acknowledges that treaty-law and customary law can be distinguished precisely because the canons of interpretation are different (para. 178). To indulge the treaty-interpretation process, in order to determine the content of a posited customary rule, must raise a suspicion that it is in reality the treaty itself that is being applied under another name.[78]

Let us look carefully at the use made of the Friendly Relations Declaration in the Court's judgment on the merits. The Court begins by making a general pronouncement about state practice:

> It is not to be expected that in the practice of States the application of the rules in question[79] should have been perfect, in the sense that States should have refrained, with complete consistency, from the use of force or from intervention in each other's internal affairs. The Court does not consider that, for a rule to be considered as customary, the corresponding practice must be in absolute rigorous conformity with the rule. In order to deduce the existence of customary rules, the Court deems it sufficient that the conduct of States should, in general, be consistent with such rules, and that instances of State conduct inconsistent with a given rule should generally have been treated as breaches of that rule, not as indications of the recognition of a new rule. If a State acts in a way *prima facie* incompatible with a recognized rule, but defends its conduct by appealing to exceptions or justifications contained within the rule itself, then whether or not the State's conduct is in fact justified on that basis, the significance of that attitude is to confirm rather than to weaken the rule.[80]

Of course, the Court was faced with two serious disabilities. In the first place, it could not pray in aid state practice under the Charter. It will be recalled that, in the *North Sea Continental Shelf* cases, the Court had to consider state practice favouring the equidistance principle for the delimitation of continental shelf boundaries. In analysing that practice, the Court discounts the practice of states parties to the 1958 Geneva Convention on the Continental Shelf:

> To begin with, over half the States concerned, whether acting unilaterally or conjointly, were or shortly became, parties to the Geneva Convention, and were therefore, presumably, so far as they were concerned, acting actually or potentially in the application of the Convention. From their action, no inference could legitimately be drawn as to the existence of a rule of customary law in favour of the equidistance principle.[81]

In the light of this dictum, one can see why the Court, in the particular circumstances of the *Nicaragua* case, is, beyond the general pronouncement just cited, singularly silent on State practice as such. In the second place, the State practice in the *Nicaragua* case would have been *negative* practice to support two prohibitory norms – the norm prohibiting the threat or use of force and the norm prohibiting intervention. It is a commonplace that it is difficult, if not impossible, to prove a negative. One can, in principle, assess evidence in State practice for the existence of an alleged *positive* norm, such as the claimed existence of a rule in customary law favouring the existence of the equidistance principle for continental shelf delimitations or the claimed existence of a rule of customary law supporting the alternative 'distance' criterion for the measurement of a State's continental shelf entitlement. But the circumstances in which a particular State may have *refrained* from resorting to the use of force or from intervening in the internal affairs of another State because of a belief that such action would constitute a breach of customary law are locked away in confidential archives.

It is, therefore, perhaps not very surprising that the Court, in the *Nicaragua* case, shrank away from any analysis of actual State practice favouring or controverting the principles of non-use of force and non-intervention as norms of customary law. Instead, the Court concentrated on the element of *opinio juris*, and here it found supporting evidence in the Friendly Relations Declaration. After recalling that the parties were agreed that the fundamental principle concerning the non-use of force is expressed in the terms employed in Article 2(4) of the UN Charter, the Court continues that it has to be satisfied that there exists in customary international law an *opinio juris* as to the binding character of such abstention:

> This *opinio juris* may, though with all due caution, be deduced from, *inter alia*, the attitude of the Parties and the attitude of States towards certain General Assembly resolutions, and particularly resolution 2625 (xxv). . . . The effect of consent to the text of such resolutions cannot be understood as merely that of a 'reiteration or elucidation' of the treaty commitment undertaken in the Charter. On the contrary, it may be understood as an acceptance of the validity of the rule or set of rules declared by the resolution by themselves.[82]

The Court's handling of the constituent elements of custom in the *Nicaragua* case has been subjected to violent criticism by some commentators.[83] Others criticise what is implicit in the passage from the Court's judgment just cited – namely, that voting for a norm-declaring resolution is an exercise in *opinio juris*, notwithstanding that actual State practice may display many instances of violations of the norms so declared:

> Traditionally, a normative principle has been thought to enter into customary law only after being confirmed by practice, that is, after it is demonstrably adhered to by the actual conduct of the large preponderance of international actors capable of violating it. The customary

> norms cited by the Court are adhered to, at best, only by some States in some instances and have been ignored, alas, with impunity in at least two hundred instances of military conflict since the end of World War II.[84]

Others again are concerned about what they see as the consequences of the passage from the Court's judgment just cited. One commentator believes that one such consequence is that:

> Every resolution that purports to express a legal norm, even a 'soft law' exhortation or aspiration, has the potential of being recognized by the Court as a binding and strictly enforceable obligation, at least for those States which did not expressly dissent from it.[85]

These views, published in the immediate aftermath of the judgment on the merits in the *Nicaragua* case, may be unduly alarmist. Still, there is cause for concern, at least if the Court, in the *Nicaragua* case, is to be taken as having downgraded (or indeed virtually dispensed with) the element of State practice in the formation of custom, relying instead on an *opinio juris* derived largely, though not exclusively, from General Assembly law-declaring resolutions adopted by consensus. It is submitted, however, that this may be to read too much into the Court's judgment on the merits. The Court had impaled itself on the horns of a dilemma, partly by assuming jurisdiction in the case at all and partly by holding that it could simply abstract from the applicable law a 'block' of multilateral treaty law and decide the case on the basis of an independent source of law, namely, customary law.[86] Then it was found that proof of customary law on the principles of non-use of force and non-intervention would be very difficult if no account could be taken of State practice in the application of the UN Charter or the Charter of the OAS. It is on this point that Judge Jennings takes issue with the majority judgment in his dissenting judgment, recalling that the relevant provisions of the Charter – and indeed also of the Charter of the OAS – have at all material times been principal elements of the applicable law governing the conduct, rights and obligations of the parties:

> It seems, therefore eccentric, if not perverse, to attempt to determine the central issues of the present case after having first abstracted these principal elements of the law applicable to the case, and which still obligate both the parties.[87]

Reverting to the passage in the Court's judgment on the merits where it invokes the Friendly Relations Declaration as evidence of *opinio juris*, Thirlway comments:

> In short, the Court begins by accepting the existence of an *opinio juris*, at least as regards the parties, and announces the need to discover practice in support; but when it looks at what States, including the

> parties, have done, it treats such action as evidence of *opinio juris* and not as practice. Either the element of practice has dropped out of the equation altogether; or else action which 'expresses an *opinio juris*' is to be treated as *ipso facto* constituting an element of practice. Neither conclusion is very satisfactory.[88]

It is difficult to gainsay the force of this criticism.

It is as well, however, to bear in mind that the tortured reasoning of the Court in the *Nicaragua* case on the constituent elements of custom stemmed from a premise which was itself questionable on the ground suggested by Judge Jennings. Moreover, the invocation by the Court of the Friendly Relations Declaration as evidence of *opinio juris* as to the content of the customary law rules prohibiting the use of force and prohibiting intervention is also open to doubt. The Friendly Relations Declaration was conceived of as an *elaboration* of seven Charter principles, taking into account subsequent practice within the United Nations. It was declaratory (so far as it went) of the law of the Charter. The qualification is necessary, since, on some points, the Declaration is deliberately neutral, precisely because those who drafted it could not agree on fundamental issues relating to the interpretation of the Charter. This applies in particular to the exceptions to the principle prohibiting the threat or use of force. At the first (Mexico City) session of the Special Committee in 1964, it rapidly emerged that there was basic disagreement between the members of the Special Committee on (*inter alia*) the following issues:

(a) whether the reference to 'force' in Article 2(4) of the Charter comprehended only armed force or whether it embraced also economic and political pressure;
(b) whether or not the legal uses of force included a right of nations or peoples to self-defence against colonial domination in the exercise of their right to self-determination;
(c) whether the use of force could be authorised by the competent organs of the United Nations (including the General Assembly) or only by the Security Council;
(d) whether the use of force could be authorised by a regional agency acting in accordance with the Charter.

It was never possible to resolve these disputed issues within the framework of the debate at successive sessions of the Special Committee. In the circumstances, the only formulation on which agreement could be reached as regards exceptions to the non-use of force principle was the anodyne formula embodied as a safeguard clause in the final statement of the principle incorporated in the Declaration: 'Nothing in the foregoing paragraphs shall be construed as enlarging or diminishing in any way the scope of the provisions of the Charter concerning cases in which the use of force is lawful'.

The Friendly Relations Declaration thus had nothing to say on the *substance* of the right of individual or collective self-defence which was one of the key issues which had to be resolved in the *Nicaragua* case. Accordingly, if the Friendly Relations Declaration is to be taken as expressive of an *opinio juris* in favour of a customary law rule prohibiting the threat or use of force, it is a very incomplete *opinio juris*, since it does not embrace, save in the most general of terms, possible exceptions to that rule.

It is of course true that the final text of the Friendly Relations Declaration purports not only to constitute an agreed elaboration or elucidation of the seven Charter principles,[89] but in addition declares in its final paragraph that 'the principles of the Charter which are embodied in this Declaration constitute basic principles of international law'. But this looks to be an afterthought, included in order to provide a basis for an appeal to all States 'to be guided by these principles in their international behaviour and to develop their mutual relations on the basis of the strict observance of these principles'.

The use made of the Friendly Relations Declaration in the Court's judgment on the merits in *Nicaragua* is therefore questionable on several grounds. The present author does not share entirely the more extreme criticisms of the judgment that have been advanced, but he would be seriously concerned if he thought that the Court in this judgment was advancing a radically new concept of custom whereby the element of State practice no longer plays a central role and is regarded as being wholly subordinate to the element of *opinio juris*, in the sense that it can be invoked only to negative a posited rule deriving from the *opinio juris* represented by a General Assembly law-declaring resolution. If some of the *dicta* in the Court's judgment on the merits can be read in this sense, that is unfortunate, and may perhaps be attributable to the very special circumstances of this case. At most, the judgment would only seem to be authority for the application of the suggested tests to *prohibitory* norms where proof of State practice favouring such norms as norms of customary law, as opposed to Charter law, is notoriously difficult.

If I have been critical of certain aspects of the Court's reasoning in its judgment on the merits of the *Nicaragua* case, it is *not* because I would affirm or defend the legality of those actions of the United States in and against Nicaragua which were at issue in the case. It is rather because I believe the Court to have been mistaken in assuming jurisdiction in the case, at least on the basis of the parallel United States and Nicaraguan Optional Clause declarations. As is well known, there was serious doubt as to the initial validity of the Nicaraguan Optional Clause declaration made in 1929, given that Nicaragua never ratified the Protocol of Signature of the Statute of the Permanent Court of International Justice. There was even more doubt as to whether the Nicaraguan Optional Clause declaration, even if initially valid, could properly be held to have continued in 1946 as an acceptance of the compulsory jurisdiction of the International Court of Justice as successor to the Permanent Court. In its judgment of 1984 on jurisdiction and admissibility in the *Nicaragua* case, these serious doubts were swept aside by the Court with reasoning which, to put it at its lowest, lacks total conviction. In its judgment on the merits in 1986, the Court might be thought to have partially redeemed these flaws in its earlier judgment by giving effect to the multilateral treaty reservation in the United States Optional Clause declaration; but it then compounded its difficulties by assuming that it could none the less still decide the case on the basis of the alternative Nicaraguan claims that the United States was in breach of its *customary* law obligations on non-use of force and non-intervention. This led the Court to embark on an unconvincing process of reasoning designed to show that the customary law principles of non-use of force and non-intervention (which undoubtedly exist) could be fitted within the Procustes bed created by the Court's ruling on the applicability of the multilateral treaty reservation. The result is unsatisfactory; and, in the context of the subject-matter of this article, it is unfortunate that the Friendly Relations Declaration should have been invoked to sustain that unconvincing process of reasoning.

Enough of the *Nicaragua* case. It remains to consider two much broader issues relevant to the significance of the Friendly Relations Declaration. The first of these relates to the continuing divisions among international lawyers as to the precise status and legal effect of law-declaring resolutions of the General Assembly. As the brief and necessarily incomplete survey of doctrinal opinion reviewed earlier in this article demonstrates, we can conclude, with Shakespeare's Caliban, that 'the isle is full of noises'. In particular, there is a wide spectrum of opinion on the legal status and effect of General Assembly resolutions, particularly of those having a law-declaring or law-developing character. The present author finds himself in the middle of this spectrum of opinion. He does not believe that there is any juridical distinction between a General Assembly resolution and a General Assembly declaration in terms of the legal status of the instrument. Nor does he regard a vote by a State in favour of a law-declaring or law-developing resolution or declaration as an instance of State practice (whether individual or collective) contributing to the material element of custom, while accepting that it can constitute an expression of *opinio juris* contributing to the psychological element. He finds himself in broad agreement (though with some qualification) with the tentative conclusions reached by the Commission of the Institut de Droit International, read in the light of the explanations given in Skubiszewki's preparatory reports. There is nothing in the Court's treatment of the Friendly Relations Declaration in its judgment on the merits in the *Nicaragua* case (if properly understood in the light of the particular circumstances of this case) which casts doubt on the essential correctness of those tentative conclusions. As Thirlway correctly points out, having analysed that part of the Court's judgment on the merits in the *Nicaragua* case which concerns the relationship between General Assembly resolutions and customary law:

> Until the Court is called upon, by the circumstances of a case before it, for a specific ruling, widely differing views as to the impact on customary law of General Assembly resolutions may thus continue to be held without inconsistency with the Court's authority.[90]

The second broader issue to which attention should be directed relates to the temporal significance of the Friendly Relations Declaration. It was drawn up in the mid- to late 1960s, and its content is redolent of the legal issues considered to be of overwhelming importance at that time. This was the 'high noon' of the process of decolonisation, and this is given explicit emphasis in the formulation of the principle of self-determination, notwithstanding that the principle itself is recognised to be universal in its application. This was also part of the 'Cold War' period between the West and the East, and many of the unresolved problems which arose in the formulation of the principle prohibiting the threat or use of force reflect what were, even at the time, long-standing differences between the two blocs over the interpretation and application of the law of the Charter. Finally, the work of the Special Committee on Friendly Relations provided an ideal opportunity for the representatives of some newly independent States to flex their muscles in the international arena, and to pursue their quest for a 'new' international law which would be responsive to their needs and which would be freed from the constraints of what they perceived to be outmoded, Euro-centric and inevitably 'colonialist' concepts.

It is interesting to speculate on what would be the content of a new Friendly Relations Declaration, assuming that work on it had commenced only at the beginning of the present decade. It is virtually certain that the emphasis would be different, if only because many of the major problems now confronting the international community had hardly surfaced in the 1960s. A prime example is the necessity for environmental protection on a global scale. A statement of the duty to co-operate, if formulated in the 1990s, could hardly fail to make explicit mention of how that duty must be regarded as applying to the solution, by international co-operation, of problems concerning the protection of the human environment. One might equally anticipate that more content would be given to the duty to protect and preserve human rights, in the light of developments in this field over the past thirty years. Many of the disputes which bedeviled the work of the successive sessions of the Special Committee on Friendly Relations in the 1960s might prove easier of solution in the changed climate of the 1990s; but, equally, new areas of dispute might arise, particularly in the context of North-South (as opposed to East-West) relations.

This is in no way to deny or to undermine the significance of the Friendly Relations Declaration as it stands. It proved to be a fertile source for the corresponding declaration of principles contained in the Helsinki Final Act which has formed the basis for the subsequent creation of the CSCE process. It has been invoked time after time in debates in various organs of the United Nations. It is not, however, holy writ. It is only a partial expression of the selected UN Charter principles, and certainly does not exhaust their content. In many respects, it is a 'conservative' formulation of those principles, omitting potential corollaries which were controversial at the time of its adoption, but which might not prove to be so controversial today. Nevertheless, it has had, and continues to have, a potent influence on the development of international law, notwithstanding the continuing doctrinal differences as to the status and legal effect of law-declaring resolutions of the General Assembly, of which the Friendly Relations Declaration is a typical example.

NOTES

1 Both published in (1974–75) 47 *B.Y.I.L.*, at pp.1–53 and 273–85 respectively.

2 UN General Assembly Resolution 2625 (XXV) of 24 October 1970, whose official (but overly cumbersome) title is 'Declaration on Principles of International Law concerning Friendly Relations and Co-operation among States in accordance with the Charter of the United Nations'.

3 At a conference of Communist parties held in Moscow in December 1960, peaceful coexistence was defined as 'a form of class struggle between socialism and capitalism' implying 'intensification of the struggle of the working class, of all the Communist countries, for the triumph of socialist ideas' (cited in Rosalyn Higgins, *Conflict of Interests*, Oxford: Oxford University Press for Royal Institute of International Affairs, 1964, p.120). See also Reports of the 47th (Dubrovnik, 1956), 48th (New York, 1958), 49th (Hamburg, 1960), 50th (Brussels, 1962) and 51st (Tokyo, 1964) Conferences of the International Law Association.

4 UN General Assembly Resolution 1815(XVII) of 18 December 1962 (paras. 1 and 2).

5 Milan Sahovic, *Principles of International Law concerning Friendly Relations and Co-operation*, Dobbs Ferry, NY: Oceana, 1972, p. 11.

6 I.M. Sinclair, in M.K. Nawaz (ed.) *Essays in International Law in Honour of Krishna Rao*, Leyden: Sijthoff, 1976, p.110.

7 That is to say, principles (a), (b), (c) and (f).

8 That is to say, principles (d), (e) and (g).

9 UN General Assembly Resolution 2103(XX) of 20 December 1965.

10 See E. McWhinney, 'The "New" Countries and the "New" International Law: the United Nations' Special Conference on Friendly Relations and Co-operation among States' (1966) 60 *A.J.I.L.* 1–33; and Luke T. Lee, 'The Mexico City Conference of the United Nations Special Committee on Principles of International Law concerning Friendly Relations and Co-operation among States' (1965) 14 *I.C.L.Q.* 1296–310.

11 Notably, G.W. Haight in (1966) 1 *International Lawyer* 96–133; and P. H. Houben in (1967) 61 *A.J.I.L.* 703–36.
12 Notably, Suzanne Bastid, 'Observations sur une "étape" dans le developpement progressif et la codification des principes du droit international', in faculté de droit de l'université de Genève *Hommage à Paul Guggenheim*, Geneva: Imprimerie de la Tribune de Genève, 1968, pp.132–45; and M. Virally, 'Le role des "principes" dans le developpement du droit international', in ibid., pp.531–54 (esp. pp.547–54).
13 G. Arangio-Ruiz, 'The Normative Role of the General Assembly of the United Nations and the Declaration of Principles of Friendly Relations' (1972-III) 137, *Hague Recueil des Cours* 419–742.
14 M. Sahovic, 'Codification des principes du droit international des relations amicales et de la co-operation entre les Etats' (1972-III) 137 *Hague Recueil des Cours* 243–310.
15 Originally published in Serbo-Croat in 1969, an English version was published in 1972 under the title *Principles of International Law concerning Friendly Relations and Co-operation*, above n.5.
16 R. Rosenstock, 'The Declaration of Principles of International Law concerning Friendly Relations: a Survey' (1971) 65 *A.J.I.L.* 713–35.
17 I.M. Sinclair, 'Principles of International Law concerning Friendly Relations and Co-operation among States', in Nawaz, above n.6, pp.107–40.
18 Arangio-Ruiz, above n.13, p.614.
19 ibid., p.615.
20 Sahovic, above *Principles of International Law*, n.15, pp.49–50.
21 Sahovic, 'Codification des principes', above n.14, p.306.
22 Rosenstock, above n.16, p.735.
23 ibid.
24 Sinclair, above n.17, p.137.
25 ibid.
26 At p.138.
27 ibid.
28 G.G. Fitzmaurice, 'The Future of Public International Law', *Livre du Centenaire 1873–1973* of the Institut de Droit International, p.233.
29 ibid., p.234. It is interesting to compare this view of the 'safeguard' clause with that of Rosenstock who believes that '. . . a close examination of its text will reward the reader with an affirmation of the applicability of the principle to peoples within existing states and the necessity for governments to represent the governed', above n.16, p.732.
30 Fitzmaurice, above n.28, pp.265–6.
31 ibid., p.269.
32 R. Falk, 'The Quasi-legislative Competence of the General Assembly', (1966) 65 *A.J.I.L.* 783.
33 Fitzmaurice, above n.28, pp.271–5. It may be noted that this scheme received little or no active support from other members of the Institut: see the debate summarised on pp.372–85, and in particular the interventions of Messrs Virally, Bindschedler, Skubiszewski, Eustathiades, Waldock and Mme Bastid.
34 E. Jimènez de Arechaga, 'International Law in the Past Third of a Century', (1978-I) 159 *Hague Recueil des Cours* 32.
35 O. Schachter, 'General Course in Public International Law', (1982-V) 178 *Hague Recueil des Cours* 111.
36 ibid., pp.116–7.
37 ibid., p.113.
38 M. Virally, 'Panorama du droit international contemporain' (1983-V) 183 *Hague Recueil des Cours* 204–5.

39 ibid.
40 O. Asamoah, *The Legal Significance of the Declarations of the General Assembly of the United Nations*, Manchester: Manchester University Press, 1966, pp.46ff.
41 B. Cheng, 'United Nations Resolutions on Outer Space: 'Instant' International Customary Law (1965) 5 *Indian Journal of International Law* 36.
42 M. Thirlway, *International Customary Law and Codification*, Leiden: Sijthoff, 1972, pp.66–7.
43 ibid., pp.70–6. Thirlway's assessment of the significance of the treatment of the Friendly Relations Declaration by the International Court of Justice in its judgment on the merits in the *Nicaragua* v *United States* case will be considered at a later stage: see p.24 below.
44 R.R. Baxter, 'International Law in Her Infinite Variety' (1980) 29 *I.C.L.Q.* 564–5.
45 ibid., p.564.
46 ibid., p.565.
47 R.Y. Jennings, 'What is International Law and How Do We Tell It When We See It?' (1981) 37 *Schweizerischen Jahrbuch für internationales Recht* 69.
48 ibid., p.71.
49 ibid., p.67.
50 M. Akehurst, 'Custom as a Source of International Law' (1974–5) 47 *B.Y.I.L.* 10.
51 Thirlway, above n.42, p.58.
52 Akehurst, above n.50 p.5.
53 ibid., pp.5–8. As we have seen, many international lawyers would not be prepared to go so far, while recognising such assertions made by or on behalf of States *in abstracto* as constituting evidence of the *opinio juris* of the State concerned.
54 Blaine Sloan, 'General Assembly Resolutions Revisited' (1987) 58 *B.Y.I.L.* 39–150.
55 ibid., p.73.
56 ibid., p.74.
57 ibid., p.75. But note that, in its judgment on the merits in the *Nicaragua* case, the Court invoked the Friendly Relations Declaration only as evidence of *opinio juris*, not as evidence of State practice.
58 ibid., p.96.
59 ibid., pp.97–8.
60 ibid., p.140.
61 See *Annuaire de l'Institut de Droit International* (hereinafter cited as *Annuaire*), vol.61-I (1985), pp.29–83 (preliminary exposé), pp.85–304 (provisional report) and pp.305–58 (definitive report). See also *Annuaire*, vol. 62-II (1987) for the records of the plenary discussion within the Institut (at pp.65–126) and for the final text of the resolution adopted by the Institut (at pp.274–88).
62 *Annuaire*, vol. 61-I (1985), pp.62–3.
63 ibid., pp.46–7. The quotations in this passage are from statements made, respectively, by the representatives of Czechoslovakia and Sweden, the United Kingdom, France, and Mali, on the occasion of the Sixth Committee debate on the final text of the Friendly Relations declaration in 1970.
64 ibid., p.111.
65 ibid., p.114.
66 [1971] I.C.J. Rep. 47. The Court was here referring to Article 60 of the Vienna Convention concerning termination of a treaty relationship on account of breach.

67 I.M. Sinclair, *Vienna Convention on the Law of Treaties*, Manchester: Manchester University Press, 2nd edn, 1984.
68 *Annuaire*, above n.61, vol. 61-I (1985), p.119.
69 Thirlway, above n.42, p.58.
70 [1969] I.C.J. Rep. 44, para.77.
71 P. Haggenmacher, 'La doctrine des deux éléments du droit coutumier dans la pratique de la Cour internationale' (1986) *R.G.D.I.P.* 124–5.
72 Chapters 2 and 5 see below.
73 [1986] I.C.J. Rep. 38, para.56.
74 [1984] I.C.J. Rep. 424, para.73.
75 [1986] I.C.J. Rep. 94, para.175.
76 ibid., p.96, para.179.
77 ibid., p.97, para.183.
78 ibid., p.532.
79 That is to say, the rules on non-use of force and non-intervention.
80 [1986] I.C.J. Rep. 98, para.186.
81 [1969] I.C.J. Rep. 43, para.76.
82 [1986] I.C.J. Rep. 99–100, para.188.
83 See, in particular, A. D'Amato, 'Trashing Customary International Law' (1987) 81 *A.J.I.L.* 101–5.
84 T.M. Franck, 'Some Observations on the ICJ's Procedural and Substantive Innovations' (1987) 81 *A.J.I.L.* 119; also E. Gordon, 'Custom on a Sliding Scale', 81 *A.J.I.L.* 147.
85 F. Morrison, 'Legal Issues in the *Nicaragua* Opinion' 81 *A.J.I.L.* 161.
86 M. Thirlway, 'The Law and Procedure of the International Court of Justice 1960–1989' (1990) 61 *B.Y.I.L.* 26.
87 [1986] I.C.J. Rep. 533.
88 Thirlway, above n.86, p.72.
89 Be it noted, however, that the Court, in the *Nicaragua* case, acknowledges specifically that the non-intervention principle was *not* strictly a Charter principle: 'Of course, statements whereby States avow their recognition of the principles of international law set forth in the United Nations Charter cannot strictly be interpreted as applying to the principle of non-intervention by States in the internal or external affairs of other States, since this principle is not, as such, spelt out in the Charter': [1986] I.C.J. Rep. 106, para.102.
90 Thirlway, above n.86, p.81.

2 The principle of non-use of force

Christine Gray

The General Assembly has passed many general resolutions on the non-use of force, from the Essentials of Peace in 1949[1] to the Declaration on the Rights of Peoples to Peace in 1984.[2] And the process continues. The General Assembly is still examining questions such as Good Neighbourliness, the Preparation of Societies for Life in Peace, and the Implementation of the Collective Security Provisions of the UN Charter.[3] But some resolutions stand out. On 18 November 1987, the General Assembly adopted the Declaration on the Enhancement of the Effectiveness of the Principle of Non-Use of Force in International Relations.[4] During the negotiating process this was referred to[5] as

> one link in the chain of precedents which include the Declaration on Principles of International Law concerning Friendly Relations and Co-operation among States in accordance with the Charter of the United Nations,[6] the Definition of Aggression[7] and the Manila Declaration on the Peaceful Settlement of International Disputes.[8]

Writers on the old question of the legal significance of General Assembly resolutions have speculated on the means of determining the relative importance of resolutions.[9] Factors such as the voting figures, the language used, the negotiating history and the intent of member states are the most popular suggestions. Despite doing well on all these tests, the Declaration on Friendly Relations did not attract much academic attention at the time of its adoption. But now – and not only because of the importance attributed to it by the International Court of Justice in the *Nicaragua* case[10] – the Declaration on Friendly Relations is central to any consideration of international law on the use of force.[11] Can the Declaration on the Non-Use of Force also play a role? Is there any need for more General Assembly resolutions on the use of force, or should the Declaration on Friendly Relations be accepted as the last word, far from perfect but marking the limits of what can be agreed between states?

The role of such resolutions with regard to the use of force in international relations has been the subject of much debate. In the negotiating process Western states, and in particular the USA and UK, have tended to adopt a sceptical, rather negative approach; on the whole they have not been enthusiastic about the series of proposals for general resolutions on the use of force. Newer states have been more positive; they have tended to stress the value of such resolutions to small states. The Soviet bloc often took the initiative in proposing resolutions. This could be seen as indicative of a more idealistic approach than that of the West, or alternatively as a cynical exercise in propaganda. China and Albania have taken the latter view: China regarded the proposal for the Declaration on the Non-Use of Force as 'sheer fraud'; Albania spoke of it as 'a hoax, an attempt to use the work of international organizations for political and propaganda purposes'.[12]

The drafting history of the Declaration on the Non-Use of Force[13] reflected deep divisions between states on the value of the whole enterprise of producing resolutions on the use of force. States were also divided on the form the end-product of the negotiating process should take: should it be a treaty or a declaration, and if the latter, what was its legal status to be?

The initiative that was to lead to the Declaration on the Non-Use of Force came from the USSR in 1976, when it proposed a Treaty on the Non-Use of Force be adopted by the General Assembly.[14] During the negotiations that followed there was some anger expressed by Western states at the apparent hypocrisy of the USSR in continuing to push such a proposal after it had invaded and occupied Afghanistan.[15] This split between what states say and what they do is seen as a fundamental problem by some writers on the use of force and has led to serious divisions in views of the law;[16] this is a question that interested Michael Akehurst and on which he made a major contribution to the debate.[17] As is common in General Assembly discussions of the rules governing the use of force, some of the sessions of the Special Committee working on the Non-Use of Force after the invasion of Afghanistan degenerated into rather bad-tempered attacks by states on each other.[18] Iran and Iraq, Cyprus and Turkey, the Arab states and Israel all engaged in these, which is worth mentioning because views on particular conflicts clearly influence states' views on general rules on the use of force.[19]

Those supporting the original project of producing a treaty on the non-use of force were in a large majority in the General Assembly and voted in 1977 to set up a Special Committee to work on this.[20] In the lengthy discussions that took place in the Special Committee, the Sixth Committee and the General Assembly as to whether the project was worthwhile, supporters described the proposed treaty as a natural continuation of the efforts of the United Nations to consolidate international peace and as strengthening and reinforcing the UN Charter. Their main concerns were with the inequality of states, the arms race and nuclear weapons.[21]

Those against the project[22] argued that it was unnecessary to repeat the UN Charter and dangerous to depart from it. They described the obligation in Article 2(4) of the UN Charter as clear and argued that any interpretation of it beyond that in the Declaration on Friendly Relations and the Definition of Aggression would detract from its cogency.[23] (It is interesting to see that those Western states which were initially sceptical about the value of both these resolutions now treat them as the last word on the interpretation of the UN Charter.) As supporters of a treaty pointed out,[24] this does not seem a very convincing argument; it would mean that the UN Charter could not be refined, and ignores the many treaties and declarations on human rights, self-determination and peaceful settlement of disputes that have done this.

Another argument put forward against the proposed treaty was that it would reduce the authority of the UN Charter by juxtaposing its provisions with those from other documents.[25] It is not clear why this should be so. A stronger argument was that the real problem facing the world was not a lack of standards but the lack of will to adhere to them.[26] Several states argued that the mandate of the Special Committee was to enhance the effectiveness of the principles on the non-use of force, not to work on restating the principles themselves. They were against any instrument that would focus on the content of the norm as opposed to ways and means of enhancing its effectiveness.[27] Belgium, France, the Federal Republic of Germany, Italy and the UK proposed instead a study of the reasons why states resort to force.[28] This was seen by some states as merely a delaying tactic;[29] by others it was rejected as a dangerous invitation to states to indulge in polemics.[30]

The split on the issue whether a treaty on the non-use of force was desirable made progress in the Special Committee slow.[31] Most of those opposed to the idea of the treaty itself declined to comment on its drafting. In spite of the fact that a majority of states supported a treaty, a small group of Western states was able to prevent the continuation of this project. The need for consensus gave these states an effective veto on the form the end-product should take.[32] The USA spoke of 'a lack of realism on the part of certain delegates in ignoring the simple political truth that the conclusion of a world treaty was unacceptable to a significant body of opinion';[33] the significance lay in the power of states concerned rather than in their number.

The deadlock between supporters and opponents of a treaty was finally broken in 1985 when the Non-Aligned Movement proposed that the Special Committee work for a declaration as an intermediate stage.[34] Also, outside the UN, Western and Eastern bloc states had been able to agree, as part of the Conference on Security and Co-operation in Europe (CSCE) process, on the Stockholm Declaration which included provisions on the non-use of force.[35] The General Assembly voted to change the instructions to the Special Committee to allow it to work for a declaration.[36] But the West continued to vote against the revised proposal and the USA and UK continued to argue that the Special Committee should be dissolved.[37] However, progress was being made on the substance of the Declaration and finally in 1987, over ten years after the initial Soviet proposal for a treaty, the Declaration on the Non-Use of Force was adopted by the General Assembly without a vote.[38]

Earlier, similar disagreements over the value of the project and the form of the end-product had arisen between states during the negotiations leading to the Declaration on Friendly Relations and to the Definition of Aggression.[39] When the Declaration on Friendly Relations was first discussed in the Sixth Committee of the General Assembly in 1962, the West had also expressed concern that the paramount role of the UN Charter should be preserved and had doubted whether a list of principles would serve any useful purpose.[40] Nevertheless in Resolution 1815 the General Assembly agreed to 'undertake a study of the principles of international law, with a view to their progressive development and codification, so as to secure their more affective application'. In 1963 there was still argument on the Sixth Committee's mandate and as to the form which the results of its work should take.[41] Many Western states, including notably the USA, opposed the proposal for a declaration. And at the end of the lengthy drafting process there were still some disagreements on the status of the Declaration. It is now largely uncontroversial to say that the Declaration on Friendly Relations represents international law; the drafting history of the Declaration on the Non-Use of Force contains repeated affirmations of this and no state seriously challenged this orthodoxy. However, when the Declaration on Friendly Relations was first adopted there was still some doubt about the legal status of General Assembly resolutions. Italy said they were not normally part of customary or general international law; Australia, Israel and Portugal said that they were only recommendations; the Netherlands regarded the Declaration as a mixture of legal and non-legal provisions and said it should not be interpreted as a carefully drafted legal document would be interpreted.[42]

The status of the Declaration of the Non-Use of Force was even more strongly challenged. The Western states took pains to play down its legal significance. The European Community and Japan repeatedly stressed the non-normative nature of the text.[43] But the Declaration contains many provisions requiring that states 'shall' behave in certain ways, and other provisions merely saying that they 'should' do so. This distinction[44] seems unnecessary if the whole declaration is non-normative. Also much of the Declaration reproduces provisions in the UN Charter, the Declaration on Friendly Relations and the Definition of Aggression; to call these 'non-normative' seems rather strange. The French statement that Part 1 of the Declaration (the part dealing with the non-use of force) sought to define legal norms but was not binding[45] seems more realistic. Its authority would be derived only from its acceptance by the international community.[46]

Other states welcomed the adoption of the Declaration. Jamaica said it had profound significance for international relations;[47] India called it an excellent achievement;[48] the Eastern bloc regarded it as an important step forward.[49] But many states were distinctly reserved or openly disappointed. Brazil said the Declaration was merely a list of generally accepted principles. It did not seem to justify the ten years dedicated to the matter.[50] Brazil, Mexico and Argentina all regretted that more consideration had not been given to the final draft.[51] The hurried drafting was the result of an agreement to end the work of the Special Committee rather than any fundamental solution to the substantive problems. Panama spoke of the defects in the Declaration because certain major countries prevented more precise and detailed provisions on what was covered by the term 'force'.[52]

That brings us – finally – to the question of the content of the Declaration on the Non-Use of Force. Was the end-product worth all the years of work it took to produce? Does it add anything to earlier resolutions?

Most states said it did not add anything. Whereas the Declaration on Friendly Relations and the Definition of Aggression had clearly added significantly to the very brief UN Charter provisions on the use of force, it is difficult to find anything new in the Declaration on the Non-Use of Force. A few states thought they could identify some innovations. Argentina said that in comparison with previous declarations, this placed more emphasis on the interrelation of general principles of law and principles on the non-use of force.[53] The Netherlands said that paragraph 6 of the new Declaration, which says

> states shall fulfil their obligations under international law to refrain from organizing, instigating, assisting or participating in paramilitary, terrorist or subversive acts, including acts of mercenaries, in other states, or acquiescing in organized activities within their territory directed towards the commission of such acts

goes beyond similar provisions in earlier instruments.[54] However, it is not obvious that there is any real difference between this and the Declaration on Friendly Relations.

Canada also attempted to find new elements in the Declaration, which it called 'a modest advance on existing instruments'.[55] It said that paragraph 3, 'No consideration of whatever nature may be invoked to warrant resorting to the threat or use of force in violation of the Charter of the UN', was a useful new provision. This builds on a similar provision in the Definition of Aggression. It was much discussed during the drafting of the Definition of Aggression and of the Declaration on the Non-Use of Force, but many states remained unconvinced that the provision had any substance. Otherwise, Canada reluctantly accepted the very general provisions on disarmament in paragraph 10 (not to be found in the two earlier resolutions) as the price to be paid for general agreement on the Declaration. And it hailed paragraph 25 – a call to UN organs to make full use of the UN Charter provisions on the maintenance of international peace and security – as new and useful. Again it hardly seems a very significant advance.

The lack of any important new provisions in the Declaration may be explained by the inability of states to resolve the fundamental controversies that remain on the use of force. As earlier with the Declaration on Friendly Relations and the Definition of Aggression problems were resolved by omission. The disagreements that had become apparent during the drafting of the Declaration on Friendly Relations and could not be resolved then can still not be settled.

Major controversies remain – these concern the meaning of 'force', on which Western states tend to take a much narrower view than the rest of the world; the right of national liberation movements to use force to which the West is opposed; the scope of the prohibition of the occupation and acquisition of territory by force; the scope of the right of self-defence; and the outlawing of the use of nuclear weapons.[56]

During the drafting of the Declaration on Friendly Relations the section on the use of force proved one of the most difficult. The Special Committee operated by consensus and there was much discussion of this method.[57] Many states were critical and said that it meant a few states could stop provisions being included even though an overwhelming majority supported them. They resented this inequality of states. But the West argued that consensus was necessary for the Declaration to achieve authoritative status. Although a majority of states would be able to pass a resolution containing a broad definition of force and outlawing anticipatory self-defence, the opposition of certain Western states would weaken these rules. Avoidance of confrontation on these fundamental issues enables both sides to maintain their positions.

Nevertheless, some controversial issues were resolved. The Report of the Special Committee on the Declaration on Friendly Relations lists the compromises that were reached: a prohibition on propaganda for wars of aggression was included; international laws of demarcation as well as international boundaries were protected against violation; and provisions on the organisation of armed bands and of acts of civil strife were included in the section on the use of force.[58]

The drafts produced by states for the Declaration on the Non-Use of Force show the gaps that still exist.[59] The West's working paper did not mention disarmament, nuclear weapons, economic and political coercion, armed force against colonial and racist domination, or propaganda. On all these points the contrast with the Non-Aligned working paper is very clear.

Unlike the Declaration on Friendly Relations and the Definition of Aggression, the Declaration on the Non-Use of Force does contain an express reference to self-defence. But paragraph 13 says only, 'States have the inherent right of individual or collective self defence if an armed attack occurs, as set forth in the Charter of the UN', a similar formulation to that in the Stockholm Declaration.[60] The drafting negotiations had shown clearly that agreement on any more elaborate provision, on any attempt to resolve the controversy over the scope of self-defence, would not be possible.[61] Several states had rejected the legality of preventive self-defence and of humanitarian intervention,[62] but of those states that have in the past asserted a wide right of self-defence only the USA spoke out.[63] A few new concerns emerged during work on the Declaration on the Non-Use of Force: Afghanistan raised the question of economic blockade of landlocked states and Trinidad and Tobago brought up environmental modification.[64]

But the crucial issues of the interpretation of Article 2(4) and of the scope of self-defence, as well as the controversies that have gained prominence since 1945 – the interrelated topics of forcible intervention, invitation by a government and self-determination – have not been illuminated by the Declaration on the Non-Use of Force.

Given the lack of any important new content in the Declaration on the Non-Use of Force, does it have any value at all? Is it fair to say that the drafting history is more valuable than the end-product in so far as it gives a clear indication of states' views and the differences between them?

For many states the Declaration has a symbolic value: it is a unanimous expression by states of the permanent validity of a number of important principles.[65] The developed states may argue that such a declaration is unnecessary, and that it weakens, rather than strengthens the UN Charter. However, at the time the Charter was adopted there were only fifty-one founding member states and it was clearly important for new states not only to become members of the UN but themselves to take part in the proclamation of fundamental rules on the use of force.[66] At the time Franck published his article 'Who killed Article 2(4)'[67] the UN General Assembly reaffirmed its commitment to the prohibition of the use of force, and elaborated on its content.

But it seems unlikely that the Declaration on the Non-Use of Force will attain a more than symbolic role. In the year after its adoption, when it might have been expected to be fresh in everyone's mind, there were no references to the Declaration in General Assembly or Security Council resolutions, or in Security Council debates or communications. It is true that the Declaration on Friendly Relations was also not invoked in Security Council resolutions or debates in that year, though there was one invocation of it in a communication by Iraq to the Security Council.[68] Express mention of it in Security Council resolutions is very unusual,[69] but the Declaration on Friendly Relations has been regularly referred to with regard to the use of force in Security Council debates.[70] The Declaration is also commonly referred to by states outside the UN. For example, it was referred to in the 1988 Afghanistan-Pakistan Agreement on the Principle of Mutual Relations,[71] by the UK over the Falklands invasion and in its foreign policy document 'Is intervention ever justified?',[72] and by the USA over the Soviet invasion of Afghanistan.[73] But perhaps the most striking instances of its invocation are in General Assembly resolutions; not so much in resolutions passed in response to particular instances of the use of force by states,[74] but in the series of general resolutions on topics involving the prohibition on the use of force. Thus, the Declaration is ritually referred to in resolutions such as those in Deepening Detente,[75] Good Neighbourliness,[76] and Implementation of the Collective Security Provisions of the UN Charter;[77] such resolutions are often reaffirmed annually or their implementation is kept under review by the General Assembly. This constant mention of the Declaration works to reinforce its status; it shares this treatment with the Definition of Aggression and the Manila Declaration.[78]

The Declaration on Friendly Relations and the Definition of Aggression have also had an important impact on the work of the International Law Commission (ILC). In their discussions of the Draft Code of Offences against the Peace and Security of Mankind,[79] the members of the Commission consistently treated the two resolutions as statements of international law to which their own work should conform. They even referred to the Declaration of the Non-Use of Force.[80] By contrast, in its protracted and increasingly unpromising work on state responsibility[81] reference is made by the ILC to the Definition of Aggression but not to the Declaration on Friendly Relations.

The Commission began its list of offences against the peace and security of mankind with aggression.[82] Although the wording of the draft is almost identical to that of the Definition of Aggression there is no express reference to it. The commentary explains that this was because some members thought that a resolution intended to serve as a guide for a political organ such as the Security Council could not be the basis for criminal prosecution before a judicial body. There were two schools of thought. One held that the international judicial function should be kept separate from that of the Security Council and that there should not be a mere transfer of the whole of the Definition of Aggression into the Code; the list of offences within the Definition should not be exhaustive as far as a judge was concerned. The other school of thought was that the whole Definition of Aggression should be reproduced in the Code, and that any judicial organ should be subordinated to Security Council decisions.[83] The question remains to be settled.

The Commission's work on the other offences – the threat of aggression, intervention and colonial and racist domination – has also been heavily influenced by the provisions of the General Assembly resolutions.[84] In its debates on these crimes and on aggression many earlier controversies have resurfaced: can economic coercion constitute aggression; should the use of nuclear weapons be an offence against the peace and security of mankind; can breach of a treaty designed to ensure international peace and security amount to aggression?

The Commission is also working on defences for individuals accused of offences against the peace and security of mankind: it is examining self-defence and errors of law and of fact.[85] Here, as in its work on 'Circumstances precluding wrongfulness' under State Responsibility, where it had dealt with consent, *force majeure* and fortuitous event, necessity and self-defence,[86] the Commission has involved itself in many of the controversies the General Assembly has found unresolvable in its years of passing general resolutions on the use of force.

Issues such as the right to protect nationals abroad, the right of a government to invite armed forces from outside onto its territory, anticipatory self-defence and the mistaken shooting down of civilian aircraft have been raised. The Commission will be on very dangerous ground if it tries to resolve issues concerning the use of force that have divided states since the foundation of the UN. To date, despite calls from some members for the Commission to adopt their own favourite views on the scope of self-defence, the right of peoples to use force against alien and colonial domination and so on, the Commission has been very cautious in its work on the draft code and on state responsibility.

In the *Nicaragua* case the International Court of Justice clearly attributed a very special status to the Declaration on Friendly Relations. Because of the US multilateral treaty reservation, the Court found that it was not able to apply the UN Charter or other multilateral treaties to the case before it.[87] It turned to customary law. Its consideration of state practice was brief; the central point was that absolutely rigorous conformity of state practice was not necessary.[88] Both the USA and Nicaragua agreed that the UN Charter principles as to the use of force correspond to those found in customary law, but the Court said that it still had itself to ascertain what rules of customary law were applicable. The Court has been strongly criticised for its rather perfunctory examination of state practice.[89] But the agreement of the parties on the rules of customary law, although by itself not enough conclusively to establish the existence of custom, made it unsurprising that the Court did not feel the need to undertake any detailed survey of state practice. Those criticising the Court seem to be those who are not willing to accept the prohibition in Article 2(4) as good law, or those who wish to undermine it by wide exceptions.

In its search for customary law the Court followed the traditional (and problematic)[90] view that *opinio juris* was a necessary element. It said,

> *Opinio juris* may, though with all due caution, be deduced from, *inter alia*, the attitude of the Parties and the attitude of States towards certain General Assembly Resolutions, and particularly Resolution 2625 (xxv) entitled 'Declaration on Principles of International Law

> concerning Friendly Relations and Cooperation among States in accordance with the Charter of the United Nations'. The effect of consent to the text of such resolutions cannot be understood as merely that of a 'reiteration or elucidation' of the treaty commitment undertaken in the Charter. On the contrary, it may be understood as an acceptance of the validity of the rule or set of rules declared by the resolution by themselves. The principle of non-use of force, for example, may thus be regarded as a principle of customary international law, not as such conditioned by provisions relating to collective security, or to the facilities or armed contingents to be provided under Article 43 of the Charter. It would therefore seem apparent that the attitude referred to expresses an *opinio juris* respecting such a rule (or set or rules), to be thenceforth treated separately from the provisions, especially those of an institutional kind, to which it is subject on the treaty-law plane of the Charter'.[91]

It is obvious why this approach is not attractive to those who have argued that the prohibition on the use of force in Article 2(4) depends on the effective functioning of the UN collective security system under Chapter VII of the Charter.[92]

It is interesting that the Court went on to mention the US acceptance of the principle of the prohibition of the use of force in the 1975 Helsinki Declaration. Again there has been criticism of the Court's use of non-legally-binding agreement to confirm the existence of *opinio juris*.[93] But this reference by the Court simply confirms that if a non-binding, or even a 'non normative', resolution or agreement contains rules of international law its label does not deprive it of legal significance.

When the Court came to apply the customary law that it had identified to the facts of the case, it referred to the detailed provisions of the Declaration on Friendly Relations. In particular it used the principle 'Every state has the duty to refrain from organizing or encouraging the organization of regular forces or armed bands, including mercenaries, for incursion into the territory of another state', in examining the legality of the US assistance to the Contras.[94] Many writers were unhappy with the Court's approach to General Assembly resolutions, in particular with the importance it attributed to the Declaration on Friendly Relations. Some also criticised the Court for excessive willingness to take account of what states say in its assessment of customary law.[95]

The Court said,

> In order to deduce the existence of customary rules, the Court deems it sufficient that the conduct of states should, in general, be consistent with such rules, and that instances of state conduct inconsistent with a given rule should generally have been treated as breaches of that rule, not as indications of the recognition of a new rule. If a state acts in a way *prima facie* incompatible with a recognized rule, but defends

> its conduct by appealing to exceptions or justifications contained within the rule itself, then whether or not the state's conduct is in fact justifiable on that basis, the significance of that attitude is to confirm rather than to weaken the rule.[96]

The criticism of the Court may be seen in the context of a wider debate – in which Akehurst was involved[97] – on the formation of international law on the use of force. There is a clear division between writers.[98] On one side are those who accept what states say (whether they call it 'commitment' or merely 'lip service') as confirming the strict prohibition on the use of force in Article 2(4). These writers look to statements by those using force to justify their own behaviour, to the world response to these uses of force as expressed in General Assembly and Security Council resolutions and to general resolutions setting out rules on the use of force.

On the other side are those who are sceptical of what states say. They refuse to accept such statements as reflecting international law. They want to 'reinterpret' Article 2(4) in order to justify the use of force to further human rights or world public order. For them it does not matter that states still say that Article 2(4) should be widely interpreted – what states using force actually do is crucial. Of this second group D'Amato is the most strident critic of the Court and of Akehurst.[99] He strongly attacks Akehurst for concentrating on what states say and ignoring what they do in his theory of customary international law.[100] Of course this misrepresents Akehurst's position;[101] but it does highlight a fundamental difference between them.

D'Amato in his search for international law on the use of force now advocates 'inferring what they [governments] *should have said* from the facts of what they did'.[102] He says

> customary law grows and changes over time as a result of the interactions of states in the international arena (the facts) and the rules we may infer from those interactions as the theory that best fits what the states did (even if it was not, or was only partly, what they said they were doing).[103]

This theory is clearly a development of the famous Reisman/Schacter debate.[104] Reisman had argued that Article 2(4) should be interpreted to allow states to use force in order to further 'world public order'; Schacter countered this by showing that states do not in practice claim such a right. States still stress their commitment to Article 2(4) and attempt to justify their use of force, generally on the basis of self-defence. D'Amato goes further than Reisman in disregarding what states say; he advises researchers to substitute what states should have said for what they did say in government claims, arguments and protests, and in Security Council and General Assembly resolutions in reaction to the use of force.

There are certain problems with the D'Amato approach.[105] He does not show convincingly why we should ignore what states actually say to justify their use of force. His theory that they 'pay lip service' to 'unchanging legal principles' in order to avoid criticism from academics seems rather farfetched. For those states and writers who are not happy to ignore the reaction of the rest of the world to a use of force simply because condemnation is not followed by effective sanctions, for those not happy to look for what the state using force should have said rather than what it did say, for those not willing to accept that the UN system and customary law should allow the prohibition on the use of force to be overridden by the alleged promotion of human rights, for those not willing to see the US actions in Grenada, Panama and Nicaragua hailed as milestones in the creation of new international law rather than condemned as breaches of the law, the Court's support for the Akehurst rather than the D'Amato approach to international law on the use of force, and its confirmation of the legal significance of the Declaration on Friendly Relations, will be very welcome.

NOTES

1 UN General Assembly Resolution 290(IV).
2 UN General Assembly Resolution 39/11.
3 UN General Assembly Resolution 41/84; UN General Assembly Resolution 33/73; UN General Assembly Resolution 38/191.
4 UN General Assembly Resolution 42/22, (1988) 27 *I.L.M.* 1672, hereafter referred to as the 'Declaration of the Non-Use of Force'. On the drafting history and content of the Resolution, see the excellent account by T. Treves (1987) 33 *A.F.D.I.* 379. See also A. Carty and V.N. Fedorov, in W.E. Butler (ed.) *The Non-Use of Force in International Law*, Dordrecht: Martinus Nihhoff, 1989, pp.53, 77.
5 Report of the Special Committee, UN General Assembly Official Records (GAOR) A/C.6/42/SR.16.
6 UN General Assembly Resolution 2625(XXV), (1970) 9 *I.L.M.* 1292, hereafter referred to as the 'Declaration on Friendly Relations'. On the drafting history see A. Tanca, in A. Cassese (ed.) *The Current Legal Regulation of the Use of Force*, Dordrecht: Martinus Nijhoff, 1986, p.397; R. Rosenstock (1971) 65 *A.J.I.L.* 713; M. Sahovic (1972. iii) 137 *Hague Recuil des Cours* 243.
7 UN General Assembly Resolution 3314(XXIX); (1974) 13 *I.L.M.* 710, (1975) 14 *I.L.M.* 588. On the drafting history see B.B. Ferencz, *Defining International Aggression: The Search for World Peace*, Dobbs Ferry, NY: Oceana 1975; A.M. Rifaat, *International Aggression* (1979); T. Bruha, *Die Definition der Aggression*, Berlin: Duncker & Humblot 1980.
8 UN General Assembly Resolution 37/10, (1982) 21 *I.L.M.* 449. For further discussion of the peaceful settlement of disputes, see ch.4 below.
9 M. Akehurst discussed this in (1974–5) 47 *B.Y.I.L.* 1, at p.5ff; more recently see, for example, B. Sloan (1987) 58 *B.Y.I.L.* 41.
10 [1986] I.C.J. Rep. 14, See p.41 below.
11 See p.39ff below.
12 *1976 UN Yearbook*, p.108 and *1977 UN Yearbook*, p.116.

13 See works cited in n.4.
14 UN Doc. A/31/243; *1976 UN Yearbook*, p.105.
15 During the work of the Special Committee in 1980 Belgium, France, FRG, Italy, Spain and the UK all criticised the USSR. The USA refused to participate in that session of the committee and opposed the renewal of its mandate: *1980 UN Yearbook*, p.174.
16 See p.43 below.
17 (1974–5) 47 *B.Y.I.L.* 1, and see p.43 below.
18 For example, on the work of the Special Committee during the 40th session of the General Assembly see UN Doc. A/C.6/40/SR.8.
19 This may be seen very clearly in the views of Arab states on the acquisition and occupation of territory.
20 UN General Assembly Resolution 32/150, passed by 111–4–27. The four states voting against were Albania, China, UK, USA: *1977 UN Yearbook*, p.115.
21 See, for example, UN GAOR A/32/181, A/C.1/32/PV 47, A/40/41, and *UN Yearbooks* from 1976. See also Treves, above n.4.
22 Mostly the Western European states, USA and Japan. See, for example, UN GAOR A/32/243, A/31/181/ Others expressed concern with the problem of enforcement: Barbados, Kuwait, Pakistan, Syria, Cyprus and Nepal. See *1977 UN Yearbook*, p.116.
23 See, for example, documents cited in n.21, and also *1977 UN Yearbook*, p.117, and *1978 UN Yearbook*, p.170.
24 For example, documents cited in n.21 and also *1977 UN Yearbook*, p.117, and *1978 UN Yearbook*, p.170.
25 Denmark and Luxembourg: UN Doc. A/32/181.
26 USA and UK: UN Doc. A/40/41; cf. *1978 UN Yearbook*, p.170.
27 On this basis Western states actually took the initiative in the Special Committee on the Charter of the UN and on the Strengthening of the Role of the UN (set up under UN General Assembly Resolution 3499 in 1975) in proposing a draft declaration on the prevention and removal of disputes and situations likely to threaten international peace and security. This Declaration was adopted in 1989 and was described as the first declaration to deal with the prevention of international disputes: UN Doc. A/43/33, cf. (1988) *UN Chronicle* 63.
28 *1979 UN Yearbook*, p.153.
29 See comments by Bulgaria: *1980 UN Yearbook*, p.176.
30 See UN GAOR A/40/41.
31 *1979 UN Yearbook*, p.154.
32 See comments by Brazil, Ethiopia, USA, Bulgaria and Vietnam: UN GAOR A/C.6/40/SR.8–9.
33 UN GAOR A/40/41.
34 UN GAOR A/C.6/40/SR.8–44.
35 (1987) 26 *I.L.M.* 190. See R. Sapienza, in Cassese, above n.6, p.423.
36 UN GAOR A/40/PV 112; UN General Assembly Resolution 40/70, passed by 119–14–12.
37 See comments by USA (UN GAOR A/C6/40/SR.8) and UK (A/C.6/40/SR.11) and Report of Special Committee (A/41/41).
38 UN General Assembly Resolution 42/22. The General Assembly had decided in 1986 (by UN General Assembly Resolution 41/76) that the Special Committee should complete a draft declaration and submit its final report in 1987. After only 3 weeks of discussion by the Special Committee in 1987 agreement was reached.
39 See works cited in n.7.
40 *1962 UN Yearbook* p.487.

41 *1963 UN Yearbook* p.514.
42 *1962 UN Yearbook*, p.487; UN Doc. A/8018.
43 See, for example, Denmark's statement for the European Community (UN GAOR A/C.6/42/SR.16); Japan (A/C.6/42/SR.20). The non-normative nature of the Declaration was apparently accepted even by some Eastern bloc and developing states. See the comments by East Germany and Romania (A/C.6/41/SR.11) and Tanzania (A/C.6/42/SR.21).
44 The draft was criticised by Greece (UN GAOR A/C.6/42/SR.20) which found it regrettable that the word 'should' rather than 'shall' was used in many parts.
45 UN GAOR A/C.6/42/SR.50.
46 UN GAOR A/C.6/41/SR.11, 13.
47 UN GAOR A/C.6/42/SR.18.
48 UN GAOR A/C.6/42/SR.19.
49 See comments by Afghanistan (UN GAOR A/C.6/42/SR.18) Yugoslavia, Czechoslovakia, Romania and Hungary (A/C.6/42/SR.20).
50 UN GAOR A/C.6/42/SR.18.
51 UN GAOR A/C.6/42/SR.17,18.
52 UN GAOR A/C.6/42/SR.20.
53 UN GAOR A/C.6/42/SR.17,18.
54 UN GAOR A/C.6/42/SR.50.
55 UN GAOR A/C./42/SR.19.
56 On the differences between states, see the contributions by R. Higgins, H. Bokor-Szego and M. Sahovic, in Cassese, above n.6, at pp.435, 453, 479.
57 *1966 UN Yearbook* p.906; *1967 UN Yearbook*, p.743.
58 UN Doc. A/8018.
59 USSR draft UN GAOR A/31/243; Western draft, A/AC.193/L.34; Non-Aligned draft, A/AC.193/L.35. For discussion of the last two, see UN Doc. A/42/41.
60 (1987) 26 *I.L.M.* 190, para.11.
61 See summary in UN Docs. A/40/41, A/41/41.
62 See comments by Spain (UN GAOR A/C.6/40/SR.11), Czechoslovakia (A/C.6/41/SR10), Pakistan (A/C.6/41/SR.11), Jordan (A/C.6/41/SR.12), Libya (A/C.6/41/SR.13) and Sri Lanka (A/C.6/41/SR.13).
63 UN GAOR A/C.6/41/SR.13; cf. UN Doc. A/40/41.
64 *1976 UN Yearbook*, p.107.
65 Brazil (UN GAOR A/C.6/42/SR.18), Mexico (A/C.6/42/SR.17), Canada (A/C.6/42/SR.19).
66 At the time work began on the Declaration on Friendly Relations there were 113 members of the UN; 127 by the time it was adopted. When the Declaration on the Non-Use of Force was adopted there were 159 member states.
67 (1970) 64 *A.J.I.L.* 809.
68 UN Doc. S/20001.
69 Security Council Resolution 330 (1973) is a rare example. This invokes the Declaration on Friendly Relations and other resolutions in urging states to refrain from coercive measures.
70 It has been invoked in the Security Council, for example, by Nicaragua against the US (9S.PV.2577), and vice versa (S/PV.2578), by Morocco against Israel (S/PV.2613), and by Israel against Libya (S/PV.2651).
71 (1988) 27 *I.L.M.* 577, at p.581.
72 (1982) 53 *B.Y.I.L.* 546; (1986) 57 *B.Y.I.L.* 614, at p.615.
73 (1980) 74 *A.J.I.L.* 418.
74 UN General Assembly Resolution 38/7 on Grenada is extremely unusual in its reference to the Declaration.
75 UN General Assembly Resolution 32/155.

76 UN General Assembly Resolution 34/99.
77 UN General Assembly Resolution 37/119.
78 On the repetition of resolutions by the General Assembly, see S.A. Bleicher (1969) 63 *A.J.I.L.* 444.
79 The ILC has been working on this since 1947. Work stopped in 1954 when the General Assembly decided to wait for the adoption of the Definition of Aggression. It resumed in 1982 and is now progressing well (*ILC Yearbook 1983*, vol. 1, p.2). The ILC has now completed its first reading of the Draft Articles of the Code of Crimes against the Peace and Security of Mankind (UN Doc. A/46/10; (1991) 30 *I.L.M.* 1584; S. McCaffrey (1991) 85 *A.J.I.L.* 703). In 1992 it also produced a draft statute for the International Criminal Court (for the earlier stages of its work on this, see UN Docs. A/CN.4/430/Add.1 and A/CN.4/435/Add.1). However, it remains doubtful whether states will be willing to implement such a code domestically, let alone accept an international criminal court.
80 See A. Yankov, *ILC Yearbook 1988* vol.1, p.95 and A. Al Khasewneh, *ILC Yearbook 1988*, vol. 1, at p.111.
81 The ILC has been working has been working on this since 1963. It is trying to produce general principles on state responsibility rather than to involve itself with primary rules of international law. Accordingly, although it has included aggression as an international crime it does not give a definition of the offence. It does not even refer to the Definition of Aggression, (*ILC Yearbook 1976*, vol. 2, part 2, p.95ff).
82 *ILC Yearbook 1988*, vol. 1, p.291; (1991) 30 *I.L.M.* 1584 (Article 15).
83 *ILC Yearbook 1988*, vol. 2, part 2, p.72. Similar disagreements arose during the drafting of the Definition of the Aggression itself. For many years states could not agree how the definition would fit into the UN system, nor on whether the definition should be exhaustive. See works cited in n.7.
84 See *ILC Yearbooks 1988 and 1989*. Also S. McCaffrey (1989) 83 *A.J.I.L.* 937; (1991) 85 *A.J.I.L.* 703.
85 See *ILC Yearbook 1987*, vol. 1, p.4, and (1991) 30 *I.L.M.* 1584. As it turned out the Commission was not able to agree on any detailed provisions on defences in the draft articles. Article 14 simply leaves it to 'the competent court' to determine the admissibility of defences. See S. McCaffrey (1991) 85 *A.J.I.L.* 703. The Commission also still has to resolve the very complex issue of the relation between the state's act of aggression or self-defence and the individual criminal responsibility of the actual people involved. The nature of the individual's involvement in the state's acts and the mental element required must be clearly spelled out. And in general the need to specify precisely the element of the offences against the peace and security of mankind faces the Commission with serious difficulties.
86 See *ILC Yearbooks 1979* and *1980*.
87 [1986] I.C.J. Rep. 14 at pp.29–38.
88 Ibid., p.98.
89 See, for example, A. D'Amato, (1987) 81 *A.J.I.L.* 101; A. D'Amato, *International Law: Process and Prospect* New York: Transnational, 1987; J. Norton Moore (1987) 81 *A.J.I.L.* 151, at p.159.
90 On the problems involved with this legal fiction, based on tradition and an argument from need, see P. Hagenmacher (1986) 90 *R.G.D.I.P.* 5.
91 [1986] I.C.J. Rep. 99–100.
92 See W.M. Reisman (1987) 81 *A.J.I.L.* 166. For discussion of this passage see R. St. J. Macdonald (1986) 24 *Canadian Yearbook of International Law* 127.
93 M.H. Mendelson, in Butler, above n.4, p.85.
94 [1986] I.C.J. Rep. 14, at p.117.

95 T.M. Franck (1987) 81 *A.J.I.L.* 116; Mendelson, above n.93; D'Amato, above n.89; W. Czaplinski (1989) 38 *I.C.L.Q.* 151. Others supported the Court's approach: Macdonald, above n.92; H. Hohmann and P.J.I.M. de Waart (1987) 34 *Neth. I.L.R.* 162.
96 [1986] I.C.J. Rep. 98.
97 Akehurst, above n.9.
98 See D'Amato, above n.89; T.J. Farer (1991) 85 *A.J.I.L.* 117; R.A. Mullerson (1989) 83 *A.J.I.L.* 494, at p.505.
99 D'Amato, above n.89.
100 D'Amato, *International Law* above n.89, p.230.
101 As set out in (1974–5) 47 *B.Y.I.L.* 1.
102 D'Amato, *International Law*, above n.89.
103 Ibid., p.231.
104 W.M. Reisman (1984) 78 *A.J.I.L.* 642; O. Schachter (1984) 78 *A.J.I.L.* 646.
105 There is no space here for a full reply. See Mullerson, above n.98, for some criticisms of D'Amato's approach.

3 The principle of peaceful settlement of disputes

J.G. Merrills

The second principle of the Declaration on Friendly Relations is 'that States shall settle their international disputes by peaceful means in such a manner that international peace and security and justice are not endangered'. Coming immediately after the principle dealing with the use of force, this part of the Declaration echoes the words of Article 2(3) of the UN Charter, as the first principle recalls those of Article 2(4). The juxtaposition of the two principles in both instruments is, of course, not accidental. If force, the traditional means of settling international disputes, is to be enjoined, there must be a corresponding obligation to resolve differences peacefully. The second principle of the Declaration is thus complementary to the first principle and this is also the position in the Charter.

It is, however, not enough merely to prescribe the use of peaceful means of settlement. Just as a prohibition of the use of force requires elaboration if it is to provide a meaningful guide for action, so an obligation to settle disputes peacefully is of limited value without more detailed arrangements. In the Charter this requirement is fulfilled by Article 33(1) which lists the means available, and by the rest of Chapter VI which is mainly concerned with the role of the Security Council. There is no equivalent of the latter in the Declaration, but, after laying down the general principle of peaceful settlement, it does provide that States shall 'seek early and just settlement of their international disputes by negotiation, inquiry, mediation, conciliation, arbitration, judicial settlement, resort to regional agencies or arrangements or other peaceful means of their choice'. This corresponds closely to Article 33(1).

With dispute settlement, then, as with a number of its other principles, the Declaration is in large measure a confirmation of the Charter. It is worth noting, however, that after listing the means available, the Declaration states that in the event of failure to reach a peaceful solution the parties have a duty to continue to pursue this objective; that all States shall refrain from actions that may aggravate disputes; and that disputes shall be settled 'on the basis of the sovereign equality of States and in accordance with the principle of free choice of means'. These precepts, although implicit in the Charter, are not emphasised in its provisions on disputes. They therefore constitute a clarification of the position and are also a reflection of international practice where, as we shall see, sovereign equality and the principle of free choice of means are regarded as especially important.

So much for the background. What is the current scope of this part of the Declaration and in particular what developments have there been in this field since 1970?[1] To answer these questions it is necessary to look more closely at the Declaration and to consider the different means of settlement separately.

NEGOTIATION AND MEDIATION

The Declaration on Friendly Relations does not set out the various methods of peaceful settlement in any order of priority, but the first mentioned, negotiation, is the principal means of handling all international disputes.[2] In fact, negotiation is used more frequently in practice than all the other methods put together. Often, indeed, negotiation is the only means employed, not just because it is always the first to be tried and is often successful, but also because States may believe its advantages to be so great as to rule out the use of other methods, even in situations where the chances of a negotiated settlement are slight. On the occasions when another method is used, negotiation is not displaced but is directed towards instrumental issues, the terms of reference for an inquiry or conciliation commission, for instance, or the arrangements for implementing an arbitral decision.

Mediation is essentially an adjunct of negotiation and involves a third party.[3] If the latter does no more than encourage the disputing States to resume negotiations, or simply acts as a channel of communication, he is said to be contributing his 'good offices'. A mediator, on the other hand, is an active participant authorised, and indeed expected, to advance his own proposals and to interpret, as well as to transmit, each party's proposals to the other. Mediation thus resembles conciliation, although a mediator usually makes his proposals informally and on the basis of information supplied by the parties, rather than through independent investigations which are a feature of conciliation. In practice, however, these distinctions tend to be blurred. In a given case it may therefore be difficult to draw the line between mediation and conciliation, or to say exactly when good offices ended and mediation began.

Although negotiation, often supplemented by mediation, is usually involved at some stage in every international dispute and is therefore related to all the other methods of peaceful settlement, its relation to the legal methods of arbitration and judicial settlement is particularly significant. This can be seen in a number of recent cases in which the International Court of Justice has had to decide whether the possibilities of negotiation have been exhausted where this has been laid down as a condition of its jurisdiction.[4] In the *Aegean Sea Continental Shelf* case,[5] on the other hand, it addressed another aspect of the relation between negotiation and adjudication, and held that when negotiation has not been given formal priority, the fact that negotiations are being pursued during litigation is no bar to the exercise of the judicial function.

Negotiation, as these cases suggest, cannot guarantee a settlement and is subject to important limitations. It may be impossible if the parties to a dispute refuse to speak to each other, or ineffective if their positions are too far apart, although in both situations mediation or good offices can often help. Negotiation may also be inappropriate if a different procedure has already been agreed. It may be noted in this connection that the terms of a negotiated settlement will usually reflect not the merits of each party's case, but their relative power. Negotiation in a situation of grossly unequal power is thus scarcely conducive to the 'just settlement' of disputes which the Declaration and the Charter prescribe. Accordingly, while negotiation is often called for by the strong, the weak may have excellent reasons for declining the invitation.

A State can of course bind itself to negotiate by treaty,[6] or find itself in a situation where an obligation to negotiate arises under the general law. In the year before the Declaration on Friendly Relations the International Court decided that according to customary international law, the delimitation of continental shelf boundaries between neighbouring States 'must be effected by agreement in accordance with equitable principles'.[7] Similarly, in 1974 it found that the United Kingdom and Iceland were 'under mutual obligations to undertake negotiations in good faith for the equitable solution of their differences', concerning their respective fishing rights in the waters off Iceland.[8] In both cases what the Court was concerned to emphasise was that as each party had rights in the disputed areas, the issues were not open to unilateral regulation, but had to be negotiated.

It is clear, then, that in some situations there is a duty to negotiate. Moreover, sometimes the parties to a dispute may have a lesser obligation such as to 'proceed expeditiously to an exchange of views', as is prescribed in the 1982 Law of the Sea Convention with reference to the means of settlement to be used.[9] However, it is worth stressing that just as there is no general duty to consult other States before taking action which affects them,[10] so there is no general duty to attempt to settle disputes by negotiation. The various means of settlement in the Declaration are listed as alternatives and so, unless there is a specific obligation to negotiate, a State is entitled to suggest that another procedure should be used. Negotiation is simply one means of settlement and in the absence of a duty to negotiate, States are entitled to use it or not as they see fit.

Despite the above qualifications, negotiation is an extremely important means of dealing with international disputes. In almost all cases diplomatic exchanges will be necessary before a disagreement becomes sufficiently specific to be called a dispute,[11] and once a dispute has arisen negotiation will often provide the best prospect of a solution. It is evident, however, that although this method must be regarded as basic, negotiation, even when assisted by mediation, may not be enough to resolve an international dispute. The other methods referred to in the Declaration must therefore now be considered.

INQUIRY AND CONCILIATION

Inquiry, as a distinct procedure, involves referring a dispute to a tribunal with a view to obtaining an independent investigation of the facts. Conciliation, on the other hand, has been defined as:

> A method for the settlement of international disputes of any nature according to which a Commission set up by the Parties, either on a permanent or an ad hoc basis to deal with a dispute, proceeds to the impartial examination of the dispute and attempts to define the terms of a settlement susceptible of being accepted by them, or of affording the Parties, with a view to its settlement, such aid as they may have requested.[12]

If mediation is essentially an extension of negotiation, conciliation puts third party intervention on a formal footing and institutionalises it in a way comparable, but not identical, to inquiry or arbitration. For the fact-finding exercise that is the essence of inquiry may or may not be an element in conciliation, while the search for terms 'susceptible of being accepted by the parties', but not binding on them, provides a sharp contrast with arbitration and forms a link between conciliation and mediation.

In the two decades since the Declaration on Friendly Relations, inquiry in the general sense of fact finding has been regularly performed in the course of arbitration and adjudication, and as part of the work of international organisations. But there have been no formal inquiry commissions of the type set up following the 1899 and 1907 Hague Conventions.[13] Conciliation, however, has been used on several occasions and is also provided for in a number of recent treaties. Although, therefore, the Declaration, following the formula in the Charter, mentions both procedures as available to States, conciliation now seems largely to have displaced inquiry in international practice.

Like other institutional methods, conciliation is normally entrusted to commissions containing several members. It is, however, open to States to refer a dispute to a single conciliator and this was the procedure adopted in 1977 when Kenya, Uganda and Tanzania asked the experienced Swiss diplomat, Dr Victor Umbricht, to make proposals for the distribution of the assets of the former East African Community.(EAC)[14]

The dispute had arisen because the partner States, having integrated their economies, had now decided to split up. Before this could be done it was necessary to determine the extent of the EAC's assets and liabilities and, more contentiously, their distribution. As these matters could not be resolved by negotiation, they were referred to Dr Umbricht for his assistance. In this case the conciliator had to begin by conducting a wide-ranging inquiry, then, having identified the assets and valued them, he succeeded in finding a formula for allocation which the parties could use as a basis for negotiation. Although the final division of assets differed slightly from that originally proposed, it is clear that the activities of the conciliator, which eventually included mediation, as well as conciliation and inquiry, made a vital contribution to the settlement.

A more straightforward dispute which was recently resolved by conciliation involved a commission of the type familiar from earlier conciliations. In 1980 Iceland and Norway set up a commission to make recommendations with regard to the dividing line for the area of continental shelf between Iceland and Jan Mayen Island.[15] The Commission was directed to take into account Iceland's 'strong economic interests' in the sea areas in question, along with various other factors. Following a detailed investigation of geological and other evidence, the Commission proposed both a boundary line and a joint development agreement covering almost all of the area offering any significant prospect of hydrocarbon production. This recommendation, typical of the constructive compromise which conciliation can produce, was accepted by the parties and in 1981 incorporated in a treaty which ended the dispute.[16]

Bilateral arrangements providing for conciliation in future disputes, though common in the League of Nations era, are now rare. Where States employ conciliation in a bilateral treaty it is therefore usually for the purposes of resolving a specific dispute, as in the cases just mentioned. Multilateral treaties, however, show a quite different pattern and in the period since 1970 arrangements utilising conciliation, often in conjunction with other procedures, have been concluded in significant numbers. Among the agreements which show how conciliation can be relevant to many different types of disputes are the Vienna Convention on Succession of States in respect of Treaties (1978),[17] the African Charter on Human and Peoples' Rights (1981),[18] the Treaty establishing the Organisation of Eastern Caribbean States (1981)[19] and the Vienna Convention for the Protection of the Ozone Layer (1985).[20]

Mention must also be made of the elaborate and potentially very important treatment of conciliation to be found in the 1982 Law of the Sea Convention. Details of the Convention must be sought elsewhere,[21] but it is relevant to note here that conciliation is specifically mentioned in section 1 of Part XV as a procedure which the parties to a dispute may select in accordance with the principle of free choice of means. Moreover, whereas certain disputes cannot, or need not, be submitted to a binding procedure of settlement under section 2, sea boundary disputes and certain other issues are made subject to compulsory conciliation. This is valuable because although conciliation produces a result which the parties are free to accept or reject, and so cannot be guaranteed to settle a dispute, the prospect of any compulsory procedure discourages unreasonableness and so can often prevent disputes from arising.

The Law of the Sea Convention, like the other treaties mentioned, lays down the procedure to be followed in setting up conciliation commissions and supplies details of their organisation and jurisdiction. It also establishes a process called 'special arbitration'.[22] Though primarily arbitral, as the name indicates, this is flexible enough to function as conciliation, or inquiry, or both, and emphasises the close relation between them.

ARBITRATION

Arbitration and judicial settlement are procedures which are employed when what is wanted is a binding decision, usually on the basis of international law. Judicial settlement involves the reference of a dispute to the International Court of Justice or another permanent tribunal such as the European Court of Human Rights. Arbitration, in contrast, requires the parties themselves to set up the machinery to handle a dispute, or a series of disputes between them. In the Declaration and in most other instruments concerned with dispute settlement the two methods are mentioned together and have much in common. Historically, however, arbitration was the first to develop and retains a distinct character.[23] Practice since 1970 demonstrates that governments are fully aware of its potential and that across a range of international disputes it still has an important role to play.

Traditionally, arbitration has been used for disputes in which the issues are legal, or can be presented in legal terms, and in which there is need to remove an obstacle to friendly relations which makes the idea of a binding settlement attractive. Territorial and boundary disputes, for example, often fall into this category. Because it is open to the parties to define the question to be answered and to specify the basis of the decision, they can exercise a degree of control over the process of resolution which is a further advantage. Moreover, as already mentioned, the parties are required to choose the arbitrators. Although this, like other elements of an arbitration, requires agreement and so can be a source of difficulty, it means that the dispute can be decided by a tribunal which the parties believe they can trust, a factor of fundamental importance in international litigation.

In the period under review arbitration has continued to be used in territorial disputes and to resolve other disputes within its established sphere of operation. Thus in 1977 Argentina and Chile referred the

Beagle Channel case[24] to arbitration and in 1988 an arbitral tribunal decided the *Taba* dispute[25] between Egypt and Israel. Maritime boundaries, which have become increasingly significant as a result of dramatic changes in the law of the sea, were the subject of arbitrations in the *Maritime Delimitation* case[26] between Guinea and Guinea-Bissau (1985) and the earlier *Channel* arbitration[27] between the United Kingdom and France (1976–7). Notable arbitrations involving other issues of a type which would have been familiar to an earlier generation of international lawyers include the *Air Services Agreement* arbitration[28] between the United States and France (1978), the *La Bretagne* case[29] between Canada and France (1986) and the two arbitrations in the *Rainbow Warrior* case[30] between France and New Zealand (1986 and 1990).

The type of arbitration set up by States to decide a case between them must be distinguished from another type which deals with disputes in which individuals or corporations are involved as parties. This kind of arbitration is known as private (as opposed to public) international arbitration, or international commercial arbitration. To the extent that it involves litigation between private individuals or corporations, commercial arbitration is not concerned with international disputes in the sense of the Declaration on Friendly Relations and need not be discussed further. However, when the dispute is between a private party and a foreign State which is accused of taking over property or interfering with a contract, the position is likely to be different. Details of the complex legal issues which such cases give rise to cannot be examined here,[31] but it is relevant to note that these arbitrations often combine features of both public and private arbitration and that cases of this type continue to be decided in significant numbers.[32]

In this connection special mention must be made of the Iran-US Claims Tribunal.[33] Set up in 1981 after the diplomatic hostages crisis to deal with a large number of claims arising out of the Islamic revolution in Iran, the Tribunal has jurisdiction over three types of cases. It can hear 'national claims', that is claims of Iranian and United States nationals against each other; 'official claims' of Iran and the United States against each other, arising out of certain contractual arrangements; and 'interpretative disputes', that is disputes between the two States relating to the interpretation or application of the two Declarations concerned with the Tribunal and its work. Of the three, the first, adjudication of national claims, is by far the most important and the Tribunal's decisions, which already run to more than twenty volumes, not only show the value of arbitration in resolving disputes with serious implications, but also form a significant contribution to international law.

No outline of the contemporary role of arbitration would be complete without mention of the fact that arbitration, like conciliation, occupies a prominent place in the provisions on the settlement of disputes in the 1982 Law of the Sea Convention.[34] In accordance with the principle of free choice of means in section 1 the parties to a dispute can decide to set up an arbitration tribunal in the traditional way. Under the provisions relating to compulsory settlement in section 2 both parties may make declarations nominating arbitration as a preferred means of settlement, in which case arbitration will be governed by the provisions of the Convention. Alternatively, if there is no common declaration under section 2, arbitration under the Convention will be deemed to have been accepted as the relevant obligatory procedure. Arbitration is thus a central feature of the Convention's procedures.

The Convention includes the necessary provisions for constituting a tribunal and arrangements covering procedure and related matters. Disputes relating to certain articles of the Convention, for example, fisheries and the preservation of the marine environment, can be dealt with under the provisions relating to special arbitration which, as noted earlier, is a procedure closely related to conciliation. The maritime activities of States, like many aspects of the contemporary international scene, are so complex that disputes require arbitrators with technical qualifications. The Law of the Sea Convention is thus a recognition that here, as in other fields, a functional approach to international arbitration is a way to enhance its usefulness.

JUDICIAL SETTLEMENT

Judicial settlement involves the reference of disputes to permanent tribunals for a legally binding decision. It is listed in the Declaration on Friendly Relations after arbitration, from which it developed historically, and for most of the present century has been available to State through a number of courts of general or specialised jurisdiction. The only court of general jurisdiction is the International Court of Justice at The Hague, whose role has been subject to intensive scrutiny in the period under review.[35] There have also been a number of developments in other tribunals which are both interesting in themselves and indicators of the status of judicial settlement.

The powers of the International Court to decide disputes are defined in its Statute and are based on the principle of consent. This principle, which is, of course, a further illustration of the underlying principle of free choice of means contained in the Declaration, gives rise to a number of questions on which recent practice has been significant. One question is how States may manifest their consent and the related question of how many have done so. On the issue of means the Court has decided several cases relating to the scope of its jurisdiction, of which its controversial decision in the *Nicaragua* case is certainly the most important.[36] On the issue of numbers, acceptances of the Court's jurisdiction under Article 36(2) have grown slightly, while treaty acceptances have also increased, with the revolutions in the former communist States of Eastern Europe exercising a positive influence in both cases.[37]

A second issue relating to consent concerns the relation between legal and political consent to adjudication. Adjudication works best when the two coincide. When they do not, legal tribunals are likely to find themselves presented with the argument that a case is not justiciable because it is political and with a refusal on the part of the respondent to recognise the Court's authority.[38] The *Nicaragua* case provides a particularly depressing example of a situation of this kind and others in the period since the Declaration include the *Fisheries Jurisdiction* cases[39] (1973), the *Aegean Sea Continental Shelf* case (1978) and the *Diplomatic Hostages* case (1980).[40] There is little a judicial tribunal can do in such a case other than to apply the law. This the Court has done. However, the fact that the political aspect of justiciability is at least as important as its legal aspect obviously limits the value of judicial settlement in practice.

The other aspect of the Court's work which has been prominent recently relates to its organisation and specifically its composition for particular cases. Cases are normally heard by the full Court. However the Statute also provides for the creation of smaller chambers and in 1972 as part of an effort to encourage greater use of its facilities the Court revised its Rules so as to enable prospective litigants to influence the composition as well as the size of the bench.[41] Experience so far indicates that this has been quite successful. States have recognised that they now have an opportunity to combine the convenience of the Court with several of the advantages of arbitration. Several cases have been referred to chambers[42] and suggest that the new procedure is seen as particularly useful for disputes which involve complex evidence, and perhaps also issues with a strong regional dimension. The decisions themselves, though inevitably lacking some of the weight which attaches to judgments of the full Court, can certainly stand comparison with them. Moreover, in each of the cases to date the Court's decision settled the case, something which unfortunately cannot be said of every decision of the full Court. The revitalisation of the chambers procedure is thus a positive step for the Court and for the student of peaceful settlement, a reminder of the link between judicial settlement and arbitration.

Among courts of specialised jurisdiction the most spectacular developments have unquestionably been those associated with human rights tribunals, notably the European Court of Human Rights at Strasbourg and the Inter-American Court in San José. In 1970 the former was rarely used, while the American Court was not inaugurated until 1979. Today, however, the European Court has a flourishing jurisprudence,[43] and, though the American Court is nothing like as busy, it has begun to make its mark with a number of important advisory opinions and its first contentious cases.[44] The work of these courts is mainly concerned with the rights of individuals under the respective regional conventions and not with inter-State disputes. However, both courts have jurisdiction over such cases and deal with them from time to time. More importantly, as human rights are now an international issue, procedures for enabling claims to be heard at the international level help to consolidate friendly relations, whether or not they are brought by States. In the broader sense, then, the activities of human rights courts certainly fall within the Declaration.

Courts with specialised jurisdiction of a quite different type are to be found in the Law of the Sea Convention.[45] For among several new institutions created by the Convention is a new court, the International Tribunal for the Law of the Sea (ITLS), and an independent subsidiary organ, the Sea-Bed Disputes Chamber (SBDC). The ITLS reflects the preference of many States for a special tribunal to handle disputes arising out of the 'new' law embodied in the 1982 Convention, and a corresponding lack of confidence in the International Court. In the same way the SBDC was set up because the complex arrangements envisaged in the Convention for the exploration and exploitation of the deep sea-bed were thought unsuitable for adjudication in the ITLS.

The arrangements pertaining to the organisation and jurisdiction of both tribunals and the choice of law to be applied are set out in great detail in the Convention and provide a good guide to the thinking behind them. Among points which are particularly worth noting are that the jurisdiction of the ITLS is based on the principle of free choice of means in the sense that it depends upon States making a declaration nominating it under section 2. The SBDC, on the other hand, has a jurisdiction which is automatically accepted by all the parties to the Convention.[46] Both tribunals, unlike the International Court of Justice, are open not just to States, but also to other entities; and both tribunals, at the request of the parties, can split into smaller chambers. This last facility parallels almost exactly what we have seen is one of the more significant elements in the recent history of the International Court of Justice. In a more general way, the fact that so much attention is given in the Law of the Sea Convention to the ITLS and the SBDC supports the view that in the settlement of international disputes permanent judicial organs still have an important part to play.

INTERNATIONAL ORGANISATIONS

The reference in the Declaration on Friendly Relations to 'resort to regional agencies or arrangements' relates to bodies such as the Organization of American States, the Organization of African Unity, NATO and the European Economic Community, which are recognised in Article 52(2) of the Charter as having a contribution to make to the settlement of local disputes. There is no reference in the Declaration's list to the United Nations' own procedures, although the phrase 'or other peaceful means of their choice' is plainly wide enough to include these, provided there is agreement. Moreover, the final paragraph of the Declaration states that nothing in the preceding paragraphs 'prejudices or derogates from the applicable provisions of the Charter, in particular those relating to the pacific settlement of international disputes'. Thus the Declaration recognises the role of international political organisations at both the regional and universal levels.

The work of the United Nations in the field of dispute settlement has numerous facets, only some of which can be mentioned here.[47] The primary responsibility is assigned to the Security Council which is given extensive powers with regard to peaceful settlement in Chapter VI of the Charter, and authority to take action to maintain international peace and security in Chapter VII. As is well known, the Council, though not totally ineffective, has not been conspicuously successful in discharging these functions, a point which was made in a General Assembly Declaration of 1988 in which the Council was urged to be more active in these areas.[48] With the ending of the Cold War, and in the light of the impressive response to the invasion of Kuwait, it appears that for the first time in the history of the United Nations there is a real possibility of this happening.

If the Security Council has often been slow to act, the same cannot be said of the Secretary-General whose work under Articles 98 and 99 of the Charter has often formed the main, or even the only, element in a United Nations response. It has been pointed out, however, that apart from political and constitutional constraints which will always be present, the work of the Secretary-General in the field of dispute settlement has often been hindered by a lack of resources both in the sense of inadequate funds and as regards the no less vital commodity of information.[49] It is therefore encouraging to see that in 1987 Secretary-General Pérez de Cuellar set up an Office for Research and the Collection of Information (ORCI) within the Secretariat with the specific function of providing early warning in relation to the Secretary-General's preventive diplomacy and good offices.[50] The ORCI has not, as yet, received much attention from international lawyers and the nature of its work is probably such that its successes will rarely be acknowledged. It is, however, the kind of measure which can act as a 'force multiplier' in the cause of peace and, as such, is to be welcomed.

A final aspect of United Nations involvement in dispute settlement which should be mentioned concerns the relation between political and legal methods of settlement and the role of the Organisation in encouraging the use of legal methods. The first of these issues has already been touched on and was also discussed by the International Court in the *Diplomatic Hostages* case, where adjudication was found to be compatible with the Secretary-General's exercise of his functions, and in the *Nicaragua* case, where the conclusion was the same as regards the role of the

Security Council under Chapter VII.[51] On the question of encouraging the use of legal methods, developments worthy of note are that in 1989 the Secretary-General announced the creation of a Trust Fund to assist States in settling disputes through the International Court[52] and three years earlier himself acted as arbitrator in the *Rainbow Warrior* case.

Turning now to 'regional agencies or arrangements' the large volume of practice, much of it naturally concerned with disputes which also involved the United Nations, again makes it necessary to be very selective.[53] As regards the handling of specific issues, however, reference must be made to the diplomatic treatment of the problems of Central America through the Contadora process and the involvement of the European Community in what used to be Yugoslavia. The former demonstrates that regional initiatives are sometimes best pursued through subregional groupings and that persistence may be needed, sometimes over years, for useful results to be achieved. The EC initiative, on the other hand, took the form of mediation first by Lord Carrington, then by Lord Owen and the sending of official EC 'monitors'. This activity, which began well before the United Nations became involved in the area, not only represents the extension of a regional organisation's activities into an entirely new field, but is also a reminder of the fact that peaceful settlement embraces internal as well as external disputes. The evolution of the EC and the instability of Eastern Europe make it likely that there will be similar cases in the future.

In relation both to Eastern Europe and the European region generally developments of potential significance for the settlement of disputes have recently been initiated through the Conference on Security and Co-operation in Europe.[54] The 'CSCE process', as the Conference and its associated activities are known, began with the Helsinki Agreement in 1975 and has been progressively developed and refined through subsequent meetings in Belgrade (1977), Madrid (1980), and Vienna (1986), with a return to Helsinki in 1992. The meetings have been concerned with three main issues: questions relating to security in Europe; co-operation in the fields of economics, science, technology and the environment; and co-operation in humanitarian and other fields. The peaceful settlement of disputes was one of the ten fundamental principles set out in the original Helsinki Agreement and has been elaborated in two ways in subsequent instruments.

The Concluding Document of the Vienna meeting, which was finally agreed in 1989, includes, for the first time in a CSCE text, a human rights monitoring procedure.[55] This is a diplomatic, not a legal, procedure with four possible stages. The first stage involves exchanging information and responding to requests and representations; the second holding bilateral meetings concerning situations and cases with a view to resolving them; the third drawing the attention of other CSCE States to those situations and cases; and the fourth and final stage, bringing the matter to one of the conferences in the CSCE process. Thus what begins as a discreet diplomatic exchange can be escalated, if necessary, to a major political confrontation. As with any system for protecting human rights, success cannot be guaranteed, but the 'Human Dimension mechanism', as it is known, was improved at a subsequent meeting in Copenhagen and has already been extensively used.

The other development arose not from one of the main CSCE meetings, but from the Paris Summit of Heads of State and Government which was held in November 1990.[56] The outcome of that meeting was the Paris Charter for a New Europe[57] which, as part of a new institutional framework for the CSCE, set up a Conflict Prevention Centre in Vienna to assist the Council of Foreign Ministers 'in reducing the risk of conflict' in ways which were left to be determined. As part of this exercise a group of governmental experts met in Malta in 1991 to draw up a report dealing with principles of dispute settlement and suggest CSCE procedures for consideration at Helsinki in 1992.[58]

A question which may arise in relation to CSCE procedures and arrangements under other regional instruments is the compatibility of political with legal methods for handling disputes. As noted earlier, in the period since the Declaration on Friendly Relations the International Court has considered this question in the context of UN action and the issue has also arisen in relation to regional measures. In the *Border and Transborder Armed Actions* case[59] between Nicaragua and Honduras, the Court concluded that it had jurisdiction under the Part of Bogatá, notwithstanding the on-going Contadora process. The point which the International Court was making here, and earlier in the *Nicaragua* case, was not that judicial settlement has a privileged status, but rather that the overriding objective is a peaceful settlement, and so, in principle, unless they have established clear priorities, the parties to a dispute are free to employ any of the means recognised by international law, without prejudice to their juridical position.[60]

CONCLUSION

Michael Akehurst, whose writing on international law was notably free from cant and wishful thinking, was well aware that in the field of dispute settlement the gulf between rhetoric and reality is conspicuously wide. All too often governments express support for general propositions, like those to be found in the Charter, the Declaration on Friendly Relations, and the Helsinki Agreement, only to follow quite different precepts in their international behaviour. But realism is not cynicism and Michael, who was alert to the significance of international law as well as to its limitations, would also have recognised that in the years since the Declaration progress has been made in refining the means available to States for resolving their disputes and in developing their obligations. The challenge for the next century, and for the remaining years of this one, is to see that the arrangements which unquestionably provide the means for settling disputes, continue to be used in international practice.

NOTES

1 Detailed surveys of the subject of dispute settlement can be found in J.G. Merrills, *International Dispute Settlement*, Cambridge: Grotius, 2nd edn, 1991; C.M.H. Waldock (ed.) *International Disputes: The Legal Aspects*, London: David Davies, 1972; and F.S. Northedge and M.D. Donelan, *International Disputes: The Political Aspects*, London: David Davies, 1971.

2 See Merrills, above n.1, ch.2; Waldock, above n.1, ch.2A; Northedge and Donelan, above n.1, ch.12 and the specialist works cited therein.

3 See Merrills, above, n.1, ch.1; Waldock, above n.1, ch.2B; Northedge and Donelan, above n.1, ch.13; and S. Touval and I.W. Zartman (eds) *International Mediation in Theory and Practice*, Boulder: Westview Press, 1985.

4 See *United States Diplomatic and Consular Staff in Tehran*, Judgment, [1980] I.C.J. Rep. 3; *Applicability of the Obligation to Arbitrate under Section 21 of the United Nations Headquarters Agreement of 26 June 1947*, Advisory opinion, [1988] I.C.J. Rep. 12; and *Border and Transborder Armed Actions, Jurisdiction and Admissibility*, Judgment, [1988] I.C.J. Rep. 69.

5 *Aegean Sea Continental Shelf*, Judgment, [1978] I.C.J. Rep. 3.

6 See, for example, Article 41 of the 1978 *Vienna Convention on Succession of States in Respect of Treaties*, which provides: 'If a dispute regarding the application or interpretation of the present Convention arises between two or more Parties to the Convention, they shall, upon the request of any of them, seek to resolve it by a process of consultation and negotiation'.

7 *North Sea Continental Shelf*, Judgment, [1969] I.C.J. Rep. 3.

8 *Fisheries Jurisdiction (United Kingdom v Iceland) (Merits)* Judgment, [1974] I.C.J. Rep. 3.

9 *United Nations Convention on the Law of the Sea* (1982) Article 283. For further examples see S.L. Kass, 'Obligatory Negotiations in International Organisations' (1965) 3 *Canadian Yearbook of International Law* 36.

10 On consultation, which can be way of using negotiation to avoid disputes, see F.L. Kirgis, *Prior Consultation in International Law*, Charlottesville: University Press of Virginia, 1983.

11 For a recent case raising this issue see *Application for Revision and Interpretation of the Judgment of 24 February 1982 in the Case concerning the Continental Shelf* (*Tunisia* v. *Libyan Arab Jamahiriya*) Judgment, [1985] I.C.J. Rep. 192.

12 The quotation is from Article 1 of the Regulations on the Procedure of International Conciliation, adopted by the Institute of International Law in 1961. See (1961) 49 (ii) *Annuaire* 385–91. For a more recent version see the 1990 United Nations Draft Rules for the Conciliation of Dispute between States in (1991) 30 *I.L.M* 229. For discussion of conciliation see Merrills, above n.1, ch.4; and J.P. Cot, *International Conciliation*, London: Europa, 1972.

13 See N. Bar-Yaacov, *The Handling of International Disputes by Means of Inquiry*, Oxford: Oxford University Press for Royal Institute of International Affairs, 1974; and Merrills, above n.1, ch.3.

14 See V. Umbricht, 'Principles of International Mediation. The Case of the East African Community' (1984) 187 *Hague Recueil des Cours* 307. Although

termed by the parties a 'mediator', Dr Umbricht was clearly engaged in conciliation.

15 See R.R. Churchill, 'Maritime Delimitation in the Jan Mayen area' (1985) *Marine Policy* 16.

16 For the Commission's Report see (1981) 20 *I.L.M* 797 and 62 I.L.R. 108. For the treaty which substantially incorporated the Commission's recommendations see (1982) 21 *I.L.M.* 1222. For reflections on the case by the chairman of the Commission see E.L. Richardson, 'Jan Mayen in Perspective' (1988) 82 *A.J.I.L.* 443.

17 Text in (1978) 73 *A.J.I.L.* 971.

18 See A.H. Robertson and J.G. Merrills, *Human Rights in the World*, Manchester: Manchester University Press, 3rd edn, 1989, pp. 100–22.

19 Text in (1981) 20 *I.L.M.* 1166.

20 Text in (1987) 26 *I.L.M.* 1516.

21 See Merrills, above n.1, ch.8 and A.O. Adede, *The System for Settlement of Disputes under the United Nations Convention on the Law of the Sea*, Dordrecht: Martinus Nijhoff, 1987.

22 See Merrills, above n.1, pp. 168–70.

23 See Merrills, above n.1, ch.5; J.G. Wetter, *The International Arbitral Process Public and Private*, 5 vols., New York: Oceana 1979; and J.L. Simpson and H. Fox, *International Arbitration: Law and Practice*, London: Stevens, 1959.

24 *Beagle Channel Arbitration* (*Argentina* v. *Chile 1977*) (1979) 52 I.L.R. 93. See M. Shaw, 'The Beagle Channel Arbitration Award' (1978) 6 *Int. Rel.* 415.

25 *Arbitral Award in the Dispute concerning Certain Boundary Pillars between the Arab Republic of Egypt and the State of Israel* (1988) 80 I.L.R. 224, summarised in (1989) 83 *A.J.I.L.* 590.

26 *Guinea-Guinea-Bissau Maritime Delimitation Case* (1985) 77 I.L.R. 636.

27 *Delimitation of the Continental Shelf* (United Kingdom of Great Britain and Northern Ireland and the French Republic) (1977) 54 I.L.R. 6. See J.G. Merrills, 'The United Kingdom-France Continental Shelf Arbitration' (1980) 10 *California Western International Law Journal* 314.

28 *Case Concerning the Air Services Agreement of 27 March 1946* (1978) 54 I.L.R. 304. See L.F. Damrosch, 'Retaliation or Arbitration – or Both? The 1978 United States France Aviation Dispute' (1980) 74 *A.J.I.L.* 785.

29 *Canada-France Arbitration on the Dispute concerning Filleting within the Gulf of St Lawrence* (1986), French text in (1986) 90 *R.G.D.I.P.* 713. See J.M. Arbour, 'L'Affiare du Chalutier-usine "La Bretagne" ou les droits de l'État côtier dans sa zone économique exclusive' (1986) 24 *Canadian Yearbook of International Law* 61.

30 *Ruling Pertaining to the Differences between France and New Zealand Arising from the Rainbow Warrier Affair* (1986) 74 I.L.R. 241. See M. Pugh, 'Legal Aspects of the *Rainbow Warrior* Affair' (1987) 36 *I.C.L.Q.* 655 and on the second arbitration in 1990, J.S. Davidson, 'The Rainbow Warrior Arbitration Concerning the Treatment of the French Agents Mafart and Prieur' (1991) 40 *I.C.L.Q.* 446.

31 See S.J. Toope, *Mixed International Arbitration*, Cambridge: Grotius, 1990.

32 Important cases of this type in the period under review include *B.P. Exploration Company (Libya) Limited* v. *Government of the Libyan Arab Republic* (1973) 53 I.L.R. 297; *Texaco Overseas Petroleum and California Asiatic Oil Co.* v. *Libya* (*TOPCO*) (1977) 53 I.L.R. 389 and *Government of Kuwait* v. *American Independent Oil Co.* (*AMINOIL*) (1982) 66 I.L.R. 518.

33 See D.D. Caron, 'The Nature of the Iran-United States Claims Tribunal and the Evolving Structure of International Dispute Resolution' (1990) 84 *A.J.I.L.* 104; and J.A. Westberg, *International Transactions and Claims involving*

Government Parties. Case Law of the Iran-United States Claims Tribunal, Washington: International Law Institute, 1991.

34 See Merrills, above n.1, pp. 166–70.

35 See Merrills, above n.1, chs.6 and 7; L. Gross (ed.) *The Future of the International Court of Justice*, New York: Oceana for American Society of International Law, 1976; L.F. Damrosch (ed.) *The International Court of Justice at a Crossroads*, New York: Transnational for American Society of International Law, 1987; and E. Lauterpacht, *Aspects of the Administration of International Justice*, Cambridge: Grotius, 1991.

36 *Military and Paramilitary Activities in and against Nicaragua, Jurisdiction and Admissibility*, Judgment, [1984] I.C.J. Rep. 392. See H.W. Briggs, '*Nicaragua v United States*: Jurisdiction and Admissibility' (1985) 79 *A.J.I.L.* 373.

37 In a letter to the Secretary-General in February 1989 the Soviet Union announced its acceptance of the compulsory jurisdiction of the International Court of Justice in respect of six international human rights conventions, without reservation. See T.M. Franck, 'Soviet Initiatives: U.S. Responses – New Opportunities for Reviving the United Nations System' (1989) 83 *A.J.I.L.* 531, at p.539. In September 1990 Poland deposited a declaration under Article 36(2) accepting the Court's jurisdiction, becoming the first Eastern European State to do so. For a survey of other States' acceptances see J.G. Merrills, 'The Optional Clause Today' (1979) 59 *B.Y.I.L.* 8.

38 See Sir Gerald Fitzmaurice, 'The Problem of the "Non-appearing" Defendant Government' (1980) 51 *B.Y.I.L.* 89.

39 *Fisheries Jurisdiction (United Kingdom* v. *Iceland) Jurisdiction of the Court*, Judgment, [1973] I.C.J. Rep. 3.

40 *United States Diplomatic and Consular Staff in Tehran*, Judgment, [1980] I.C.J. Rep. 3.

41 See R. Ostrihansky, 'Chambers of the International Court of Justice' (1988) 37 *I.C.L.Q.* 30.

42 See *Delimitation of the Maritime Boundary in the Gulf of Maine Area*, Judgment, [1984] I.C.J. Rep. 246; *Frontier Dispute*, Judgment, [1986] I.C.J. Rep. 554; *Case concerning Elettronica Sicula S.p.A. (ELSI)*, Judgment, [1989] I.C.J. Rep. 15. At the time of writing several other cases are before the full Court.

43 See J.G. Merrills, *The Development of International Law by the European Court of Human Rights*, Manchester: Manchester University Press, 2nd edn, 1993.

44 See Robertson and Merrills, above n.18, 2nd edn, 1993.

45 See Merrills, *International Dispute Settlement*, above n.1, pp.170–5.

46 However, in respect of certain disputes alternative procedures may be used by agreement. Thus the principle of free choice of means is relevant here also.

47 See Merrills, *International Dispute Settlement*, above n.1, ch.9; K.V. Raman (ed.) *Dispute Settlement through the United Nations*, New York: Oceana for UNITAR, 1977; and A. Roberts and B. Kingsbury (eds) *United Nations, Divided World*, Oxford: Oxford University Press, 1988. Also the valuable analysis and recommendations in Secretary-General B. Boutros-Ghali's 1992 report, *An Agenda for Peace*, New York: United Nations, 1992; text in (1992) 31 *I.L.M.* 953.

48 *Declaration on the Prevention and Removal of Disputes and Situations which may threaten International Peace and Security and on the Role of the United Nations in this Field* (1988) quoted in B.G. Ramcharan, *International Law and Practice of Early-Warning and Preventive Diplomacy: The Emerging Global Watch*, Dordrecht: Martinus Nijhoff, 1991, p.92.

49 See J. Pérez de Cuellar, 'The Role of the UN Secretary-General', in Roberts and Kingsbury, above n.47, p.61.
50 See Ramcharan, above n.41, ch.4.
51 See Merrills, *International Dispute Settlement*, above n.1, pp.191–6.
52 Text in (1989) 28 *I.L.M.* 1584.
53 For more detailed treatments see Merrills, *International Dispute Settlement*, above n.1, ch.10 and Northedge and Donelan, above n.1, ch.11.
54 For the background to recent developments and the origins of the Conference see Robertson and Merrills, above n.18, pp.148–56.
55 See A. Bloed and P. Van Dijk (eds) *The Human Dimension of the Helsinki Process*, Dordrecht: Martinus Nijhoff, 1991, chs 4 and 5; and D. McGoldrick, 'Human Rights Developments in the Helsinki Process' (1990) 39 *I.C.L.Q.* 923.
56 See E. Schlager, 'The Procedural Framework of the CSCE: From the Helsinki Consultations to the Paris Charter, 1972–90' (1991) 12 *Human Rights Law Journal* 221.
57 Text in Bloed and Van Dijk, above n.55, p.269; (1990) 11 *Human Rights Law Journal* 379; and (1991) 30 *I.L.M.* 190.
58 For the Report of the meeting see Bloed and Van Dijk, above n.55, p.301; and (1991) 30 *I.L.M.* 382. For the response of the CSCE Council meeting in Berlin shortly afterwards see (1991) 30 *I.L.M.* 1349.
59 *Border and Transborder Armed Actions, Jurisdiction and Admissibility*, Judgment, [1988] I.C.J. Rep.69.
60 See Merrills, *International Dispute Settlement*, above n.1, pp.22–6.

4 The principle of non-intervention: use of force

Vaughan Lowe

[Non-intervention] C'est un mot métaphysique, et politique, qui signifie à peu près le même chose qu'intervention.

(Talleyrand)

On one of the last occasions on which I met him, Michael Akehurst intervened at a conference to question my view that international law showed some signs of an acceptance of a right of humanitarian intervention. In his view all the alleged instances – Uganda, Bangladesh and so on – were merely instances of States acting with little regard for the law in order to protect their own interests. While he was by no means a cynic or lacking in compassion, Michael resisted my attempt to draw idealistic rules from cases where selfish motives had led to action advancing the common good.

The difference between our approaches has many facets: different weights given to explicit justifications and inferred motives in the characterisation of State practice; different conceptions of the weight of practice needed to establish qualifications to the rules contained in articles 2(4) and 51 of the UN Charter; and different perceptions of the position of moral imperatives in the contemporary legal order. But in a sense the difference between us was one to be measured in centuries. Unconsciously, I harked back to an approach to international law rooted in the eighteenth century; Michael was thoroughly modern. It is that difference, nowhere more evident that in the context of the principle of non-intervention, that is the subject of this personal tribute to the memory of Michael Akehurst.

Much has been written on the minutiae of the detailed formulations of the principle of non-intervention,[1] and that exercise is not repeated here. It is with the more fundamental question of the central driving force of the principle that this paper is concerned. And it looks to a more distant past than other papers in this collection – a past where legal and moral argument were more closely attuned than they have since become. The paper begins with a brief account of postwar attempts to define the principle in the face of a body of inconsistent State practice. It then argues that the attempts to rationalise the practice and principle mark a return to an earlier conception of non-intervention, which was abandoned during the nineteenth century. Finally, the prospects for the resurgence of that earlier conception are discussed.

THE DEFINITION OF NON-INTERVENTION IN CONTEMPORARY INTERNATIONAL LAW

The most interesting question regarding the principle of non-intervention in international law is why on earth anyone should suppose that it exists. From the most cursory review of the international history of the past two centuries it is apparent that intervention in foreign States is quite normal. Indeed, if international history is thought of as the analysis of the influences of nations upon each other, it is arguable that the very terrain of history is mapped out on the grid of intervention.

This does, of course, presuppose a wide conception of what intervention might be. As Percy Winfield once remarked, 'A reader, after perusing Phillimore's chapter upon intervention, might close the book with the impression that intervention may be anything from a speech of Lord Palmerston's in the House of Commons to the partition of Poland.'[2] That remark retains much validity.

The principle is stated in its classic modern form in UN General Assembly Resolution 2625, as follows:

> No State or group of States has the right to intervene, directly or indirectly, for any reason whatever, in the internal or external affairs of any other State. Consequently, armed intervention and all other forms of interference or attempted threats against the personality of the State or against its political, economic and cultural elements, are in violation of international law.

The Resolution goes on to make it clear that it is not only military intervention, but any form of intervention whatever, that is proscribed:

> No State may use or encourage the use of economic, political or any other type of measures to coerce another State in order to obtain from it the subordination of the exercise of its sovereign rights and to secure from it advantages of any kind.

It is the intention, rather than the means adopted, which may qualify a State's action as unlawful intervention. None the less, this paper will concentrate on interventions involving the use of force, which present the most urgent and difficult problems in contemporary international relations.

The implications of the principle as commonly conceived by international lawyers have been succinctly summarised by Galina

Shinkaretskaya, who wrote of the domain of domestic jurisdiction which the principle of non-intervention protects:

> Clearly, domestic jurisdiction refers to the right of each State to freely – independently of other States and international organizations – exercise its own legislative, executive and judicial jurisdiction. Its exercise is the consequence of State sovereignty and the right of nations to self-determination.'[3]

Here there are two major threads evident in the principle. First, the right of each State freely to choose its own destiny; and second, the correlative duty of every other State and international organisation not to impede the effective exercise of that choice. To these two threads we must add two more. The first – the right to choose the State's destiny – includes both what now passes for the principle of domestic jurisdiction proper, and the historically distinct principle of self-determination. The second – the correlative duty – comprehends both the prohibition on what used to be called 'dictatorial intervention' and more specifically the prohibition on the threat or use of force in international relations, and also what might be termed the non-justiciability under public international law of certain issues. These different aspects of the principle are intimately intertwined; and most can be discerned in the instances where the principle has arisen in practice.

The principle of non-intervention, in its various guises, has arisen frequently during the postwar era. The United Nations has on several occasions sought to state the principle of non-intervention in a general manner. The UN Charter itself contains prohibitions on the use of force (Article 2(4)), and on intervention in matters essentially within the domestic jurisdiction of any State by the United Nations (Article 2(7)).[4] Both are framed in general terms. But, as was pointed out by the United States' delegate during attempts to draft what became UN General Assembly Resolution 2131, the Charter does not explicitly set out a general obligation of non-intervention, and the principle's main claim to international authority derived from its inclusion in Article 18 of the Charter of the Organization of American States.[5]

The first detailed formulation of the principle of non-intervention was adopted by the General Assembly in 1965 as Resolution 2131(XX).[6] That Resolution begins with a general statement of the principle:

> No State has the right to intervene, directly or indirectly, for any reason whatever, in the internal or external affairs of any other State. Consequently, armed intervention and all other forms of interference or attempted threats against the personality of the State or against its political, economic and cultural elements are condemned.

Subsequent paragraphs go on to condemn the use of 'economic, political or any other type of measures to coerce another State' and the assisting or inciting of subversive or armed activities aimed at the overthrow of the State, and the use of force to deprive peoples of their national identity; and to reassert the obligation to respect the principles of non-intervention and self-determination. In protecting peoples and nations against intervention, the Resolution extended the conception of the principle beyond the Western States' proposals to limit it to intervention in civil wars and unrest in foreign States.

The question of definition of the duty of non-intervention inevitably arose again during the drafting of General Assembly Resolution 2625, which aimed to set out the fundamental rules of contemporary international law.[7] Discussions focused on Resolution 2131 and on a British draft[8] which proposed to limit the principle to the narrower and more traditional ground of a prohibition on intervention by States in matters within the domestic jurisdiction of other States. However, the broader approach prevailed, and Resolution 2625 adopted a definition which is substantially the same as that adopted as Resolution 2131(XX), and which has been quoted above.

A further and even more detailed elaboration of the concept was adopted in 1981, as General Assembly Resolution 36/103, the Declaration on the Inadmissibility of Intervention and Interference in the Internal affairs of States.[9] In addition to the usual assertion of the duty of non-intervention and right of self-determination, it prescribes a striking series of more specific duties which went far beyond the traditional boundaries of the principle. For example, Resolution 36/103 asserts

> The right of States and peoples to have free access to information and to develop fully, without interference, their system of information and mass media..

and

> The duty of States to refrain from any measure which would lead to the strengthening of existing military blocs or the creation or strengthening of new military alliances, interlocking arrangements, the deployment of interventionist forces or military bases and other military installations conceived in the context of great-Power confrontation;[10]

and again,

> . . . the duty of a State not to use its external economic assistance programme or adopt any multilateral or unilateral economic reprisal or blockade and to prevent the use of transnational and multilateral corporations under its jurisdiction and control as instruments of political pressure or coercion against another State, in violation of the Charter of the United Nations.

It is not surprising that the Resolution was opposed by most developed States.

The Principle has also arisen in international litigation.[11] The International Court of Justice has declined to decide one case on the basis that the question asked of it was non-justiciable and that the answer lay within the discretion of the litigating States.[12] It has been faced with the question of the scope of the 'domestic jurisdiction' reservation in acceptances of the Court's jurisdiction under Article 36(2) of its Statute.[13] In each case, the existence of the principle appears to have been accepted, albeit without establishing an explicit link between either non-justiciability or domestic jurisdiction and the more general principle of non-intervention. Such a link has, however, been established in cases where what would in the past have been called 'dictatorial' intervention was in issue. Thus, for example, in the *Corfu Channel* case the Court condemned the British minesweeping operation in Albanian territorial waters as an unlawful act of intervention.[14]

The most notable contribution of the International Court on the subject is the judgment in the *Nicaragua* case.[15] There it seems to have held that

> action in support of opposition forces within another state may constitute intervention, even if the support itself is of a non-military kind; if it has military character but is limited to such indirect support as the supply of weapons or logistic support, it may constitute not only intervention but also an unlawful threat or use of force, but would not amount to an armed attack; and if it involves direct military action by the supporting state (whether on the part of its regular forces or through the dispatch of armed bands on a significant scale) it is in addition likely to constitute an armed attack . . . [16]

The message from the United Nations and the International Court is clear: intervention is unlawful.

INTERVENTION IN CONTEMPORARY PRACTICE

History tells a different tale. The postwar division of Europe and the establishment of the Soviet satellite States can now be characterised even in the most diplomatic of circles as an exercise in wholesale intervention, in which the more remarkable interventions in Hungary (1956), Czechoslovakia (1968), and Afghanistan (1980) stood out only by virtue of their overtly military nature. Neither they, nor Soviet 'involvement' in countries such as Angola, Cuba, Ethiopia and Vietnam, added anything to the explicit Leninist policy of defending revolutionary gains which found its clearest expression in the 'Brezhnev doctrine' and the concept of the Socialist Commonwealth.[17] As it was put in an article in *Pravda* on 26 September 1968, 'every communist party is responsible not only to its own people but also to all the socialist countries and to the entire Communist movement' for the defence of revolutionary gains.

The United States has been no less active in intervening in foreign

States. In 1947, President Truman announced that 'it must be the policy of the United States to support free peoples who are resisting attempted subjugation by armed minorities or by outside pressures.'[18] This was by no means the last such statement. After the Soviet invasion of Afghanistan in 1980, President Carter stated that '[a]n attempt by any outside force to gain control of the Persian Gulf region will be regarded as an assault on the vital interests of the United States. It will be repelled by any means necessary, including military force.'[19] Despite the provisions of Article 18 of the Charter of the Organization of American States, which affirms the duty of non-intervention in much the same terms as were adopted in Resolution 2625,[20] the United States intervened in Guatemala (1952), Cuba (1961), the Dominican Republic (1965), Chile (by subversion, in 1973), Argentina/Malvinas (1982), Grenada (1983), and Panama (1989), as well conducting the long-running intervention which formed the subject of the *Nicaragua* case before the International Court. Further afield, the United States intervened in Lebanon (1958), Congo (1964), Zaire (1978), and, of course, in Vietnam.

Both the Soviet Union, in the Brezhnev doctrine, and the United States, in the Monroe doctrine and the Polk Corollary,[21] adopted general policies justifying intervention in order to maintain their regional influence – a logical extension into the era of Superpower politics of the concept of the Balance of Power, which dominated European politics in the eighteenth and nineteenth centuries.[22] Other States have intervened, too. Among the more notable modern examples are the Anglo-French action in Egypt (1956), Belgian interventions in Congo (1960, 1964) and Zaire (1978), India in Bangladesh (1971), Turkey in Cyprus (1974), Israel's action in Uganda (1976), Germany in Somalia (1977), Tanzania in Uganda (1978), Egypt in Cyprus (1978), Vietnam in Kampuchea (1978), Israel in Lebanon (1982) and India in Sri Lanka (1987) and the Maldives (1988). This list is, of course, by no means exhaustive, and covers only the more significant military interventions.

The pattern continues, and the range of States involved increases. In 1990 the States members of ECOWAS (the Economic Community of West African States) intervened militarily in the Liberian civil war, where troops remain at the time of writing; and in the late 1980s a number of Western States put themselves in a position where they were able to invoke rights of self-defence against the States involved in the Iran-Iraq war (but chiefly against Iran). The recent events in Iraq/Kuwait, Yugoslavia and Somalia will be discussed below.

RECONCILING THE PRINCIPLE AND THE PRACTICE

What is going on here? On the one hand, we have a continuous tradition of legal formulations of the principle of non-intervention. On the other hand, there is an equally continuous tradition of intervention in the affairs of foreign States. There is plainly a long-standing contrast between the word and the deed. Non-intervention is preached, but not practised. Why is this? Why do States choose repeatedly to assert a principle with which they do not comply?

Part of the answer lies in the dynamics of the creation of international law. For all the methodological rigour of positivism it does not, and never has, given an adequate account of how international law is generated. Rules do not simply emerge from State practice; they are drawn from State practice – and the ambiguity of the word 'drawn' is entirely apposite. Raw practice exercises no more than a pressure to conform with expectations derived from the previous actions of States, which expectations may be confused and ambivalent. It is only when some attempt is made to systematise the law that rules are produced in a clear form. International Law, in the sense of a systematic body of rules, is a by-product of the jurists, the international organisations and the tribunals which set themselves the task of articulating those rules. Until that task is attempted, conflicting and uncertain practices coexist. Even in relation to matters as apparently straightforward as diplomatic immunity and the breadths of maritime zones, it is only at the point where an attempt is made to reduce to writing the rules immanent in State practice that a coherent body of law emerges.

So it is with non-intervention. In legal terms it began as an abstract and amorphous principle. With the advent of the League of Nations, the United Nations and the International Court, the pressure for the precise articulation of the principle as a legal norm began. The establishment of the League of Nations brought one aspect of the principle into clear focus. If States were obliged to refrain from non-intervention in the conduct of their respective foreign policies, it made no sense to permit the evasion of that duty by authorising an international organisation (and hence, the States in effective control of it[23]) to intervene in the domestic affairs of member States. It was necessary to mark out a sphere of domestic jurisdiction, within which the international organisation was incompetent and the State exclusively competent. The League Covenant thus sought to preserve matters within the domestic jurisdiction of States from League interference.[24]

This notion of domestic jurisdiction was applied not only to international organisations, but also to international tribunals. Logically, the notion operates differently in the two cases. Organisations are established without authority to enter the reserved domain: matters of domestic jurisdiction are *ultra vires* the organisation.[25] In international tribunals, on the other hand, certain matters cannot be investigated because they are not regulated by international law. The former is a limitation on the powers of an organisation; the latter is a limitation inherent in the nature of the subject matter, and introduces the element of non-justiciability into the principle of non-intervention. Indeed, that element can be seen to operate also in municipal tribunals.[26]

The United Nations' attempts to define the principle were noted above. Once articulation was attempted, there was a tendency to establish a definition of the principle which cohered with other principles, such as the sovereign equality of States, which together constitute the understanding of the international legal order. Coherence with other principles tended to be more important that the conformity of the putative principle with State practice. And once a coherent formulation of the legal principle had been adopted, the further elaboration of that principle became a matter of exegesis – the explanation of the meaning and significance of earlier 'authoritative' texts, rather than an exercise based upon a return to State practice and the inference of rules therefrom.

Moreover, it seems to be a characteristic of the General Assembly that it cannot cope with anything more than the shortest of intellectual agendas and the simplest of principles. It appears, for the most part, constitutionally incapable of articulating sophisticated legal concepts. This is no reflection on the ability of its members: it is a limitation evident whenever a large group attempts to draft an agreed text. So, in the early postwar years, the General Assembly was able to go as far as adopting texts prohibiting the use of force. Subsequently, it could adopt texts on self-determination and non-intervention. In each case it responded to the political pressures of the day.[27] In neither case did it proceed by the cautious inference of norms from State practice or in any other way refine the basic principles so as to take account of the exceptions and qualifications to those principles which were, and are, so clearly embedded in State practice. It achieved doctrinal coherence and purity at the expense of accuracy and compliance.

More importantly, concentration upon the text – and Resolution 2625 is a perfect example of this phenomenon – diverts attention away from the location of the real source of normative force in international relations. To the extent that States consider normative principles at all in the context of intervention, they surely look to the actual practice of States and to principles of moral and political philosophy which may be thought to justify departures from previous practice. In elaborating legal concepts by the expansion of definitions adopted in earlier texts, there is a tendency for the international community to look inward, turning its back on the practice and the underlying moral basis which the concepts should express.

So it is that texts such as Resolution 2625 become detached at once from State practice and from moral principle.

In fact, the same State practice which appears to undermine the principle of non-intervention ought to be seen as an indication that States have a more sophisticated understanding of the principle than do the drafters of the United Nations resolutions. Interventions have not, in general, been presented as exercises of naked power in total disregard of international law. They have been justified as exercises of power in pursuit of exceptions to that principle, which exceptions are accepted in international law.

A recent, and authoritative, text identifies five common justifications for intervention.[28] First is intervention to protect the lives of citizens abroad, in circumstances where the 'host' State is unable or unwilling to provide the degree of protection demanded by international law. The interventions in the Congo (1960, 1964) and Uganda (by Israel, at Entebbe in 1976), are perhaps the clearest examples of this.

Secondly, it is said that

> a substantial body of opinion and of practice has supported the view that. . . . when a state commits cruelties against and persecution of its nationals in such a way as to deny their fundamental human rights and to shock the conscience of mankind, the matter ceases to be of sole concern to that state and even intervention in the interests of humanity might be legally permissible.[29]

The interventions in Bangladesh (by India, 1971) and Uganda (by Tanzania, 1978), are probably the best examples here; although it must be conceded that in both cases the intervening State was at least as much concerned with the impact of the human rights violations in its own territory, in the form of refugee movements and the general creation of civil unrest, as with the humanitarian issues.

The third justification for intervention is that the action constituting intervention is an exercise of the right of self-defence. This justification formed part of the American pleadings in the *Nicaragua* case and was accepted by the Court as a matter of law, but rejected on the facts.

Fourth, there is sometimes said to be a right to intervene in order to assist the process of self-determination. This was one element of the Vietnamese justification for the intervention in Kampuchea in 1978.

And fifth, there is said to be a right to intervene in pursuance of a treaty commitment or otherwise at the request of the government of the State concerned. The German intervention in Mogadishu at the request of the Somali government in 1978, the American, French and Italian action in Lebanon in 1982, and the Indian interventions in Sri Lanka (1987) and the Maldives (1988), offer examples here.

The elegance of this analysis in *Oppenheim* cannot conceal the enduring truth of Winfield's observation that 'the non-intervention rule appears to be a patent consequence of independence with a host of disorderly exceptions fastened upon it.'[30] States have indeed sought to justify their actions in these and other instances by claiming the benefit of exceptions to the principle of non-intervention. But in many, if not most, cases their actions have provoked criticism and controversy in the United Nations, and the repeated and continuing appeal to exceptions to the principle has not led to the modification of the principle of non-intervention. It is high time that the principle were modified; and were that done, the principle could once more be placed in the proper moral context from which it sprang.

A RETURN TO THE ROOTS OF NON-INTERVENTION

Vattel is commonly credited with the first clear articulation of the principle of non-intervention.[31] It is usual to focus upon Vattel's significance in terms of the development of the positivist approach to international law (in which the will or consent of States is the source of obligation) as a replacement for the earlier natural law foundations of the international legal system. This is something of a misconception. Despite the emphasis given to Vattel in the development of the positivist approach to international law, he was essentially a theorist. Indeed, the full potential of the crucial role of consent in stripping away alleged principles of international law unsupported by State practice was not really felt until a substantial body of non-European States gained independence in the twentieth century and insisted upon their rejection of some of those traditional principles. Vattel's insistence upon the equality and independence of States, which was a natural development of Hobbes' theories,[32] arose in reaction against the background of a medieval order in which States and princes jostled for precedence, and of the feudal system in which intervention was both an undisputed right and a duty. Both sovereign equality and non-intervention were principles which he derived by abstract reasoning from a conception of how the world was properly to be ordered. They were not principles or rules painstakingly inferred from the actual practice of States in the manner that is (or, according to the dictates of positivism, should be) practised today. While Vattel rejected Wolff's conception of international law 'déduit de l'idée d'une espéce de grande République (*Civitatis Maximae*) institutée par la Nature elle-même, & de laquelle toutes les Nations du Monde sont les Membres',[33] he himself deduced international law from a conception of the world, less fanciful but no less abstract. That needs to be borne in mind in assessing Vattel's view of non-intervention.

Eighteenth-century international lawyers, including Vattel, conceived of their subject in terms which embrace both what we now understand by public international law and what would now be called public law. Vattel began his book *Le Droit des Gens* with an exposition of the concepts of the nation, the State, and the sovereign; and he followed this with a lengthy discussion of the duties of a government within the State. Only then did he turn to the question of relations between States – to what is now understood as public international law proper. In Vattel's scheme the sovereign (whether personal or institutional) derives its authority from the individuals who constitute the State.[34] The sovereign is bound to act in the best interests of the State, providing the basic conditions for the conduct of civilised life and commerce, and defending the State against attacks from the outside. States may, as Vattel clearly recognises, choose to pursue different paths: and since all States are equal, the principle of non-intervention is a logical consequence of the scheme of things. Hence Vattel wrote:

> C'est une conséquence manifeste de la Liberté & de l'indépendance des Nations, que toutes sont en droit de se gouverner comme elles le juge à propos, & qu'aucune n'a le moindre droit de se mêler du Gouvernement d'une autre.'[35]

Note that Vattel's proposition is perfectly general, and not limited to questions of armed intervention. He continued:

> Il n'appartient donc à aucune Puissance étrangere de prendre connaissance de l'administration de ce Souverain, de s'ériger en Juge de sa conduite & de l'obliger à y rien changer. S'il accable ses sujets d'impôts, s'il les traite durement, c'est l'affaire de la Nation; nul autre n'est appellé à le redresser, à l'obliger de suivre des maximes plus équitables & plus sages.'[36]

It may be noted in passing that a similar progression of thought appears in the UN Charter itself. The Charter's preamble opens with the words 'We the peoples of the United Nations. . . . .have resolved to combine our efforts' to accomplish the aims of the Organization, and goes on to assert that 'our respective governments, through representatives assembled in the city of San Francisco, have agreed to the present Charter'. As one member of the US Senate Committee on Foreign Relations (Senator Thomas of Utah) observed, 'the reference to the role of "We the peoples" might imply acceptance of the idea of popular sovereignty'. In reply to his question whether the Preamble meant that 'the governments represented at the Conference were actually the agents of the people of those countries represented there', Leo Pasvolsky, the Special Assistant to the Secretary of State for International Organization and Security Affairs, replied that he did not know that the question was discussed in that form, but he was able to assure the Senator that 'there is nothing offensive to the thinking of Americans' in the reference to 'We the peoples'.[37] Only after the preamble has established the democratic credentials of the UN in this way does the Charter move on to the enumeration of the Principles of the Organization, including the sovereign equality of States and the principle of non-intervention. Inchoate and inarticulate it may be, but the Charter treads the same path from internal legitimacy and 'public law' to international law as had been trodden by Vattel.

There is a continuum embracing the municipal and international public orders. To the extent that the claim to freedom from interference resulted from the right of each society to regulate itself, the claim was clearly undermined in circumstances where a despotic sovereign suppressed the will of the citizens. This consequence of the link between internal legitimacy and the right to external independence was recognised by Vattel:

> Mais si le Prince, attaquant les Lois fondamentales, donne à son peuple un légitime sujet de lui résister; si la Tyrannie, devenuë insupportable, soulève la Nation; toute Puissance étrangère est en droit de sécourir un peuple opprimé, qui lui demande son assistance.[38]

The right to intervene depended upon large-scale abuse of the population by the sovereign: maltreated individuals could be expected to seek their remedy before the courts of the State. But where the despotism and maltreatment reached the point where the population was justified in rising up against the sovereign, that option would, almost by definition, not be available. Then, intervention would be justified.

The dangers of this were apparent: as de Martens noted later, 'there is hardly a civil war anywhere in which foreign powers do not find a pretext for taking part when they think fit'.[39] But the dangers do not justify abandoning the principle that the right of a sovereign to be free of foreign intervention cannot stand where the sovereign engages in large-scale transgressions of the elementary dictates of humanity.

THE DISTORTION OF THE PRINCIPLE OF NON-INTERVENTION

Somehow, this crucial qualification to the duty of non-intervention shrank into the background during the nineteenth century. Writers began to take a more absolute view of the duty. The British theorists Cobden and Mill were prominent among them. Cobden is notable for his wedding of the principles of free trade and non-intervention.[40] A central theme in his writings is his belief that prosperity and liberty can be best secured in circumstances where international dealings take place primarily between individuals, rather than governments. This requires governments to assume only those minimal powers necessary for the discharge of functions, such as national defence, which cannot be organised on the individual plane.

There is an important point raised by Cobden's approach. It is arguable that the State as an institution has an inherent tendency towards intervention. To sit someone at the desk in the imperial grandeur of the Foreign Secretary's room in Whitehall and tell them that their constitutional duty is to advance British interests abroad is tantamount to a direction to them to intervene in foreign States; and it is a direction the pursuit of which has varied in vigour in relation to British power and influence rather than in relation to any changes in the legal or moral climate. British gun-boats may now be dispatched less frequently than in the past, and to show the flag rather than to shoot; armed intervention may have yielded to the cutting of diplomatic or trade links, or the blocking of credits and loans from international organisations; but the principle remains unchanged. All States seek to influence the conduct of other States. That is what the international system of nation States signifies.

The wider the powers of government, the wider the scope for the deployment of State power in order to reward or punish the policies of other States: non-intervention and minimal government are intimately linked. Cobden failed to anticipate the quasi-governmental power and role which some multinational corporations have achieved in this century. He also drew the wrong inference from the existence of extensive governmental powers: while those powers did, indeed, provide a propensity towards intervention, Cobden underestimated the force of factors favouring reticence in their exercise and the advantages for States of the principle of non-intervention. But his basic insight – that intervention is an inevitable concomitant of powerful government – is sound.

Sixteenth- and seventeenth-century Europe had abounded in instances of interventions in foreign States for religious reasons. The practice was continued in the doctrine of the balance of power and in the form of humanitarian interventions in the eighteenth and early nineteenth centuries.[41] A right of intervention was also asserted in order to stave off the threat of contagion from foreign revolutions: in a celebrated circular letter in 1821, in which he refused to involve Britain in a planned intervention in Naples, Lord Castlereagh stated

> [I]t should be clearly understood that no government can be more prepared than the British government is to uphold the right of any state or states to interfere, where their own immediate security or essential interests are seriously endangered by the internal transactions of another state. But as they regard the assumption of such right as only to be justified by the strongest necessity, and to be limited and regulated thereby, they cannot admit that this right can receive a general and indiscriminate application to all revolutionary movements, without reference to their immediate bearing upon some particular state or states, or be made prospectively the basis of an alliance. They regard its exercise as an exception to general principles of the greatest value and importance, and as one that only properly grows out of the circumstances of the special case; but they at the same time consider that exceptions of this description never can, without the utmost danger, be so far reduced to rule as to be incorporated into the ordinary diplomacy of states, or into the institutes of international law.[42]

That statement is a good reflection of the views which prevailed amongst politicians in the first part of the nineteenth century. Intervention for the protection or advancement of important political values remained the norm.

Later in the nineteenth century the principles of sovereign equality and non-intervention came to be asserted in State practice in a more recognisably modern form. They were pressed with particular vigour by the Latin American republics: non-intervention underlay the Drago doctrine, the doctrine of *uti possidetis* and the elaboration of the Calvo clauses. After the European revolutions of the mid-nineteenth century and the Congress of Berlin, the Powers reached a point where they had more to gain by agreeing to respect each other's spheres of influence and to abstain from intervention than they had by asserting a right of intervention. Interventions tended to occur less frequently, in peripheral areas, and in circumstances where some clear justification (such as maltreatment of nationals or reneging on international obligations) provided a political justification clear enough for the intervention to be seen as limited in scope and not intended to disturb the balance of power.

This tendency in State practice found support in theoretical writings. Like Cobden,[43] John Stuart Mill regarded non-intervention as not merely a right, related to the right of self-determination, enjoyed by States, but a burden which they must bear.[44] Mill pushed this principle to its extreme conclusion: the people of a State had, in his view, to struggle for their own political freedom; and if they failed to secure it, there could be no resort to external intervention to win it for them. It is, perhaps, no accident that the principle of non-intervention was asserted in a purer form and with greater vigour by those who were outside government than by those who actually made and implemented foreign policy (although even Mill conceded that there were some circumstances in which intervention might be justified).[45] Even so, among the Great Powers the desirability of mutual respect for the sovereign independence of States carried the principle of non-intervention to the fore.

The product of these developments was a view of non-intervention which saw it as a defence of State sovereignty. Inevitably, the governments which made international law sought to defend their own position, and the principle became more absolute, detached from its roots in principles of internal political legitimacy. That detachment is a dominant characteristic of twentieth-century attempts to define the principle, and prepares the ground for the absolute prohibition on intervention in contemporary international law.

A REVERSION TO LEGITIMACY?

It might be said that the principle has survived in its absolute form because States think it preferable to retain whatever constraining force the principle might have, so as to make States the more cautious in departing from it, rather than to risk the instability which might follow from the ready concession of a right to intervene. On the other hand, there is a growing feeling that it is doubtful whether more good has been done by compliance with the principle than by violation of it. Certainly, it is difficult to argue against the moral desirability of the interventions which helped to put an end to the shocking human rights abuses in Bangladesh, Uganda and Vietnam.

The latter view, which sees a moral justification for intervention in circumstances where the bond uniting ruler and ruled is violated by the unconscionable conduct of the ruler, harks back to Vattel's crucial precondition for the application of the principle of non-intervention, which was described in the opening pages of this paper. Many closet natural lawyers (myself included) have yearned for the day when the international community becomes capable of distinguishing between justifiable and unjustifiable intervention, and of modifying the prescriptions of international law accordingly. That day may be closer than any of us thought. The collapse of the Soviet 'empire' and the radical upheaval in international relations of the past three years has presented an opportunity in which it seems possible that the law on non-intervention might develop so as to be more closely attuned to moral imperatives.

There are several indications of this trend which deserve comment: the UN action against Iraq; the UN resolutions concerning the rendition by Libya to the United Kingdom or the United States of two men accused of terrorist offences against civilian aircraft; and the 'humanitarian' interventions in Yugoslavia and Somalia. In each case the international community has sought to take steps to promote international peace and security by intervening in the internal affairs of a sovereign State.

The handling of the Iraq crisis is the clearest example. Having restored, by a military intervention whose precise legal basis remains unclear,[46] Kuwait to independence, the United Nations went on to impose a variety of measures upon Iraq which go to the heart of Iraqi sovereignty. Thus, Security Council Resolution 687 (1991) required the unconditional acceptance by Iraq of the internationally supervised destruction of all its chemical, biological and nuclear weapons and its ballistic missiles having a range of over 150 km. This, and the imposition of zones in the north and south of Iraq for the protection of Kurds and Shi'ites respectively, within which Iraqi aircraft are forbidden to fly, goes far beyond a mere requirement that Iraq conform to its international obligations. It creates special obligations for Iraq concerning the internal order and policies of the State. It is a classic example of (collective) intervention in the pursuit of overarching humanitarian aims.

The *Lockerbie* case[47] is similar. The decision of the Security Council to oblige Libya to surrender to the United Kingdom or the United States the two men suspected of involvement in the bombing of a US civilian aircraft over Lockerbie amounts to the creation of a *lex specialis* for Libya. Under the 1971 Montreal Convention for the Suppression of Unlawful Acts Against the Safety of Civil Aviation,[48] Libya appears to have the choice of surrendering or trying suspected hijackers, and the decision to order it to surrender the suspects is a perfect example of intervention in what Quincy Wright once called 'the residuum of discretionary authority remaining outside of a state's international obligations' which is domestic jurisdiction. The claim that the Security Council was exercising its powers in relation to the maintenance of international peace and security in this case might appear dubious as a matter of fact; but the important point in the present context is that, even granting the competence of the Council to act, the episode represents a startling incursion into Libya's internal affairs.

Again, the decisions of the United Nations to deploy UN troops to guarantee the provision of humanitarian aid to Yugoslavia and Somalia in the midst of civil wars in those countries demonstrates the increasing willingness of the international community to make limited military interventions for humanitarian purposes. Quite how those limited interventions will develop, and whether it will prove necessary to use force in order to safeguard the delivery of food and medical supplies and so change the character of the intervention, remains to be seen.

What is clear is that the international community no longer regards an absolute prohibition on intervention as desirable even in theory. The principle, which has been used so often in the past in attempts to insulate domestic oppression from international scrutiny and sanctions, may be entering a new phase. There is a clear reluctance on the part of States to intervene unilaterally. States have a strong preference for cloaking interventions with the authority of regional organisations, such as ECOWAS and the OAS, or the United Nations. While unilateral action may remain subject to a principle of non-intervention in a strict form, the international community has at long last reached the point where it has the confidence to decide that there are circumstances where the protection of life is more important than the protection of abstract values such as sovereign equality and independence. That, I am sure, is a development which Michael Akehurst would have applauded, had he lived to see it.

NOTES

1 See, for example, Milan Sahovic (ed.) *Principles of International Law Concerning Friendly Relations and Cooperation*, Dobbs Ferry, NY: Oceana, 1972: Tomislav Mitrovic submitted the chapter on 'Non-Intervention in the Internal Affairs of States' (pp.219–76). And see the bibliography in Sir Robert Jennings and Sir Arthur Watts (eds) *Oppenheim's International Law*, London: Longmans, 9th edn, 1992, p.427.

2 P.H. Winfield, 'The History of Intervention in International Law' (1922–23) 3 *B.Y.I.L.* 130–50, at p.130. The reference is to Phillimore's *Commentaries upon International Law*, London: Butterworths, 3rd edn, 1879, vol.I.

3 Galina G. Shinkaretskaya, 'Content and Limits of "Domaine Reservée" ', in G. Tunkin and R. Wulfrum (eds) *International Law and Municipal Law*, Berlin: Duncker & Humblot, 1988, 121–31, at p.123.

4 The Charter does not explicitly forbid intervention by States in matters within the domestic jurisdiction of other States. However, when a member of the United Nations seeks to have the domestic affairs of another State discussed within the United Nations, intervention by the Organization and by the State coalesce: examples can be found readily in the Security Council debates on, for instance, the Dominican Republic (1965), Bangladesh (1971), and Czechoslovakia (1968), cf. the *Nicaragua* case [1986] I.C.J. Rep. 14, at p.106.

5 UN Doc. A/AC.119/SR.29, 30. The OAS Charter is reprinted in 119 *U.N.T.S.* 3. The International Law Commission had proposed in 1949 a Draft Declaration on the Rights and Duties of States, Article 3 of which provided that 'Every State has the duty to refrain from intervention in the internal or external affairs of any other State': UN GAOR, 4th Sess., Supp. 10, A/925, p.7. The General Assembly commended the draft to member States in Resolution 375(IV).

6 Text in (1966) 60 *A.J.I.L.* 662. The Resolution was adopted by 109 votes to 0, with one abstention (United Kingdom).

7 On the drafting of that Resolution see Sahovic, above n.1, pp.219–76.

8 UN Doc. A/5746, A/AC.119/L.8.

9 The Resolution was adopted by 120 votes to 22, with 6 abstentions. Many developed States including Australia, Canada, France, FRG, the Netherlands, UK and USA, voted against the Resolution. (1981) 35 *UN Yearbook* 145–9.

10 Quite apart from the apparent conflict with the right of collective self-defence under Article 51 of the Charter, this provision itself seems to be an attempt to interfere with the right of States to develop their own international relations.

11 For arbitral practice, see, for example, the *Spanish Zones of Morocco Claims* (1925) 2 R.I.A.A. 615, 2 I.L.R. 157; *ITTSA* v. *OPIC* (1974) 59 I.L.R. 366, at pp.383–9.

12 *Haya de la Torre* [1951] I.C.J. Rep. 71.

13 *Norwegian Loans* [1956] I.C.J. Rep. 9; *Interhandel* [1959] I.C. J. Rep. 6; and cf. the Permanent Court decision in *Nationality Decrees in Tunis and Morocco* (1923) P.C.I.J. Rep., Series B, No.4.

14 *Corfu Channel* case [1949] I.C.J. Rep. 35.

15 [1986] I.C.J. Rep. 14. See further chapter 2 in this volume.

16 Jennings and Watts, above n.2, pp.431–2 (footnotes omitted).

17 On the Brezhnev doctrine see, for example, R.R. James (ed.) *The Czechoslovak Crisis 1968*, London: Wiedenfeld & Nicolson, 1969, p.114.

18 Message to Congress, 23 March 1947: quoted in (British) Foreign and Commonwealth Office, *Is Intervention Ever Justified*?, Foreign Policy Document No.148, 1984, 23.

19 State of the Union Address, 23 January 1980. Quoted in *Is Intervention Ever Justified*?, ibid., p.26.

20 But note Article 22, which provides that '[m]easures adopted for the maintenance of peace and security in accordance with existing treaties do not constitute a violation' of the principle of non-intervention.

21 Under the Monroe Doctrine the United States 'would consider any attempt on the part of [the European Powers] to extend their system to any part of this hemisphere as dangerous to our peace and security': quoted, T.D. Woolsey, *Introduction to the Study of International Law*, London: Stevens and New York: Scribner, Armstrong, 6th edn, 1888, p.53. Under the Polk Corollary, the United States claimed the right to take all necessary steps to prevent any non-American power from obtaining control over territory in the hemisphere, regardless of whether the foreign intervention occurs with the consent of the inhabitants of the territory affected. See Memorandum for the Attorney General *re* Legality Under International Law of Remedial Action Against Use of

Cuba as a Missile Base by the Soviet Union, reprinted in A. Chayes, *The Cuban Missile Crisis*, London: Oxford University Press, 1974, p.111.

22 See H. Butterfield, 'The Balance of Power', in Herbert Butterfield and Martin Wight (eds) *Diplomatic Investigations: Essays in the Theory of International Politics*, London: George Allen & Unwin, 1966, ch.6.

23 It is an interesting question why the activities of companies are commonly considered to be the actions of their controlling shareholders, but the actions of international organisations are not.

24 Article XV of the Covenant excluded matters within the domestic jurisdiction of States from the League's dispute settlement procedure. On the other hand, the Covenant expressly recognised the continuing validity of the Monroe Doctrine (Article XXI).

25 But see Rosalyn Higgins, *The Development of International Law through the Political Organs of the United Nations*, London: Oxford University Press, 1963, part II, where the determination of the United Nations not to allow its jurisdiction to be unreasonably curtailed by the invocation of Article 2(7) is noted. She concludes that 'the question of whether or not a matter is in fact one of domestic jurisdiction must be open for discussion and vote, and so must the issue of whether it should be inscribed upon the agenda', ibid., p.62.

26 See, for example, *Buttes Gas and Oil Co* v. *Hammer* [1981] 3 W.L.R. 787 (HL); F.A. Mann, *Foreign Affairs in the English Courts*, Oxford: Clarendon Press, 1986, 63–83. The US 'Act of State' doctrine overlaps with this principle, but is not driven by the conviction that international law places foreign laws beyond review by municipal tribunals; see, for example, *Banco Nacional de Cuba* v. *Sabbatino* (1964), 376 U.S. 398.

27 See Louise Doswald-Beck, 'The Legal Validity of Military Intervention by Invitation (1985) 56 *B.Y.I.L.* 189.

28 Jennings and Watts, above n.2, 439–47. Sir Robert Jennings is President of the International Court of Justice. Sir Arthur Watts was formerly Legal Adviser to the British Foreign and Commonwealth Office.

29 Ibid., p.442 (footnotes omitted).

30 Winfield, above n.2, p.137.

31 For example, Tomislav Mitrovic, 'Non-Intervention in the Internal Affairs of States', in Sahovic above n.1, p.219 at p.224. Others had taken a similar view before Vattel: see, for example, C. Wolff, *Jus Gentium Methodo Scientifica Pertractatum* (1749), §§255–7 (Classics of International Law, Np.13, Oxford: Clarendon Press, 1934). Wolff wrote: 'Since by nature no nation has a right to any act which pertains to the exercise of the sovereignty of another nation, since, moreover, the ruler of a state exercises the sovereignty of a state, and since government consists in the exercise of sovereignty; no ruler of a state has the right to interfere in the government of another, consequently cannot urge that another should establish anything in its state or do anything, or not do anything, and the government of the ruler of one state is not subject to the decision of the ruler of any other state', ibid. §257, trans. Joseph H. Drake (1934).

32 *Leviathan*, ch.xiii ff, 1651, (ed. John Plamenatz, London: Collins, 1962).

33 Emmerich de Vattel, *Le Droit des Gens*, 1758 (Classics of International Law No.4, Washington: Carnegie, 1916), Preface, p.xvii.

34 Ibid., Liv. I, chs I-IV.

35 Emmerich de Vattel, *Le Droit des Gens, ou Principes de la Loi Naturelle, Appliqués à la conduite & aux affaires des Nations & des Souverains*, London, 1758, above n.33, Liv. II, ch.IV, §54.

36 Ibid., Liv. II, ch.IV, §55.

37 *Hearings before the Committee on Foreign Relations, United States Senate,*

Seventy-Ninth Congress, First Session on the Charter of the United Nations, [Revised] July 9, 10, 11, 12 and 13, 1945, pp.227–8. The phrase had, in fact, been proposed by the US delegation, and was modelled upon the opening words of the Constitution of the United States; ibid., p.51.

38 Vattel, *Le Droit des Gens*, above n.33, Liv II, ch.IV, §56.

39 *Précis*, §74, quoted in Sir Geoffrey Butler and Simon Maccoby, *The Development of International Law*, London: Longmans, Green, 1928, p.72.

40 Richard Cobden, *Free Trade as the Best Human Means for Securing Universal and Permanent Peace*, London; 1842, cf. F.H. Hinsley, *Power and the Pursuit of Peace: Theory and Practice in the History of Relations between States*, Cambridge: Cambridge University Press, 1963, pp.96–100, pp.109–10.

41 See, for example, Butler and Maccoby, above n.39, p.69.

42 Quoted in L. Oppenheim (ed.) *The Collected Papers of John Westlake on Public International Law*, Cambridge: Cambridge University Press, 1914, p.125. As Westlake noted, two years later Canning propounded a modified version of this position, disavowing any claim to intervene in response to purely internal changes in a foreign State and limiting the right of intervention to cases where a revolutionary State sought to propagate its principles abroad, ibid., p.126.

43 Cobden took the principle of non-intervention so far as to refuse to sanction any organisation formed in England for the purpose of interfering in the domestic affairs of foreign States, including anti-slavery organisations concerned with the slavery question in the United States.

44 See J.S. Mill, 'A Few Words on Non-Intervention' (1859). This article is the subject of a penetrating discussion by Michael Walzer, *Just and Unjust Wars: A Moral Argument with Historical Illustrations*, New York: Harper Collins, 2nd edn, 1991, ch.6.

45 He argued that Britain should have intervened in Hungary in 1849 to counter the invasion of Hungary by the army of Tsar Nicholas I.

46 The legality of the action, Operation Desert Storm, is not in doubt. But it is unclear how far the military alliance against Iraq was acting on the basis of rights of collective self-defence and how far it was acting on the basis of an authorisation of the use of force by the United Nations.

47 [1992] ICJ Rep. See F. Beveridge, 'The Lockerbie Affair' (1992) 41 *I.C.L.Q.* 907.

48 (1971) 10 I.L.M. 1151.

5 The principle of non-intervention: human rights

Dominic McGoldrick

INTRODUCTION

The concept of 'international human rights' has brought about a revolution in the discipline of international law since 1945. That revolution has challenged much of the pre–1945 international law order in which the doctrine of 'non-intervention' had developed into something approaching a fundamental principle. An examination of the relationship between the two doctrines will reveal that they were developed to protect rather different interests. International human rights developed to protect the interests of individuals and groups, minorities and peoples. Non-intervention developed historically (in Latin America) as a protection for states from the involvement in their affairs of other states. Within the concept of non-intervention there is a subconcept of 'domestic jurisdiction'. This concept serves a different purpose again. It seeks to delineate the line of jurisdiction between matters of international law and matters of domestic law. The different purposes served by the different doctrines leads to varying degrees of complexity when their relationships are considered. This complexity is heightened because developments in one concept have tended to have a corresponding effect on the interests protected by the other concepts, and ultimately on the other concepts themselves.

This essay will try to analyse the concepts of domestic jurisdiction, intervention and international human rights and the relationships between them. It examines them briefly and identifies the interests they purport to protect. It then considers how the concepts and the relationships between them have developed and how there has been an evolution in the interests protected by the concepts. In the course of the analysis we will attempt to illustrate the relationship between human rights and non-intervention by examining the current practice in international law. The focus is very heavily on the development of procedures, practices and institutional machinery rather than on the human rights performance of any particular state or group of states. We will try to present the picture as it stands in 1993 and predict how it is likely to develop in the future.

The contribution of Resolution 2625 to these developments is considered when relevant.

DOMESTIC JURISDICTION

At its simplest, the question raised is one of drawing a line between matters of international law and matters of domestic law.[1] The dominant role of states in the creation of international law (partly through the increasing number of international organisations) ensures that they largely determine which matters are to be regulated by international law.[2] Both the Covenant of the League of Nations (1919) (Article 15) and the United Nations Charter (1945) (Article 2(7)) make reference to the concept of 'domestic jurisdiction'. However, the UN Charter also makes explicit reference to human rights (Articles 1, 55 and 56) whereas the Covenant did not.[3] Therefore, while the concept of 'domestic jurisdiction' may be broadly the same one, its content may have been affected by the inclusion of the human rights provisions of the Charter.

As for the concept of 'domestic jurisdiction' itself, the Permanent Court of International Justice indicated in its advisory opinion in the *Nationality Decrees* case that the question was a *relative* one.'

> The question whether a certain matter is or is not solely within the jurisdiction of a State is an essentially relative question; it depends on the development of international relations . . . it may well happen that, in a matter which . . . is not, in principle, regulated by international law, the right of a State to use its discretion is nevertheless restricted by obligations which it may have undertaken towards other States. In such a case, jurisdiction which, in principle, belongs solely to a State is limited by the rules of international law.[4]

Closely analysed this is a complex passage. The 'development of international relations' makes it difficult to determine whether a matter is 'in principle' regulated by international law. Similarly the 'obligations' which a state may have undertaken towards other states may reflect customary obligations, treaty obligations or both. The Court did not indicate whether the undertaking of international obligations could, and if so in what circumstances, irrevocably take a matter into the field of international law. This is important because the principal argument that will be made in this essay is that because of the 'development of international relations', the existence of human rights obligations, both under treaty and custom, are such that the matter of human rights protection is no longer regulated 'in principle' by the state.[5] If this is correct, then there has been a substantial departure from the traditional rule of international law that, apart from the treatment of aliens, and possibly humanitarian intervention, the rights of individuals were not matters regulated by international law. This is not to say that the most appropriate place for ensuring human rights protection is not at the national level in the first instance.[6]

In rather simpler terms, it is a matter of analysing how far international law has developed in relation to human rights, and in consequence, how much the scope of domestic jurisdiction has diminished. Wherever the line is drawn at a particular point in time represents the line of permissible intervention in states. It may be found that it is not a case of a single line, but of a whole series of lines drawn in different areas. One general comment that should be made is that the line is clearly moving in one particular direction, namely in the direction of greater regulation of, and interest in, the human rights practices of states. This is evidenced in various regimes both under the UN Charter, for example Resolutions 1235 and 1503 operated by the Human Rights Commission, and in the increasingly intrusive levels of human rights regimes based on treaties, for example, under the International Covenants on Human Rights (1966).[7]

Having established the nature of domestic jurisdiction we can now consider it in the context of its relationship with the broader concept of intervention.

NON-INTERVENTION AND DOMESTIC JURISDICTION

The concept of intervention is a complex and difficult one.[8] Analysis of it is assisted by its reflection in Article 2(7) of the UN Charter, the terms of Resolution 2625, and the consideration of the concept by the International Court of Justice in the *Nicaragua* case (1986). We consider the development of the principle and then these aspects in turn.

Non-intervention in general

The development of international rules of non-intervention was historically linked to the response of the Latin-American states in the nineteenth century to intervention by the United States and by European powers.[9] Classically, discussion of the principle of *intervention* has proceeded from Oppenheim's definition of it as 'dictatorial interference by a State in the affairs of another State for the purpose of maintaining or altering the actual condition of things'.[10] The principle does not directly appear as a separate principle in the UN Charter.[11] It does appear in a more limited form in Article 2(7) of the Charter.

Article 2(7) of the UN Charter

Article 2(7) provides that,

> Nothing contained in the present Charter shall authorise the United Nations to intervene in matters which are essentially within the

> domestic jurisdiction of any state or shall require the Members to submit such matters to settlement under the present Charter; but this principle shall not prejudice the application of enforcement measures under Chapter VII

The interpretation and application of this provision was crucial to the development of international human rights law. A wide interpretation of 'intervention', or of matters 'essentially within the domestic jurisdiction' of a state, would have substantially limited the scope of application of international human rights. Exactly the opposite has occurred. Of critical importance to this was the practice of United Nations organs since 1945.[12] This is examined below.[13]

Article 2(7) has been described as an affirmation of the Westphalian Legal Order, that is, a world legal order which is state-centred.[14] In its terms Article 2(7) is merely a rule of constitutional competence for an international organisation. However, it is generally regarded as reflecting the general rule of non-intervention. Professor Brownlie has commented that, 'While there is some difference of opinion, Article 2(7) of the UN Charter is probably in substance a restatement of the classical rule'.[15] He also comments that the reservation is inoperative when a treaty obligation is concerned.[16] He further states that,

> the domestic jurisdiction reservation does not apply if the United Nations agency is of the opinion that a breach of a specific legal obligation relating to human rights in the Charter itself has occurred. In practice, organs of the United Nations further reduce the effect of the reservation by construing certain provisions relating to human rights, which might seem only hortatory, as presenting a definite and active legal obligation.

He notes that the 'liberal practice' under Articles 55 and 56 could drastically change the concept of domestic jurisdiction. 'The extent to which "defendant" states can now rely on some type of formal interpretation of Article 2, paragraph 7 is in doubt. If care is not taken, too much can be proved, and the substance of Article 2(7) will disappear'.[17]

It seems clear, then, that a state will not be able to rely on the terms of Article 2(7) if it has undertaken a treaty obligation relating to human rights, either within or without the UN Charter (in principle the same should be true of obligations under customary international law). The effect of this interpretation of Article 2(7) is to render crucially important the determination of the human rights obligations imposed on states by the Charter itself. This was originally a matter of controversy, but there is now substantial practice and judicial authority for the view that the Charter does impose human rights obligations on states.[18]

A further problem in interpreting Article 2(7) is its relationship with the prohibition on the use of force in Article 2(4) of the UN Charter.

Subsequent practice and the two leading General Assembly Resolutions of 1965 and 1970 (considered below) have made it clear that the principle of non-intervention went well beyond the concept of intervention using force.[19] The use of force is only the most extreme form of intervention.[20] This conclusion was confirmed in the *Nicaragua* case (1986).[21]

Resolution 2625 – The Declaration of Principles (1970)

In 1965 the General Assembly had offered some guidance on 'intervention' in the 'Declaration on the Inadmissibility of Intervention in the Domestic Affairs of States and the Protection of their Independence and Sovereignty' (Resolution 2131).[22] The very title of the Declaration indicates that the interests it was concerned with protecting were those of states.[23] The 1965 Declaration provided the substantial basis for the text of the Declaration of Principles of International Law in Resolution 2625.[24] Both Declarations were treated as reflecting customary law in the *Nicaragua* case.[25] The 1970 Declaration is to be understood in a rather sophisticated way. It has to be considered as a frame of reference, a guide to the development of the law under the UN Charter, and as the basis for subsequent development.[26] However, it should not be understood simply as a picture frozen in time.

An initial question that has to be considered is whether the 1970 Declaration can only be considered in the light of developments under the UN Charter system on the basis that it was a reflection thereof, or whether the analysis can be more broadly put and therefore involve consideration of human rights under customary law and under the now extensive human rights treaty network, for example, under the two International Covenants.[27] The Declaration states that it contains 'basic principles of international law'.[28] It is submitted that the 1970 Declaration was a reflection of the general principles of international law embodied in the Charter, but that those principles themselves go beyond the purely treaty basis of the Charter. This is partly in the nature of the Charter's constitutional status.[29] Thus viewed, the Declaration sets forth the parameters of developments in international law both within the UN system and without on the basis of the general principles of international law. It follows that both custom and treaty-based human rights regimes can be analysed. The Declaration may, in addition to its role as an aid to interpretation of the Charter, also serve as evidence of *opinio juris* with respect to the customary law norm of non-intervention.[30]

In the Declaration three principles in particular are relevant to human rights.

Principle III: The principle concerning the duty not to intervene in matters within the domestic jurisdiction of any state, in accordance with the Charter

This principle makes no direct reference to human rights. The prohibition on intervention covers 'armed intervention and all other forms of interference or attempted threats against the personality of the State or against its political, economic and cultural elements.' The 'forms of interference' and the 'attempted threats' referred to are very hard to define in positive terms. The Principle continues, 'No State may use or encourage the use of economic, political or any other type of measures to coerce another State in order to obtain from it the subordination of the exercise of its sovereign rights and to secure from it advantages of any kind'. Clearly 'coerce' and 'subordinate', are strong terms. 'Coercion' was the expression which the ICJ focused upon in the *Nicaragua* case (see below).

Finally for these purposes, 'Every State has an inalienable right to choose its political, economic, social and cultural systems, without interference in any form by another State.'

Principle IV: The duty of states to co-operate with one another in accordance with the Charter

'States shall cooperate in the promotion of universal respect for and observance of human rights and fundamental freedoms for all, and in the elimination of all forms of racial discrimination and all forms of religious intolerance.' As Rosenstock has commented, 'this is an anodyne statement which accords a commendable importance to universal respect for and observance of human rights'.[31]

Principle V: The principle of equal rights and self-determination of peoples

Under this principle, *inter alia*, 'Every State has the duty to promote through joint and separate action universal respect for the observance of human rights and fundamental freedoms in accordance with the Charter'. This goes no further than the express provisions of the UN Charter.

The 1970 Declaration is a difficult and infuriating document to interpret. It may be helpful as regards specific aspects of other general principles, for example, concerning reprisals involving the use of force. It is much less so in relation to human rights. In relation to human rights and non-intervention, it is basically not very helpful. It is certainly much less helpful than the Helsinki Final Act (1975) which devotes a specific principle to non-intervention (Principle VI) and a specific principle to human rights (Principle VIII). It then, in a further principle, declares that the principles are to be equally applied (Principle X).[32] Similarly the political element in the drafting work of Resolution 2625 was very strong and the *travaux préparatoires* are therefore not very helpful. There was relatively little substantive discussion of the non-intervention principle. The academic commentaries on Resolution 2625 are almost uniformly critical.[33] Moreover, Resolution 2625 was very much a child of its time: a time marked by the depths of the Cold War, decolonisation, a world divided both East and West and North and South.[34] Developments since 1970 have been very much more constructive and progressive (see below).[35] There has been an increasing pace of change, but it is difficult to argue convincingly that the Resolution has played any significant part in that. In retrospect, the Declaration appears rather conservative and cautious. A declaration drafted in 1993 would be much stronger and more explicit in the prominence it would give to the principle of human rights (see the Vienna Declaration and Programme of Action adopted by the UN World Conference on Human Rights, 25 June 1993).

The *Nicaragua* case (1986)

The non-intervention principle

The Court stated that this principle involved the right of every sovereign state to conduct its affairs without outside interference and although violations of the principle were not infrequent it was part and parcel of customary international law.[36] It stated that expressions of *opinio juris* regarding the existence of the principle of non-intervention and customary international law were numerous and not difficult to find. This is quite true. It then noted that the principle was not, as such, spelt out in the Charter. Its explanation for this was that the Charter was not intended to embody written confirmation of every essential principle of international law which was in force. It stated that the existence of *opinio juris* of states on the principle of non-intervention was backed by established and substantial practice.[37] It also stated that the principle has been presented as a corollary of the principle of the sovereign equality of states. The example given was Resolution 2625.[38] The Court then referred to its ruling in the *Corfu Channel* case (1949),[39] Resolution 2131,[40] practice in inter-American relations and the principles of the Helsinki Final Act.[41]

It then dealt with the questions of the content of the principle and the requirements of sufficient state practice. As regards the contents of the principle, the Court would only define those aspects of it necessary to resolve the dispute before it. It stated that,

> in view of the generally accepted formulations, the principle forbids all states or groups of states to intervene directly or indirectly in internal or external affairs of other states. A prohibited intervention must accordingly be one bearing on matters on which each state is permitted, by the principle of state sovereignty, to decide freely. One

> of these is the choice of a political, economic, social and cultural system and the formulation of foreign policy. Intervention is wrongful when it uses methods of coercion in regard to such choices which must remain free ones. The element of coercion which defines and indeed forms the very essence of prohibited intervention is particularly obvious in the case of intervention which uses force.[42]

The affairs referred to by the Court are strikingly similar to those covered by the principle of sovereign equality and the principle or right of self-determination.[43] What is more interesting is the reference to 'coercion'. The expression appeared in both Resolutions 2131 and 2625. In the Court's view, this is the 'essence' of intervention. Presumably then, if something is intervention but not coercive intervention, it is not prohibited. This may be the situation of human rights criticism and procedures directed against a state.

The Court then went on to consider the complaints with regard to Nicaragua's and America's conduct in the light of this principle. The Court did not refer to specific cases of intervention. It simply stated that when states had intervened, they did not do so on the basis of a novel right or an unprecedented exception to the principle of non-intervention. Reasons given by the US had referred to the domestic policies of the country concerned, its ideology, its level of armaments, or the direction of its foreign policy. The Court stated that these were 'statements of international policy and not an assertion of rules of existing international law'. This raises the difficult question of the interplay between what is international policy and what is international law. In many cases a state's statement of its international policy is a reflection of its international practice and therefore a formative element in the creation of customary international law rules and evidence of subsequent practice under a treaty.[44]

Another general argument in the case concerned the nature of the Nicaraguan government. The US had taken exception to it being a totalitarian communist dictatorship. The Court stated that,

> however the regime in Nicaragua be defined, adherence by a state to any particular doctrine does not constitute a violation of customary international law; to hold otherwise would make a nonsense of the fundamental principle of State sovereignty, on which the whole of international law rests, and the freedom of choice of the political, social, economic and cultural systems of a State. . . . The Court cannot contemplate the creation of a new rule opening up a right of intervention by one state against another on the ground that the latter has opted for some particular ideology or political system.[45]

The Court referred to Resolution 2625 for support for its view of relations among states being based on coexistence amongst their various ideologies.

Finally, for our purposes, the Court also considered the question of human right violations. America accused Nicaragua of very serious violations of human rights commitments which it had undertaken since the 1979 revolution in Nicaragua. There was good evidence of very serious human rights violations in Nicaragua. The Court stated that, 'Where human rights are protected by international conventions, that protection takes the form of such arrangements for monitoring or ensuring respect for human rights as are provided for in the Convention themselves'.[46] The Court noted that Nicaragua had ratified a number of instruments on human rights, including the American Convention on Human Rights, and that the 'mechanisms provided for therein have functioned'.[47] The Court then expressed the view that,

> In any event, while the United States might form its own appraisal of the situation as to respect for human rights in Nicaragua, *the use of force could not be the appropriate method to ensure such respect*.[48]

When the Court dealt with state practice on non-intervention, it looked at cases of state conduct prima facie inconsistent with the principle in terms of the nature of the ground offered as justification. It commented that states had not justified their conduct by reference to a new right of intervention or a new exception to the principle of its prohibition.

Adopting this approach it can be argued that the states have asserted their right to criticise the human practices and situations in states as consistent with the scope of the non-intervention principle, or as an exception to the principle. The arguments have not simply been that the action has been politically justified but also that it is legally justified. The Court noted that the principle of non-intervention has been presented as a corollary of the principle of the sovereign equality of states, for example in Resolution 2625.[49] In its application of the principle of non-intervention the Court concluded that it was clearly established that the United States intended, by its support of the Contras, to coerce the government of Nicaragua in respect of matters in which each state is permitted, by the principle of state sovereignty, to freely decide.[50]

The Court considered whether there was anything in the conduct of Nicaragua which might have legally warranted countermeasures by the United States.

> The questions as to which the Nicaraguan Government is said to have entered into a commitment are questions of domestic policy. . . . A state's domestic policy falls within its exclusive jurisdiction, provided of course that it does not violate any obligation of international law. Every state possesses a fundamental right to choose and implement its own political, economic and social systems.[51]

The Court then considered the question of the possibility of a state binding itself by agreement in relation to a question of domestic policy, such as that relating to the holding of free elections on its territory.[52] The Court could not discover,

> within the range of subjects open to international agreement, any obstacle or provision to hinder a state from making a commitment of this kind. A state, which is free to decide upon the principle and methods of popular consultation within its domestic order, is sovereign for the purpose of accepting a limitation of its sovereignty in this field.[53]

The Court then looked at the evidence and found no evidence that Nicaragua had accepted such a limitation as a legal undertaking.[54]

INTERNATIONAL HUMAN RIGHTS AND NON-INTERVENTION

We now consider how the international law of human rights has developed in practice and the effect of this on the concepts of 'domestic jurisdiction' and 'intervention'. The simplest argument is that the 'development of international relations' this century has made human rights a matter of international law. Although there were significant developments prior to the UN Charter it seems indisputable that the human rights provisions of the Charter were a watershed.[55] A vast network of bilateral, regional and multilateral human rights treaties has been built on the foundations of the Charter. If it is accepted that human rights are matters of international law, the issue then to be considered is whether there is any continuing role and function for the doctrine of 'domestic jurisdiction'. Are all issues of human rights matters of international law? If so, then there could never be a breach of the non-intervention rule because, although there might be 'intervention', it could never be within the 'domestic jurisdiction' of a state. If not all issues of human rights are matters of international law, what criteria are applied to determine the threshold between domestic jurisdiction and international law? Does it depend on the level and degree of the obligation violated, or on who is intervening – a state or an international organisation? What is the approach when international human rights treaties have been ratified, particularly when they contain some kind of international implementation machinery? To answer these questions we will consider in turn developments within and without the United Nations, and the relationship between them.

Developments within the United Nations system[56]

Within the UN system an astonishing array of human rights activities have taken place.[57] We focus on the development of concepts, standards, procedures, practices and institutional machinery. Consideration is only given to the actual human rights performance of any particular state or group of states when this has a wider significance in terms of the development of the UN system.

Concepts and standard-setting

The three generations of rights

The story of the development of rights through civil and political to economic, social and cultural and the third generation rights is well known.[58] The debate was very much a classic one of primacy, immediacy and the relationship between the rights. The compromise position eventually reached and reflected in the famous General Assembly resolution was that the first two sets of rights are of equal importance and are interdependent. Resolution 32/130 of 16 December 1977 states that 'all human rights . . . are inter-related and indivisible'. The Declaration of the World Conference on Human Rights in 1993 stated that, 'All human rights are universal, indivisible and inter-dependent and inter-related'.

While in one sense this was an important step for those states which had argued for the importance of second generation rights, in particular Third World states and Eastern European states, it carried with it the consequence that the international concern with human rights extended beyond civil and political rights to the economic and social policies of states. This has also carried through to third generation rights such as the right to development and to a healthy environment.[59] For example, states are now concerned with their respective economic policies in terms of their effects on the national, regional and international environment.[60]

Indigenous people/populations

Whereas minorities have continued to make little progress even after 1970, indigenous people have directed a much cleverer and more orchestrated campaign to secure recognition of their rights.[61] The curious problem they have is whether they accept the existence and relevance of international law in the first place.[62] The Working Group of the UN Human Rights Commission's Sub-Commission on the Prevention of Discrimination and Protection of Minorities on Indigenous Populations has become a major focal point for the advancement of the interests of indigenous people. The establishment of the Working Group was a 'major triumph' in international efforts to protect the rights of indigenous peoples. It has given them a much higher profile and a vital forum for the expression and consideration of their arguments, values and views.

The Working Group is drafting a Universal Declaration on the Rights of Indigenous Peoples.[63] The International Labour Organisation updated an earlier Convention to reflect more contemporary understandings of the situation of indigenous people.[64] Similarly, the United Nations Convention on the Rights of the Child (1989) includes reference to indigenous peoples as a separate category of status.[65] Indigenous peoples represent a particular challenge because of the degree to which they challenge the very primacy and legitimacy of international law in its application of rules to them. It acutely raises questions as to the relationship between self-determination and territorial integrity.[66]

Standard-setting

Although the UN Charter made specific reference to human rights, it did not define them or set them out. The task of drafting an international bill of rights was given to the UN Human Rights Commission established under Article 68 of the Charter.[67] The Commission is the central UN organ on human rights.[68] When the Commission initially took the view that it could not take any action on complaints of human rights violations, its standard setting role became its principal function.[69] The standards developed by the Human Rights Commission and other bodies, often in parallel with developments at the regional level, range in nature from treaties to declarations, recommendations, codes of conduct and guidelines.[70] There is a continuing interrelationship between standard-setting and implementation.[71] As the concepts or generations of human rights have been developed, each level of human rights standard setting reaches a greater level of specificity. The consequence is that the practices of states are subject to more rigorous analysis from national and international human rights bodies.[72] The standards have also been used by the Human Rights Commission, the General Assembly, states generally, and academic writers to assess the human rights performance of states even if they have not at the particular time accepted the standards concerned as treaty obligations.[73] For example, they have been used in this way in relation to South Africa, Israel and Iran.[74]

Practices and procedures of UN organs – from promotion to protection[75]

Although the UN Charter refers only to the 'promotion' of human rights, the practices and procedures of UN organs evidence a development towards 'protection'. The history of the Human Rights Commission in particular shows a movement from standard-setting and promotion to implementation.[76] This development involved a reversal of the Human Rights Commission's position on its competence. The Commission's view, affirmed by the Economic and Social Council (ECOSOC), was that it had 'no power to take any action in regard to any complaints concerning human rights'.[77] The shift from this position was evidenced by two famous resolutions of ECOSOC (the Commission's parent body) in 1967 and 1970.

Resolution 1235 (1967)[78]

Under this Resolution the Commission was authorised 'to examine information relevant to gross violations of human rights and fundamental freedoms' and to

> make a thorough study of situations which reveal a consistent pattern of violations of human rights, as exemplified by the policy of apartheid as practised in the Republic of South Africa and the Territory of South West Africa. . . . and racial discrimination as practised notably in Southern Rhodesia, and report, with recommendations thereon, to the Economic and Social Council.[79]

On the basis of this Resolution the 'public procedure' of the Commission takes place during which alleged human rights violations by particular states are considered.[80] It is important to note that, although the Resolution refers to particular human rights violations and particular countries, it is not limited to them. It establishes a general principle for consideration of human rights situations. In practice, the early history of the Resolution was characterised by concentration on three states, namely Israel (in relation to the Occupied Territories), South Africa and Chile.[81] These three were often referred to as the 'pariah states'.

The Chile case is particularly important because it was a watershed in terms of the international attention it attracted from human rights bodies, in particular, the Human Rights Commission.[82] Israel has particular features in terms of the question of the very existence of Israel as a state, the issue of the Palestinians' right to self-determination, and the issues relating to the lands occupied by Israel in the various Middle East wars.[83] Similarly, South Africa is characterised by the issue of apartheid. What makes Chile of particular significance is that it was a straightforward case of massive violations of civil and political rights, but had no other political or ideological factor to distinguish it.[84] Again, it marks the 'crack in the citadel' which allowed subsequent cases to be considered that were similar in factual terms, and provided the political will was there.[85]

The defendant or respondent state has generally argued by reference to intervention in their domestic jurisdiction but to no avail. The co-operation given by the states concerned has varied widely. The Working Group on Chile established in 1975 received co-operation to allow a visit only in 1978.[86] Sometimes co-operation is only extended after the existence of the rapporteur for example for a number of years, as happened with Iran and Afghanistan.[87] Some degree of co-operation and permission to visit have now become the rule rather than the exception.[88]

Even though the UN may be faulted for concentrating excessively on this limited number of states, it none the less established the principle of international concern for high-level human rights violations. The subsequent practice has seen the extension of the public procedure to other states.[89] Particularly important is the extension of human rights criticism and comment to the rest of Africa and to Asia.[90] The effectiveness of public debate on alleged human rights violations is difficult to gauge. In general, however, governments are increasingly sensitive about their international reputations. One authoritative writer has suggested that, 'Public debate does seem, in most instances, to have a mitigating effect upon the scale of violations of human rights in a country. It often contributes towards amelioration in a situation, particularly when it leads to a mobilisation of international opinion.'[91] Alston is more critical:

> [I]t is difficult to escape the conclusion that the glass is at best half full. Although it is an achievement that should not be underestimated it is nevertheless difficult to accept that, after almost half a century of concerted efforts, the principal UN procedures for responding to violations are quite as embryonic, marginally effective and unevenly applied as they are.[92]

As this public procedure had begun before 1970 it cannot be argued to have stemmed from the 1970 Declaration although it may be consistent with it. The Resolution may be of significance, however, in suggesting that, in state and UN practice, domestic jurisdiction would not be regarded as a defence to 'gross violations' or a 'consistent pattern of violations'.

Resolution 1503 (1970)[93]

This Resolution established a complex three-stage procedure for the consideration of communications from individuals and non-governmental organisations. On the basis of the communications the Sub-Commission can refer to the Commission 'particular *situations* which appear to reveal a *consistent pattern of gross and reliably attested violations of human rights* requiring consideration by the Commission'.[94] The Commission may decide to undertake a 'thorough study' under Resolution 1235 (above) or to appoint an *ad hoc* committee to conduct an investigation. The latter can only be done, *inter alia*, with the express consent of the state concerned and has never in fact been done. The whole of the Resolution 1503 procedure remains 'confidential' until the Commission decides to make recommendations to ECOSOC.

Resolution 1503 was a major step in the jurisdiction of the Commission.[95] The importance of the Resolution 1503 procedure is that it is universally applicable to all UN members. Its terms deal with 'situations which appear to reveal a consistent pattern of gross and reliably attested violation of human rights'.[96] If the Human Rights Commission can consider these situations without the consent of the state concerned, it suggests that at least such violations are a matter of international law and are not within the purely domestic jurisdiction of the state. However, the practice under Resolution 1503 has been disappointing. The political element in the Commission has been very strong. Also, the confidentiality attached to it has allowed consideration of alleged gross human rights violations to be conducted in secret over many years, thereby avoiding public consideration under the Resolution 1235 procedure (above). However, as Professor Humphrey has pointed out, the confidentiality problem can be overstressed and the taking of each step in the procedure is itself viewed as a sanction.[97] The involvement of the Sub-Commission and the number of governments represented on the Commission limit the extent of the confidentiality. Since 1978, at the commencement of the public debate on the question of violations of human rights in any part of the world, the chairman has announced the names of the countries in respect of which the Commission has taken decisions in private meetings under Council Resolution 1503. However, everything else remains confidential. The Commission has considered the situation in over forty different countries under the Resolution 1503 procedure. In 1991 the Sub-Commission's Pre-sessional Working Group reportedly transmitted cases relating to ten countries to the full Sub-Commission. In a confidential session the Sub-Commission reportedly transmitted to the Commission the cases of Bahrain, Chad, Myanmar, Somalia, Sudan, Syria and Zaire. The cases of Bhutan and Turkey were reportedly left pending, while that of Guatemala was dropped.

Notwithstanding its historical significance, Resolution 1503 has been subjected to punishing criticism.[98] Alston concludes that although states respond to 1503 communications 'there is little if any evidence that these responses have led to significant reversals of existing policy or practice in such states' and that the Resolution needs major reform.[99]

Resolution 1503 was adopted in the same year as Resolution 2625. Therefore, the procedures in Resolution 1503 have to be understood as being consistent with the principles of Resolution 2625.[100]

Implementation – the thematic approach[101]

The thematic approach, was principally developed in the 1980s through the establishment of working groups or special rapporteurs who prepare public reports to provide a basis for public discussion. The beginning of what is termed the thematic approach, in contrast to the country-oriented approach, was the Commission's establishment of a Working Group on Missing Persons in February 1980. Although it is not state-specific, it does involve criticism of individual states. There are now four thematic procedures, two working groups and two special rapporteurs.[102] All four report to the Commission. A major feature of the most recently established working group's mandate is that it is required to investigate cases. This is a totally new concept since similar mechanisms in the past have only been given mandates to examine certain questions or phenomena.

The reasoning behind the establishment of thematic enquiries is to obtain more information on certain issues, to avoid the difficulties encountered when trying to consider particular situations because of the opposition and diplomatic power of the governments concerned, for example, Argentina over disappearances, and to discover the dimensions of problems with a view to being better able to deal with them.[103]

Thematic procedures are obviously less 'interventionist' than a complaints procedure seeking to respond to violations like Resolution 1503. Also they are not country-specific in the sense of a Resolution 1235 study. On these bases they are more acceptable to states. However, the procedures have developed in ways that have made them more effective and 'interventionist' than expected. They 'examine questions' by considering individual cases, overall country situations and the way the phenomena are developing.[104] They rely on extensive sources of information, request information from governments on alleged violations, make urgent action representations in relations to individual cases, and conduct on-site country visits. Their reports to the Commission have often been authoritative and critical. Despite these merits, however, the thematic procedures 'do not succeed in putting much pressure on individual countries'.[105]

As well as their individual features it is also important to note the inter-relationship between the various UN procedures. Most country-orientated public procedures have been preceded by a decision of the Sub-Commission to forward communications to the Commission within the framework of the confidential procedure. Similarly, the thematic procedures grew out of the country-oriented practices. These could decrease the importance somewhat of the confidential procedure, particularly its inability to act quickly. This procedure may lead to the adoption of resolutions and, in exceptional cases, to the establishment of special procedures such as the Special Working Group of Experts on Southern Africa.[106]

The roles of the Human Rights Commission and the Sub-Commission[107]

The UN Human Rights Commission is a political body, while the Sub-Commission is composed of independent experts.[108] As the role of the Commission and its working groups (see above) has evolved from standard-setting to implementation and consideration of specific countries, its relationship with the Sub-Commission has been severely strained. The functions of the Sub-Commission and its working groups[109] have been established by the various resolutions of the Commission, ECOSOC and the General Assembly. It includes standard-setting and studies on human rights,[110] roles in the operations of ECOSOC Resolutions 1235 and 1503 (above) and other specific mandates from the Commission, ECOSOC and the General Assembly.[111] The relationship between the Commission and the Sub-Commission has been under pressure because the independent experts on the Sub-Commission have strongly asserted its separate role in discussing and assessing the human rights performance of specific countries. It passes resolutions on specific country situations under the Resolution 1235 procedure (see above).[112] Indeed, it has reformed its procedural rules to ensure secret voting on those situations.[113] The Commission has complained of duplication and inefficiency, has pressed the Sub-Commission to reform its working methods, and has even considered abolishing the Sub-Commission.[114]

The role of the General Assembly[115]

The practice of the General Assembly (principally in its Third Committee) has evolved to reflect the human rights priorities of its changing majority. This has affected both conceptual issues and the development of procedures (see above). Initially, consideration by the Assembly of a country-specific human rights situation was justified by reference to an existing international agreement or the likelihood of the situation impairing friendly relations among states. These were soon replaced by criteria of 'large-scale', 'gross', or 'massive and flagrant' violations of human rights, as particularly, but not exclusively, exemplified by the policy of apartheid.[116] Although for political reasons only a limited number of countries have been subject to country-specific resolutions, the legitimacy of General Assembly consideration is now clearly established.[117]

In normative terms the General Assembly has repeatedly based its work on human rights on the Charter and the Universal Declaration (1948). In General Assembly Resolution 34/175 (1979) it 'Reaffirm[ed] that mass and flagrant violations of human rights are of special concern to the United Nations'.[118] Since 1979 its resolutions have referred to 'various international instruments'. It has particularised the international covenants in some cases. It has also urged all states to be bound by the principles of the Covenant. Individual cases and smaller scale violations have rarely been dealt with in Assembly resolutions although they are increasingly referred to in the debates.[119] The General Assembly does not generally deal with communications alleging human rights violations except for communications concerned with human rights in non-self-governing territories and concerning the policy of apartheid.[120]

The General Assembly also has a broader policy and strategic role in determining the human rights programme and budget of the UN. Therefore, its requests, and responses to the work of the many UN bodies and treaty organs dealing with human rights questions have been important. The positive (or at least not negative) responses from the Assembly to proposed human rights standards,[121] new procedures like Resolutions 1235 and 1503 and the thematic procedures,[122] the annual reports of the treaty organs like the Human Rights Committee,[123] and new strategies like the increasing focus on advisory services and public information campaigns,[124] have done much to ensure their development.

The treaty organs

Of particular importance are the various international human rights implementation bodies such as the Human Rights Committee (HRC), the Committee on Economic, Social and Cultural Rights, the Committee on the Elimination of Discrimination Against Women, the Committee on the Elimination of Racial Discrimination, and the United Nations Committee Against Torture. These are independent organs established under multilateral treaties.[125] These have only come into existence since 1970. In terms of the concepts of domestic jurisdiction and non-intervention there is a simple response. This is that the states parties to the treaties have expressly *consented* to the degree of intervention permissible under the terms and procedures of the particular treaty. This consent removes the otherwise 'coercive' nature of the intervention.[126] The degree of intervention varies from treaty to treaty but the trend is clearly towards more intrusive verification and analysis. Resolution 2625 remains of importance as a frame of reference for the interpretation and application of the founding treaties and the jurisdiction of those implementation bodies. For example, in relation to the Human Rights Committee, various aspects of its work have raised questions of how the substantive rights in the International Covenant on Civil and Political Rights (ICCPR) should be interpreted,[127] the role of the Committee,[128] and the extent of its jurisdiction.[129] In the early years of the Human Rights Committee's practice the classic East/West approaches to the interpretation of the concepts of domestic jurisdiction and non-intervention were clearly detectable.[130] To some extent these have been resolved, although not to the satisfaction of some. A leading example is that of the question of the HRC's jurisdiction under Article 40 of the ICCPR to make 'general comments'. Could the HRC make general comments that were country-specific? If they could, it would represent a much more intrusive and powerful weapon for the protection of human rights. The debate on this question continued for a number of years. To date, all of the General Comments of the HRC have been addressed to all states parties and not to individual states.[131]

An increasing number of the treaty organs operate communication (petition) systems under their governing treaties. They include the First Optional Protocol to the Civil and Political Rights Covenant (1966),[132] the Convention on the Elimination of Racial Discrimination (CERD) (1965),[133] and the UN Convention Against Torture.[134] However, there are still many of them which do not contain such a system. These include the International Covenant on Economic, Social and Cultural Rights (ICESCR) (1966), the Convention on the Elimination of Discrimination

Against Women (CEDAW) (1979) and the Convention on the Rights of the Child (1989).[135]

The historical trend is for more and more states to be willing to participate in the multilateral treaty system. The ICCPR, the ICESCR, the CERD, the CEDAW and the Children's Convention all have in excess of 100 states parties. The First Optional Protocol to the ICCPR has sixty-five states parties. Major recent breakthroughs were the accession by Russia to the Optional Protocol to the ICCPR in 1991 and the accession by the USA to the ICCPR in 1992.[136] This clearly constitutes significant evidence of the states parties' willingness to accept increasingly higher levels of international supervision of their human rights performance. It is also noteworthy that some governments which did not co-operate with the United Nations in the framework of the special public procedures do co-operate with the Human Rights Committee, for example, Afghanistan, Chile and Iran.

International protection: a synopsis[137]

In the practice of the UN the limited provisions of Articles 1, 55 and 56 of the UN Charter have been dynamically interpreted while that in Article 2(7) has been greatly reduced in significance.[138] That practice has clearly gone well beyond 'promotion'. The focus has shifted to how far the UN will go in 'protecting' human rights. The further the UN goes towards protection the more it effectively limits the sovereignty of states and the scope of their domestic jurisdiction. The scope and variety of the UN's human rights activities are astonishing. As well as the practice of its own organs and subsidiary bodies, a kaleidoscope of procedures, techniques and mechanisms have been used. These include, individually or in combination, reporting systems, inter-state and individual communication (petition) systems, working groups, special committees, special rapporteurs or representatives, public debate, confidential procedures, good offices, conciliation, direct contacts, humanitarian activities, urgent response systems, intercession by the Secretary-General of the UN or his representatives, advisory and technical assistance, and publicity.[139] Crucial to the shift to protection has been the practice of the treaty organs like the Human Rights Committee and the Committee on Economic, Social and Cultural Rights.[140] Many of them have taken a very positive and dynamic approach to their jurisdiction and competence, and subjected the practices of states to searching analysis and criticism.[141] Similarly the jurisprudence developed by these bodies on specific rights is increasingly significant.[142] Ramcharan comments that,

> There can be little doubt that the United Nations is competent to act for the protection of human rights, particularly in situations where there exists a consistent pattern of gross violations of human rights

> and fundamental freedoms. . . . While it may be doubtful whether States can be called to account for every alleged infringement of the rather general Charter provisions, there can be little doubt that responsibility exists under the Charter for any substantial infringement of the provisions, especially when a class of persons, or a pattern of activity are involved.[143]

Situations of gross violations of human rights have been considered within the General Assembly, Security Council, ECOSOC,[144] the Human Rights Commission and the Sub-Commission. 'Protection' is still secondary to promotion but it is becoming increasingly less so. However, '[m]easures of international protection, which are commonly referred to as means of implementation, are still at a relatively primitive stage and in most instances can hardly satisfy the test which international law has set for national protection namely, the test of effectiveness.'[145]

Developments outside the United Nations – regional human rights protection[146]

Of major importance to the development of international human rights protection has been the development of systems outside the UN. The most highly developed and effective system is that under the European Convention on Human Rights (1950).[147] This has served as something of a model for other systems. European Community Law has also evolved incrementally into a relatively developed human rights system.[148] The system under the American Convention on Human Rights (1969) is increasingly significant and influential.[149] The African Charter on Human and Peoples' Rights (1981) was hailed as a major step for the African continent both for its content and its procedures.[150] There are now wide ranging sets of regional petition procedures open to individuals, groups of individuals, or non-governmental organisations.[151] In many systems, however, there is still no right of individual petition; for example, under the European Social Charter (1961).[152]

These regional systems have often developed more rapidly and further than the UN system. They can constitute evidence of regional custom. The consensual nature of their operation makes it difficult to assess their significance in terms of Resolution 2625. Their cumulative effect, however, is to reduce yet further the scope of the defence of domestic jurisdiction and to expand the range of co-operation between states on human rights matters.

The Conference on Security and Co-operation in Europe (CSCE, 1975-)[153]

The CSCE is another regional development.[154] It is treated separately here because it has been argued to have been a fundamental development in terms of removing the argument of the Eastern European states, and in particular the then USSR, that human rights questions were purely questions of domestic jurisdiction.[155] As noted above, the Helsinki Final Act (HFA) elevated the principle of respect for human rights to a position alongside those of state sovereignty and domestic jurisdiction.[156] The HFA also made provision for follow-up meetings to review its implementation and to negotiate new agreements.[157] The HFA was an important political and psychological breach.[158] It also follows the pattern of where a small breach has led to a subsequent substantial development in terms of the level and range of international interest in the human rights practices of other states.[159] The evolution of the CSCE system bears characteristics similar to those of the UN human rights system. A period of standard-setting and promotion is being followed by an increasing focus on implementation. A four-stage 'Human Dimension Mechanism' has been developed under which 'cases and situations' can be considered.[160] The mechanism is not limited to consistent patterns of gross violations.[161] The CSCE's guiding principle of consensus has been changed to deal with 'cases of clear, gross and uncorrected violations of relevant CSCE commitments' (relating to the human dimension).[162] A CSCE High Commissioner for Minorities has been appointed.[163] The CSCE has also been at the forefront of those advocating the interrelationship between human rights and economic development.[164] Again, states pay the price of increased human rights intervention by other states in return for their interest in economic development and assistance.

Although the CSCE does not have a treaty basis, we have already noted that it can, in the opinion of the International Court of Justice, 'with all due caution' be used as evidence of the practice and *opinio juris* of states.[165] Respect for the human rights provisions of the CSCE has also been one of the conditions (or criteria) for recognition of new states emerging from the revolutions in Central and Eastern Europe.[166] The CSCE has become a major European forum. The early effects of Western and Eastern states uniting in human rights initiatives, for example, in the UN, have already been felt.[167] There is a clear trend in international law towards the idea of the democratic legitimacy of states.[168] The concept is being advanced, for example, in the UN, the CSCE, the European Community, the Council of Europe and in the human rights and economic policies of states and international institutions.[169]

GENERAL PRINCIPLES – SOVEREIGNTY, RESPONSIBILITY

Discussions on human rights in international law have always proceeded from a consideration of the status of the individual in international law. The non-status or limited status of the individual has reflected the limited acceptance of the idea of individuals possessing international human rights. The various developments outlined above cannot but have had a significant effect on the status of the individual in international law. Each advance in terms of concepts, standards-setting, procedures and mechanisms leads to a realignment of the position of individuals, minorities and peoples in relation to states.

If the above analysis is broadly correct then it has clearly changed the concept of state sovereignty (and within that, of course, domestic jurisdiction). State sovereignty may be equal but it is increasingly limited.[170] Sovereignty is no longer, if it ever was, absolute.[171] In the decolonisation and post-decolonisation period states have used sovereignty as a defensive shield. However, with the passage of time its force is weakening. The sovereignty of states is limited by their obligations under the UN Charter, the multilateral human rights treaty network, and under customary international law to respect human rights.[172] Those obligations are increasingly being asserted in a positive manner by states and international organisations. The stress has shifted to a more positive conception of sovereignty based on co-operation with the UN and between states to protect human rights.

There has also been an increasing focus on the responsibility of states (and individuals) for human rights violations.[173] Under Article 19 of the International Law Commission's draft articles on state responsibility, there may be international criminal responsibility, *inter alia*, for,

> a serious breach of an international obligation of essential importance for safeguarding the right of self-determination of peoples, such as that prohibiting the establishment or maintenance by force of colonial domination,

and for

> a serious breach on a widespread scale of an international obligation of essential importance for safeguarding human beings, such as those prohibiting slavery, genocide and apartheid.[174]

An internationally wrongful act which is not an international crime in accordance with the provisions of Article 19 will constitute an international delict.[175]

The provisions of Article 19 were influenced by the concept of 'obligations *erga omnes*' developed by the International Court of Justice in the *Barcelona Traction* case (1970).[176] According to the Court,

> all States can be held to have a legal interest in their protection; they are obligations *erga omnes*. Such obligations derive, for example, in contemporary international law, from the outlawing of acts of aggression, and of genocide, as also from the principles and rules concerning basic rights of the human person including protection from slavery and racial discrimination. Some of the rights of protection have entered into the body of general international law . . . others are

> conferred by international instruments of a universal or quasi-universal character.[177]

Does the *erga omnes* character of these obligations give greater support for intervention? Professor Schachter suggests that, 'Declaring these obligations erga omnes adds marginally to the right of states to criticise infringements in the international political organs. . . . Whether this will extend into the judicial area so that an *actio popularis* will emerge is still uncertain.'[178] He thinks that states will be hesitant to do this.[179]

The story of human rights and non-intervention is very much one of David and Goliath. The citadels of sovereignty are being destroyed. There is an increasing concept of the international promotion and protection of human rights and responsibility, including the criminal responsibility of individuals and states, for violations.

CONCLUSION

Limits for the future

There are undoubtedly still political limits on the development of international human rights protection; when CEDAW requested the promotion of UN studies on status of women under Islamic law it was subjected to strong criticism in ECOSOC and the General Assembly asked it to reconsider.[180] The Commission has recently increased significantly in size to give increased representation for Third World states. It is too early to assess whether this will reduce the political will on human rights issues in the Commission.[181] Similarly, political forces can prevent the consideration of the human rights record of a state, most notably in recent years Iraq, through a strange coalition in the Human Rights Commission.[182] However, states are particularly sensitive even when they initially plead the classic argument of domestic jurisdiction. Such was the case with China over the Tiananmen Square incident,[183] which they initially simply argued as a matter of domestic jurisdiction. However, the importance of China's relationships, particularly in economic terms, with other states demanded that it permitted visiting delegations to discuss the human rights situation in China. So, for example, American delegations eventually went to China to talk about human rights.

There are also substantial practical constraints on the further development of international human rights protection. The under-resourcing of the UN human rights programme is scandalous. Only 1 per cent of the UN budget is spent on the human rights programme (the World Conference on Human Rights in 1993 asked for substantial increases). The excessive confidentiality evident in procedures like that in Resolution 1503 undermine the credibility of the UN.[184] There are still reports prepared which exclude country names.[185] Non-governmental organisations continue to have a vital role in the system but their ability to contribute to some forums is very limited.[186]

What's left for states?

The answer to this question bears some similarities to the concept of the 'margin of discretion' developed in international human rights law. The human rights practices of states are subjected to an ever-increasing array of analysis by other states, international organisations, and human rights bodies. A defence of 'domestic jurisdiction' will be of little effect. They may refuse to co-operate but the political and economic pressures on them will be immense and few will be able to hold out. However, armed force will not generally be used against them except in two situations. First, if the Security Council judges the situation to be a threat to international peace and security under Chapter VII of the UN Charter. Such a situation is expressly exempted from the domestic jurisdiction provision in Article 2(7) of the Charter.[187] If the human rights policies of a state are judged to be such a threat the state may be subject to economic sanctions, as in the cases of Rhodesia and South Africa.[188] In the Iraq-Kuwait war of 1991 the Security Council resolution authorising measures to 'restore international peace and security to the area' has been interpreted by the allied coalition as authorising the establishment of 'safe-havens' for Kurds (an alternative or co-existing justification is humanitarian intervention).[189] Secondly, there is increasing evidence that states are interpreting the protection of nationals as within the concept of self-defence in Article 51 of the UN Charter and using force accordingly.[190]

States will be held accountable whether or not they join in regional or universal treaty regimes (or the CSCE). United Nations regimes will still apply, for example, Resolutions 1235 and 1503. There is no 'safe-haven' for states which engage in human rights violations.

Notes

1 See A. D'Amato, 'Domestic Jurisdiction', in R. Bernhardt (ed.) *Encyclopedia Public International Law*, Amsterdam: North Holland, vol.10, pp.132–7. The relationship between the two systems is a different question.

2 See Article 38 of the Statute of the International Court of Justice. 'The principal intellectual instrument in the last century for providing objective standards of legal validation has been the doctrine of sources', O. Schachter, *International Law in Theory and Practice*, Dordrecht: Martinus Nijhoff, 1991, p.35. As well as inter-state pressure, States are, of course, subject to great pressure from national and international non-governmental interest groups, particularly in the human rights field.

3 See Articles 1(3), 13(1)(b), 55(c), 56, 62, 68 and 76 of the UN Charter. On the drafting see R. Russell, *A History of the United Nations Charter*, Washington: Brookings, 1958, pp.777–807, 900–10.

4 *Nationality Decrees issued in Tunis and Morocco* (1923) P.C.I.J. Rep., Series B, No.4, 27.

5 This argument raised some complex questions concerning how customary international law can be changed and also the denunciation and termination of treaties in a human rights context. See E. Schwelb, 'The Law of Treaties and Human Rights', in M. Reisman and B. Weston (eds) *Towards World Order and Human Dignity*, New York: Free Press, 1976, pp.262–90.

6 See also Schachter, above n.2, pp.332–3 where he considers questions of domestic jurisdiction. He suggests that even though a matter may be governed by an international obligation, it may, under some circumstances, be regarded as appropriate for domestic action alone.

7 See pp.96–9, 102–3 below; P. Alston (ed.) *The United Nations and Human Rights – A Critical Appraisal* Oxford: Oxford University Press, 1992.

8 See T. Opperman, 'Intervention', in Bernhardt, above n.1, vol.3, pp.233–6. The following statement by Mr Sinclair, the UK delegate to the Drafting Committee on the Declaration, is often cited in works on intervention,

> In considering the scope of 'Intervention', it should be recognised that in an inter-dependent world, it is inevitable and desirable that States will be concerned with and will seek to influence the actions and policies of other States, and that the objective of international law is not to prevent such activity but rather to ensure that it is compatible to the sovereign equality of States and self-determination of their peoples. The United Kingdom delegation wishes to state its understanding that the concept of intervention in the 'external affairs' of States was to be construed in the light of that commentary.
>
> UN Doc. A/AC.125/SR.114.

9 'There can be no doubt that the principle of non-intervention is an autonomous principle of customary law; indeed it is very much older than any of the multilateral Treaty regimes in question. It is, moreover, a principle of law which in the inter-American system has its own peculiar developments, interpretation and importance', Separate Opinion of Judge Jennings, *Case Concerning Military and Paramilitary Activities In and Against Nicaragua* (hereinafter the *Nicaragua* case) [1986] I.C.J. Rep. 14, at pp.534–4. See also G. Arangio-Ruiz, 'The Normative Role of the General Assembly of the United Nations and the Declaration of Principles of Friendly Relations' (1972-II) 137 *Hague Recueil des Cours* 419–742, at pp.547–9.

10 H. Lauterpacht (ed.) *Oppenheim's International Law*, London: Longmans, 1955, 8th edn, vol.I, para. 134. Non-intervention also has a kind of natural appeal in terms of self-government, self-determination and the element of democratic rule by its own government rather than by external powers. See now Sir Robert Jennings and Sir Arthur Watts (eds) *Oppenheim's International Law*, London: Longmans, 9th edn, 1992, pp.427–51.

11 It can be viewed as part of the principle of the sovereign equality of (member) states in Article 2(1) of the UN Charter. See the approach of the ICJ in the *Nicaragua* case, below.

12 See Article 33(3) of the Vienna Convention on the Law of Treaties (1969).

13 See pp.94–104 below.

14 E. Lane, 'Demanding Human Rights: A Change in the World Legal Order', (1978) 6 *Hofstra L.R.* 169–95, at p.283. See also the major article by J.S. Watson, 'Autointerpretation, Competence and the Continuing Validity of Article 2(7) of the United Nations Charter' (1977) 71 *A.J.I.L* 60–83.

15 I. Brownlie, *Principles of Public International Law*, Oxford: Clarendon Press, 4th edn, 1990, p.553. He continues by noting that, 'However, it is concerned

with the question of the constitutional competence of the organs of the United Nations, and it may be that its precise content is not therefore identical with the rule of general international law apart from the Charter.'

16 Citing the *Peace Treaties* case, [1950] I.C.J. Rep. 65, at pp.70–1, and the *Nationality Decrees* case, above n.4.

17 Brownlie, above n.15 pp.553–4.

18 See H. Lauterpacht, *International Law and Human Rights*, Cambridge: Cambridge University Press, 1950; E. Schwelb, 'The International Court of Justice and the Human Rights Clauses of the Charter' (1972) 66 *A.J.I.L.* 337–51; N. Rodley, 'Human Rights and Humanitarian Intervention: The Case Law of the World Court' (1989) 38 *I.C.L.Q.* 321–33; R. B. Lillich, *International Human Rights*, Boston: Little Brown, 2nd edn, 1991, pp.14–85.

19 'There was an eventual Western recognition that some way had to be found to cover economic and political pressures of sufficient magnitude to affect political independence', R. Rosenstock, 'The Declaration of Principles of International Law concerning Friendly Relations: a Survey' (1971) 65 *A.J.I.L.* 713–35, at p.728.

20 As Arangio-Ruiz notes, 'a sweeping prohibition such as that of Article 2(4) was bound to cover at least some of the problems met by the principle of non-intervention.' He also suggests that the coexistence of intervention with the negative general principle in Article 2(4) does anything but strengthen the prohibitions in question. It confuses the concept of intervention; above n.9, para. 66.

21 See text to n.42 below.

22 UN General Assembly Resolution 2131(XX).

23 'The text is largely orientated toward the preservation and protection of State sovereignty rather than the development of new norms and new mechanisms more suited to the increasingly inter-dependent world of today and of the future', Rosenstock, above n.19, p.735.

24 Rosenstock describes this as the greatest blunder in the drafting of Resolution 2625, above n.19, p.728. See also Arangio-Ruiz, above n.9, pp.547–61; Mitrovic, 'Non-Intervention in the Internal Affairs of State', in M. Sahovic (ed.) *Principles of International Law concerning Friendly Relations and Co-operation*, Dobbs Ferry, NY: Oceana, 1972, pp.219–75.

25 *Nicaragua* case, above n.9, para. 202 *et seq*.

26 'The legal significance of the Declaration lies in the fact that it provides evidence of the consensus among member States of the United Nations on the meaning and elaboration of the principles of the Charter.'

27 In any event the relationship between the latter and the United Nations in general is very close, see D. McGoldrick, *The Human Rights Committee – Its Role in the Development of the International Covenant on Civil and Political Rights*, Oxford: Oxford University Press, 1991, ch.2.

28 Declaration, Part III.

29 See 'The United Nations Charter: Constitution or Contract', in R. St J. Macdonald and D.H. Johnston (eds) *The Structure and Process of International Law* The Hague: Martinus Nijhoff, 1983, pp.889–912.

30 It was used in this way, 'with all due caution', by the I.C.J. in the *Nicaragua* case, above n.9, see para. 188.

31 Rosenstock, above n.19, p.729. Although at the very least the statement highlights the importance attached to the issues of racial discrimination and racial intolerance.

32 '[T]he human rights principle had become just as important as (other) fundamental principles of international law, such as the sovereign equality of states and the non-intervention in internal affairs. It was the first time that the human

rights principle had acquired such a ranking to fundamental intergovernmental documents', A. Bloed, *From Helsinki To Vienna: Basic Documents of the Helsinki Process*, Dordrecht: Martinus Nijhoff (1990), p.6. See also M. Bossuyt, 'Human Rights and Non-Intervention in Domestic Matters' (1985) 35 *Rev. I.C.J.* 42–52.

33 See Arangio-Ruiz, above n.9; Sahovic above n.24; Rosenstock, above n.19; B. Conforti, 'Non-Intervention', in M. Bedjaoui (ed.) *International Law: Achievements And Prospects* Dordrecht: Nijhoff/Unesco, 1991, pp.467–82.

34 See A. Cassese, *International law in a Divided World*, Oxford: Clarendon Press, 1986.

35 The resolution of that conflict evidenced, for example, in the *Charter of Paris*, may have significant long-term implications for the development of human rights activities in the light of the 1970 Declaration. See D. McGoldrick, 'Human Rights Developments in the Helsinki Process', in R. Beddard and D. Hills (eds) *Emerging Rights Within the New Europe*, Southampton: University of Southampton, 1992, pp.17–49.

36 *Nicaragua* case, above n.9, para.202 *et seq*.

37 The Court has been criticised for getting these requirements the wrong way round.

38 The 'sovereign equality of states' is Principle VI of Resolution 2625.

39 [1949] I.C.J. Rep. 4.

40 See text to n.22 above.

41 See text to n.32 above.

42 *Nicaragua* case, above n.9, para.205.

43 See Principles V and VI of Resolution 2625. See the formulations in Article 1 of each of the International Covenants (1966) on which see McGoldrick, *The Human Rights Committee* above n.27, ch.5.

44 The Court went on to note that the United States did not argue the case on the basis of such a right of intervention.

45 *Nicaragua* case, above n.9, para.263. Such a view clearly leaves no room for a doctrine such as the 'Brezhnev Doctrine' as applied in the Czechoslovakia case, or indeed the 'Reagan Doctrine'. The Brezhnev Doctrine was disavowed by the Gorbachev regime.

46 *Nicaragua* case, above n.9, para.267.

47 Ibid.

48 Ibid., para.268 (emphasis added). This clearly suggests that the Court would have little time for a concept of humanitarian intervention to protect individuals subject to human rights violations. Note this does not expressly exclude the concept of intervention in self-defence of nationals. However, some writers suggest that the Court's tone is against such an argument. Cf. Jennings and Watts, above n.10.

49 *Nicaragua* case, above n.9, para.207.

50 However, the Court did not find that the economic action complained of was a breach of the customary law principle of non-intervention, para.245.

51 *Nicaragua* case, above n.9, para.257.

52 Ibid., para.259. Cf. T.M. Franck, 'The Emerging Right to Democratic Governance' (1992) 86 *A.J.I.L.* 46–91.

53 *Nicaragua* case, above n.9.

54 Cf. the dissenting opinion of Judge Schwebel in the *Nicaragua* case, above n.9, p.259, at paras.241–50. He cites the Statute of the Council of Europe, 'The history of the Council of Europe demonstrates that these international obligations are treated as such by the Council; they may not be avoided by pleas of domestic jurisdiction and non-intervention'. He continues to conclude that the efforts of the United States were 'legally well-grounded efforts to

induce Nicaragua to perform its international obligations'. His argument on whether the assurances given by the government of Nicaragua to protect human rights etc. are binding would be relevant in the case of the recognition of countries in Central and Eastern Europe under the European Community's Recognition Guidelines, see C. Warbrick, 'Recognition of States' (1992) 41 *I.C.L.Q.* 473–82.

55 See text to n.18 above.

56 For ease of analysis we include the 'treaty organs' like the Human Rights Committee which were developed under and have very close connections with the UN. See McGoldrick, above n.27.

57 See *United Nations Action In The Field of Human Rights* (1988).

58 See P. Alston, 'Conjuring Up New Human Rights: Proposals For Quality Control' (1984) 78 *A.J.I.L.* 607–21; T. Van Boven, 'Distinguishing Criteria of Human Rights', in K. Vasak and P. Alston (eds) *The International Dimensions of Human Rights*, Paris: Unesco, 1982, pp.43–59.

59 See P. Alston, 'Making Space For New Human Rights' (1988) 1 *Harvard H.R.Y.* 332–81.

60 An Earth Summit on the Environment was held in Rio in 1992, see (1992) 31 *I.L.M.* 814–87. See also the Preliminary Reports by F. Ksentini, 'Human Rights and the Environment', E/CN.4/Sub.2/1991/8 and 1992/7 and Add. 1; P.W. Birnie and A.E. Boyle, *International Environmental Law*, Oxford: Oxford University Press, 1993.

61 H. Hannum, *Autonomy, Sovereignty and Self-Determination – The Accommodation of Conflicting Rights*, Philadelphia: University of Pennsylvania Press, 1990; F.M. Brookfield (ed.), I. Brownlie, *Treaties and Indigenous Peoples*, Oxford: Oxford University Press, 1992.

62 See R.A. Williams, *The American Indian in Western Legal Thought – The Discourses of Conquest*, New York: Oxford University Press 1990; D. McGoldrick, 'Canadian Indians, Cultural Rights and Human Rights Committee' (1991) 40 *I.C.L.Q.* 658–69.

63 For the latest draft see UN Doc. E/CN.4/Sub.2/1993/26. The draft declaration will therefore be sent to the Commission as a proposal from the Sub-Commission (a group of independent experts) which has had limited state input. This was a deliberate policy decision by states. The real test for the draft will be how it is received by the Commission which is composed of state representatives. In 1992 the Working Group on Indigenous Populations was attended by over 600 people.

64 See (1989) 28 *I.L.M.* 1382.

65 See D. McGoldrick, 'The U.N. Convention on the Rights of the Child' (1991) 5 *Int.J.Law and the Family* 132–69.

66 See the Draft Universal Declaration, above n.63.

67 See McGoldrick, *The Human Rights Committee*, above n.27, ch.1.

68 Most initiatives are taken there and the purpose of several human rights initiatives at the Sub-Commission and the General Assembly is to stimulate the Commission into action. From a strictly legal point of view, operational decisions are taken by the ECOSOC. However, in human rights matters, the ECOSOC functions merely as a mailbox. See D. O'Donovan, 'The Economic and Social Council', in Alston, *The United Nations*, above n.7, pp.107–25. The Commission's decision to establish special procedures is often facilitated by previous resolutions of the General Assembly and/or the Sub-Commission. There are various interactions between the UN human rights bodies and the treaty organs (like the Human Rights Committee) and between the confidential and public procedures of the Commission. They frequently exchange information.

69 See T. Meron, *Human Rights Law-Making in the United Nations – A Critique of Instruments and Process*, Oxford: Oxford University Press, 1986.

70 See *Human Rights – A Compilation of International Instruments*, New York: United Nations, 1993. Most recently see the UN Declaration on the Rights of Persons Belonging to National or Ethnic, Religious and Linguistic Minorities, GA Resolution 47/135 of 18 December 1992.

71 See Rosalyn Higgins, 'Some Thoughts on the Implementation of Human Rights' (1989/1) *UN Bull. of Human Rights* 60–6.

72 For example, note the importance of intervention in times of public emergency. Generally, in all situations there is a complicated set of roles. On states of emergency, see McGoldrick, *The Human Rights Committee*, above, n.27, ch.7; J. Oraa, *Human Rights in States of Emergency in International Law* Oxford: Oxford University Press, 1992.

73 See B. G. Ramcharan, *The Concept and Present Status of the International Protection of Human Rights*, Dordrecht: Martinus Nijhoff, ch.2.

74 Ibid. For example, the UN Ad-hoc Working Group of Experts on Southern Africa was established in 1967 and has met since 1968. South Africa objected on the basis of Article 2 paragraph 7 of the Charter. It used provisions from the Universal Declaration as well as from the Covenant. Israel had signed the ICCPR but had not ratified it. It ratified it in 1991.

75 See Ramcharan, above n.73; Vasak and Alston, above n.58; M. Bossuyt, 'The Development of Special Procedures of the United Nations Commission on Human Rights' (1985) 6 *Human Rights Law Journal* 179–210; J. Humphrey, *No Distant Millenium – The International Law of Human Rights*, Paris: Unesco 1989.

76 See H. Tolley, *The UN Human Rights Commission*, Boulder, Colorado: Westview Press, 1987, ch.6; Pastor Ridruejo, 'Les Procedures Publiques Speciales Da La Commission Des Droits De L'homme Des Nations Unies' (1991-III) 228 *Hague Recueil des Cours* 183–271.

77 See T. Zuidjwick, *Petitioning the United Nations*, New York: Gower, 1982, ch.1, especially pp.39–90.

78 See Alston, *The United Nations* above n.7, pp.155–73.

79 ECOSOC Resolution 1235(XLII), June 1967.

80 The agenda item is entitled, 'Questions of the violation of human rights and fundamental freedoms, including policies of racial discrimination and segregation and of apartheid, in *all countries*, with particular reference to colonial and other dependent territories and countries' (my emphasis). The procedure can be initiated by a member state, a group of states, or by the Sub-Commission but the decision to act is that of the Commission.

81 A standing working group was established in respect of each of these. *Ad-hoc* groups are established for other countries. On the standards used by these bodies see Ramcharan, above n.73, ch.2.

82 See F. Ermacora, 'United Nations and Human Rights in Chile', (1976) 1 *Human Rights Review* 145–56; M. Bossuyt, 'The United Nations and Civil Political Rights in Chile' (1978) 27 *I.C.L.Q.* 462–71.

83 See Security Council Resolutions 242 and 338; E. Cohen, *Human Rights in Israeli-Occupied Territories 1967–1982*, Manchester: Manchester University Press, 1985.

84 Chile objected to what it saw as the specialised procedure being applied to it. Chile argued that the procedures had no legal basis. The Special Rapporteur on Chile replied that 'the General Assembly and the Commission have based themselves expressly on the Charter of the United Nations. . . . In the long-standing practice of the United Nations it has been repeatedly confirmed that the United Nations has wide competence to deal with large scale situations of

violations of human rights. . . . Whatever the method used, it is clear that the United Nations may utilise for each situation such methods or procedures as it considers best suited to deal with that situation. . . . The decision in each case is for the United Nations. . . . The Ad-hoc Working Group was changed to a special rapporteur but with, in every sense, the same mandate. . . . On the basis of these and various other arguments, the objections of the Chilean Government to the competence of the Special Rapporteur are without any legal foundation', reproduced in Ramcharan, above n.73, pp.70–5.

85 Politics plays a substantial part in the decision to consider the human rights situation in a particular state.

86 '[I]t was the first case of a United Nations mission of enquiry carried out on the territory of a member State and, as such, was to prove an important precedent', A.H. Robertson and J.G. Merrills (eds) *Human Rights in the World*, Manchester: Manchester University Press, 3rd edn, 1989, p.81.

87 See Bossuyt, above n.75.

88 Ibid.

89 See Alston, 'The Commission on Human Rights', in Alston, *The United Nations*, above n.7, p.162 and the review of the Commission's session in n.107 below.

90 See Alston, *The United Nations*, above n.7, pp.155–64.

91 Ramcharan, above n.73, p.106. He also notes limitations in terms of political selectivity, transient effect and the consideration of the general situation rather than individual cases. 'The education of world public opinion is the end result of most existing international implementation mechanisms. . . . Public opinion is, however, something to which most governments, including authoritarian governments are sensitive. It is therefore a kind of sanction. In the present state of international law and relations, an educated world public opinion may indeed be the ultimate sanction of the international law of human rights', Humphrey, above n.75, pp.18, 19.

92 Alston, *The United Nations*, above n.7, p.173.

93 ECOSOC Resolution 1503(XLVIII) May 1970. See Alston, *The United Nations*, above n.7, pp.145–55.

94 My emphasis.

95 See H. Tolley, 'The Concealed Crack in the Citadel: The United Nations Commission on Human Rights' Response to Confidenital Communications' (1984) 6 *Human Rights Quarterly* 420–62.

96 There is no reference to apartheid or racial discrimination even as examples.

97 Humphrey, above n.75, pp.104–10.

98 See Alston, *The United Nations*, above n.7, pp.126–210; F. Newman and D. Weissbrodt, *International Human Rights: Law, Policy and Process*, Cincinnati: Anderson, 1990; R.B. Lillich, above n.18, pp.372–441; I. Guest, *Behind the Disappearances: Argentina's Dirty War against Human Rights and the United Nations*, Philadelphia: University of Pennsylvania Press, 1990.

99 Alston, *The United Nations*, above n.7, p.154.

100 Ramcharan, above n.73, also cites evidence for the view that the Commission may be competent to deal with individual cases, at least in some circumstances, at pp.80–3.

101 See Alston, *The United Nations*, above n.7, pp.173–81; Bossuyt, 'The Development of Special Procedures', above n.75; M. Kamminga, 'The Thematic Procedures of the UN Commission on Human Rights' (1987) 34 *Neth.I.L.R.* 299–323.

102 These are the Working Group on Enforced or Involuntary Disappearances, the Special Rapporteur on Summary or Arbitrary Executions, the Special Rapporteur on the Question of Torture, and the Working Group on Arbi-

trary Detention. The Working Groups and Rapporteurs regularly transmit cases to governments for their responses.

103 Ramcharan, above n.73, pp.191–6.

104 Alston, *The United Nations*, above n.7, p.176.

105 Alston, *The United Nations*, above n.7, p.181.

106 Neither it nor the 'Special Committee to Investigate Israeli Practices Affecting the Human Rights of the Population of the Occupied Territories' were admitted to the territories concerned.

107 See P. Alston, 'The Commission on Human Rights', in Alston, *The United Nations*, above n.7, pp.126–210; A. Eide, 'The Sub-Commission on Prevention of Discrimination and Protection of Minorities', ibid., pp.211–64. For reviews of recent sessions see 'An Enlarged UN Commission on Human Rights' (1992) 48 *Rev.I.C.J.* 56–68; K. Reierson and D. Weissbrodt, 'The Forty-Third Session of the Sub-Commission: The Sub-Commission Under Scrutiny' (1992) 14 *Human Rights Quarterly* 232–77; D. Weissbrodt, P.L. Parker and A.Z. Kayal, 'The Forty-Fourth Session . . .' (1993) *Human Rights Quarterly* 410–58.

108 Many writers doubt the independence of some members of the Sub-Commission, see Tolley, above n.76 pp.166–7. See also (1991) 47 *Rev.I.C.J.* 43–51. An important recent decision was to elect alternates rather than having them named by the permanent missions in Geneva. There is still pressure, however, for the Sub-Commission to reform its working methods.

109 The Sub-Commission has three working groups. One on Indigenous Populations (see text to n.63 above), one on Contemporary Forms of Slavery and one on Communications under the Resolution 1503 procedure (see above). In the first two of these working groups states are often subjected to very severe criticism from non-governmental organisations.

110 For example, a study is being prepared on the question of impunity for perpetrators of violations of human rights.

111 See Alson, *The United Nations*, above n.7, pp.126–31.

112 For example, at its 1991 session the Sub-Commission adopted resolutions on nine countries or territories. They included the human rights situation in Tibet. China denounced the resolution calling it null and void. A 1990 Resolution on Iraq was the first Sub-Commission resolution in respect of an Arab country.

113 See (1991) 47 *Rev.I.C.J.* 43–51. Voting by secret ballot has taken place since 1989.

114 See Reierson and Weissbrodt, above n.107, pp.270–5; M.B. Abram, 'Human Rights and the United Nations: Past as Prologue' (1991) 4 *Harvard H.R.J.* 70–90.

115 See A. Cassese, 'The General Assembly: Historical Perspective 1945–1989', in Alston, *The United Nations*, above n.7, pp.25–54; J. Quinn, 'The General Assembly into the 1990s', ibid., pp.55–106.

116 See Cassese, above n.115, pp.32–38; Humphrey, above n.75, p.36. 'In practice the General Assembly has acted mainly on violations if they concern or are related to, situations of gross violations of human rights' Ramcharan, above n.73, p.248.

117 'The responses of the countries which have been the subject of General Assembly Resolutions repay careful attention. All of these countries have now agreed to allow special rapporteurs and representatives to visit their territories to inspect conditions, although the extent to which these visits have been unfettered is a moot point. All have made lengthy statements in defence of their reputations. None has challenged the fundamental legitimacy

of the procedures, although all have complained about politicization', Quinn, above n.115, p.79.

118 The resolution also stressed the 'important role that the Secretary-General can play in situations of mass and flagrant violations of human rights'. See also UN General Assembly Resolution 32/130.

119 '[N]o delegation has seriously challenged the legitimacy of efforts to raise violations of the human rights of individuals at recent sessions of the General Assembly. The international prominence given to individual victims (Nelson Mandela, for example) would make it difficult for proponents of this line of reasoning to sustain their objections', Quinn, above n.115, p.85. See also Cassese, above n.115, pp.42–3.

120 See Ramcharan, above n.73, pp.247–50.

121 See pp.95–6 above.

122 See pp.96–100 above.

123 See pp.102–3 below.

124 See Quinn, above n.115, pp.89–92. On the importance of publicity and public reaction see the seminal article by R. Bilder, 'Rethinking International Human Rights: Some Basic Questions' (1969) *Wisconsin L.R.* 171–217.

125 The nature of the Committee on ESC rights (CESCR) was altered by a resolution of ECOSOC from a body of governmental representatives to one of independent experts. See the essays in Alston, *The United Nations*, above n.7, on CERD by Partsch, pp.339–68; on HRC by Opsahl, pp.369–443; on CEDAW by Jacobson, pp.444–72; on CESCR by Alston, pp.473–508; on CAT by Byrnes, pp.509–46. The most recent addition is the Committee on the Rights of the Child (CRC), see McGoldrick, 'The U.N. Convention', above n.65.

126 See pp.87–94 above.

127 On the reference to Resolution 2526 in the HRC's 'General Comment' on Article 1 ICCPR, see McGoldrick, *The Human Rights Committee*, above n.27, para.5.5.

128 See McGoldrick, *The Human Rights Committee*, above n.27, ch.2.

129 For example, under the reporting procedure, see ibid., ch.3.

130 The debates also reflected views expressed during the drafting of the Covenant on intervention in domestic jurisdiction.

131 See above n.129.

132 This has been ratified by sixty-seven States as of April 1993.

133 See N. Lerner, *The UN Convention on the Elimination of All Forms of Racial Discrimination*, Alphen aan den Rijn: Sijhoff, 2nd edn, 1980.

134 See J.H. Burgers and H. Danelius, *The UN Convention Against Torture* Dordrecht: Martinus Nijhoff, 1988.

135 See McGoldrick, 'The UN Convention', above n.65.

136 Accession was by the USSR but the Russian Federation has succeeded to its obligations. On the OP see McGoldrick, *The Human Rights Committee*, above n.27, ch.4. On US ratification of the ICCPR see 'US Senate Report on the ICCPR' (1992) 31 *I.L.M.* 645–61.

137 See above n.75.

138 See above n.18 and R. Bernhardt, 'Domestic Jurisdiction of States and International Human Rights Organs' (1986) 7 *Human Rights Law Journal* 205–16.

139 See B.G. Ramcharan, *Humanitarian Good Offices in International Law* Dordrecht: Martinus Nijhoff, 1983. Ramcharan, above n.73, states that, 'The creation of a climate of international protection and the nurturing of mechanisms for such protection are absolutely essential in the conditions existing in the contemporary world' (p.18). The different methods of international

protection he notes are anticipatory or preventive, curative or mitigatory, and remedial or compensatory. He notes that these mainly extend to civil and political rights (p.18). Many procedures perform functions belonging to more than one of these categories, see his graph on p.21.

140 See pp.87–9, 91–2 above.

141 See above n.125.

142 For example, with reference to the Human Rights Committee, Schachter, above n.2, comments 'That committee is developing an exemplary record of findings and interpretations based on objective assessments rather than political interests' (p.347).

143 Ramcharan, above n.73, pp.27, 570. 'In numerous situations the United Nations Organs have exposed and condemned violations of human rights. One is even able to detect signs of the emergence of sanctions. The UN has studied the consequences of aid given to countries in which violations of human rights were said to be taking place, such as Chile and South Africa, and published a list of collaborating institutions', ibid., p.29.

144 ECOSOC has various procedures for considering human rights complaints other than those in resolution 1235 and 1503. See Ramcharan, above n.73, p.251, n.16.

145 Ramcharan, above n.73, p.357. See also T. Farer, 'The United Nations and Human Rights: More than a Whimper, Less Than a Roar' (1987) 9 *Human Rights Quarterly* 550–85.

146 See B.H. Weston, R.A. Lukes and K.M. Hnatt, 'Regional Human Rights Regimes: A Comparison and Appraisal' (1987) 20 *Vanderbilt J.Trans.L.* 585–637.

147 See P. Van Dijk and G. Van Hoof, *Theory and Practice of the European Convention on Human Rights*, Dordrecht: Martinus Nijhoff, 2nd edn, 1990; R. Beddard, *Human Rights and Europe*, Cambridge: Gratius, 3rd edn, 1993. There are now ten Protocols to the ECHR. See also M. Evans and R. Morgan, 'The European Convention for the Prevention of Torture: Operational Practice' (1992) 41 *I.C.L.Q.* 590–614.

148 This has developed primarily through the activist jurisprudence of the European Court of Justice on the basis of 'general principles of law'. See A. Toth, *The Oxford Encyclopedia of European Community Law* Oxford: Clarendon Press, 1990, pp.277–81, 284–93.

149 See T. Buergenthal, D. Shelton and R. Norris, *Protecting Human Rights in the Americas*, Kehl, Germany: Engel, 3rd edn, 1986; S. Davidson, *The Inter-American Court of Human Rights*, Aldershot: Dartmouth, 1992.

150 The practice under the Charter has been rather limited. See C.E. Welch, 'The African Commission on Human and Peoples' Rights: A Five Year Report and Assessment' (1992) 14 *Human Rights Quarterly* 43–61.

151 See H. Hannum (ed.) *Guide to International Human Rights Practice*, Philadelphia: University of Pennsylvania Press, 2nd edn, 1992.

152 See D. Harris, 'A Fresh Impetus for the European Social Charter' (1992) 41 *I.C.L.Q.* 659–76.

153 See above n.32; D. McGoldrick, 'Human Rights Developments in the Helsinki Process' (1990) 39 *I.C.L.Q.* 923–40; n.157 below; A. Bloed and P. Van Dijk (eds) *The Human Dimension of the Helsinki Process*, Dordrecht: Martinus Nijhoff, 1991.

154 As of 1 July 1992 there were fifty-two participating states in the CSCE.

155 See A. Bloed and P. Van Dijk, 'Human Rights and Non-Intervention', in A. Bloed and P. Van Dijk (eds) *Essays on Human Rights in the Helsinki Process*, Dordrecht: Martinus Nijhoff, 1985, pp.57–78; Bossuyt, above n.32. The two socialist exceptions to the intervention principle were first, that

other states can opt in, for example into the Covenants or the First Optional Protocol, and secondly, massive and gross breaches which have a breach of the peace link to international peace and security.

156 See text to n.32 above.

157 The fourth 'follow-up' meeting was held in Helsinki in 1992. A substantial concluding document was adopted. See D. McGoldrick, 'The Development of the CSCE – from Process to Institution', in R.H. Jackson and D. McGoldrick (eds) *Legal Visions of The New Europe*, London: Graham and Trockman, 1993. pp.135–82

158 It was also of great importance to the many human rights groups in Central and Eastern Europe which used it to support their aims. Some writers have argued that the HFA was an element in the political revolutions in Central and Eastern Europe in 1989–91. Kamminga has noted that the HFA is the most widely cited text, always without reference to any specific provisions, in interstate arguments concerning human rights. 'There were many Helsinki monitoring groups in Eastern Europe but very few, if any, covenant monitoring groups. This preference of States and of dissident groups is curious. The position of the United States is one answer, further explanation is the great political significance of the HFA', M. Kamminga, 'The Role of the CSCE' (1992) 1 *European Human Rights Yearbook* 143–150.

159 See pp.96–9 above on Resolutions 1235 and 1503.

160 See McGoldrick, 'Human Rights Developments' above n.153.

161 See H. Hazewinkel, 'Paris, Copenhagen and Moscow', in Bloed and Van Dijk, above n.153, who comments that, 'The procedure was set up to make questions on the human dimension, the subject of discussion between States, to do away with the objection of non-interference and to provide an opportunity to solve problems which could not be solved in normal bilateral contacts', p.137.

162 'Prague Document on Further Development of CSCE Institutions and Structures', paras.16–17, in (1992) 13 *Human Rights Law Journal* 174–6; (1992) 31 *I.L.M.* 976, at p.987.

163 See ch.II of the Concluding Document of the CSCE Helsinki Meeting, 1992, on which see McGoldrick, 'Human Rights Development', above n.153.

164 See D.McGoldrick, 'A New International Economic Order For Europe?', (1993) 12 *Yearbook of European Law* (forthcoming).

165 See n.30 above.

166 See Warbrick, above n.54.

167 See R. Barsch, 'The Right To Development As a Human Right' (1991) 13 *Human Rights Quarterly* 322–38.

168 See Franck, above n.52.

169 See McGoldrick, n.164 above; *Democracy and Human Rights* Council of Europe, 1990; 'Harare Commonwealth Declaration' (1992) 17 *Comwth. L.B.* i-iii.

170 On the idea of sovereignty and international responsibility, see the text of the then UN Secretary-General's speech in (1991) 47 *Rev. I.C.J.* 24–7. He stresses the idea of 'sovereignty' residing in the people. 'It is not increasingly felt that the principle of non-interference with the essential domestic jurisdiction of States cannot be regarded as a protective barrier behind which human rights could be massively or systematically violated within impunity' (p.27). See also M. Reisman, 'Sovereignty and Human Rights in Contemporary International Law' (1990) 84 *A.J.I.L.* 866–76.

171 'When a hundred years from now, historians write about international law in the twentieth century, they will say that these developments were the most

important and most radical in the history of the order', Humphrey, above n.75, p.203.

172 See American Law Institute, Restatement, 3rd, *The Foreign Relations Law of the U.S.*, vol.II, pp.152–83; T. Meron, *Human Rights and Humanitarian Norms As Customary International Law*, Oxford: Oxford University Press, 1989; Schachter, above n.2, ch.XV.

173 'On the evidence of state practice to date, the customary law of human rights will generally limit international responsibility and remedies to cases of gross systematic violations of human rights', Schachter, above n.2, p.341. See also the International Law Commission's 'Draft Code of Crimes Against the Peace and Security of Mankind', Article 21 on 'Systematic or Mass Violations of Human Rights', Report of the ILC, 43rd Session, UN Doc.A/46/10 (1991).

174 *ILC Yearbook 1980* part II.

175 Article 19(4).

176 [1970] I.C.J.Rep. 3. Article 19 also bears some relation to the concept of *jus cogens*, see Article 53 of the Vienna Convention on the Law of Treaties (1969). Writers frequently argue that some human rights obligations have the character of *jus cogens*.

177 [1970] I.C.J.Rep., at paras.33–4. Some writers have viewed the concept as a reversal by the ICJ of its jurisprudence in the *South West Africa* Case (1966) on the lack of a legal interest for states in upholding the human rights provisions of a League of Nations Mandate agreement.

178 Schachter above n.2, p.344.

179 Ibid., p.345.

180 See also R. Brody, M. Convery and D. Weissbrodt, '42nd Session of Sub-Commission' (1991) 13 *Human Rights Quarterly* 260–90, at p.272.

181 See (1991) 6 *Interights Bulletin* 44–55. The reviewer of the Commission cited in n.107 above comments that the fears 'proved unfounded' (p.56).

182 A Resolution was passed the following year after Iraq had invaded Kuwait. See P. Parker and D. Weissbrodt, 'Major Developments at the UN Commission on Human Rights in 1991' (1991) 13 *Human Rights Quarterly* 589.

183 See A. Kent, 'Waiting for Rights: China's Human Rights and China's Constitutions 1949–89' (1991) 13 *Human Rights Quarterly* 170–201.

184 See pp.98–9 above.

185 An example is the Secretary-General's yearly report on human rights of persons subject to detention or imprisonment. Some NGOs have refused to submit information relating to these unless the practice is changed.

186 An example is the CSCE. Some more progress on this problem was made at the Helsinki Follow-Up Meeting in 1992, see McGoldrick, above n.157.

187 See pp.86–7 above.

188 See Security Council Resolutions 232 on Rhodesia and 418 on South Africa. Some writers have argued that these situations did not themselves threaten international peace and security. It was the reaction of other states to them that constituted the threat.

189 See Security Council Resolutions 688 on Iraq, 731 on Libya, 733 on Somalia and 743 on Yugoslavia. See B.G. Ramcharan, 'The Security Council: Maturing of International Protection of Human Rights' (1992) 48 *Rev.I.C.J.* 24–37; S. Bailey, 'The Security Council', in Alston, *The United Nations*, above n.7, pp.304–36.

190 See Jennings and Watts, *Oppenheim's International Law*, above n.10, pp.400–2.

6 The principle of co-operation: the environment

Alan E. Boyle

INTRODUCTION

It is indicative of the relatively recent emergence of international environmental law that the Declaration on Principles of International Law concerning Friendly Relations and Co-operation among States in accordance with the Charter of the United Nations, adopted in 1970, makes no reference to co-operation on environmental matters. Environmental protection might of course be included under the general heading of a duty to co-operate 'in the various spheres of international relations, in order to maintain international peace and security and to promote international economic stability and progress [and] the general welfare of nations', but the declaration's emphasis on economic sovereignty and the promotion of economic growth suggests that environmental matters were not a priority concern of the drafters of this resolution.

Twenty years later, a different perspective is evident in the management of friendly relations among nations. Disputes over natural resources, transboundary pollution and global environmental risks such as ozone depletion and climate change threaten to assume greater potential for conflict in a post-Cold War era than the use of force or other forms of aggression. The policy implications of this are indicated by the emergence during the 1980s of the concept of 'ecological security' in international diplomacy and by the growing prominence of environmental issues on the agenda of regional organisations, the United Nations and its specialised agencies.[1] Thus, environmental co-operation has proved to be one of the more successful aspects of the work of the Conference on Security and Co-operation in Europe (CSCE),[2] leading to the negotiation of protocols on air pollution,[3] the drafting of a treaty on watercourse pollution[4] the elaboration of a draft charter of environmental rights and obligations,[5] and the conclusion of a treaty on environmental impact assessment and transboundary co-operation.[6] Some of these developments are a direct response to the continuing alarm generated by the Chernobyl disaster in 1986 and the realisation, even in the former Soviet Union, that continuing disregard for shared environmental risks poses a real threat to the future of all nations.

The convening of the UN Conference on Environment and Development in June 1992 once more focused international political attention on the imperatives of securing better co-operation on global environmental problems, of addressing the sometimes conflicting perceptions of developed and developing nations on these issues and of securing a more widely acceptable relationship between environmental protection and economic development.[7] At the same time proposals have been made to strengthen the management of environmental issues by extending the powers of the Security Council, ECOSOC or the Trusteeship Council, recognising the need for some authority capable of acting in the interests of the international community as a whole.[8] Thus the absence of any explicit mention of the environment in the Declaration on Principles of Friendly Relations should not be seen as implying that the principles of law and co-operation it sets out have no importance in an environmental context.

This chapter will explore some of these principles as they relate to the environment. It examines the early development of bilateral co-operation based on customary requirements of notification and consultation over issues relating to the utilisation of shared natural resources and the management of transboundary environmental risks, and the attempts which have been made to codify and develop international law in this respect by the United Nations Environment Programme (UNEP), the International Law Commission (ILC) and regional bodies such as the UN Economic Commission for Europe. It will be argued that these essentially procedural principles of international co-operation are now an established part of international law and an important element of environmental protection policy, but that they must also be seen in the context of institutional developments which provide a means of giving effect to this form of 'good neighbourliness'. Moreover, international institutions have increasingly become the forum for more sophisticated attempts to achieve multilateral co-operation on environmental issues at global and regional levels. In some cases these institutions have gone beyond facilitating co-operation among states and have acquired powers of majoritarion decision-making and environmental management which point to the emergence of a new model of international regulation that may eventually replace or supplement the present co-operative structure.[9]

THE EXISTENCE OF AN OBLIGATION TO CO-OPERATE

The existence of an obligation to co-operate in protecting the environment can be inferred from judicial decisions, state practice, treaties, the work of the ILC and other attempts to codify aspects of international environmental law dealing with shared natural resources and transboundary environmental risks.

Shared natural resources

Probably the most important judicial precedent is the *Lac Lanoux* arbitration[10] of 1957. This award concerned the proposed diversion of a river which originated in France but subsequently flowed into Spain. After a lengthy period of consultation between the two states regarding France's proposal, which resulted in substantial modification designed to eliminate any adverse impact on Spain, the parties eventually agreed to refer to arbitration the question whether under the Treaty of Bayonne of 1866 such works could be undertaken only with the prior agreement of both governments. The tribunal noted that conflicting interests of this kind must be reconciled by negotiation and mutual concession, that both under the Treaty of Bayonne and as a matter of customary law France was required to inform Spain of its proposals, allow for consultations and give reasonable weight to Spain's interests, and that the obligation to negotiate, which arose in these circumstances, was not a mere formality but must be pursued in good faith. But it held that France had, in fact, already carried out its obligations in these respects. Moreover, although France's freedom to act within its own jurisdiction was thus limited by obligations of equitable utilisation of the watercourse, and by the requirements of procedural co-operation which this entailed, Spain had no right of veto over French action, and no claim to insist on specific precautions.

This award has rightly been treated as an authoritative statement of the law regarding co-operative utilisation of shared watercourses. The principles on which it is based have subsequently been followed, in more detailed form, by the ILC in its draft articles on the non-navigational uses of international watercourses.[11] The Commission's conclusion that international law requires states to notify and negotiate is clearly consistent with its recognition of equitable utilisation as the main basis for the allocation of rights and interests in shared water resources. Since, in effect, neither party has exclusive sovereignty over the use of such resources, a co-operative solution of this kind becomes essential as a means of reconciling conflicting rights and interests.

A similar view can be observed in the International Court's decision concerning common property resources in the *Icelandic Fisheries* cases.[12] In these cases the International Court of Justice found that States engaged in high seas fishing were under an obligation to make 'reasonable' use of the resource, which required them to take account of the needs of conservation and of coastal States' preferential rights in the allocation of high seas stocks. Here too, all parties were required to negotiate in good faith with a view to reaching an equitable solution; co-operation was thus again the only basis on which this complex balancing process could be performed.[13] Although international fisheries law has radically changed since this decision, following endorsement of the 200 mile exclusive economic zone in the 1982 UNCLOS, that convention continues to require states to co-operate in the management of shared and straddling stocks, and remaining high seas common property resources.[14] Thus, although its application has changed, the principle of co-operation on which the 1974 case is based remains unaltered, and several subsequent conventions have sought to establish regional co-operation schemes for fisheries management, although these have not proved conspicuously successful.[15]

Several attempts have been made to codify some of these requirements of co-operation in respect of shared resources generally. Article 3 of the 1974 Charter of Economic Rights and Duties of States[16] provides that 'in the exploitation of natural resources shared by two or more countries, each state must co-operate on the basis of a system of information and prior consultation in order to achieve optimum use of such resources without causing damage to the legitimate interests of others'. Though the Charter is in other respects controversial, Article 3 is a conservative formulation which closely reflects the earlier international case-law. It provided the basis for subsequent efforts by UNEP to adopt a more detailed set of 'Principles of Conduct in the Conservation and Harmonious Utilisation of Natural Resources Shared by Two or More States'.[17] Although adopted by UNEP in 'soft law' form, which avoids the use of language implying existing legal obligation, these principles follow closely the rules on co-operation applied in the *Lac Lanoux* arbitration, and are 'without prejudice to the binding nature of those rules already recognised as such in international law'. Thus their form, and the General Assembly's reluctance to do more than call on States to use the principles as 'guidelines and recommendations',[18] in deference to the continued controversy and opposition encountered by earlier resolutions on natural resources, should not detract from the implication that in certain respects at least UNEP's principles are a statement of existing law.

Transboundary environmental risks

A second area where co-operation is required by international law concerns transboundary environmental risks. Principle 24 of the Stockholm Declaration on the Human Environment recognised that 'co-operation through multilateral or bilateral arrangements or other appropriate means is essential to effectively control, prevent, reduce and eliminate adverse environmental effects resulting from activities conducted in all spheres, in such a way that due account is taken of the sovereignty and interests of all states'. No agreement could be reached on more detailed rules, however, and a General Assembly resolution[19] endorsing Principle 24 merely called on states to exchange information 'in a spirit of good neighbourliness', while noting that it should not be construed as enabling them to delay or impede programmes and projects of exploration, exploitation and development of natural resources within the territory of other states.

Yet it is clear from subsequent developments that the basic principles of co-operation articulated in the *Lac Lanoux* arbitration have now been extended to the management of transboundary, and in some cases global, environmental risks in treaties dealing with various hazardous or potentially harmful activities. These include nuclear installations near borders, continental shelf operations, transboundary air pollution and marine pollution from land-based sources or dumping at sea. In each of these situations some measure of prior notification, consultation and co-operation has been called for.

Bilateral agreements dealing with nuclear installations all require a full exchange of information on the proposed installation so that other states may review the decision-making process and data and offer comments on safety and health protection.[20] In many cases permanent commissions are established to consider these issues. As in the *Lac Lanoux* arbitration, however, neighbouring states are not given a veto over proposed developments; co-operation, not consent, is required, with a view to ensuring reasonable regard for the rights and legitimate interests of other states. Yet the narrowness of the principle's application in these cases must be observed; most of the treaties in question relate only to installations within 30 km of an international border. Moreover, state practice on consultation and co-operation with regard to nuclear installations is generally also limited to border installations, such as Cattenom;[21] the Chernobyl reactor was not in a border area, and states have not consulted in such cases, save in emergency. In contrast, as we shall see, the ILC's proposed articles,[22] and the 1991 ECE Convention considered below, are considerably broader in scope, and require consultation regarding all activities creating an appreciable transboundary risk, wherever located.

With regard to transboundary air pollution the requirements of co-operation found in regional treaties are also relatively weak. The 1979 Geneva Convention on Long Range Transboundary Air Pollution, to which some thirty states in Eastern and Western Europe are party, together with the USA and Canada, obliges states to notify and consult in respect of 'major' changes in policy or industrial development likely to cause 'significant' changes in long-range air pollution.[23] Apart from this, consultations must also be held at the request of other parties 'actually affected by or exposed to a significant risk of long-range transboundary air pollution'.[24] This latter provision comes closest to reflecting the customary rule found in the *Lac Lanoux* arbitration, but it makes no reference to notification and consultation in cases of *proposed* activities likely to create a risk of air pollution, and is thus concerned with existing pollution. This is a significant limitation which largely deprives the article of any real impact. The omission is, however, rectified by the 1991 ECE Convention.

The 1979 Convention, despite the looseness of its terminology, has proved in practice more successful than originally anticipated; its importance lies less in its specific provisions than in providing an institutional framework for co-operation and the development of further measures of pollution control.[25] Moreover, a bilateral agreement concluded in 1991 between the USA and Canada commits these states to co-operate in the reduction of transboundary air pollution, to assess the likely impact of activities within their respective jurisdictions and to notify, consult and take measures to mitigate the potential risk.[26] For this purpose the agreement confers appropriate powers on the existing International Joint Commission which regulates border problems under the 1909 Boundary Waters Treaty.

Co-operation between states with regard to protection of the marine environment from pollution is in certain respects particularly well developed. Article 197 of the 1982 UNCLOS requires states to co-operate on a global or regional basis, either directly or through international organisations, in formulating international rules, standards and recommended practices and procedures for the protection of the marine environment. Such rules have already been adopted in respect of many sources of marine pollution; the 1973/78 MARPOL Convention, the 1972 London Dumping Convention and the 1991 Oil Pollution Preparedness Readiness and Response Convention are in effect global rules governing pollution from ships, dumping and maritime emergencies,[27] while at regional level there is a series of treaties dealing with land-based pollution, regional seas, maritime emergencies and dumping.[28] Other provisions of the 1982 UNCLOS also require co-operation with regard to enclosed or semi-enclosed seas,[29] and as we have seen, in respect to fisheries.

But regulation is only part of the answer to the problem of protecting the marine environment; once again, procedural obligations of notification and consultation are an important aspect of co-operation in the management of environmental risks. These assume particular importance in those regional seas where no agreement on co-ordinated regulatory standards exists, since they are then the only mechanisms for controlling unilateral decisions which disregard the interests of other states. It is a serious omission from the 1982 UNCLOS and from UNEP's regional seas treaties that they contain no provision requiring notification and consultation with other states likely to be affected by activities which pose a risk of marine pollution. Such an obligation is, however, recognised by the 1974 Paris Convention for the Prevention of Marine Pollution from Land-based Sources, and by other regional agreements on this form of pollution, including the Quito Protocol and the Athens Protocol. In these cases, where other states are at risk, regional commissions are empowered to recommend solutions to parties in dispute.[30] UNEP guidelines and a few regional treaties also apply a rule of prior notification and consultation to continental shelf operations,[31] although it is not clear how far such co-operation normally takes place in these circumstances.

In contrast to the situation where other states are at risk, no prior consultation or dispute settlement is required by any of the treaties on land-based sources of pollution where only the marine environment is affected. At most, states are then required only to co-operate through relevant international commissions by reporting the results of environmental impact assessments and monitoring the condition of the oceans. This may give other parties the opportunity for comment and review, but it does not give them the right to prior consultation.

The principle that other states likely to be adversely affected must be consulted is also found in treaties dealing with dumping at sea. Meetings of the Consultative Parties to the London Dumping Convention (LDC), and regional conventions, provide forums for general multilateral consultation and co-operation, but states are also required by the LDC to consult others likely to be affected by emergency dumping of prohibited waste,[32] and by the 1982 UNCLOS to consult others who may be adversely affected by dumping in maritime zones.[33] An OECD scheme provides for prior consultation among NEA members proposing to dump radioactive waste in the North Atlantic.[34] But, provided they follow the prescribed procedures, the LDC leaves parties free to make their own determination of where and whether to dump. They do not need the permission of the consultative meeting or of any other party. In this respect the new policy of the Oslo Dumping Commission represents a radical departure, and comes closer to a prior consent regime. Under this scheme, which applies to North Sea dumping, parties seeking to dump (which means in practice the United Kingdom only) must justify in advance to the Commission that no harm to the marine environment will result and that no alternative exists.[35] In effect this gives the Oslo Commission a role in approving dumping not possessed by the parties to the LDC. As we shall see below, this kind of 'precautionary approach' has significant advantages over one based on co-operation and self-restraint.

The ILC and regional codification

Since 1978 the International Law Commission has been engaged in the codification and development of principles of international law concerning the 'Injurious Consequences of Acts Not Prohibited by International Law'. The character of this topic has changed quite radically since its initial characterisation as an aspect of the law of state responsibility.[36] In its present form it is now much closer to a codification of certain principles of environmental law.[37] The proposed articles cover liability for environmental damage, both in private law and in public international law, but also include rules on the control of harmful activities and co-operation in the management of environmental risks.

The 1990 draft articles apply to 'activities involving risk', defined to mean those involving dangerous substances, radiation or dangerous genetically altered organisms. States within whose territory or under whose jurisdiction or control such activities are undertaken are required to co-operate in preventing such activities from causing transboundary harm, and to minimise the effects of any harm which does occur. For this purpose, the draft articles then go on to require environmental impact assessment of activities with potential transboundary effects, and notification and consultation with the states likely to be affected. A state with serious reason to believe that it has been or will be affected may also request information and consultation.

These articles are very close to a codification of the main principles examined earlier, and their requirement of prior impact assessment reflects provisions found in the 1982 UNCLOS, in UNEP guidelines on the subject, and in an increasing number of regional treaties.[38] The practice of many states and of the World Bank now also favours some form of prior environmental impact assessment before major projects are undertaken.[39] Such assessments are, in effect, essential if notification and consultation are to be effective, since they ensure that co-operation takes place on an adequate basis of information. Thus the ILC's articles, although in other respects controversial, do incorporate principles of transboundary co-operation which have now been widely endorsed both judicially and in treaties and codifications. Similar provisions are found in the Commission's articles on international watercourses, where there are, of course, more extensive precedents and practice on which to draw.[40]

A novel feature of the ILC's 'Injurious Consequences' articles, however, is the involvement of international organisations in the consultation process. The proposed article would require states to notify an international organisation 'with competence in that area' whenever more than one state is likely to be affected, or if the states likely to be affected cannot be determined precisely. The organisation in question may then use whatever powers it possesses in the matter, or facilitate a solution through its good offices. This is in practice what a number of organisations already do informally, and, as we have already seen, a comparable provision is found in some of the treaties on land-based sources of pollution.

Unlike some of the ILC's work on environmental law, these proposed articles on co-operation are not only soundly based in existing law and developing practice, but sensible in themselves. They do contain the basis for necessary co-operation in the management of transboundary risks, not only bilaterally, but at a multilateral level. But the ILC articles do more than compel a measure of co-operation. Their ultimate purpose is to secure an equitable balance of interests among the states concerned in relation to potentially hazardous activities, taking into account a variety of factors listed in the draft. Although this is comparable to the concept of equitable utilisation applied to the exploitation of shared resources, the introduction of equitable balancing as a test for the permissibility of environmentally harmful activities is much more controversial, and there is little support for such an approach except in some academic writings.[41] It goes well beyond most of the precedents dealing with the risk of transboundary harm and is not followed in other codifications.[42] In effect it does give neighbouring states a veto unless an equitable solution is negotiated, but as we have seen, such a prior consent rule is exceptional in international environmental law. The ILC's proposals would, however, benefit other states by requiring fuller account to be taken of the transboundary costs of risky activities, something which the present law fails to achieve.

A different approach is found in the 1991 ECE Convention on Environmental Impact Assessment in a Transboundary Context. This Convention stems from efforts made by the CSCE to extend its earlier work on air and water pollution, and the Convention represents the first regional treaty to establish a general framework for environmental management comparable to the ILC's draft articles. The Convention is intended to provide the basis for enhanced environmental co-operation in Europe. It is not confined to environmental impact assessment but requires parties individually or jointly to take 'all appropriate and effective measures' to prevent, reduce and control significant adverse transboundary environmental impacts of proposed activities. The activities covered include oil refineries, power stations, nuclear installations, smelters, chemical installations, dams and reservoirs, groundwater abstraction and deforestation of large areas.

In each of these cases prior environmental impact assessment is to be undertaken, affected parties must be notified, consultations held without undue delay, and the final decision must take due account of the assessment and consultations. This is very similar to the requirements of the *Lac lanoux* arbitration. It stops short of giving other parties, or the ECE itself, a veto over the final decision, nor does it compel an equitable balance of interests in the manner of the ILC draft articles. Thus it is very likely that the basic principles of the ECE Convention can be regarded as a reflection of existing law; they are unlikely to be controversial in the same manner as the ILC articles. What is different about them, however, as we saw earlier, is that they are not limited to border activities, or to the actual impact of pollution, as were the treaties on nuclear installations and air pollution respectively which we considered above. To that extent they provide a more satisfactory general regime for facilitating co-operative management of transboundary environmental problems. Where activities not listed in the convention pose a risk of harm the parties may agree to treat them as subject to the convention;

where they cannot agree on whether an activity falls with those listed, an inquiry procedure to determine the matter is provided for.

The ECE Convention is not yet in force and it is premature to determine what impact it will have. Its more straightforward character is likely to make it more appealing to states than the ILC articles, however, since it leaves the final decision to the proposing state. Moreover it is consistent with policies already adopted by OECD,[43] the Nordic states[44] and the EEC. But it does not give effect to the so-called 'precautionary principle' which is emerging as an important limitation on environmentally harmful activities,[45] still less does it adopt the stronger approach of the Oslo Dumping Convention in requiring states to demonstrate the harmless character of their activities to an international body, and thus it falls some way behind emerging concepts of environmental management.

The contrast between the ILC's more far-reaching proposals, and the more conservative ECE instrument demonstrates something of a conflict of values and ideology at the heart of international environmental law. This can best be summarised as a choice between co-operative models which stress the ultimate freedom of states to pursue their own environmental policies and priorities, subject to whatever substantive limits and consequences international law places on harmful activities, and a more authoritarian model, under which states ultimately surrender their power of decision to international management or trusteeship exercised by international institutions. It is this approach to which we must now turn.

CO-OPERATION THROUGH INTERNATIONAL INSTITUTIONS

Historically, multilateral environmental co-operation has been organised either through *ad hoc* intergovernmental commissions or meetings of parties established under individual treaties, or through international organisations such as IMO, the International Atomic Energy Authority (IAEA) or UNEP. The latter organisations essentially facilitate policy-making, co-ordinate technical advice and assistance, and sponsor the negotiation of relevant treaties, soft-law instruments and recommendations.[46] Their impact can be seen in such international conventions as the 1973 MARPOL Convention, the 1985 Vienna Convention for the Protection of the Ozone Layer, the 1989 Basel Convention for the Control of Transboundary Movement of Hazardous Wastes and the 1985 Vienna Conventions on Notification and Assistance in Cases of Nuclear Accidents and Emergencies.

Ad hoc commissions and meetings of parties are, however, in many ways more important in facilitating the implementation of environmental agreements and providing the forum for negotiating specific co-operative arrangements.[47] Almost all modern environmental treaties make provision for institutional support and co-operation in this way; the absence of any such component is a clear indicator of weakness and limited effect in a treaty. Such bodies perform a variety of roles, and their powers vary considerably. Typically, however, three main functions can be identified.

The first involves a legislative role in adopting amendments to conventions and their related annexes, in adopting detailed regulations on, for example, emissions standards or safety measures, and in negotiating additional protocols or treaties necessary to deal with new problems or respond to improved scientific information regarding pollution or species loss. The 1979 Geneva Convention on Long Range Transboundary Air Pollution is an example of a regulatory treaty of this framework kind. Under it, a series of protocols has been adopted to set specific emission standards for differing kinds of air pollution, enabling the very general provisions of the main treaty to be implemented.

Their second role is one of treaty enforcement. Treaties can, of course, be enforced in various ways, including termination for material breach, actions for reparation in case of non-compliance and retaliatory action. But none of these is particularly appropriate to multilateral environmental protection treaties where the continued co-operation of all parties is the most important consideration, and the major task is therefore one of trying to bring all parties into compliance. For this purpose the virtue of multilateral institutions is their capacity to act as a forum for focusing a sense of community pressure on states. This may be done through formal non-compliance complaints procedures, as provided for in the Montreal Protocol to the Ozone Convention,[48] or it may be left to informal operation as in most treaties, but it should not be underestimated as a method of political rather than judicial enforcement, which leads directly into the third role these institutions may perform, that of dispute settlement.

This role can involve formal powers to act as a mediator, provide good offices or conciliation, or it may simply occur informally. Some treaties on environmental matters go further and provide for arbitration or judicial settlement of disputes concerning interpretation or application of the treaty. Only a few make resort to such procedures compulsory,[49] however, and third party dispute settlement provisions in environmental treaties are often weak. Once again the emphasis tends to be on negotiated settlements using political institutions.

Through institutions of this kind other forms of co-operation can also be facilitated. In particular, such bodies are often given power to organise and co-ordinate scientific research and the dissemination of information among the parties. In some cases the institution's secretariat may be empowered to verify independently information provided by states, and to receive information from other sources, such as non-governmental organisations.[50] As we have also seen, multilateral institutions may provide a forum for notification and consultation in cases where proposed activities may be harmful to other states or to the global commons. Secretariats of such bodies can co-ordinate responses to emergencies and facilitate co-operation in the provision of assistance.

At a global level bodies such as the meetings of parties of the Ozone Convention, or the consultative meeting of the London Dumping Convention in effect provide a form of environmental trusteeship or stewardship. They represent an expression of community interests, rather than simply those of individual states, and this function is particularly apparent whenever membership comprises diverse groups of states with competing interests. The LDC, with an approximate balance of dumping and non-dumping states, illustrates this phenomenon; by contrast, fisheries commissions, usually composed of states whose only interest is to maximise their fish catches, are not convincing representatives of the interests of a wider community. Yet, even when they do attempt to act in the interests of the international community, such bodies are limited in their role as trustees by the limitations of their powers. Their law-making role depends on consensus and is vulnerable to the persistent objector who can legitimately opt out of regulations adopted by a majority and binding only on non-objectors. Their law enforcement and dispute settlement roles are also dependent on consent, and rarely allow serious sanctions to be imposed on recalcitrants.

Underlying these limitations is a deeper problem, that of the 'free-rider', the state which refuses even to become a party to the treaty, and thus stays outside its rules. While there are methods of tackling this problem, including trade sanctions and the offer of financial and technical assistance to parties,[51] the essential voluntarism of the treaty structure of environmental co-operation emphasises that states retain their freedom of action. A failure to co-operate may, of course, lead to legal consequences, such as violation of primary obligations of diligent control of transboundary harm in customary law, but the inability to agree co-operative solutions, unless evidence of bad faith, is not itself a breach of international law. Thus the difficulty of securing co-operative solutions in a diverse international society of over 170 states whose environmental perceptions and priorities differ greatly should not be underestimated. A primary difficulty of global environmental management is precisely that there is no consensus on what is good for the globe. Moreover, the need to find a co-operative solution encourages delayed response to environmental problems, by enabling a few significant states to postpone action until there is 'clear and convincing' proof of the cause and the consequences.

One response to this predominant model of environmental decision-making is to remove from states their freedom of action. To some extent this has begun to happen in the EEC, where directives and regulations on certain environmental matters can now be adopted by weighted majority vote in the Council of Ministers,[52] and compliance is policed by the Commission and the European Court of Justice. Comparable models at the international level are the International Seabed Authority,[53] and the proposed Antarctic Mineral Resources Commission.[54] What these bodies share is that they are given responsibility for the management of resource exploitation and the regulation of its environmental consequences. Decisions would be taken by weighted majority vote binding on all participants. Neither institution at present exists, however, and both have encountered considerable opposition. The one functioning example of a stronger form of environmental decision-making is the Montreal Protocol to the Ozone Convention. As we saw earlier, this body may adopt a limited range of decisions involving amendment of production and consumption limits by weighted majority. The measures adopted in this way are binding on objectors, whose only remaining option is to give one year's notice of withdrawal. Withdrawal will, however, entail loss of financial and technical benefits, and the possible application of trade sanctions for non-parties. Though at present a unique example, the Montreal Protocol does overcome some of the problems of the excessive voluntarism of the present system of environmental law by building a stronger decision-making capacity onto a basically co-operative structure.

Moreover, a similar development can be observed in the Oslo Dumping Convention. As we have seen, states wishing to dump in the North Sea must justify their proposal to this body, enabling it to refuse its agreement if it cannot be proved that no harm will result. This has the effect of reversing the normal presumption that states are free to act unless there is some proof of harm or potential harm. It amounts to the adoption of a strong form of the precautionary principle, and enables the parties collectively to control the creation of environmental risks. Although it cannot be said that this approach represents international law, since it has few parallels, nevertheless it has the significant advantage of moderating the freedom of states to take unilateral decisions affecting their neighbours, without subjecting them to the kind of prior consent regime rejected in the *Lac Lanoux* arbitration.

CONCLUSIONS

Customary international law would seem at present to require neighbouring states to co-operate in the management of transboundary environmental risks and shared natural resources, largely within limits modelled on the *Lac Lanoux* arbitration, and to that extent it limits the freedom to create risks affecting neighbouring states. But this obligation of co-operation is a relatively weak one, entailing no veto for other states, and no loss of the ultimate power of decision for the proposing state. This leaves individual states with very little protection against harmful activities pursued by their neighbours, and gives them no opportunity to influence decisions affecting global commons.

The advantages of co-operation at a wider multilateral level, whether regional or global, through international institutions, are more readily apparent and not as such in doubt. They have been widely accepted by states in numerous treaties dealing with various aspects of the environment. In this sense, co-operation is at the heart of contemporary international environmental law, and represents perhaps the key strategy for its implementation. This form of co-operation has facilitated co-ordinated action on a wide scale and provided opportunities for influencing state behaviour, harmonising policies and national laws and responding to environmental threats.

Yet as we have seen, the co-operative model on which the development of environmental law has been based has certain inherent weaknesses. Its voluntarism has the advantage of necessitating consensus in which the interests of all states must be accommodated; at the same time, however, it may slow the pace of necessary law-making and inhibit rational action, as in the case of many fisheries regimes. The acceptance of more advanced models of institutional management and control remains limited, however, and does not yet justify the conclusion either that the 'precautionary principle' has replaced national freedom to act in the absence of proof of harm, or that a system of majoritarian decision-making has supplanted the existing techniques of ensuring friendly relations among states through co-operation and consent. Whether such a system can ultimately achieve the amelioration of environmental decay which it seeks remains to be seen.

NOTES

1 See further A.S. Timoshenko, 'Ecological Security and International Law' (1988) *Soviet Yearbook of International Law* 23; P. Sand, "International Law on the Agenda of the United Nations Conference on Environment and Development: Towards Global Environment Security" (1991) 60 *Nordic Journal of International Law* 5.

2 CSCE, Final Act, Helsinki, 1975, Cmnd. 6198; Concluding Document, Madrid 1980–83, Cmnd. 9066; Concluding Document, Vienna, 1989; Report on Conclusions and Recommendations of the Meeting on Protection of the Environment, Sofia/Vienna 1989–90; Charter of Paris, 1991, (1991) 30 *I.L.M.* 193; and see generally E. Chossudovsky, *East-West Diplomacy for Environment in the United Nations*, New York: Unitar, 1990.

3 1985 Sulphur Dioxide Protocol, (1988) 27 *I.L.M.* 707; 1988 Nitrogen Oxide Protocol, (1988) 18 *E.P.L.* 228.

4 UN Economic Commission for Europe, 1992 Convention on the Protection and Use of Transboundary Watercourses and International Lakes, (1992) *31 I.L.M.* 1312.

5 1990 Draft ECE Charter on Environmental Rights and Obligations.

6 1991 Convention on Environmental Impact Assessment in a Transboundary Context, (1991) 30 *I.L.M.* 802.

7 See Report of the United Nations Conference on Environment and Development, UN DOC. A/CONF. 151/26/Rev. 1 (vol. 1), 1992. The present chapter should be read in the light of the extensive provisions on co-operation now found in the Rio Decloration on Environment and Development adopted by the 1992 Conference

8 See A. Hurrell and B. Kingsbury, *The International Politics of the Environ-*

ment, Oxford: Oxford University Press, p.6; G. Plant in R. Churchill and D. Freestone (eds) *International Law and Global Climate Change*, Dordrecht: Martinus Nijhoff, 1991, ch.10.

9 See generally P.W. Birnie and A.E. Boyle, *International Law and the Environment*, Oxford: Oxford University Press, 1992.

10 (1957) 24 I.L.R. 101.

11 1991 Draft Articles, *Report of the ILC to the UN General Assembly*, UN Doc. A/46/10 (1991), p. 161, Articles 11–19, and commentary in *Report of the ILC to the UN General Assembly*, UN Doc. A/43/10 (1988) pp.114ff. Cf., however ILA, Helsinki Rules on the Uses of the Waters of International Rivers, 1966, Articles 29–30 and see C. Bourne, 'Procedure in the Development of International Drainage Basins' (1972) 10 *Canadian Yearbook of International Law* 212.

12 [1974] I.C.J. Rep.

13 See also *North Sea Continental Shelf* case [1969] I.C.J. Rep. 3, at pp.46–7.

14 Articles 63, 64, 117–19.

15 For example, the 1978 Convention on Future Multilateral Co-operation in the North-West Atlantic Fisheries; 1980 Convention on Future Multilateral Co-operation in North-East Atlantic Fisheries.

16 UN General Assembly Resolution 3281 (XXIX) (1974).

17 (1978) 17 *I.L.M.* 1091.

18 UN General Assembly Resolution 34/186 (1979) merely 'takes note of the principles'.

19 UN General Assembly Resolution 2995 (XXVII) (1972).

20 For example, 1980 Agreement between Spain and Portugal on Co-operation in Matters Affecting the Safety of Nuclear Installations in the Vicinity of the Frontier, B. Ruster and B. Simma, *International Protection of the Environment*, vol.27, p.420 New York: Oceana, 1975; 1977 Netherlands-FRG Memorandum on Exchange of Information and Consultation in Border Areas, ibid., p.275; 1977 Denmark-FRG Agreement Regulating the Exchange of Information on the Construction of Nuclear Installations along the Border, (1978) 17 *I.L.M.* 274; 1966 Belgium–France Convention on Radiological Protection, 988 *U.N.T.S.* 288; 1982 Switzerland-FRG Agreement on Mutual Information on Construction and Operation of Nuclear Installations in Border Areas, (1983) II *Bundesgesetzblatt* 734.

21 See K. Lenaerts, in P. Cameron, L. Hancher and W. Kühn, *Nuclear Energy Law After Chernobyl*, London: Graham & Trotman, 1988, p.49.

22 ILC, Draft Articles on Injurious Consequences of Acts Not Prohibited by International Law, UN Doc. A/CN.4/L.438 (1989), Article 1.

23 Article 8(b).

24 Article 5.

25 See Birnie and Boyle, above n.9, ch.10.

26 1991 Agreement Between the Government of the USA and the Government of Canada on Air Quality, (1991) 30 *I.L.M.* 678.

27 See further, Birnie and Boyle, above n.9, chs 7 and 8.

28 For example, 1974 Paris Convention for the Prevention of Marine Pollution from Land-based Sources; 1976 Barcelona Convention for the Protection of the Mediterranean Sea Against Pollution with protocols on Co-operation in Cases of Emergency, Dumping and Land-based Sources of Marine Pollution; 1974 Helsinki Convention on the Protection of the Marine Environment of the Baltic Sea Area; 1978 Kuwait Convention for Co-operation on the Protection of the Marine Environment from Pollution, with protocols on Co-operation in Emergency and Land-based Sources of Marine Pollution; 1972 Oslo

Convention for the Prevention of Marine Pollution by Dumping, and other agreements in UNEP's 'Regional Seas' series.

29 Articles 122–3.

30 1974 Paris Convention, Art. 9; 1983 Quito Protocol for the Protection of the South-East Pacific Against Pollution from Land-based Sources, Art. 12; 1980 Athens Protocol for the Protection of the Mediterranean Sea against Pollution from land-based sources, Art. 12.

31 1983 Canada-Denmark Agreement for Co-operation Relating to the Marine Environment, (1984) 23 *I.L.M.* 269; 1988 Kuwait Protocol Concerning Marine Pollution Resulting from Exploration and Exploitation of the Continental Shelf, (1989) 19 *E.P.L.* 32; 1981 UNEP Principles Concerning the Environment Related to Offshore Drilling and Mining within the limits of National Jurisdiction, (1981) 7 *E.P.L.* 50.

32 Article 5(2) and Annex 6.

33 Article 210(5).

34 OECD Rec. C(77)115, in *OECD and the Environment*, Paris: OECD 1986, p.181.

35 OSCOM Decision 89.1. But cf. R. Churchill (1991) 18 *Journal of Legal Studies* 166, who points out the UK's failure to comply fully with this procedure.

36 See generally A.E. Boyle, 'State Responsibility and International Liability for Injurious Consequences of Acts Not Prohibited by International Law: A Necessary Distinction?' (1990) 39 *I.C.L.Q.* 1.

37 For the 1990 draft articles see Un Doc. A/CN.4/428 (1990).

38 1982 UNCLOS, Articles 204–6; 1991 Protocol to the Antarctic Treaty on Environmental Protection; 1991 Convention on Environmental Impact Assessment in a Transboundary Context; 1983 Convention for the Protection and Development of the Marine Environment of the Wider Caribbean, Article 12; 1985 ASEAN Agreement on Conservation of Nature and Natural Resources, Articles 14, 19, 20; UNEP, 1987 Guidelines on Environmental Impact Assessment.

39 EEC, Council Directive 85/337, OJ 1985 L175, p. 40; Germany, 1990 Act Concerning Environmental Impact Assessment; US, 1969 National Environmental Policy Act, 42 U.S.C. ss. 4321–47; World Bank, Operational Directive on Environmental Assessment 1989, summarised in *The World Bank and the Environment*, Washington: International Bank for Reconstruction and Development, 1991, pp. 66–72.

40 See further Birnie and Boyle, above n.9, ch.6 and literature cited there.

41 See, for example, G. Handl, 'International Legal Perspectives on the Conduct of Abnormally Dangerous Activities in Frontier Areas' (1978) 7 *Ecology Law Quarterly* 50.

42 See, for example, the ILA's 1982 Montreal Rules on Transfrontier Pollution.

43 See OECD Recommendations C(74) 224; C(76) 55; C(77) 28 reprinted in *OECD and the Environment*, Paris: OECD 1986.

44 1974 Nordic Convention on Protection of the Environment.

45 For analysis of this principle, which has diverse meanings, see D. Freestone, in Churchill and Freestone, above n.8, ch.2; E. Hey, *The Precautionary Approach and the LDC*, annexed to LDC 14/4 (1991).

46 See generally L.K. Caldwell, *International Environmental Policy*, North Carolina: Duke University Press, 1991 2nd edn.; Birnie and Boyle, above n.9 ch.2.

47 See A.E. Boyle, 'Saving the World? Implementations and Enforcement of International Environmental Law through International Institutions' (1991) 3 *Journal of Environmental Law*, p.229; A.C. Kiss, in F. Kalshoven, F. Kuyper and J. Lammers (eds) *Essays on the Development of the International Legal Order*, Alphen aan den Rijn: Sijhoff and Noordhoff, 1980), p.99.

48 Article 8. An interim procedure was agreed in 1990 which any party may invoke unilaterally. See Decision II/5 and Annex III, UNEP, OzL.Pro.2/3 (1990); UNEP/OzL.Pro/WG.3/2/2 (1991); UNEP/OzL.Pro/WG.3;3/2 (1991) and see T. Gehring, 'International Environmental Regimes: Dynamic Sectoral Legal Systems' (1990) 1 *Yearbook of International Environmental Law* 35, at pp.50–4.

49 See, for example, 1974 Paris Convention for the Prevention of Marine Pollution from Land-based Sources, Article 21; 1976 Convention on the Protection of the Rhine against Pollution from Chemicals, Article 15.

50 See, for example, 1989 Basel Convention for the Control of Transboundary Movements of Hazardous Wastes, Article 19.

51 See, for example, the 1987 Montreal Protocol to the Vienna Convention on the Ozone Layer, as revised in 1990.

52 1986 Single European Act, Articles 100A, 130S.

53 1982 UNCLOS, Articles 156–69. See especially Articles 159(8), 160(2)(f)(ii) and Annex III, Article 17(1)(b).

54 See 1988 Convention for the Regulation of Antarctic Mineral Resource Activities.

7 The principle of co-operation: terrorism

David Freestone

INTRODUCTION

The increasing incidence and impact of acts of political terrorism over the last twenty-five years have demonstrated that independent, national attempts to deal with the problem are not adequate. External support for terrorist operations, the possibility of terrorists escaping to safe havens across international boundaries and the switching of targets by terrorists to less well-protected persons and property abroad as security at home improves are indicators of the transnational nature of much political terrorism. Some rules of international law, like those on territorial sovereignty and non-intervention, have stood in the way of unilateral action by States to pursue and apprehend transnational terrorists. Existing regimes of criminal co-operation have proved inadequate or incomplete to meet the problems posed by terrorism. To some extent also, the deficiencies of the legal response to terrorism are the intrinsic limitations of domestic law: favoured terrorist techniques, like hijacking of aircraft, were not specifically criminal; even where the terrorist activities were embraced by existing criminal offences, those offences were often not extraterritorial, particularly for common law States; even rules of national criminal procedure proved to be substantial handicaps in investigating terrorist offences. States could, and did, take steps by themselves to address these problems but even here, international legal considerations impinged, making difficult or legally dubious some of the responses States wished to make. The rules on criminal legislative jurisdiction under customary international law limited the powers of States to criminalise extraterritorial activity. The law of international human rights was also a restraint on some changes in criminal procedure that States wished to introduce.[1]

International legal action to meet the threat of transnational terrorism requires the co-operation of States. That co-operation cannot be assumed and has not always been forthcoming. Not all States have equally been the object of, or equally affected by, terrorist activities. Not all States strike the same balance between the prosecution of crime and the protection of defendants. Most fundamentally, States are still not agreed on what constitutes international terrorism and before co-operation can be achieved to deal with it, some degree of precision about what is involved is required. One feature of terrorism is that it involves illegitimate violence. For States, the right of legitimate violence, occasionally for international purposes, always for domestic purposes, is an essential aspect of their statehood. Some States remain concerned that proposed understandings of terrorism would fetter their capacity to respond to illegitimate violent action. Others, seeking to establish the international legitimacy of force in the cause of self-determination – force which was frequently irregular and low-intensity in nature – feared that other proposals would deprive national liberation movements of their only effective manner of taking military action. Even where a modicum of agreement was reached that certain activities of certain persons did constitute terrorism, States differed about what should be done about it. Western States were generally of the view that the answer was to be found in increasingly concerted action by governments against the perpetrators of what these States regarded as wholly inexcusable activities. Other States, mainly developing countries, considered that terrorism was ineradicable by the means proposed. They saw terrorism as a consequence of conditions of political exploitation or impoverishment, which would persist so long as these conditions were allowed to continue. The attack on terrorism would be successful only if it were directed at the conditions which gave rise to it. Since some of the situations which generated substantial terrorist activity were among the most intractable of political disputes, the prospects for dealing with terrorism if this prescription were adopted were remote. At the general international level, these difficulties were so profound that the UN General Assembly's *Ad Hoc* Committee on Terrorism was not able to reach a definition of terrorism on the basis of which a general scheme of co-operation could proceed.[2]

Instead, the main thrust of the legal response of States has been to isolate particular problems, such as the hijacking of aircraft or attacks against diplomats, which were widely regarded as reprehensible, and to conclude treaties which establish regimes of criminal co-operation between the parties so as to increase the chances of successful prosecution of the perpetrators of such acts.[3] Central to those arrangements have been provisions seeking to regulate, harmonise and/or extend the criminal jurisdiction of the contracting States. This chapter will therefore concentrate on the methods developed by these conventions to co-operate in this way. To appreciate the way in which they operate, however, some understanding is necessary of the pre-existing framework within which those conventions operate. The following sections therefore address the problems of obtaining custody over offenders or offences committed outside national jurisdiction and the framework of basic principles within which such co-operation takes place.

EXTRATERRITORIAL JURISDICTION AND OBTAINING CUSTODY OVER OFFENDERS OUTSIDE THE JURISDICTION

It has already been explained that much political terrorism has been of an extraterritorial character. This has required that States extend the jurisdictional reach of their criminal law in order to be able to prosecute persons accused of terrorist offences. However, under general international law, States do not have an unlimited capacity to criminalise the acts of non-nationals beyond their territory. It is not necessary to rehearse these rules.[4] It will become apparent that the international agreements and State practice have stretched them to the limit. Equally, having established extraterritorial jurisdiction, States have been faced with the difficulty of obtaining custody over defendants who are in a foreign State. This is a problem not unique to extraterritorial offences but arises as well where defendants have fled the territorial jurisdiction of the State, before or after having being convicted of an offence. Unless the fugitive is willing to surrender volutarily, States may only gain custody lawfully over such defendants by extradition or following deportation.

Although there has been some progress towards common standards for extradition, there are wide differences in national laws and there is no general right of States to have a fugitive returned in the absence of an extradition treaty.[5] Deportation, which is the right of the removing State, does not involve an international obligation to return a fugitive to a State which wants to prosecute him/her. Both extradition and deportation procedures have important constitutional constraints upon them, again varying from State to State.[6] Domestic extradition law can be very technical and is sometimes as concerned to protect the defendant against unfair rendition as to secure international criminal co-operation.[7] Two aspects of extradition law have been of particular significance in the context of terrorist offences. The first is the requirement of double criminality, that is the need for the requesting State to demonstrate that the conduct constituting the extraterritorial) crime in the requesting State would also, *mutatis mutandis*, constitute a crime by the law of the requested State. The result is that mutuality of jurisdiction over terrorist crime is as important for extradition as it is for the exercise of primary jurisdiction.[8] The other matter is the political offence.

The exclusion of political offenders from extradition has its roots in nineteenth-century practice, the first such exclusion being found in a Belgian treaty of 1833. It can now be found in the overwhelming majority of extradition treaties and national extradition laws. The two main limbs of the 'political offence' exclusion can be seen clearly in Article 3 of the European Convention on Extradition[9] which allows contracting States the option of refusing extradition for a 'political offence' or 'an offence connected with a political offence' (i.e. criteria relating to the nature of the offence itself) or in circumstances where 'the requesting state has substantial grounds for believing that a request for extradition for an ordinary criminal has been made for the purpose of prosecuting or punishing a person on account of his race, religion, nationality or political opinion or that that person's position will be prejudiced for any of these reasons' (i.e. criteria relating to the circumstances of trial). The latter limb has been called the humanitarian exclusion and can be found in a number of other treaties including Article 5 of the European Convention on the Suppression of Terrorism, discussed further below.[10] Important as such safeguards appear to be, they may in fact be of limited utility to the individual fugitive, for courts have again had difficulty utilising provisions of this kind because of the fact that making such a finding involves casting a major aspersion on the objectivity and fairness of the criminal justice system of another State, and bona fides of the requesting authorities.[11]

Equally difficult is the traditional 'political offence' exception. There is no international law definition of such an offence and State practice varies widely on the variety of factors – some subjective, some objective – which may be taken into account by national courts in deciding whether a crime may be classified as 'political'.[12] It is even possible to discern crude foreign policy considerations in some decisions.

GENERAL LEGAL FRAMEWORK

The general framework of international law within which the jurisdictional rights of States operate involves a number of general principles of wider application. These are the principle of sovereign equality of States; the principle of territorial integrity (codified in Article 2(4) UN Charter) and the principle of non-intervention in the internal affairs of other States (codified in the 1970 General Assembly Resolution around which this book is organised).

Jurisdiction is a basic concept of State sovereignty and mutual recognition of State jurisdictional powers represents an important aspect of sovereign equality. Similarly in the exercise of its rights of jurisdiction a State must respect the territorial integrity of other States. In the absence of specific agreement,[13] the exercise of enforcement jurisdiction by one State in the territory of another will be a breach of international law. For example, after the kidnap of Adolph Eichmann, former head of the Jewish Office of the Nazi Gestapo, from Argentina allegedly by the Israeli Secret Service (Mossad) case and his subsequent appearance for trial in Jerusalem for crimes against humanity, the Argentine government lodged a complaint with the UN Security Council that 'the transfer of Adolph Eichmann to the territory of Israel constitutes a violation of the sovereignty of the Argentine Republic . . . incompatible with the Charter of the United Nations'.[14] After a reported apology from Israel the matter was said to be closed. However, it is unclear whether as a matter of international law the obligation to make reparation for such a violation of territorial sovereignty includes an obligation to return the offender illegally abducted. If such an obligation exists it is not, as Fawcett has explained, unqualified.[15] Certainly the illegality of an offender's arrest in such circumstances does not appear to undermine the right of a national court to try him/her.

In relation to prescriptive jurisdiction, that is, the promulgation of a claim to exercise jurisdiction, it is unlikely that such a claim could in itself (in the absence of enforcement action) constitute a violation of another State's integrity, although it could be argued that the promulgation of a claim to exercise enforcement jurisdiction in another State might in itself constitute a threat to the territorial integrity or political independence of the latter. Indeed it might even be argued that such a claim constitutes an indirect violation of the norm of non-intervention in the internal affairs of another State. The 1970 Declaration states

> No State . . . has the right to intervene, directly or indirectly, for any reason whatever, in the internal or external affairs of any other State. . . .
> Every State has an unalienable right to choose its political, economic, social and cultural systems, without interference in any form by another State.

A number of difficulties surround the application of this principle to jurisdictional claims. While it could be accepted that (for reasons of economic self-determination) certain types of extraterritorial jurisdiction – notably those relating to anti-trust legislation[16] – might conflict with this principle, it is not easy to extend this concept *en bloc* to jurisdiction over terrorist offences. Indeed, a State may well feel inhibited from protesting at the assertion of extraterritorial jurisdiction over offences committed in its territory or by its nationals if those offences were terrorist offences precisely because those offences were directed *ex hypothesi* at the political, economic, social or cultural system of another State.[17]

THE FRAMEWORK FOR CO-OPERATION

Given the sensibilities which exist in relation to the existing framework of national jurisdictional rules, the response of the world community has not been to the development of international terrorist courts – as was proposed by the League of Nations in 1937[18] – but toward the functional co-ordination and extension of existing powers in the field of jurisdiction and extradition. Like most crimes, transnational crimes have an important fashion or 'copy-cat' element. Also, as certain types of counter-terrorist measures become more effective, terrorists turn to other forms of activity. Briefly traced, the 1960s saw the emergence of the aerial hijacker – a form of activity previously unknown and largely 'non-criminal' in the sense that hijacking was not a crime known to national criminal laws and it was difficult to apply the existing rules of piracy *mutatis mutandis* to it. This issue was not directly addressed by the 1963 Tokyo Convention on Offences and Certain Other Acts committed on Board Aircraft[19] which, although concerned with extending national jurisdiction, did not seek to define hijacking so as to ensure co-ordination of national laws. It was clearly the intention of the Tokyo Convention that hijacking be treated as aerial piracy but it does not expressly provide this.[20] Perhaps because the Convention did not provide a clear lead on this – as well as because of its unusual jurisdictional provisions, which appear to sanction executive jurisdiction over aircraft in flight according to the territorial, passive personality and protective principles[21] – the Convention did not reach the required number of ratifications to bring it into force until 1969. By this time it had been overtaken by the initiatives resulting in the International Civil Aviation Organization (ICAO) Hague Convention for the Suppression of Unlawful Seizure of Aircraft of 1970[22] and the Montreal Convention for the Suppression of Unlawful Acts against the Safety of Civil Aviation of 1971.[23]

It was probably not the conventions themselves that actually reduced the flood of hijacking in the late 1960s and early 1970s. They seem to be more symptoms of a generally stronger, more united, stance taken by the States most affected: increased airport security, threats of boycotts like the Bonn Declaration of 1978 of non-cooperating States.[24] The 1970s saw a slight decrease in hijacking but an increase in the number of kidnappings, and often murder, of prominent politicians, diplomats and industrialists. Then the mechanisms already developed in response to hijacking were simply redirected at these new forms of terrorism by the 1973 UN Convention on the Prevention and Punishment of Crimes against Internationally Protected Persons, including Diplomatic Agents (IPP Convention)[25] and the 1979 UN Convention against the Taking of Hostages (the Hostages Convention).[26] By then the 'formula' developed in these conventions could be relatively easily applied to new potential terrorist threats and it was used by the International Atomic Energy Agency in the development of its 1980 Convention on the Physical Protection of Nuclear Material[27] and in 1988 after a single incident – the *Achille Lauro* Affair – the same general formula was quickly adapted to apply to vessels (and offshore installation) in the IMO International Convention for the Suppression of Unlawful Acts against the Safety of Maritime Navigation (and its protocol on fixed platforms).[28] The 1980s saw an increase in the use of remote controlled bombs, some of them placed on aeroplanes resulted in disasters such as that at Lockerbie in Scotland in December 1988 in which 270 passengers and crew lost their lives when a bomb alleged to have been planted by Libyan agents exploded on a Pan-American 747 jumbo jet. Ironically the Lockerbie incident – which raises rather different issues which are covered in the final section of this chapter

– occurred after the conclusion by ICAO in February 1998 of a Protocol to the Montreal Convention specifically directed at airport security.

Each of these conventions has its own particular aspects and idiosyncrasies but broadly the 'formula' that they develop adopts three main devices:

1 The targeted offences are defined in as comprehensive a manner as possible, and contracting States are obliged to make them punishable by severe penalties in their national criminal laws.
2 Contracting States are then obliged to extend their jurisdictional rules over these targeted offences in order to create as comprehensive a network of national jurisdictions as possible to avoid offenders slipping through.
3 Contracting States accept an obligation of *aut dedere aut judicare* – to extradite or try offenders falling within their jurisdiction.

The following section looks at the way in which the global counter-terrorist conventions address these issues.

Defining terrorist offences

It was suggested above that the failure of the Tokyo Convention to define hijacking or related offences may have been one of the reasons for its lack of support among States. However, this was remedied by the approach taken by The Hague and later the Montreal Conventions. The Hague Convention defined unlawful seizure of aircraft as:

> Any person who on board an aircraft in flight:
> a) unlawfully, by force or threat thereof, or by any form of intimidation, seizes, or exercises control of, that aircraft, or attempts to perform any such act, or
> b) is an accomplice of a person who performs or attempts to perform any such act commits an offence.

The following year, in the Montreal Convention, a longer list of proscribed offences was laid down covering a range of some seven primary offences from acts of violence against persons on board aircraft to communicating false information, endangering the safety of aircraft in flight, together with the ancillary offences of attempting, or being an accomplice, or even being an accomplice to an attempt.[29] For the Montreal Convention most of the activities covered were already offences under national criminal laws. This comprehensive listing of relevant offences had another significance – it engaged for those offences (whatever they were called under various national laws) all the consequential mechanisms of the treaty network, including extradition and extended extraterritorial jurisdiction. This technique of listing the activities covered by the convention in as comprehensive a manner as possible was utilised by all the later conventions. Article 2 of the 1973 IPP Convention lists offences relating to the murder, kidnapping or other attacks on the person or liberty of IPPs and attacks on official premises, private accommodation or means of transport of such persons, together with ancillary offences. The offences covered by the 1979 UN Convention against the Taking of Hostages were even more specific[30] but the more general approach is taken by both the 1980 IAEA Convention on the Physical Protection of Nuclear Material (Article 7 of which lists some eight offences) and the 1988 IMO Convention for the Suppression of Unlawful Acts against the Safety of Maritime Navigation (Article 3 lists at least seven offences).

Extending jurisdictional competence

The basic approach taken in all the counter-terrorist conventions under examination here is primarily that of a treaty regime aimed at apprehending and punishing individual terrorists. Therefore the co-ordinated extension of powers of criminal jurisdiction provides a means of ensuring that the powers which existing international law already permits States to exercise are utilised to the full. State claims to criminal jurisdictions vary quite widely. Common law countries favour criminal jurisdictions based on the territorial principle – even though contemporary interpretations of this principle often take it far from its most obvious form – that of a State to prosecute offences committed within its territory by offenders also within its territory.[31] Civil law countries favour personal jurisdiction, based on the nationality of the offender. For historical and political reasons some suspicion still attaches to many forms of extraterritorial jurisdiction even though it seems difficult to sustain the argument that they are actually contrary to international law. In fact, the conventions under examination here have themselves contributed to the development of State practice in that it can be argued that they constitute an important public recognition of permissive rules of extraterritorial jurisdiction.

It was in recognition of the sensitivities surrounding extraterritorial jurisdiction that the Tokyo Convention recognised in Article 3 the primary jurisdictional rights of the State of registration of the aircraft over offences committed on board and obliged parties to 'take such measures as may be necessary' to establish such jurisdiction. It sought, however, to supplement this with Article 4 which appears to recognise the right to exercise criminal jurisdiction over an aircraft in flight according to the territorial, the active and the passive personality and protective principles.[32] Again it was the Hague Convention which took a more measured view of the extension of jurisdictional powers. It obliged contracting States (by Article 4) to claim jurisdiction: (a) as the registering State,[33] (b) as the State where an aircraft lands with an offender aboard, and (c) as the State of place of business or residence of lessee in case of leases without crew. In addition Article 4(2) obliged States to establish jurisdiction where the offender was in their territory and they did not extradite him. Custody jurisdiction, known in customary international law as universality jurisdiction, has traditionally only been recognised in relation to a few offences, such as piracy or slave trading, although in recent years it has been claimed in relation to a growing number of offences, including war crimes and genocide.[34] There is a well-known controversy as to whether this Article establishes a form of universality jurisdiction. On the basis that it is only binding on contracting parties to the Hague Convention it has been called quasi-universal, but it is worth pointing out that the Hague Convention now has over 140 parties, which places it among the most widely ratified of all global conventions.

The significance of the use of custody (or universal) jurisdiction in Article 4(2) of the Hague Convention should not be underrated, for it has been echoed by all the subsequent global conventions.[35] The very wide adherence to the hijacking conventions – Tokyo, The Hague and Montreal – suggests that, for hijacking at the very least, the right to try on the basis of universality has now moved into the realm of customary law.[36]

It is probably still true to say that 'terrorism' is not itself a crime triable according to the universality principle under customary international law, if only because of the intrinsic difficulty of defining 'terrorism'.[37] It would not, however, be true to say that terrorist *offences* are not so triable, for the treaty-making practice here would gainsay that. Indeed, in relation to the core of offences which are covered by those multilateral conventions which have achieved wide adherence (e.g. hijacking and hostage taking) it might be argued that this general pattern of treaty practice which includes custody jurisdictional provisions within its obligatory forms of jurisdiction (and which seeks to extend its ambit to the nationals of signatories and non-signatories alike) suggests that not simply hijacking, but also a wider core of 'terrorist offences' are subject to jurisdiction according to this principle under customary international law.[38] The readiness with which the 1988 IMO Conference on Maritime Safety was prepared to accept this principle in relation to the offences it proscribes in the IMO Convention might perhaps support such an argument.

Traditionally even more controversial is the passive personality principle of jurisdiction – where jurisdiction is exercised by the State of nationality of the victim of an offence. It has been condemned by common law writers[39] and its legality was challenged – albeit unsuccessfully – by France in the *Lotus* case in 1927.[40] More recently it has been used with increasing frequency by national criminal law as well as by treaty arrangements. The counter-terrorist conventions deal gently with it, either in the discretionary jurisdiction paragraphs, or with phrases such as 'if the State considers it appropriate'. In the Tokyo Convention – as already pointed out above – it was an 'optional' form of jurisdiction under Article 4. The IPP Convention, the Hostages Convention and now the 1988

IMO Convention and its Protocol all permit its use. In addition, the implementation of these conventions and other counter-terrorist measures by a number of States, including those such as the United States and France[41] with a history of opposition to the concept, make it difficult to maintain the argument that the principle is *per se* contrary to international law.[42]

A technical device which has also been developed in the counter-terrorist conventions has now been identified as a new discrete jurisdictional principle by the Council of Europe Committee on Crime Problems.[43] This is the representational principle. A good example is Article 10(4) of the Hostages Convention which reads:

> The offences set forth in Article 1 shall be treated, for the purpose of extradition between States Parties, as if they had been committed not only in the place in which they occurred but also in the territories of the States required to establish their jurisdiction in accordance with paragraph 1 of Article 5.

This 'jurisfictional' device is designed to allow states to extend their jurisdictional network without necessarily having to accept the more controversial principles of jurisdiction. The territorial principle is obviously one which all States accept, this treaty device seeks to extend the territorial network to the territories of all the States parties.

Aut dedere aut judicare

The obligation to extradite an alleged terrorist offender or to submit him/her to the normal internal processes of prosecution is a crucial part of the strategy adopted by all these international conventions after Tokyo. The ultimate success of this 'no hiding place' approach does, of course, depend upon the number of States which accept this obligation by becoming parties to the conventions; nevertheless the obligation to extradite or try is an interesting jurisdictional device because it hooks the newly proscribed offence(s) into the existing network of extradition treaties and procedures.

The law of extradition is particularly complex and technical.[44] However, to appreciate the strategy of the counter-terrorist conventions some regard must be paid to aspects of it here. For extradition to take place it is necessary to fulfil the requirements of national extradition law. Most national systems will not permit extradition unless the request satisfies the dual criminality principle. This requires that the extraditable offence be a crime in both requesting and requested States. This rule applies in both its substantive and procedural aspects. Substantively this is done by requiring each contracting State to make the relevant offences punishable under its national law (and incidentally extradition treaties are deemed to be amended where this is necessary and/or possible). Procedurally the problem is more difficult because of the differences between national jurisdictional rules. One State may, for example, request extradition according to a principle of jurisdiction which is not recognised by the requested State (e.g. the passive personality principle). The UK would traditionally not recognise such a request. Here the representational principle formula used by the UN conventions and discussed above minimises this difficulty.

So, to take a hypothetical and perhaps controversial example, a request by Germany to the UK for the extradition of an offender over which Germany seeks to exercise jurisdiction according to the passive personality principle (i.e. where a German national has been the hostage) will be deemed to be based upon the territorial principle (i.e. will be deemed to have been committed in Germany) and thus be recognisable by the UK courts. It should be noted that Article 5(1)(d) of the Hostages Convention does confer discretion on States as to whether or not to espouse jurisdiction under the passive personality principle by the use of the phrase 'if that State considers it appropriate'. However that discretion appears to be conferred only on the State with primary jurisdiction, not that State which exercises 'representational' jurisdiction, which appears to be obliged to accept any form of jurisdiction legitimately exercised under the Convention for these purposes. This does incidentally appear to be the interpretation put upon these provisions by the British Government, for the UK Taking of Hostages Act 1982 appears to extend to such a situation.[45]

REGIONAL APPROACHES

The two regional conventions, one concluded under the auspices of the Organization of American States (OAS), the other within the Council of Europe, adopt a similar pattern but with additional refinements reflecting to some extent the greater degree of political agreement which can be found at a regional level.

The 1971 OAS Convention to Prevent and Punish Acts of Terrorism taking the form of Crimes against Persons and related Extortion that are of International Significance[46] was negotiated before the main global conventions. It has an 'extradite or try' clause: 'if extradition is refused because the person sought is a national' or for some other 'legal or constitutional impediment' then there is an 'obligation to prosecute as if the act had been committed in its territory.' (Article 5)

It also imposes obligations on States parties to extend their national criminal jurisdiction in order to meet this obligation. Under Article 8 contracting States simply accept the obligation 'to endeavour to have the criminal acts contemplated in this Convention included in their penal laws, if not already so included'.

The most notable feature of the Convention, however, is the fact that it takes the important step of removing or restricting the political offence exception – thus addressing what is perceived to be a major impediment to the extradition of terrorists. Article 2 requires that the listed offences:

> Kidnapping, murder and other assaults on life or personal integrity of those whom the State has to give special protection according to international law, as well as extortion in connection with those crimes, shall be considered 'common crimes of international significance regardless of motive'.

This deprives terrorist offenders of the protection of the political offence exception.

The 1977 European Convention on the Suppression of Terrorism[47] (ECST) negotiated under the auspices of the Council of Europe uses a mixture of the techniques which have been discussed and is possibly the most sophisticated of the treaties discussed here. It seeks to establish the closest kind of jurisdictional net both quantitatively (in the sense of the number of offences which it covers) and also qualitatively, in that its drafters obviously felt able to address some of the issues which the global conventions ignore. It lists the 'terrorist offences' covered by the Convention. These are:

a) an offence within the scope of the Convention for the Suppression of Unlawful Seizure of Aircraft, signed at The Hague on 16 December 1970;
b) an offence within the scope of the Convention for the Suppression of Unlawful Acts against the Safety of Civil Aviation, signed at Montreal on 23 September 1971;
c) a serious offence involving an attack against the life, physical integrity or liberty of internationally protected persons, including diplomatic agents;
d) an offence involving kidnapping, the taking of a hostage or serious unlawful detention;
e) an offence involving the use of a bomb, grenade, rocket, automatic firearm or letter or parcel bomb if this use endangers persons; and
f) an attempt to commit any of the foregoing offences or participation as an accomplice of a person who commits or attempts to commit such an offence.

Contracting States also have the discretion to extend its regime to any serious offence involving violence against life, physical integrity or liberty of a person or against property if it creates a collective danger for persons.[48]

The ECST follows the global pattern rather more closely, for having defined the offences covered by the regime, it establishes the, by now familiar, principle of *aut dedere aut judicare.*[49] It also requires contracting States to extend their domestic jurisdiction so as to be able to try offenders found in their territory whom they do not extradite.[50] However, like the OAS Convention it takes advantage of closer relations at regional level to seek to deprive those accused or convicted of such offences of the opportunity of using the political offence exception to extradition (Article 1).

Two aspects of the ECST are particularly interesting: first, the obligation to extend jurisdiction to meet the *aut dedere aut judicare* obligation and second, the elimination of the political offence exception.

Extended jurisdiction

The first issue arises from Article 6(1) which requires that:

> Each Contracting State shall take such measures as may be necessary to establish its jurisdiction over an offence mentioned in Article 1 in the case where the suspected offender is present in its territory and it does not extradite him after receiving a request for extradition from a Contracting State whose jurisdiction is based on a rule of jurisdiction existing equally in the law of the requested State.

It has been suggested by Lowe and Young[51] that this creates a form of rolling extraterritorial jurisdictional claim. They pose the problem of a State which has passed legislation conferring extraterritorial jurisdiction upon itself in order to meet the obligations of the Convention, then being faced with the suggestion that these extra-territorial assertions of jurisdiction have themselves to be taken into account in determining the reciprocity of interest for the purposes of Article 6.

This might explain the unusual way that the ECST has been implemented in the UK by the use of both fiction and double fiction. Under the 1978 Suppression of Terrorism Act a scheduled offence committed within a Convention country is deemed to have been committed in the UK – a fiction.[52] But also an offence committed outside another Convention country, but according to a principle which is accepted in that Convention country (provided that the offender is a national of a Convention country) is also deemed to be committed within the UK – a double fiction. By the use of this method of implementation the UK has rather neatly avoided addressing this issue. This is presumably deliberate, for the UK courts already have wide jurisdiction over some of the listed offences under, for example, the Aviation Security Act,[54] although the object of this clause was probably to maximise jurisdiction without forcing States to accept new principles.

The political offence exception

Article 1 of the ECST obliges parties to remove the political offence exception in extradition proceedings relating to persons charged with the listed offences. The effect of this restriction of the political offence is, however, restricted by two other provisions: Articles 13 and 5, which will be considered in turn.

First, Article 13 allows parties to enter a reservation permitting them to reject a request for extradition on the grounds that it is a political offence, notwithstanding that it is a listed offence. This seems to negate one of the main objectives of the Convention and has come in for a great deal of vigorous criticism.[55] It was included so as not to deter those States which felt themselves unable to renounce the political offence exception unequivocally – most obviously Ireland. It has been utilised by 5 of the 14 parties. The right of reservation is, however, itself subject to two further provisions:

1 the requirement of reciprocity in Article 13(3);
2 the obligation on a reserving State when deciding whether to invoke its reservation to take into account the following factors:
   a) that it created a collective danger to the life, physical integrity or liberty of persons; or
   b) that it affected persons foreign to the motives behind it; or
   c) that cruel or vicious means have been used in the commission of the offence.[56]

Second, the important provision of Article 5 – included it is said at the instigation of the UK – also permits a State to refuse extradition of an offender in relation to a listed offence if the requested State has substantial grounds for believing that the request for extradition for an offence mentioned in Article 1 or 2 has been made for the purpose of prosecuting or punishing a person on account of his race, religion, nationality or political opinions, or that person's position may be prejudiced for any of these reasons. This has been called the 'political asylum' proviso to distinguish it from the 'political offence' exception. It concentrates on the circumstances of the likely trial or punishment, rather than the motives or circumstances of the offence itself. This is an important human rights clause, but in so far as it presumably involves judicial or political determination of the lack of impartiality or discriminatory behaviour of the judicial system of another State (*ex hypothesi* a friendly State) the courts and the executive may find it difficult to apply.

The ECST, then, utilises the same basic model as the global conventions, but seeks to go further by addressing the difficult issue of the political offence and by using innovative techniques to extend even further jurisdiction over fugitive terrorists.

It has to be said that the ECST has not been an outstanding success. It has attracted criticism from many sides of the political spectrum[57] and it was slow to receive wide ratification within the Council of Europe. It was, however, the subject of a most unusual and interesting arrangement negotiated under the auspices of the European Community (EC): the

1979 Dublin Agreement.[58] This agreement has yet to come into force but it is an unusual, if not actually unique, arrangement under which a group of States (the EC members) agreed to apply an existing treaty regime (the ECST) in a modified form among themselves, despite the fact that some were not even parties to it.

The Dublin Agreement was negotiated outside EC law and is therefore governed by international law. The (at that time) nine EC member States agreed to apply the regime of the ECST between themselves without reservation, despite the fact that not all the EC States were parties to the ECST, and one had already made a reservation to the Convention. Denmark had made a reservation under Article 13 (reserving the right to allow the political offence exception) on ratifying the ECST and Ireland had not even signed it. Under the Dublin Agreement, if EC members wished to reserve the political exception in extradition between themselves they were required to lodge a reservation to that effect with the Irish Foreign Ministry (Article 3). The Agreement specifically permits Ireland (Article 3 (3)) as a non-signatory to the ECST to refuse extradition on the grounds that it accepts the obligation to try domestically. This unusual arrangement required ratification by all nine of the then members of the EC to come into force. It has, however, to date received only five.

The Dublin Agreement was hailed in some quarters as the first step in the creation of a European judicial area. This originated from a French proposal of 1977. The exact form this judicial area would take has not always been made clear, but it has encompassed a number of proposals including a European Terrorist Court or a Criminal Chamber of the European Court of Justice in Luxembourg to hear all terrorist cases where extradition is involved, or cases referred to it by member States reluctant to extradite an accused terrorist offender.[59]

There have also been calls for a common system of extradition between member States of the EC. The EC has concluded some agreements – notably the TREVI 'arrangements for cooperation and exchanging information and techniques for dealing with terrorist incidents'. The working party of senior officials which produced the Dublin Agreement also produced in 1980 a Draft Convention concerning Cooperation in Criminal Matters which was never opened for signature.[60] Internal EC politics appear to have prevented this idea from progressing,[61] although they have been kept alive by the Legal Affairs Committee of the European Parliament which in 1982 produced a report arguing the case that the EEC Treaty itself provides a legal basis for the conclusion of such arrangements under Community law.[62] In 1984 the Draft Treaty on European Union provided for the establishment of a 'Homogeneous Judicial Area',[63] but this concept was not accepted by the Single European Act in 1986. Since then, discussions have centred on the issue of police cooperation, which has now been the subject of the Schengen Convention, between all the ES States except the UK, Eire and Denmark (Greece is an observer).[64] The 1992 Treaty on Political Union concluded at the Maastricht Summit on 7 February 1992 includes 'Provisions on Co-operation in the Spheres of Justice and Home Affairs' under which member States declare that they regard a number of areas as 'of common interest'. These include 'judicial co-operation in criminal matters' (Article A(6)) and 'police co-operation for the purposes of preventing and combating terrorism . . . in connection with the organisation of a Union wide system for exchanging information within a European Police Office (EUROPOL)' (Article A(8)).[65]

THE LOCKERBIE CASE[66]

It should have become clear from the previous discussion that the term 'terrorism' is not a term of art in international law. Hence the notion of 'State' or 'State-sponsored' terrorism should similarly not cause any formal difficulties for international lawyers. The description of acts as 'terrorism' adds nothing to the general and pre-existing obligations of States not to interfere by acts of their officials or agents with the rights of other States. At a State-to-State level, acts such as hijacking or destruction of ships or aircraft, assault on diplomats or hostage taking engage the normal principles of State responsibility. Difficulties that have arisen have been of a different order. There is the mundane forensic one of proving the involvement of the State in the activity. Another is a symbolic one: is state terrorism adequately condemned by treaty if it is only classified as an ordinary international wrong? In an international legal system that as yet sets little store by State criminality, seeking reparation for damage done by State activities may appear insufficient, given the abhorrence with which terrorism is regarded.[67] It might be contended that the obligation of reparation for an international wrong does, in such cases, include a duty to punish the offenders. Hence, the prospect of a State discharging this obligation if it were implicated in the wrong is probably remote.[68] Even if the offenders were brought before a court, what chance of a vigorously pursued prosecution, what chance of a fair trial? However, the positions with respect to the counter-terrorist treaties is not much different: how are States to be made to discharge the duties imposed upon them by the treaties?[69] Thus understood, the problem is a general one of the enforcement of anti-terrorist law.

Against this background, it might be tempting to see the actions of the Security Council in the Lockerbie case as an innovation which may be relied upon for the enforcement of the counter-terrorism treaties. There are obstacles in the way of doing so. It will be recalled that the United States and the United Kingdom demanded the rendition of two named Libyans, accused of involvement in the placing of a bomb on the Pan American airliner which blew up over the Scottish town of Lockerbie, so that they could face trial in New York or Scotland. Libya rejected the demand, saying that it would investigate the case itself and asking for the evidence in the hands of the American and British prosecutors to help it to do so.[70] Libya noted that it was not in a position to extradite its own nationals. It is far from clear that Libya is in breach of its obligations under the Montreal Convention.[71] A State's primary duty is to submit a case to its prosecutor if it does not extradite the fugitive.[72] Libya has made elaborate gestures of its willingness to do this. Even if there were a duty to extradite that duty is to be exercised in accordance with national extradition law and Libya may not, according to that law, surrender its nationals.[73] In any event, the fugitives have an arguable case that the offences are political. Certainly, Libya had questioned whether they would have a fair trial if they were surrendered. However, this is to some extent irrelevant because the Security Council's request in Resolution 731 and its demand in Resolution 748 that the men be handed over makes no reference to the Montreal Convention. Resolution 748, which makes express reference to Chapter VII, is concerned with the threat to international peace and security posed by Libya's support for terrorism.[74] The rendition of the men is only one of the steps required to be taken by Libya with the object of removing the threat to international peace. The International Court of Justice's treatment of Libya's request for provisional measures showed that it was alive to this point.[75] It may yet be that there are legal questions to be raised on the merits about the right of the Security Council to proceed in the way that it has, and political questions about the influence of the Western permanent members on the Council's decision-making. None of this goes to the enforcement of the counter-terrorist treaties. Rather, it represents one more step towards regarding some instances of State-supported terrorism as posing threats to international peace and security.[76] The Security Council has not gone so far as some States would like and determined that all terrorist attacks are armed attacks for the purposes of Article 51. If anything, the *Nicaragua* judgment suggests that they are not. Rather, it appears that if the involvement of the State in activities, by reason of its degree of control over the terrorists, is such that there is an armed attack, then nothing is added to the right of the 'attacked' State to respond by way of self-defence by categorising the action as terrorist as well as an attack.[77] Where the involvement of a State with the terrorists is insufficient to implicate it an armed attack or where there is no involvement at all, then the action is not an armed attack and another State has no right of forcible action to terminate the action, even if it involves breaches of the standards of the counter-terrorist treaties.

CONCLUSIONS

This then is the limit of international co-operation. Initially, it must be achieved by treaty. Successful co-operation on one matter or between a few States may lead to its imitation on other matters or between different States. Widespread co-operation may even lead to modification of the customary standards which made the treaty action necessary in the first place – it appears that this may have happened on the reach of criminal jurisdiction. Certainly the extent of the treaty network, the uniformity of approach and the number of States parties suggest that the counter-terrorist treaties represent a significant pattern of jurisdictional State practice. As Michael Akehurst himself wrote with some prescience in 1972, before many of the conventions discussed above were concluded: 'if other States do not protest against the conclusion or execution of such treaties, one is entitled to infer that there is a permissive rule of international law authorising such action'.

There is, however, no evidence to suggest that there has been a similar development in relation to the move to establish a general obligation of extradition of terrorists. However intense co-operation has become, it has not disturbed the fundamental principles of international law: States are to refrain from unilateral acts of armed force and to respect the territorial integrity and right of non-intervention of other States. If further action to enforce co-operation be required (and if the notion is comprehensible), it must be done under the authority of the Security Council within the limits of its competence under Chapter VII.

NOTES

1 See David Freestone, 'Legal Responses to Terrorism', in J. Lodge (ed.), *Terrorism: a Challenge to the State*, London: Martin Robertson, 1981, pp.195–224.

2 Among several, see General Assembly Resolution 3034(XXVII), 40/61, 42/159 and debate in Sixth Committee A/C.6/42/SR29–34; Security Council Resolution 579. A. Cassese, 'The International Community's "Legal" Response to Terrorism' (1989) 38 *I.C.L.Q.* 589; A. Sofaer, 'Terrorism and the Law' (1986) 64 *Foreign Affairs* 901.

3 Among an extensive literature, see particularly Nancy D. Joyner, *Aerial Hijacking as an International Crime*, Dobbs Ferry, NY: Oceana, 1974; Lewis M. Bloomfield and Gerald F. Fitzgerald, *Crimes against Internationally Protected Persons: Prevention and Punishment*, New York: Praeger, 1975; Joseph S. Lambert, *Terrorism and Hostages in International Law*, Cambridge: Grotius, 1990; Natilano Ronzitti (ed.) *Maritime Terrorism and International Law*, Dordrecht: Martinus Nijhoff, 1990.

4 For a brief but contemporary assessment, see *Extraterritorial Criminal Jurisdiction: Report of the European Committee on Crime Problems*, Strasbourg: Council of Europe, 1990. For a more detailed account, see M. Akehurst, 'Jurisdiction in International Law' (1972–73) 46 *B.Y.I.L.* 145.

5 In general, see G. Gilbert, *Aspects of Extradition Law*, Dordrecht: Martinus Nijhoff, 1991.

6 For the United Kingdom, see I. Macdonald, *Immigration Law and Practice in the United Kingdom*, London: Butterworths 1991, ch.15.

7 C. Wijngaert, 'Applying the European Convention on Human Rights to Extradition: Opening Pandora's Box' (1990) 39 *I.C.L.Q.* 757.

8 United Kingdom Extradition Act 1989, s.2.

9 E.T.S. No.24 (1957).

10 See p.148 below.

11 For example, *R* v. *Governor of Winson Green Prison Birmingham ex parte Littlejohn* [1975] 1 W.L.R. 893; *Kelly and McFarlane* v. *Netherlands* European Commission of Human Rights, App. No.12543/86, 10 E.H.R.R. 161.

12 A. Connelly, 'Ireland and the Political Offence Exception to Extradition' (1985) 12 *Journal of Law and Society* 153; T. Carbonneau, 'The Political Offence Exemption as Applied in French cases dealing with the Extradition of International Terrorists' (1983) *Michigan Yearbook of International Legal Studies* 109.

13 For example, in the case of the Irish government agreement in October 1979 (concluded after the murder of Lord Mountbatten in August 1979) to permit UK helicopters to fly 10 km into Irish airspace. For general discussion see J. Lodge and D. Freestone, 'The European Community and Terrorism', in Y. Alexander and K. Myers (eds) *Terrorism in Europe*, London: Croom Helm, 1982, pp.79, 91. See also the Schengen Agreement, below n. 64.

14 The Israeli trial court in *Attorney-General of the Government of Israel* v. *Eichmann* (1961) 36 I.L.R. 5 (at para. 41, citing the English case *Ex parte Elliott* [1949] 1 All E.R. 373) found 'an established rule of law that a person being tried for an offence against the laws of the State may not oppose his trial by reason of the illegality of his arrest or of the means by which he was brought within the jurisdiction of that State.'

15 In the *Lawler Incident* (McNair, *Law Officers Opinions*, (1956) vol.1, 78) the British Law Officers found such a duty, but in the *Savarkar* case (Scott, *Hague Court Reports* 275, 279) the Permanent Court of Arbitration refused the return of a fugitive who had been illegally handed over to the UK authorities as a result of a mistake by a French policeman. J.E.S. Fawcett (1962) 38 *B.Y.I.L.* 181, suggests some important limitations on the right to demand the return of a fugitive in such circumstances which are particularly germane for the present discussion, namely 'that the State [demanding reconduction] is the *forum conveniens* for his trial, and that it declares an intention to put him on trial. If these conditions are not satisfied, then the State must accept reparation in another form, since otherwise the interests of justice would be defeated.'

16 See, for example, A.V. Lowe (ed.) *Extraterritorial Jurisdiction*, Cambridge: Grotius, p.198.

17 *Quaere*, does silence in the face of an assertion of extraterritorial criminal competence constitute acquiescence for the purpose of the evolution of customary law? Does the promulgation of a law claiming jurisdictional competence constitute a claim for these purposes or does a trial (or even a conviction or sentence of punishment) have to take place? On this see Akehurst, above n.4, cited p.154 below.

18 For text of proposed League of Nations Convention see M. O. Hudson (ed.) *International Legislation*, Washington: Carnegie Endowment for International Peace, 1950, vol.7, pp.865. This is also reproduced in M. Cherif Bassiouni, *International Crimes: Digest and Index of International Instruments, 1815–1985*, 2 vols, Dobbs Ferry, NY: Oceana, 1985, at vol.2, p.44. The idea of an International Criminal Court has, of course, persisted, see Benjamin Ferencz, *An International Criminal Court*, 2 vols, Dobbs Ferry, NY: Oceana, 1980.

19 (1969) *U.K.T.S.* 126, Cmnd. 4230; Bassiouni, above n.18, vol.2, p.47. Entered into force 4 December 1969. At 1 January 1991, 138 parties.

20 This was clearly recognised by the UK implementing legislation. The 1967 UK Tokyo Convention Act included Articles 15–17 (on piracy) of the 1958 Geneva Convention on the High Seas as a schedule and s.5 of the 1982 Consolidation Act specifically uses the term 'air piracy'.

21 Article 4, Tokyo Convention.

22 (1971) 10 *I.L.M.* 133; (1972) *U.K.T.S.* 39, Cmnd. 4965; Bassiouni, above n.18, vol.2, p.50. Entered into force 4 December 1971. At 1 January 1991, 144 parties.

23 (1971) *U.K.T.S.* 10, Cmnd. 5524; Bassiouni, above n.18, vol.2, p.54. Entered into force 26 January 1973. At 1 January 1991, 143 parties. The Montreal Convention now has a 1988 Protocol for the Suppression of Unlawful Acts of Violence at Airports serving International Civil Aviation, signed 24 February 1988, Misc. 6 (1988) Cm 378; ICAO Doc 9518. At 1 January 1991, 28 parties. It is noteworthy that 1969 and 1970 were the worst two years for aerial hijackings, see A. E. Evans and J. F. Murphy, *Legal Aspects of International Terrorism*, Lexington, Mass.: American Society of International Law, 1978.

24 Reproduced (1978) 17 *I.L.M.* 1285.

25 Misc. 19 (1975) Cmnd. 6176; Bassiouni, above n.18, vol.2, p.75. Entered into force 20 February 1977. At 1 January 1991, 78 parties.

26 (1979) 18 *I.L.M.* 1456; Bassiouni, above n.18, vol.2, p.89. Entered into force 4 June 1983. At 1 January 1991, 62 parties.

27 (1979) 18 *I.L.M.* 1419; Misc. 27 (1980); Bassiouni, above n.18, vol.2, p.306. Entered into force 8 February 1987. At 1 January 1991, 28 parties.

28 Reproduced (1988) 3 *International Journal of Estuarine and Coastal Law* 317. At 1 January 1991, 9 parties to Convention and Protocol. For detailed comments on the Convention see D. Freestone (1988) 3 *International Journal of Estuarine and Coastal Law* 305 and G. Plant (1990) 39 *I.C.L.Q.* 27.

29 Article 1 reads:

> 1. Any person commits an offence if he unlawfully and intentionally:
> (a) performs an act of violence against a person on board an aircraft in flight if that act is likely to endanger the safety of that aircraft; or
> (b) destroys an aircraft in service or causes damage to such an aircraft which renders it incapable of flight or which is likely to endanger its safety in flight; or
> (c) places or causes to be placed on an aircraft in service, by any means whatsoever, a device or substance which is likely to destroy the aircraft, or to cause damage to it which renders it incapable of flight, or to cause damage to it which is likely to endanger its safety in flight; or
> (d) destroys or damages air navigation facilities or interferes with their operation, if any such act is likely to endanger the safety of aircraft in flight; or
> (e) communicates information which he knows to be false, thereby endangering the safety of an aircraft in flight.

30 Article 1:

> 1. Any person who seizes or detains and threatens to kill, to injure or to continue to detain another person (hereinafter referred to as the 'hostage') in order to compel a third party, namely a State, an international intergovernmental organisation, a natural or a juridical person, or a group of persons, to do or abstain from doing any act as an explicit or implicit

condition for the release of the hostage commits the offence of hostage-taking within the meaning of this convention.

31 See, for example, G. Williams, 'Venue and Ambit of the Criminal Law' (1965) 81 *L.Q.R.* 276. See also J. D. M. Lew, 'The Extraterritorial Criminal Jurisdiction of the English Courts' (1978) 27 *I.C.L.Q.* 168.

32 Article 4 provides:

A Contracting State which is not the State of registration may not interfere with an aircraft in flight in order to exercise criminal jurisdiction over an offence committed on board *except* [emphasis added] in the following cases:
a) the offence has effect on the territory of such State;
b) the offence has been committed by or against a national or permanent resident of such State;
c) the offence is against the security of such State;
d) the offence consists of a breach of any rules or regulations relating to the flight or manoeuvre of aircraft in force in such State;
e) the exercise of jurisdiction is necessary to ensure the observance of any obligation of such State under a multilateral international agreement.

33 It was understood at the Hague Conference that aircraft need not be registered in a contracting State for the Convention to apply.

34 In relation to war crimes, universality jurisdiction was claimed by the UN War Crimes Commission, (1949) 15 *War Crimes Reports* 26. The Israeli court claimed universality jurisdiction over genocide in *Attorney-General of Israel* v. *Eichmann* (1961) *I.L.R.* 5, but this claim does involve a controversial interpretation of Article VI of the 1948 Genocide Convention (see para. 22 of judgment). Note also such claims in 1961 Single Convention on Narcotic Drugs, 520 *U.N.T.S.* 204, and Convention on the Suppression and Punishment of Apartheid, (1974) 13 *I.L.M.* 50.

35 Article 5(2), Montreal Convention; Article 5(2), Hostages Convention; Article 5(2), IPP Convention; Article 8(2), IAEA Convention; Article 6(4), IMO Convention.

36 The *North Sea Continental Shelf* cases [1969] I.C.J. Rep. 3 contain a classic formulation of the requirements for the establishment of a rule of custom, namely evidence of a uniformity or consistency of practice; of a generality of practice; of duration of that practice over time (although if the first two have been established, the short passage of time will not in itself be a obstruction); and, arguably the most significant in the establishment of new rules, of the psychological element '*opinio juris sive necessitatis* – the 'conception that the practice is required by, or consistent with, prevailing international law'. See also *Nicaragua* v. *US (Merits)* [1986] I.C.J. Rep. 14 and, for comment I. Brownlie, *Principles of Public International Law*, Oxford: Clarendon Press, 4th edn, 1991, p.7.

37 See p.138 above.

38 This argument is developed by the present author in 'International Cooperation against Terrorism and the Development of International Law Principles of Jurisdiction', in M. Flory and R. Higgins (eds) *Terrorism and International Law: Anglo-French Perspectives*, forthcoming 1994.

39 See, for example, J.L. Brierly, *The Law of Nations*, Oxford: Oxford University Press, 6th edn, 1963, pp.299–304; and (1928) 44 *L.Q.R.* 154, 161.

40 [1927] P.C.I.J., Series A, No. 10.

41 US legislation s.1203, 18 USC, Pub.L. No. 98–473, ch.9, and 2.2002(a) 98 Stat. 1976, 2186, and France, see n. 38 above. For a wider discussion see C.R. Blakesley, 'Jurisdictional Issues and Conflicts of Jurisdiction', in M.

Cherif Bassiouni (ed.) *Legal Responses to Terrorism: US Procedural Aspects*, Dordrecht: Martinus Nijhoff, 1988, pp.131–79.

42 Whether the principle may only be utilised in relation to certain offences would require an examination of state practice outside the scope of this paper.

43 *Extraterritorial Criminal Jurisdiction*, above n. 4.

44 On extradition generally see M.C. Bassiouni, *International Extradition and World Public Order*, Dobbs Ferry, NY: Oceana Leiden: Sijthoff, 1974; and I.A. Shearer, *Extradition in International Law*, Manchester: Manchester University Press, 1971.

45 Section 1(1) provides: 'A person, whatever his nationality, who, in the United Kingdom *or elsewhere*, – (a) detains any person ("the hostage"), and (b) in order to compel a State, international organisation or person to do or abstain from doing any act, threatens to kill, injure or continue to detain the hostage commits an offence' (emphasis added).

Section 3(4) reads: '(4) For the purposes of the [Extradition] Act of 1870 any act, wherever committed, which – (a) is an offence under this Act or an attempt to commit such an offence, and (b) is an offence against the law of any State in the case of which that Act is applied . . . shall be deemed to be an offence committed within the jurisdiction of that State.'

46 Text in Bassiouni, above n.18, vol.2, p.72. Entered into force 16 October 1973.

47 E.T.S. No. 90; (1977) *U.K.T.S.* 93; Bassiouni, above n.18, vol.2, p.58. Entered into force 4 August 1978. At 1 January 1991, 21 parties. For a more extended discussion see D. Freestone, in Lodge, above n.1, pp.211ff, and D. Freestone, 'The EEC and Common Article on Terrorism' (1984) *Yearbook of European Law* 207, at pp.211ff.

48 Article 2. Note that both Articles 1 and 2 include attempts to commit, participation as an accomplice in, and participation as an accomplice in attempts to commit such offences.

49 By Article 7.

50 Article 6.

51 A.V. Lowe and J.R. Young, 'Suppressing Terrorism under the European Convention: a British perspective' (1978) 25 *Neth. I.L.R.* 305.

52 1978 Suppression of Terrorism Act (cap. 26), section 4(1).

53 Ibid., section 4(3).

54 1982 Aviation Security Act consolidates the Hijacking Act.

55 See, for example, P. Wilkinson, 'Problems of Establishing a European Judicial Area', Report to *Conference on Democracy against Terrorism in Europe: Tasks and Problems*, Strasbourg, November 1980, AS/Pol/Coll/Terr(32)6, p.4.

56 These are, in fact, the terms of the 1974 Resolution of the Council of Europe Committee of Ministers.

57 See, for example, Wilkinson, above n.55, and contra J.J.A. Salmon, 'La Convention européene pour la repression du terrorisme: un vrai pas en arriere' (1977) *J.T.* 497 (24 September 1977); and G. Soulier, 'European Integration and the Suppression of Terrorism' (1978) *Review of Contemporary Law* 21.

58 Cmnd 7823. See further M. C. Wood (1981) 1 *Yearbook of European Law* 307; and D. Freestone (1984) 4 *Yearbook of European Law* 207. At 1 January 1991, 5 parties (Belgium, France, Italy, Luxembourg and Netherlands).

59 See further Freestone, ibid.

60 It was alleged that this was the result of Dutch opposition – ostensibly because of certain technical provisions of the Convention – but *Le Monde* reported that this was, in fact, in retaliation for French blocking of Dutch proposals for the desalination of the Rhine. As a result of the failure of the 1980 draft, it was reported that France refused to ratify the ECST or the Dublin Agree-

ment. See further J. Kelly, 'Problems of Establishing a European Judicial Area', *Report to Conference on Democracy against Terrorism in Europe*, Strasbourg, November 1980, AS/Pol/Coll/Terr(32)8.

61 Mention should also be made of another EC arrangement concluded after the Libyan Embassy siege which covers, one presumes, attacks by diplomats rather than against them. On 11 September 1984 the EC Foreign Ministers in Dublin concluded a set of measures 'to combat terrorism and abuse of diplomatic immunity' (*The Times*, 1 September 1984 and (1983–4) *H.C.* 499-iii, 51).

62 Report drawn up on behalf of the Legal Affairs Committee on the European Judicial Area (Extradition), Rapporteur A. Tyrrell, EP Doc. 1–318/82. For an extended discussion see D. Freestone (1984) 4 *Yearbook of European Law* 207ff.

63 Article 46 of the draft treaty provided: 'In addition to the fields subject to common action, the co-ordination of national law with a view to constituting a homogeneous judicial area shall be carried out in accordance with the method of co-operation. For further comments see, for example, D. Freestone and S. Davidson, in J. Lodge (ed.) *European Union: the EC in Search of a Future*, New York: St Martins Press, 1984.

64 Convention applying the Schengen Agreement of 14 June 1985 between the governments of the States of the Benelux Economic Union, the Federal Republic of Germany and the French Republic on the gradual abolition of checks at their common border, 19 June 1990, Schengen. (1991) 30 *I.L.M.* 68, see particularly Title III on Police and Security which provides a number of mechanisms for co-operation for, *inter alia*, counter-terrorist work, and Article 41 which allows police a reciprocal right of 'hot pursuit' across frontiers. Under ch.4 parties also agree to apply the European Convention of Extradition between themselves even if one State is not a party (Article 60).

65 Text in 1992 C.191, 29 July 1992.

66 *Aerial Incident at Lockerbie* (*Libya* v. *US, UK*) (*Provisional Measures*) [1992] I.C.J. Rep. 3, text in (1992) 31 *I.L.M.* 662. See M. Weller, 'The Lockerbie Case: a Premature End to the New World Order?' (1992) 4 *Revue Africaine de Droit International et Compare* 302; F. Beveridge, 'The Lockerbie Affair' (1992) 41 *I.C.L.Q.* 907.

67 'Terrorism' is included in the Draft Code of Crimes being prepared by the International Law Commission. See draft articles on the Draft Code of Crimes against the Peace and Security of Mankind, Article 24, text in (1991) *I.L.M.* 1584, at p.1592.

68 A good indication of what might be expected can be gained from the French reaction to the *Rainbow Warrior* affair, see Memorandum of France, in *Ruling of the Secretary-General in the Rainbow Warrior Affair* (1987) 74 I.L.R. 256, at p.264.

69 See Cassese, above n.2.

70 See Libyan letter to the UN Secretary-General, 8 January 1992, text in (1992) 31 *I.L.M.* 725–7.

71 *U.K.T.S.* No.10 (1974), Cmnd. 5524.

72 Article 7.

73 See Weller, above n.66, pp.309–12.

74 See Beveridge, above n.66, pp.912–16.

75 *Lockerbie* case, above n.66, paras.42–44.

76 On this question in general, see Richard J. Erikson, *Legitimate Use of Military Force against State-Sponsored International Terrorism*, Maxwell Air Force Base, Alabama: Air University Press, 1989.

77 *Case Concerning Military and Paramilitary Activities in and against Nicaragua (Merits)* [1986] I.C.J. Rep. 14.

8 The principle of co-operation: United Nations peacekeeping

Alan James

Insofar as its central purpose – the maintenance of peace – is concerned, the UN Charter speaks in an authoritative rather than a co-operative mode. Responsibility for the achievement of this purpose is 'primar[ily]'[1] bestowed on the Organization's Security Council, initially composed of five permanent and six non-permanent members. All members agree that in this matter the Council 'acts on their behalf',[2] and, therefore, that they will 'accept and carry out'[3] its decisions. When the Security Council has 'determine[d]'[4] the existence of any threat to or breach of the peace or an act of aggression, it is empowered to 'decide what measures not involving the use of armed force are to be employed to give effect to its decisions'.[5] And, in the event of such measures proving insufficient, it may 'take such action by air, sea, or land forces as may be necessary to restore international peace and security'.[6] On the face of it, the international society of states has placed the key issue of the maintenance of peace under centralised control. Something which looks very like the scaffolding for a world state has apparently been erected.

In 1945 this scheme was widely acclaimed on the ground that it would supply the UN with what its unhappy predecessor, the League of Nations, was deemed fatally to have lacked: teeth. A leading international lawyer, however, expressed dissent. Professor James Brierly suggested that in moving from what he characterised as the co-operative to the corporative or organic[7] approach, the world had saddled itself with an inappropriate arrangement. As he put it, 'what we have done is to exchange a scheme which might or might not have worked for one which cannot work'.[8] His argument was that by making the operation of the Charter's security provisions dependent on the Council taking 'an affirmative vote of seven members including the concurring votes of the [five] permanent members',[9] an obstacle of huge magnitude had been placed in the way of strong UN action in support of international peace. In his view, the co-operative emphasis of the League Covenant, under which it was up to each member state to decide whether a member had unlawfully gone to war and had therefore made itself liable to sanctions, was much more realistic and therefore satisfactory.

The early onset of the Cold War underlined the validity of Brierly's analysis – with a vengeance. For this development transformed the Security Council from the Charter's intended band of law-enforcing brothers into an acrimonious debating chamber, generating much heat but little action – and none of the powerful peace-maintaining kind which had been envisaged. The war-time unity of the permanent members had been deeply fractured, and each of the two political camps emerging from the erstwhile alliance regarded the other as the main threat to peace. The UN's members no longer being united, they could not act together to keep the peace. Accordingly, as a means to this end the UN was soon seen as not much better than useless.

Had Brierly been writing a little later than 1946, he might have seen some unintended virtue in the UN's security scheme. For the voting provisions which governed all decision-making did make it very hard for the Organization's mantle to be hijacked in East-West confrontations by the camp – the West – which was then firmly in the majority in the Security Council, and also in the UN as a whole. Something of this kind did take place, in unusual institutional circumstances, in the Korean Crisis of 1950.[10] Had such stratagems been easier, the West would almost certainly have taken advantage of them. This could well have resulted in the Soviet Union and associates walking, *de facto,*[11] out of the UN, and perhaps being suspended or even expelled from it. The UN would thereby have lost its claim to be, at least potentially, a world-wide organisation.

Any such addition to Brierly's argument, however, would in no way have diminished its basic thrust. For what in essence he was saying, and very rightly so, was that in a world of sovereign states there are sharp limits to the extent to which important functions can be centralised. Such an arrangement implies a willingness on the part of states to accept the decisions which emanate from the centre. But as a practical matter, this willingness is absent on issues of any significance. Accordingly, either the decision-making procedures will be difficult to operate, due to certain states being given a veto (as was done in the UN Charter), or decisions are likely to be flouted. Putting the matter the other way around, the majority voting which is implicit in effective centralisation only works where there is a high measure of social harmony, such as enables the minority to have trust in the behaviour of the majority. This was not the position in 1945, not even among the members of the victorious alliance.

In this sort of context, joint action best emerges not in consequence of dictates from above but as the outcome of individual decisions from below, taken by the several states concerned. In other words, the key to collaboration is voluntary co-operation. Individual states, in the light of their own conceptions of their obligations and interests, will from time to time come together on a bilateral or multilateral basis to advance their common purposes. It may be that they will do so in response to the initiative of an international organisation, such as the UN; or they may themselves decide to try to channel their co-operation through such a body. In either case the resultant action reflects the fundamental character of the international society of states – where jurisdiction is not concentrated at the centre but is divided up on a territorial basis.

Maybe, therefore, it was not by chance that the UN, having perforce abandoned the unrealistic enforcement scheme set out in the Charter, found itself adopting other measures to assist in the maintenance of international peace which were unquestionably rooted – and rooted very firmly – in the principle of co-operation. Such measures were, before long, characterised as 'peacekeeping'.

UN PEACEKEEPING FORCES AND OBSERVER GROUPS

From the point of view of their composition, such operations fall, broadly speaking, into two categories: forces and observer groups. The latter are made up of individual military officers; the former consist, or have at their core, a number of national battalions. Both will be under the direction of an individual who, in that capacity, will be a member of the UN Secretariat. In the past this individual has generally been a military man, but in the case of missions where civilians play a large operational part, the overall leadership will also be in civilian hands. Whether military or civilian, the commander will be under the immediate authority of the UN Secretary-General. In turn, the Secretary-General will be responsible to the UN political organ, almost invariably the Security Council, which established the operation in question.

Since 1970 the UN has established seven peacekeeping forces, and an eighth, in Cyprus (1964–), dates from before that time. These are the Second Emergency Force in Egypt between her forces and those of Israel (1973–9); the Disengagement Observer Force between Israeli and Syrian forces (1974–); the Interim Force in (South) Lebanon (1978–); the Transition Assistance Group in Namibia (1989–90); and the Mission for the Referendum in Western Sahara, which was established in 1991 but the full deployment of which has, been postponed; the Transitional Authority in Cambodia (1992–); and the Protection Force in parts of former Yugoslavia (1992–). A relatively large civilian element was, or will be, included in the Namibian, Western Sahara, and Cambodian missions. It is expected that the latter is likely to be 'the biggest and most complex'[12] in the UN's history. (The biggest hitherto was that in the Congo – now Zaire – in the early 1960s. It included 20,000 troops and a large civilian component.)

If a broad definition of peacekeeping is adopted, thirteen new observer groups can be identified since 1970, with two continuing from the earlier period. The latter two are in the Middle East (1948–) and Kashmir (1949–). The new ones relate to allegations of attacks on purely civilian targets in the Iran-Iraq war (1984–8), and the supervision of the subsequent cease-fire (1988–91); the monitoring of a demilitarised zone between Iraq and

Kuwait (1991–), and the provision of security in relief centres in northern Iraq (1991–)[13]; the supervision of the withdrawal of Soviet troops from Afghanistan (1988–90), and the search for a solution to the continuing conflict in that country (1990–); the withdrawal of Soviet-supported Cuban troops from Angola (1988–91), and the ending of the Angolan civil war (1991–); the peace process in Central America (1989–); the supervision of elections in Nicaragua (1989–90) and Haiti (1990–1); the ending of the civil war in El Salvador (1991–) and a cease-fire and humanitarian operation in Somalia (1992–).

THE CO-OPERATIVE NATURE OF UN PEACEKEEPING

The use of the term 'peacekeeping' to designate and describe the UN's main direct contribution to international peace is perhaps somewhat unfortunate, for it suggests a more forceful and authoritative activity than that which takes place under this rubric. In fact, the activity which has been conceptualised as peacekeeping is in essence and at all levels of a secondary nature, in the sense that it is dependent, in respect of its origin, operation, and success, on the willingness of various of the UN's member states to co-operate with the Organization. This can be seen in each of the following five key areas: the process of authorisation for a peacekeeping mission; the provision of personnel for it; its financing; the presence of such a mission on the territory of a particular state or states; and its effectiveness.

Authorisation

As with any notional or corporate entity, the UN can only act through an individual or a group of persons, and legitimate action requires the receipt of authorisation so to proceed from an appropriate UN organ. It happens that in this respect the UN Secretary-General is in a slightly ambiguous position – but only very slightly, for while he is quite widely seen as in some way embodying the UN as a whole, and in possession of a quasi-independent political base, in fact his independence is very limited.[14]

Especially is this so with regard to the establishment of peacekeeping operations. If they are exceedingly small, and politically innocuous, it may be that they can be set up by the Secretary-General without specific authorisation. In the case of the inspection teams sent to Iran and Iraq in 1984, for example, the Secretary-General simply informed the Security Council of what he was doing. This procedure was even followed over the establishment of the Mission regarding Afghanistan, although that was more a result of concern about Soviet sensitivities than of independent action by the Secretary-General (and the Council came formally into the picture six months later). On the mission's withdrawal, the retention of some military personnel by the diplomatic body which took its place was a consequence of a decision by the Secretary-General, the Council being informed. The civilian mission to supervise the Nicaraguan elections was also set up in this way, except that here it was the General Assembly which was the organ to whom the Secretary-General made an immediate report.

However, two points must be borne in mind. The first is that in all these matters there would assuredly have been close contact between the Secretary-General and the key member states of the relevant political organ. In other words, the Secretary-General would in effect have obtained political clearance in advance for what he proposed. Secondly, had any of these operations become politically controversial, the Assembly or the Council would either have done a lot of public hand-washing or, in one way or another, have ensured its involvement, and hence its control. States are unwilling to let the Secretary-General lose sight of the fact that the UN is an association of sovereign states who, collectively, are going to call all the significant tunes. The Secretary-General has no real option but to dance to them.

Thus virtually all the peacekeeping operations itemised above have been established by the UN's political organs, and of those all but one – the supervision of elections in Haiti (which was authorised by the General Assembly) – by the Security Council. Moreover, none of these authorisations were, in point of time, open-ended. All set a defined and fairly limited period for the operation in question. This means that any extensions have also to be specifically approved by the political organ in question. Consequentially, 9 of the 15 Security Council members have to vote in favour of setting up a mission and for each extension of its mandate, and a negative vote from any of the Council's five permanent members has at all times to be avoided. In 1979, for example, it was the knowledge that the Soviet Union would veto the renewal of the mandate of the Second UN Emergency Force in Sinai, which had had an important future mapped out for it in the Egyptian-Israeli Peace Treaty of that year, that led to the demise of the Force.[15] In this formal sense, therefore, co-operation is necessary for the authorisation of UN peacekeeping missions.

In deciding how to vote, each state will, of course, consult its own interests, and they will be the overriding determinant. But it is also the case that there will be extensive private discussion among the Council's members before a matter comes to a public session of the Council. This has been particularly marked in recent years, and among the 'Permanent Five' it has been taken to the extent of institutionalisation.[16] Indeed, and in sharp contrast to the years of the Cold War, public sessions of the Council tend nowadays to be brief and colourless affairs. But in the prior private occasions there will almost certainly have been a good deal of give and take regarding the details of the draft resolutions. There is, therefore, not just a formal but a very real sense in which international co-operation between certain states is an integral part of the authorisation process.

Personnel

Having a large Secretariat, there are certain elements of a peacekeeping operation which the UN is itself able, or might be able, to provide. The Field Operations Division is staffed by people who have accepted the contingency of service abroad, and can therefore supply the basic administrative and some of the technical backing which a peacekeeping mission will require. *Ad hoc* recruitment in the marketplace is also possible for certain types of work.

For operations which require a relatively large professional-level civilian component, the Headquarters staff can be asked if they want to be considered for such a role. The Transition Assistance Group in Namibia is an outstanding instance of this, a staff of about 450 international officials being mustered (perhaps 'plundered' would be a better word) not just for the general administration of Untag but also to run the network of regional and district offices which were established throughout Namibia. Their job was to explain what was going on, assist in the much needed process of internal reconciliation, and provide Untag's headquarters with a steady flow of reliable information about local developments. Additionally, for the election which was, in one sense, the culminating point of the transition period, about 500 Secretariat members from outside Namibia were recruited to assist with the task of supervising the South African-run process.[17] Something of the same kind, albeit on a much lesser scale, will happen in respect of the operation in Western Sahara. And if the Cambodian operation gets off the ground, it is likely to make large requests of Headquarters staff – although whether they will be as willing to serve there with the same readiness with which many of them volunteered for Namibia remains to be seen.

Another way in which the UN is able to draw on its own staff for peacekeeping duties is seen in the putting together in mid–1991 of its Guard Contingent in northern Iraq (although this is not seen at UN Headquarters as a peacekeeping operation). The Contingent was sent to the Kurdish refugee camps – the 'safe havens' as they were called – to provide some kind of substitute for the American, British and French troops which had been guarding the camps since their establishment in the aftermath of the expulsion of Iraq from Kuwait. By agreement with Iraq, a limit of 500 was placed on the Contingent,[18] and it was hoped that the necessary personnel could be recruited from security staff at the UN's offices in New York, Geneva and Vienna, plus other staff with some experience in security duties.[19] However, not many more than 100 signed up, and for the rest the UN turned to its member states.[20]

This last experience draws attention to the basic point that for certain kinds of specialised personnel the UN is entirely dependent on its member states. Most notably this is so in respect of the military, who are at the core of (virtually) all operations which can be seen as having a connection with international peace. It is also true of police, who in the last few years have made increasingly frequent appearances in peacekeeping missions – in Namibia,[21] Western Sahara,[22] the second Angolan operation,[23] and El Salvador,[24] and possibly also in the guise of 'security experts'[25] in Haiti. Such people are not on the UN payroll, and as the Organization has no territorial jurisdiction it cannot assert a claim to their services. Accordingly, it has to go to its members.

In so doing certain limitations have to be borne in mind. It used to be the case in respect of UN forces that the permanent members of the Security Council were not looked to for contingents, except in very special circumstances, of which the United Kingdom battalion in the Cyprus Force and that of France in Lebanon were the two exceptions. Such a restriction does not now apply. However, in each particular case the Secretary-General has to have an eye to any political factors which bear on the desirable composition of a force or observer group; to the technical requirements of the mission in question, especially the provision of specialist services for a UN force, such as signalling and engineering; to linguistic needs and competences; and to the political susceptibilities of the host state or states (on which more will be said below). The fact that some contingents will come better equipped than others may also need to be considered.

However, there is no question of simply calling up particular national contingents, or of telling a state how many military observers are needed. Essentially, the UN is a suppliant. In practice, there has been little overall problem on this score, as a large number of states have, for one understandable reason or another, shown a willingness and even a keenness to get involved in peacekeeping missions. This has found reflection in the increased number of contributors in recently established operations: the military in Namibia came from 20 states and the police from 25;[26] the observers in the Iran-Iraq Observer Group came from 26 states,[27] and in that on the Iraq-Kuwait border from no less than 33, including all five permanent members of the Security Council (a 'first');[28] and 24 states are contributing observers to the second Angolan mission.[29] Moreover, 36 states have agreed to contribute to the military unit of the Referendum Mission in Western Sahara – including, again, the Permanent Five,[30] and 28 to the Transitional Authority in Cambodia.[31] One 'traditional' peacekeeper – Canada – did decline to contribute to the UN Guards in northern Iraq. It remains to be seen whether, in the light of the difficulties being experienced in former Yugoslavia, and ones which may yet be encountered in Cambodia and elsewhere, some desirable contributors will be less than enthusiastic over responding positively to an enquiry from the Secretary-General about the availability of their personnel.[32] But even if that proves not to be so, it must be remembered that the UN, as such, has no carrots to wave or sticks to wield in this connection, but must rely, wholly, on the co-operation of its relevant member states.

Financing

In law, the financing of peacekeeping operations is not usually a voluntary matter. As with personnel (and even more so), the UN has to turn to its member states for the necessary resources. But in respect of the costs of peacekeeping the Organization generally has a clear right to claim the relevant sums, and the members an equally clear obligation to make payment.

There can be exceptions to this position. Due to the financial position of the UN at the time of the establishment of the UN Force in Cyprus, it has, thus far, been financed on a voluntary basis.[33] And the Guard Contingent in northern Iraq, being seen as part of the UN's humanitarian work in that country, is similarly supported. In general, the costs of peacekeeping – which, like all UN expenditures, have to be approved by the General Assembly – are treated as 'expenses of the Organization', and hence are to be borne by 'the Members as apportioned by the General Assembly'.[34] This is done in one of two ways. Small operations may be financed as part of the regular budget, in which case the liability of members will be in proportion to their general liability for the UN's expenses (which ranges from 25 per cent to 0.01 per cent). But differential apportionments may be made on other bases in respect of expenditures which are included in special (i.e. separate) accounts. Larger operations tend to be given such special accounts, and it has become customary in these cases to adopt a modified version of the usual budgetary scale, requiring the permanent members of the Security Council to pay more so as to provide some relief for their less well-off brethren.[35]

Payment is due within 50 days of the receipt of the letter informing members of their financial obligations, or the first day of the year to which those obligations relate, whichever is the later. Unfortunately that is frequently the beginning rather than the end of the matter, for an appreciable number of members are, to understate, slow to pay up. Some may have difficulty in finding the money or – in the notable case of the United States – have problems in getting it authorised by their legislative bodies. Others may withhold payment for as long as possible, so as to have the money available for their own use. And yet others may refuse to pay on some political ground connected with the operation in question. The result is that the UN's large long-running peacekeeping operations are in financial disarray, which in turn means that the UN is way behind in reimbursing states who contribute personnel to these operations for the extra costs which their co-operation has brought them. Thus in the case of the Interim Force in Lebanon, which has an annual budget of in the region of $US150 million, the deficit on the account amounted in mid–1991 to about $US300 million.[36] And in the case of the voluntarily-financed Cyprus Force, the comparable figures are an annual budget of about $US31 million and a deficit of $US179 million.[37]

In respect of sums which are obligatory, the UN Charter does provide that a member which is in arrears by a sum which 'equals or exceeds the amount of the contributions due from it for the preceding two full years . . . shall have no vote in the General Assembly',[38] unless the arrears are deemed to be beyond the member's control. But this has so far been a totally ineffective sanction in relation to peacekeeping costs. In effect, therefore, the financing of such operations can be said to be on a basis which to almost all intents and purposes is voluntary. Thus this becomes another area where the UN must rely on the co-operation of its member states.

It must be added, however, that here the lack of co-operation does not have the consequences which could be imagined. The withdrawal of two states from participation in the Cyprus Force may not have been unconnected with their financial dissatisfaction.[39] But in general troop contributors to UN peacekeeping bodies do not make a large issue of their inadequate reimbursement. And the operations themselves have not been significantly hindered, let alone closed down, on account of the fragility of their finances. Evidently, the political will to keep them going outweighs the financial embarrassments to which they give rise.

Presence

As peacekeeping operations are not in the business of enforcement, they are not established under the provisions of the Charter referred to at the beginning of this chapter, which allow the Security Council to deploy a force where it wishes. It follows that a state has no obligation to accept a peacekeeping mission on its soil, for the UN has no general authority over its sovereign members.[40] The agreement of the potential host state is therefore a pre-condition of the despatch of a peacekeeping mission, and consent must also be sought for an extension of its presence beyond the period for which permission has been given. This is so even if the state concerned is in no position to resist an unauthorised presence on its soil. For much of the life of the UN's Lebanese Force, for example, the government of Lebanon has had very little effective authority, and none where the Force operates. Yet its permission has always been sought, and received, prior to an extension of the Force's mandate.[41] Correspondingly, on the morrow of its crushing defeat in 1991, Iraq's refusal to accept a UN 'police presence'[42] to watch over Kurdish refugees in the northern part of its country led to the end of that idea – and to the lesser scheme for a Guard Contingent, which was accepted.

It is also the case that if a peacekeeping mission is to be based or operate on territory which is under occupation, or to which the state in control has an unclear title, the permission of that state to its presence is, practically speaking, necessary. Thus the consent of the unrecognised (except by Turkey) Turkish Republic of Northern Cyprus is, *de facto*, a requirement of the periodic continuation of the UN's Cyprus Force. The same is true of Israel in respect of the UN Force which patrols between the Syrian territory occupied (and purportedly annexed) by Israel, and the rest of Syria.[43] Likewise, the Referendum Mission in Western Sahara requires the co-operation of Morocco. The co-operation of the potential host states is indeed fundamental, as in its absence there would, quite simply, be no UN peacekeeping at all.

In the theory of the matter, what the host state agrees to is the presence of a UN body, with the composition of that body being the responsibility of the UN. But it is in no way surprising, given the present nature of the political world, that the host will also have a keen eye to the national make-up of the body in question, especially as soldiers are involved. This means that in practical terms agreement has to be obtained to the composition of the mission, giving hosts a veto over particular national contingents or observers of a particular nationality. There may be room for discussion between the UN Secretariat and the host over aspects of this question, as happened in respect of the Transition Assistance Group in Namibia. Initially, South Africa objected to the inclusion of Canadian troops, but was persuaded to accept them. The South African government also raised certain questions about the appropriateness of Australian military participation, but was satisfied by the UN's response. They persisted, however, in blackballing Nigeria and Sweden – making this one of the very few UN peacekeeping bodies to which Sweden made no military contribution.[44] In the case of the Observer Group set up in 1988 to watch over the Iran-Iraq cease-fire, Australians could be deployed only in Iran, because of Iraq's refusal to have them on the Iraqi side of the line.[45] Analogously, Israel has for many years refused to co-operate with contingents or observers from states which have not recognised Israel or have broken off diplomatic relations with the country. One result of this is that the relatively large group of Soviet nationals in the UN's Middle East Observer Group has been markedly underemployed.

There is a final twist to the link between co-operation and the presence of peacekeeping bodies. It concerns their withdrawal. Much ink and emotion was expended on this subject following the 1967 departure from Sinai, at the host's – Egypt's – request, of the (First) UN Emergency Force, and the outbreak shortly thereafter of the Six Day War. Many took the view that the UN Force had gone too quietly or, indeed, that it should not have gone at all. But at the level of practicalities it seems very clear that a peacekeeping body, which will be relatively small and at best lightly armed, cannot maintain itself against the will of the host state. And in terms of law, unless the host state(s) has specifically agreed to the contrary (as Egypt and Israel did in their abortive plan for a post-Peace Treaty role in Sinai for a UN force), there seems no ground on which the UN can resist a request for the withdrawal of a peacekeeping body when its mandate runs out, and perhaps not even a request for an earlier departure. Here, therefore, is another aspect to the key point that the presence of a peacekeeping mission is indicative of an ongoing co-operative relationship between the UN and the host state or states.

Effectiveness

Co-operation is also of the essence in so far as the effectiveness of peacekeeping is concerned, for it is a cardinal aspect of what has come to be termed peacekeeping that this activity is of a non-threatening kind. The contingents making up a peacekeeping force will bring some weapons with them, but they will be of a sort which are suitable only for personal self-defence or for the defence of the positions which the force takes up. And the officers making up an observer group will almost certainly not be carrying any arms at all. A peacekeeping mission is not mounted to knock heads together or to expel an aggressor. Instead it plays the secondary – but by no means unimportant – role of assisting the parties to live for the time being together in peace or to settle an issue which has soured their relations. The parties are the primary actors. Accordingly, it is on their cooperation that the effectiveness of a peacekeeping mission turns.

This point deserves emphasis because it is often misunderstood. Peacekeeping bodies are neither intended nor equipped to impose themselves on the situations to which they are sent. It follows that there is no legitimate ground for criticising them for not achieving what they are not meant to achieve. It is not their purpose to make a pair of states behave in a peaceful way, or to insist on a problem's solution. Rather, it is to help the states concerned to move in one or other, or both, of these directions.

In consequence, the criterion of a body's effectiveness must be related to the end which it was set up to serve. In, for example, the case of the UN Force which sits between Israel and Syria, its efforts since 1974 have not in any obvious way diminished the bitter hostility of the two states in question. But this was not its aim. It might have been hoped in a number of quarters that the presence of the Force would have this indirect result, but its immediate job was to contribute towards calm by patrolling an area between the forces of the two sides. That it has done – and has been able to do because the parties have co-operated with it. While, therefore, a settlement of this aspect of the Arab-Israeli dispute is not in sight, that is not an adverse reflection on the Force. The same general point is applicable to the Force which occupies a buffer zone in Cyprus, and the Observer Mission which now sits in a demilitarised zone between Iraq and Kuwait.

Correspondingly, the UN was able to provide assistance of probably an essential kind in the solution of the long dispute over Namibia. Its role in the territory was not to throw South Africa out but to work with the South African government in implementing the agreed transitional agreement. This was not an entirely straightforward task, but because of South Africa's basic co-operation the UN was able to usher the new state of Namibia on to the international stage. In a similar way, the resolution of the dispute over Western Sahara will only be advanced to the extent to which the local parties amend their attitudes to each other. In that process the UN Referendum Mission can offer assistance, but unless those immediately concerned – Morocco and the Polisario movement – co-operate towards the agreed goal, the Mission will have no significant impact on the situation. The same is true of the Transitional Authority in Cambodia, except that there the parties whose co-operation will be required are internal and not international.

The importance of this point is underlined where co-operation is insufficient. The UN's Observer Group in Kashmir, for example, has been unable to make much of a contribution towards calm since, in 1972, the Indian government withdrew her co-operation. India allows the Group to remain; but in operational terms ignores it. Likewise, the UN's Force in Lebanon has, since its inception, suffered from the fact that Israel, by refusing ever to make a genuine withdrawal from that country, is less than fully co-operative. In the normal way, a peacekeeping operation would not be mounted without adequate assurances of co-operation. But in 1978 there was great political urgency about getting a formal Israeli withdrawal from Lebanon, so this aspect of the matter was not attended to with adequate care. The UN's caution in the early months of 1992 about sending a force to Yugoslavia was, in no small measure, a reflection of its awareness of the need for full co-operation from all concerned for a peacekeeping body to be effective.

THE FUTURE OF UN PEACEKEEPING

The forceful ejection of Iraq from Kuwait early in 1991, in an operation which at every stage was legitimised by the UN, has led some to envisage that a new and more powerful type of peacekeeping is at hand. This is certainly a conceptual mistake, and probably a substantive one too. Substantively, it may be doubted whether there will be many 'Kuwaits', or even authoritative interventions in states' internal affairs. Kuwait will be unusual, it may be conjectured, in respect of both the nature of the aggressive act and of the strength of the response to it.

Conceptually, co-operation is at the heart of peacekeeping. Therefore enforcement measures and the like cannot, by definition, qualify as peacekeeping. If it happens that there is a widespread move to speak of them as such, it will be necessary, at the least, for academics to distinguish between two quite different types of peacekeeping, only one of which depends wholly on the co-operation of the parties. (Both would presumably still depend on co-operation in regard to personnel and finance, and to some extent also for authorisation.) But, for the reason just given, it may be doubted whether the need for that distinction is likely to be urgent. There are, however, two grounds on which some emphasis on the co-operative nature of peacekeeping would none the less be no bad thing.

The first is that there is a widespread tendency to expect more of peacekeeping operations than, given their basis in international co-operation, they can possibly deliver. The second is that any such emphasis is a very useful reminder of the huge importance of co-operation for any bilateral or multilateral international activity. For better or ill the political world is made up of sovereign states, each of them constitutionally separate from the others and each therefore having a distinct territorial jurisdiction. Various means are available, some of them sometimes very potent, through which states can try to persuade their fellows to accept a point of view. But ultimately, and in the absence of any legal obligations to the contrary, it is for each state to decide what to do. This is another way of saying that international relations very largely consist of a myriad of co-operative enterprises or, more generally, that co-operation is a – indeed, arguably *the* – fundamental principle in the relations of states. Of this truth, the peacekeeping practice of the UN is a splendid example.[46]

NOTES

1 Article 24.1
2 Ibid.
3 Article 25.
4 Article 39.
5 Article 41.
6 Article 42.
7 See James Brierly, 'The Covenant and the Charter', in Hersch Lauterpacht and C.H.M. Waldock (eds) *The Basis of Obligation in International Law and Other Papers by the late James Leslie Brierly*, Oxford: Clarendon Press, 1958, pp.316–17. This lecture, given in Cambridge in 1946 (and published by Cambridge University Press), also appeared in (1946) 23 *B.Y.I.L.* 83.
8 Brierly, ibid. p.324.
9 UN Charter, Article 27.3. In 1966, with the coming into operation of a Charter amendment enlarging the Security Council to fifteen members, the number of affirmative votes necessary for a decision to be taken was increased to nine.
10 See Leland M. Goodrich, 'Korea: Collective Measures against Aggression', (October 1953) 494 *International Conciliation* 140.
11 The UN Charter does not allow a member formally to withdraw, on its own volition, from the Organization.

12 The UN Secretary-General, quoted in UN Information Centre, London, Press Release, 23 October 1991.
13 Although Iraq's consent for this operation ran out in June 1992, the mission never really ceased and on 22 October 1992, Iraq agreed to its continuation. *UN Monthly Chronicle* December 1992, p.29.
14 See further, Alan James, 'The Secretary-General as an Independent Political Actor', in B. Rivlin and L. Gordenker (eds) *The Challenging Role of the UN Secretary-General*, New York: Praeger, 1993.
15 See *The Blue Helmets. A Review of United Nations Peace-keeping*, New York: United Nations, 2nd edn, 1990, pp.97–8.
16 See Erik Jensen and Thomas Fisher (eds) *The United Kingdom – The United Nations*, London: Macmillan, 1990, pp.54–5, 276, and 282. See also A.J.R. Groom and Paul Taylor, *The United Nations and the Gulf War, 1990–91: Back to the Future?* London: Royal Institute of International Affairs, 1992, pp.3–4.
17 See, Alan James, *Peacekeeping in International Politics*, London: Macmillan, in association with the International Institute for Strategic Studies, 1990, pp.260–1.
18 See UN Doc. S/22663, 31 May 1991, Annex, para.4.
19 See UN Information Centre, London, News Summary 19/91, 23 May 1991.
20 Private information.
21 See *The Blue Helmets*, above n.14, pp.445–7.
22 See UN Doc. S/21360, 18 June 1990, para.79.
23 See UN Doc. S/22627, 20 May 1991, para.15.
24 See UN Doc. S/22494, 16 April 1991, para.12.
25 *United Nations Electoral Assistance to Haiti*, UN Department of Public Information, March 1991.
26 See *The Blue Helmets*, above n.14, pp.445–7.
27 Ibid. pp.442–3.
28 See UN Doc. S/23106, 2 October 1991, para.4.
29 See UN Doc. S/23191, 31 October 1991, para.11.
30 See UN Doc. S/22771, 9 July 1991.
31 See UN Doc. S/23773 and S/23774, both 2 April 1992.
32 Private information.
33 This has caused serious difficulty and much discontent. In June 1991 the Security Council resolved to put the Force on a better financial basis, but no immediate progress was made towards that end. The Representative of Canada observed in the Security Council that this was because 'once again most of the permanent members of the Council opposed the use of assessed contributions to finance UNFICYP and indicated that they would not support the establishment of such a system at this time': UN Doc. S/PV.3022, 18 December 1991.
34 UN Charter, Article 17.2.
35 See further, Alan James, 'The Security Council: Paying for Peacekeeping', in David P. Forsythe (ed.) *The United Nations in the World Political Economy. Essays in Honour of Leon Gordenker*, London: Macmillan, 1989; see also, Susan R. Mills, *The Financing of United Nations Peacekeeping Operations. The Need for a Sound Financial Basis*, New York: International Peace Academy, Occasional Paper, No. 3, 1989.
36 See UN Doc. S/22829, 21 July 1991, para.26.
37 See UN Doc. S/22665, 31 May 1991, paras.36–38. Because some of the contributor states have foregone their right to charge the UN for certain items, these figures do not reflect the full cost of the operation.
38 UN Charter, Article 19.
39 See James, *Peacekeeping in International Politics*, above n.17, p.231.

40 For a general discussion of sovereignty, see Alan James, *Sovereign Statehood. The Basis of International Society*, London: Allen & Unwin, 1986, part I and ch.11.

41 See, for example, UN Doc. S/22791, 15 July 1991, and S/22829, 21 July 1991, para.34.

42 *UN Chronicle*, vol.XXVIII, no. 3 (September 1991), p.17.

43 See UN Doc. S/22631, 21 May 1991, para.24.

44 Private information.

45 See Hugh Smith (ed.) *Australia and Peacekeeping*, Australian Defence Studies Centre, 1990, p.133.

46 In view of the fast-moving peacekeeping scene, it should be noted that this essay was written in January 1992; some small revisions were made in order to update it in August of that year.

9 The principle of self-determination

Patrick Thornberry

PRELIMINARY REFLECTIONS

Self-determination is the right of all peoples to govern themselves. By way of initial and prescriptive generalisation, the external dimension defines the status of a people in relation to another people, State or empire, whereas the democratic or internal dimension should concern the relationship between a people and 'its own' State or government. Those who expound democratic self-determination describe it as a challenge to governments that oppress their peoples. External self-determination may best express a discontinuous aspect, called up to define new externalities, new identities, in convulsive times, but also continuous defence against external intervention. Internal self-determination would translate the achievement of freedom by a people into authentic self-rule.

A major problem is that States have sometimes indicated that internal self-determination has no distinctive existence or role.[1] Another judgment is that it makes sense, but requires elaboration.[2] The debate is situated in contemporary discussions of peoples' rights. An International Meeting of Experts on Further Study of the Concept of Peoples Rights organised by Unesco in November 1989 made instructive observations. On peoples' rights in general, the Experts noted: 'the debate . . . is no longer *whether* [original emphasis] peoples' rights are recognised by international law, . . . [it] is about their content.'[3] Self-determination was listed first among peoples' rights in the light, *inter alia*, of its recognition in the UN Charter; it was a right 'universally accepted'.[4] None the less, dynamic change in the international community indicated that Unesco should extend its reflection on peoples' rights to new areas, including 'the implications of peoples' rights . . . to internal self-determination, especially democratic forms of government'.[5] The Unesco proposal is directed to elucidation and clarification rather than 'establishment' of a principle, and searches for common ground among diverse views. The work of elaboration of peoples' rights includes rights to peace, environmental rights and development: the UN Global Consultation on Development has made it clear that development in particular intersects with self-determination.[6]

The Declaration on Principles of International Law incorporates a paraphrase of the decolonisation process to 1970, the *summum bonum* of which was the formation of an independent State, since there could be no true freedom under alien rule. The self-determination section in the Declaration also makes implicit reference to South Africa, its construct of racial hierarchies, its gross violation of democratic principles.[7] The passions that once animated Afro-Asian colonies now energize the peoples of the former Soviet Union, Yugoslavia, Ethiopia and myriad other groups seeking 'an act of self-determination', from the Basques of Euskadi to the islanders of Bougainville.[8] The desired acts of self-determination would 'externalize' the groups from existing sovereignties.

The present challenge to international order has other aspects, perhaps more important in the long term. 'Classical' colonialism is now almost dead, as is stark ideological polarization of left and right.[9] Reforms of uncertain outcome are under way in South Africa. North-South divisions exacerbate and new fundamentalisms emerge. In terms of the potential contribution of self-determination to 'colonize the future', it is obvious that while self-determination liberates, it can also unhinge. Every secession creates new complexities, oppositions, new minorities, new totalitarian or authoritarian temptations, new purities of nation and tribe.[10] Addressing democratic or internal self-determination may enable us to consider whether we can grasp the sense of popular empowerment without the new tribalism. In this chapter the first focus is on the core of global instruments on self-determination culminating in the Declaration on Principles and then on legal developments which may extend their possibilities.

WILSON AND LENIN

Throughout its history, self-determination has exhibited elements of 'nationalism' and elements of 'democracy', and political change may demonstrate both.[11] In the French Revolution, the goal was exercise of power by the people and not the expulsion of a foreign government; the American revolutionaries cast off an 'external' power and proclaimed popular rule. In the nineteenth century, fundamentalist nationalism often prevailed over the ethic of democracy, as nations discovered themselves and empires unravelled. After the war of 1914–18, the principles of self-determination put forward by President Woodrow Wilson divided and created States, but they also proposed democracy, in the light of Wilson's belief that any universal instruments would be modelled on the Constitution of the United States.[12] Cobban wrote that: 'To Wilson, self-determination was almost another word for popular sovereignty . . . *vox populi* was *vox dei*.'[13] Lenin supported self-determination as the maximum of democracy and the minimum of nationalism, in the sense that self-determination promoted the proletarian interests in the class struggle.[14]

Self-determination did not play the major role in the postwar settlement. The use of plebiscites to ascertain democratic preferences was limited. Many groups demanding self-determination had to be satisfied with recognition as minorities. Self-determination and minority rights were essentially confined to Europe.[15] Colonial systems remained outside the sweep of the principle.

CORE INSTRUMENTS ON SELF-DETERMINATION

(i) The Charter of the United Nations

The new order of the United Nations was to be different. In the 1941 declaration of principles by the President of the United States and the Prime Minister of the United Kingdom, the Atlantic Charter, aspects of self-determination are amalgamated:

> they [the signatories] respect the right of all peoples to choose the form of government under which they will live; and they wish to see sovereign rights and self-government restored to those who have been forcibly deprived of them.[16]

The Yalta Declaration of 1945 reaffirmed the principles of the Atlantic Charter and pledged signatories to the 'earliest possible establishment through free elections of governments responsive to the will of the people.'[17] Choice of government figured in initial understandings of the United Nations Charter:

> an essential element of the principle . . . is a free and genuine expression of the will of the people, which avoids cases of the alleged expression of the popular will, such as those used for their own ends by Germany and Italy.[18]

Totalitarian government of right or left is incompatible with self-determination. The Charter does little to develop the content of self-determination, though it can provide the substratum for rights of peoples. The opening phrase is: 'We the Peoples of the United Nations'. Falk reads the Charter to mean that governments and States derive authority from the peoples.[19] Articles 1(2) and 55 refer to self-determination in the context of friendly relations among nations and in conjunction with 'equal rights' of peoples. Linkage with friendly relations and peace is apparently regarded as a limitation by Cassese, for whom it means that self-determination must be set aside 'when its fulfilment would give rise to tension and conflict among States'.[20] But the Charter should be read to underline the contribution of the principle to 'universal peace' (Article 1(2)), impossible without the principle of self-determination: the Charter outlines a comprehensive concept linking interdependent factors of security, stability and human rights.[21] There is no contradiction between a principle which is instrumentally useful and one which represents an independent value. The Charter is important for the reason that self-determination is brought into relationship with human rights and fundamental freedoms, though the convoluted syntax of articles obscures the point of connection.[22] It is also related to development and international co-operation. Humanitarian and democratic elements in chs XI and XII are of high significance, including the injunction in Article 76(c) 'to encourage recognition of the interdependence of the peoples of the world', a point sometimes lost when rights are asserted. The combination of explicit articles on self-determination and chapters on non-self-governing and trust territories ensured that the first fruits of self-determination fell to colonial territories in the empires of the Western Powers through emergence as independent States.

The Colonial Declaration

The Charter story is continued in the 1960 Declaration on the Granting of Independence to Colonial Countries and Peoples, General Assembly Resolution 1514(XV).[23] The Resolution is in the form of an interpretation of the Charter and is usually taken to characterize the Afro-Asian account of self-determination. It stresses independence as the principal means through which self-determination is implemented, demanding in paragraph 5 that:

> Immediate steps shall be taken, in Trust and Non-Self-Governing Territories or all other territories which have not yet attained independence, to transfer all powers to the peoples of those territories, without any conditions or reservations.[24]

The form of self-determination is multifaceted, with political, economic, social and cultural components, the target is colonialism, and the Charter principle has become a right:

> All peoples have the right to self-determination; by virtue of that right they freely determine their political status and freely pursue their economic, social and cultural development [para. 2].

Paragraph 6 combines self-determination with territorial integrity, an insistent linkage in self-determination discourse at the United Nations:

> Any attempt aimed at the partial or total disruption of the national unity and then territorial integrity of a country is incompatible with the purposes and principles of the Charter of the United Nations.

There are other nuances. Self-determination is associated with human rights in preambular paragraphs 1 and 2, and operative paragraphs 1 and 7.[25] For many States, the text recorded the simple statement that colonialism violated human rights and should be dismantled immediately. Self-determination, in often repeated language, was a 'prerequisite' for human rights[26] and the Declaration did not purport to control post-independence parameters of human rights in new States. But while the text is heavily conditioned by repeated and narrowing references to colonialism, there are intimations of an open field of action: the right is for 'all peoples'. There is a powerful resonance to this transcendent claim.

The Declaration has been an article of faith for many States and is often treated as second only to the Charter in importance. It is still quoted. The representative of China explained to the 1992 session of the Human Rights Commission:

> The principles contained in the Declaration were still of practical significance and would continue to serve as an important legal basis for countries to safeguard their independence, sovereignty and territorial integrity and defend their economic, social and cultural rights.[27]

This amounts to a demand for non-interference, not for democratic self-determination: the 'democratic' theme is absent from the speech except for a commonplace reference to 'racist rule' in South Africa. The 'liberating' anti-colonial Declaration is treated as part of the armoury of concepts to defend developing countries from the machinations of unnamed Powers.

The Covenants on Human Rights

Self-determination is presented as a human right in the common article 1 of the UN Covenant on Civil and Political Rights and the Covenant on Economic, Social and Cultural Rights:

> 1. All peoples have the right of self-determination. By virtue of that right they freely determine their political status and freely pursue their economic, social and cultural development.

Paragraph 2 deals with free disposal by peoples of natural wealth and resources, adding that 'In no case may a people be deprived of its own means of subsistence'. Paragraph 3 clearly indicates the universal scope of self-determination by mandating States, 'including those having responsibility for Non-Self-Governing and Trust territories', to promote and respect self-determination.

This complex statement of the treaty-right of self-determination was explicated by the Human Rights Committee at its 21st session in General Comment 12.[28] The main points are:

1 The right of self-determination is of particular importance 'because its realization is an essential condition for the effective guarantee and observance of individual human rights and for the promotion and

strengthening of those rights' (para.1). The right is placed 'apart from and before all of the other rights' in the two Covenants (para.1).

2 Self-determination is an inalienable right of all peoples and imposes corresponding obligations (para.2). The text does not stand alone: 'The right and . . . obligations concerning its implementation are interrelated with other provisions and rules of international law (para.2). The Comment refers in particular to the Declaration on Principles of International Law in connection with 'other instruments' on self-determination (para.7).

3 Although the Comment (like the text of Article 1) does not refer to democratic self-determination as such, it may refer to it in the point that many State reports 'completely ignore' Article 1, provide inadequate information in regard to it or confine themselves to a reference to election laws (para.3).

4 Instead of thus limiting themselves, the States parties 'should describe the constitutional and political processes which in practice allow the exercise of this right' (para.4).

The Comment also addresses the economic content of the right in Article 1(2), advising that States should indicate any factors or difficulties in the way of 'free disposal' and to what extent it affects the enjoyment of other rights in the Covenant (para.5). Although not contained in a 'general comment' by a treaty body, a further valuable point in the context of the Covenant on Economic, Social and Cultural Rights is that references in common Article 1 to 'economic, social and cultural development' and 'a people's own means of subsistence' have a particular significance in the context of that Covenant, and, to the extent that they are not dealt with adequately in reports under the Civil and Political Rights Covenant, should be included in reports under the Economic, Social and Cultural Covenant.[29]It should be recalled that self-determination underlies both UN Covenants, so that any democracy to which it relates has economic as well as political elements.

Text and Comment assert a general relationship of reciprocity between self-determination and human rights; an ongoing right of self-determination touching independent States; a minimal indication of the importance of processes and structures in the elaboration of self-determination; and a concern with economic control and the peoples' right to development.[30] The Comment intimates what has been 'elaborated' and what has not. There is, in particular, no attempt to define a people, not even in relation to the 'lesser' rights of minorities set out in Article 27:

> In those States in which ethnic, religious or linguistic minorities exist, persons belonging to such minorities shall not be denied the right, in community with the other members of their group, to enjoy their own culture, to profess and practise their own religion, or to use their own language.[31]

The Declaration on Principles of International Law

This Declaration presents itself as evidence of the consensus of States on the meaning and elaboration of the principles of the Charter. For some, the Declaration on Principles is now simply 'customary law', by virtue of the consensus.[32] Self-determination is described in a manner that transcends the colonial context and the obsession with independence. By virtue of self-determination, 'all peoples have the right freely to determine, without external interference, their political status and to pursue their economic, social and cultural development'. Both 'status' and 'development' aspects are incorporated in self-determination, following the pattern of the Colonial Declaration. Open-ended modes of exercise are attached to the right:

> The establishment of a sovereign and independent State, the free association or integration with an independent State or the emergence into any other political status freely determined by a people constitute modes of implementing self-determination by that people.[33]

The self-determination section includes a free-standing paragraph on human rights, implicitly recalling UN Charter Articles 55 and 56.[34] A territorial integrity paragraph protects a State or country from the actions of other States. The overall integrity principle is qualified in a penultimate paragraph on peoples in existing States:

> Nothing in the foregoing paragraphs shall be construed as authorizing or encouraging any action which would dismember or impair, totally or in part, the territorial integrity or political unity of sovereign and independent States conducting themselves in compliance with the principle of equal rights and self-determination of peoples as described above and thus possessed of a government representing the whole people belonging to the territory without distinction as to race, creed or colour.

Although brief, this has clear possibilities of elaboration. Cassese finds therein a limited concept of 'internal' self-determination, which consists in the possession by a sovereign and independent State of a government representing the whole people on a non-discriminatory basis.[35] 'Race, creed or colour' can be collapsed into a reference to race and religion, though 'creed' might be associated with a philosophical system of beliefs or principles. The phrase is also found in operative paragraph 5 of the Colonial Declaration, but in the narrower context of Non-Self-Governing and Trust Territories. The text refers to 'the whole people', so it seems that self-determination benefits the people of the State as a unified group. A draft by the United States pointed towards a less constricted concept of 'people':

> The existence of a sovereign and independent State possessing a

> representative government, effectively functioning as such to all distinct peoples within its territory, is presumed to satisfy the principle of equal rights and self-determination as regards those peoples.[36]

The clear difference between this and the agreed version is the replacement of 'all distinct peoples' in the US draft by 'the whole people'.[37] On the other hand, despite the holistic terminology, a more flexible argument can be made. Thus, the 'non-distinction' reference would be redundant if it did not apply to distinct racial or religious groups in the State, groups which are a component part of the people. The groups are not necessarily minorities: the paragraph could apply to South Africa which is a case of rule by minority and not persecution of a minority.[38] The government is to represent the people without a specific group bias. So self-determination directs itself to State organisation, going beyond the protection of individuals as such. A State organisation that works to exclude racial or religious groups violates self-determination, as does one which denies the groups representation on a non-discriminatory basis – 'distinction' being synonymous with 'discrimination'.[39] Some idea of group equality may be present here, possibly indicating that groups should be represented according to the extent of their presence in the State. What is the significance of 'representation'? It can hardly mean a particular pattern of organisation, or a specific politics or ideology. The paragraph could be read to state that the formal organisation of the State is a matter of choice provided it conforms to the principle of representation. To represent means 'to stand for'. We may further distinguish between true and false representation so as not to undermine the ethics of the concept. A merely formal idea will not do; representation should be representation in substance, parallel to the difference between equality in law and equality in fact.[40] This may direct us from representation to participation of groups in the government of a State, if not necessarily 'the government' in the narrow sense of the Executive. Representation and participation may be experienced as part of a continuum: representation is light, participation is heavy. On the other hand, representation has a static quality, while participation is an active principle, and other international instruments have striven to individuate a right of participation in more explicit terms.[41] The idea of representing is amenable to the notion that self-determination will be exercised with regard to the interests of various racial/religious groups in 'the territory', going beyond the case of 'simple' majority rule.

And what if a government is not 'representative'? Then it appears that territorial integrity is not guaranteed. Group autonomy does not interfere with territorial integrity, so the 'non-guarantee' leads logically to the possibility of secession. There is little relationship between secession and religious groups so that in practice it would apply to racial groups or groups where a 'race' is identified with a specific religion.[42]

Many objections are possible to this sketch of arguments. One is to look at the total effect of the paragraph, which is predominantly negative in terms of forbidding secession by affirming territorial integrity. This is reinforced by the Declaration read as a whole, including preambular paragraph 15. The maxim *expressio unius, exclusio alterius* is relevant in view of the narrowing of 'people': broader descriptions – 'all distinct peoples' – were ruled out.[43]'Race, creed or colour' may or may not be susceptible to intelligent interpretation in view of its obvious slogan-like quality, or, if it is, may restrict rather than expand the scope of the paragraph. The interpretation as a whole may simply be too 'theoretical', at some distance from diplomatic reality. Objections and fears expressed by States often relate to the idea of secession by sub-State groups. Secession, to the extent that it is recognised in the Declaration, is probably a defensible right since the reform of the State to make it more representative satisfies the principle of self-determination. The thrust of the text is towards the implementation of self-determination through State organisation. There is some attraction in intimating an 'ultimate sanction' to despotic governments of secession. But as a general 'right', it is difficult to see how it can be accepted by States, however nuanced the criteria suggested.[44] Most groups that achieve it do so through struggle without benefit of 'rights'.[45] For others, secession will be unrealisable, perhaps counterproductive in threatening governments, and may deflect attention from potentially more productive approaches to group protection.

REVIEW OF THE PRINCIPLE

The self-determination referred to in the UN Charter has undergone a process of development through the core instruments and attendant State practice, resulting not so much in the resolution of ambiguities as in the actualisation of some of its potential. The following is a summary of progress to date:

1 There is a general right and principle of self-determination in international law.[46]
2 It has inherent value, and an instrumental value in underpinning international peace through the development of friendly relations among nations.
3 Self-determination applies to all peoples.
4 Colonial peoples have benefited from the application of self-determination through the process of decolonisation.
5 The basic form of self-determination has been the achievement of independence, the most desirable 'political status'.
6 In essence, this meant that the 'nationalist' aspect of the principle prevailed over the 'democratic', though the nationalism is whole territory nationalism rather than that of ethnic or 'racial' divisions.[47]

7 The 'democratic' aspect of self-determination is present in muted form, through the idea of representation in the Declaration on Principles, and by indeterminate 'connection' with human rights.

This does not amount to a complete code of self-determination and the interpretation of the core instruments demands consideration of elements of unclarity affecting normative coherence. An overview must also pay attention to contemporary developments sketched out in the introduction. It is clear that independence remains an attractive goal for many groups. A cursory comparison of international reaction to the plight of Kuwait and the efforts on behalf of more numerous but 'minority' Kurds suggests reasons for the enduring attraction of independence.[48] Democracy is also resurgent. A democratic order is demanded in Eastern Europe, Saharan and Sub-Saharan Africa, Latin America and parts of Asia. The demand for democracy has the aspect of a general claim, the various dimensions of which are emphasised through the matrix of different cultural systems, though it is not a claim that is always satisfied. The point is that the achievement of independence is not enough for authentic expression of peoples' rights. The sources of the stream of democracy are many.

Among the regional developments, international lawyers will note the significant contribution of the CSCE process as a whole as an engine of democratic change and a repository of democratic principle.[49] The non-treaty nature of CSCE instruments should not detract from their standard-setting power and the importance of the underlying political will to implement them. The role of the Council of Europe in the service of democracy, human rights and the rule of law also deserves underlining,[50] as does that of the European Community through, *inter alia*, its ACP policies of 'democratic adjustment',[51] the Organization of American States,[52] and the Organization of African Unity in its adoption of the African Charter on Human and Peoples' Rights.[53]Regional enhancement of democracy has been prompted and complemented by developments at United Nations level which encompass the concept of economic democracy and a concern for development and the very poor,[54] and growing respect for pluralism, diversity, and group rights or the collective dimensions of individual rights.[55] The axial role of non-governmental organizations and associations in the articulation and promotion of a democratic culture also characterizes contemporary international society.[56] In this ferment of movement, the standard of democracy is increasingly taken as universal human rights as opposed to ideologies of narrower range. The preamble to the CSCE Paris Charter[57] recites the 'steadfast commitment' of the heads of State or government to 'democracy based on human rights and fundamental freedoms'. Under the rubric of 'Human Rights, Democracy and Rule of Law', the Charter states that

> Human rights and fundamental freedoms are the birthright of all human beings, are inalienable and are guaranteed by law. Their protec-

> tion and promotion is the first responsibility of government. Respect for them is an essential safeguard against an over-mighty State. Their observance and full exercise are the foundation of freedom, justice and peace.

It is also asserted that 'Democracy has as its foundation respect for the human person and the rule of law.' The linkage of democracy and human rights is almost a commonplace in the instruments of the CSCE and allied processes.[58]

These developments feed into self-determination. The succeeding sections of this chapter examine the impact of new concepts on the basic structure and substance of self-determination, taking textual nuances in core instruments as a point of departure. Comment is offered on the extent to which self-determination is a valid and continuing right, a query which has still some, if diminishing, force; on the extent to which it can present a democratic concept of the people; and in what ways it interrelates with the spectrum of recognised human rights. The contemporary interpretation of democratic self-determination is not resolved through simple contrast between *lex lata* and *lex ferenda*. The relationship between what is and what ought to be is fluid and dynamic, conditioned alike by perceptions of diplomatic reality as well as what is useful, necessary and appropriate for the vocation of our age.

CONTINUANCE

This is is an essential presupposition to any further self-determination . While it cannot be categorised as a 'non-question',[59] it requires emphasis because the continuance of self-determination as a principle of international law is a fundamental statement in all relevant texts. It seems obvious, despite objections,[60] that they propose it as a continuing right that is not exhausted by the achievement of independence. Other instruments reflect this perception. The Helsinki Final Act provides the clearest expression:

> By virtue of the principle of equal rights and self-determination of peoples, all peoples always have the right, in full freedom, to determine, when and as they wish, their internal and external political status, without external interference, and to pursue as they wish, their political, economic, social and cultural development.[61]

The principle is recalled in subsequent instruments of the CSCE. The African Charter on Human and Peoples' Rights, to which some forty African States are parties,[62] provides in Article 20 that

> 1. All peoples shall have the right to existence. They shall have the unquestionable and inalienable right to self-determination. They shall

> freely determine their political status and freely pursue their economic and social development according to the policy they have freely chosen.

Paragraph 2 makes specific provision for 'colonized or oppressed peoples' who have the right to 'free themselves from the bonds of domination'. There is therefore both a general and a specific proposition and nothing to qualify the ambit of the right of all peoples.[63]

Self-determination can be understood as process and event – the 'act' of self-determination at the heart of important contemporary demands. This continuance need not presuppose, prima facie, a particular meaning of self-determination. There are ways in which self-determination functions as 'external' defence of sovereignty through non-interference, economic self-determination and claims on the international community in terms of development.[64] These aspects are more crucial than ever, in view of widening gaps between North and South in major indicators of human development.[65] On the other hand, arguments limiting self-determination to colonial situations are often formulated in terms of a threat: the dismemberment of the State. The question of continuance of self-determination is rolled up *in practice* with questions of who holds the right and what it means. The 'threat' conception of self-determination has been underlined by the representative of India to the Human Rights Commission, reflecting a continuing preoccupation:

> The right to self-determination had always been taken by the United Nations to apply to non-self-governing territories and not to integral parts of sovereign and independent States . . . the application of the right . . . to constituent units of sovereign States could not but undermine the principle of the territorial integrity of sovereign States and was thus a threat to democracy everywhere.[66]

It may be noted that the contrast drawn by the representative is between the application of self-determination to 'non-self-governing territories' and to 'constituent units' of sovereign States. This is different from the contention in the Indian declaration on the Covenant on Civil and Political Rights which states that self-determination does not apply to 'sovereign and independent States'.[67] It is important not to reject the Indian contentions out of hand, but to see if they can be reconciled with existing and developing law. The first can possibly be reconciled with that law, the second cannot.

PEOPLE AND TERRITORY

Changing notions of democracy can change our view of the people. The Unesco Experts describe people as a mutable concept, possibly carrying different meanings for different rights.[68] The difficulty with that view is: who is to be excluded in the computation of rights? Periodic agonising about a definition of people has not produced consensus and the various instruments do not attempt a definition. This is not a failure of the ethnographer, the lawyer or the lexicographer to 'fix' a subject. The meaning of people is distilled from changing complexities of the political and diplomatic process. A move from definition to 'softer' description is superficially attractive. The Unesco Experts discussed characteristics 'inherent in a description (but not a definition) of a 'people':

1. a group of individual human beings who enjoy some or all of the following common features:
(a) a common historical tradition;
(b) racial or ethnic identity;
(c) cultural homogeneity;
(d) linguistic unity;
(e) religious or ideological affinity;
(f) territorial connection;
(g) common economic life.

The description makes reference to number – 'more than a mere association of individuals'; will or consciousness to be a people; and possibly institutions to express characteristics and identity.[69] The approach may not carry far. The 'description' can be compared (and confused) with definitions of 'minority': the definitions revolve around essentially the same characteristics.[70] The draft UN Declaration on the Rights of Persons Belonging to Minorities [71] does not reproduce any definition but prefaces 'minority' with the adjectives 'national or ethnic, religious and linguistic', regarded as sufficient in themselves.[72]

For much of the Charter period, people has apparently meant the whole people in a non-self-governing territory, effectively the majority therein.[73] The Declaration on Principles respects the whole people view, though ambiguously while also intimating differentiation. The self-determination choice has almost inevitably been described in terms of a people *or* an ethnic group possessing the right. These are incompatible oppositional prescriptions. The result is the perception of minorities as rivals in self-determination, as a permanent threat to the people, and their marginalisation and suppression in many States. In this, the Unesco Experts' points on the characteristics of people are not helpful, at least as the basis of a general rule *of international law*. They say in effect that complex States incorporate many 'peoples'. Under current international practice, this means that there are many candidates for self-determination, since once a people is identified, the self-determination inference is almost irresistible. This may diminish possibilities of accommodation between majorities and minorities in most societies, producing a self-determination that divides where it should reconcile.[74]

Other possibilities emerge if core texts are developed even if State practice is not yet adequate to this.[75] One is to consider a less monolithic meaning of people. A more differentiated approach to the meaning of people has been understood but needs underlining and new stress.[76] Most human groups will continue to live in ethnically rich societies and concepts of the people should take account of this. The description of people need not mimic the meaning of State and its themes of unity and indivisibility. A differentiated meaning of people is not equivalent to attributing the right of self-determination to ethnic components but encourages participation in the self-determination of the whole. The participation of these and other groups has gained increasing recognition in a range of international instruments at various levels from the United Nations to the CSCE.[77] In these, minorities are not described as peoples but have their own role and status in the life of nations . Peoples' rights to self-determination, existence, development and peace must therefore include them. This is without prejudice to designated rights of minorities, as it is without prejudice to the rights of all persons. In this last respect, the democratic embrace of the people needs to go beyond electoral ritual and to empower classes of individuals marginalised not on account of ethnic affiliation but through extreme poverty, a condition found in developed as well as in developing States.[78]

A less majoritarian, more differentiated, participatory and communitarian meaning of people carries opportunities and few risks if it is placed in a spectrum of rights and the participation is genuine and not simply asserted. A mature concept of people respects and incorporates diversity and takes strength from it. The proposition that diversity increases the potency of the whole is made in a range of international instruments which channel and reflect the currents of democratic pluralism that wash around us.[79] The inclusive notion may assist in restraining the overweening power of majorities to identify *their* interests as the interests of the people. It does not *per se* identify new peoples. This may reassure States in their concern for integrity, but will not restrain the recognition of new peoples through struggle or dialogue and negotiation between groups and States, or, like many peoples in Eastern Europe, from implicit recognition as such in constitutional law.[80] The propositions in this section state a possible but *general* normative development, one which could make the emergence of 'new' peoples less of a necessity than has been the case through a narrowing of the gap between the rights of peoples and component groups.

Indigenous peoples in their attempts at self-assertion and recognition have taken the first steps along a different path of principled legal change. The validity of their self-definition as peoples is becoming more generally accepted, though the full legal implications of this have yet to be determined. The groups were described as 'populations' in International Labour Organisation (ILO) Convention No. 107, 1957; they became 'peoples' in ILO Convention No. 169. Even here, Article 1(3) states that 'The use of the term "peoples" in this Convention shall not be construed as having any implications as regards the rights which may attach to the term under international law.' This gives States the choice of accepting 'peoples' but refusing its implications, including self-determination. Paragraph 1 of the UN draft Declaration on the Rights of Indigenous Peoples is bolder but also holds back:

> Indigenous peoples have the right to self-determination, in accordance with international law. By virtue of this right, they freely determine their relationship with the States in which they live, in a spirit of co-existence with other citizens, and freely pursue their economic, social, cultural and spiritual development in conditions of freedom and dignity.[81]

This is an approach which recognises self-determination but seeks to confine its exercise within States. The respect for territorial integrity is a feature which may recommend itself.[82] The draft is at an early stage and has uncertain prospects of success.[83] Indigenous peoples appear to be the only *general* category of sub-State group with an emerging right to self-determination. In this, they are differentiated from minority groups in general who are unlikely to receive general international recognition as peoples. The possible line of development for the indigenous – recognition as peoples with self-determination but with its exercise confined within States – is assisted by the fact that secession is not an issue for most groups. Many other questions such as protection from genocide and ethnocide, land rights, respect for their distinctive world view, and rectification of historical injustices, are more pressing.

TERRITORY

Territorial integrity is fundamental to international law and its respect is called for in three of the core instruments. In turn, the Covenants are connected with the UN Charter and the General Comment connects them with the Declaration on Principles of International Law. Paragraph 4 of the Colonial Declaration refers to the integrity of the territory of dependent peoples; paragraph 6 warns against disruption of the 'national unity and the territorial integrity of a country'; paragraph 7 requires respect for 'the sovereign rights of all peoples and their territorial integrity'. The principle of the integrity of colonies through to independence has been maintained with only minor inconsistencies throughout the decolonisation process. Among contemporary political settlements, the resolution of the Cambodian crisis involves among other instruments, the 'Agreement concerning the Sovereignity, Independence, Territorial Integrity and Inviolability, Neutrality and National Unity of Cambodia'.[84] The integrity to be respected is in general the integrity of colony or State even if the terminology is variable. Other cases push the concept on. The EC approach to recognition of new States in Eastern Europe and the Soviet

Union employs certain guidelines: they refer, *inter alia*, to 'respect for the inviolability of all frontiers which can only be changed by peaceful means and by common agreement'.[85] The Summary of Conclusions of the Prague Meeting of the CSCE Council requires in the context of the Yugoslav crisis 'respect for the inviolability of all borders, whether internal or external, which can only be changed by peaceful means and by common agreement'.[86] The Eastern European cases demonstrate that, even in cases of apparently freewheeling secession, some form of framework remains crucial. Also at a sub-State level, recognition and demarcation of indigenous territories has assumed prominence in international instruments. For some purpose, internal boundaries have international significance.

From a humanitarian point of view, the attachment to integrity is often and rightly seen as a cover for iniquitous policies of governments under challenge from the international community. Its role is negative. A more positive role for the principle in the context of peoples' rights is reflected in the Declaration on the Right to Development which proposes in the preamble that the elimination of threats to, *inter alia*, 'national unity and territorial integrity . . . would contribute to the establishment of circumstances propitious to the development of a great part of mankind' (para.9).[87] This contains a thought which should be taken further. Thinking on self-determination has largely been concerned with the spectre of secession. In essence, this follows from the logic of decolonisation, a process now under way in Eastern Europe. Like Russian dolls, each determined unit contains within it a smaller scale replica of itself. States have not accepted secession as a principle of international law – any message to the contrary in the Declaration on Principles is almost unreadable.[88] This is despite attempts to define general criteria for secession, though in specific politics, States may be constrained to proposing secession as a *sui generis* solution to a particular problem.[89]

Faced with the inscription of integrity and national unity in texts and the intransigent nature of its support in State practice, it may be productive to respect its ratio as a general principle and consider its virtues. After every breach of integrity comes a demand for it. In terms of a more participatory concept of peoples and a less oppositional view of the rights of peoples and other communities, the integrity principle can manifest opportunity as well as limitation. A constructive reading of the principle can promote accommodation between groups and implicate them in common concerns. The draft Declaration on Minorities relates some of this sentiment through a demand in Article 4(4) that 'Persons belonging to minorities should have adequate opportunities to gain knowledge of the society as a whole'.[90] Mutuality can be promoted more directly by encouraging tolerance, good-neighbourliness, etc., which is increasingly the case in international instruments.[91] The trouble with secession is that it is rarely an answer to anything and creates new difficulties; it can only be an exceptional not a normal response to events. The stress on integrity can promote solutions to problems by indicating that existing territorial arrangements are the first framework for examination, dialogue, negotiation, confidence-building and possible disposition. It can also function as a defence of groups that comprise the people, since the integrity of the whole is disturbed by policies of forced resettlement, population transfer, mass expulsions, etc. These should be seen as violations of self-determination. The increasing stress on internationalisation of human rights does not disturb these principles. Augmentation of the role of international organisations in human rights and humanitarian assistance is not the same as promoting secession and may work against it. This mirrors the sentiment in the Universal Declaration on Human Rights that rights are a substitute for rebellion against tyranny, that democratic culture is the ultimate prize.[92]

A reconceptualization of people towards more inclusive meanings demolishes barriers between part and whole and helps to combat tribalism. Recognition of group and individual participation in communitarian self-determination assists the search for structures and modalities of accommodation. It does not mandate particular organisational outcomes, though active participation may move towards decentralised, autonomist structures as individuals and groups find levels of organisation appropriate to continuing involvement.[93] A more participatory concept of people may therefore supply some of the democratic deficit of majority-rule self-determination. For the rest, the core instruments point to a relationship between self-determination and human rights, but do little to clarify it.

HUMAN RIGHTS: THE DEMOCRATIC SUBSTANCE

The connection between human rights and self-determination has been the subject of frequent comment. At the time of drafting the General Comment on self-determination, individual members of the Human Rights Committee made observations. The Comment avoids prerequisite language in favour of a claim that self-determination is 'an essential condition' for individual human rights and is interrelated with other articles. The relationship was variously described: it was 'one of interdependence'. It was not one-sided. 'For the right of self-determination to be freely exercised, it was essential that there should be freedom of opinion, of expression, of movement and of assembly.'[94] And,

> There was probably no one who believed that none of these rights . . . could be implemented without previous implementation of the right to self-determination. But there was probably no one who believed that all of those rights could be implememented . . . as a whole, unless the right to self-determination had also been implemented.[95]

Cassese has written extensively on the connection between human rights and self-determination. In the Covenants, self-determination

> presupposes freedom of opinion and expression (article 19), the right of peaceful assembly (article 21), the freedom of association (article 22), the right to vote (article 25(b)), and more generally the right to take part in the conduct of public affairs, directly or through freely chosen representatives (article 25(a)). Whenever these rights are recognized for individuals, the people as a whole enjoy the right of internal (political) self-determination; whenever these rights are trampled upon, the right of the people to self-determination is infringed.[96]

J.B. Marie writes that self-determination is the essential condition for human rights but is not synonymous with human rights. It is not enough for peoples' rights to be a collectivisation of human rights; there is need for a specific substance. Peoples are not free under colonialism but neither are they free under governments denying human rights: systematic violations of human rights bring into play the right to self-determination – 'the right of a people to appeal against oppression and dicatorship'.[97] Ramcharan refers to 'critical internal dimensions' of self-determination and states that it 'must be a human right in its individual as well as in its collective dimension, for reasons which lie, for example, in article 21 of the Universal Declaration of Human Rights'.[98]

In terms of the practical application of the Covenant on Civil and Political Rights, the self-determination article has been addressed consistently under the system of State reporting and effectively excluded from the Optional Protocol.[99] In this, as for peoples' rights in general, the narrow language of procedural justiciability may be inadequate or inappropriate. As Cancado Trindade has observed:

> rights pertaining to human collectivities seem to call for a distinct approach to the means and the institutional arrangements for their implementation or vindication . . . . Violations of these rights may affect so many individuals that individual litigation may prove unsuitable . . . it is clearer that the 'justiciability' of a right cannot be erected as a conditio sine qua non of its existence and recognition.[100]

Notions of representation may overcome the impasse faced by the Committee. The General Comment is very limited, though at least the language of reciprocity and interrelationship is to be preferred to self-determination as prerequisite for human rights. It would appear that self-determination should be understood in terms of the generality of rights, the unity, indivisibility and interrelatedness of which are constantly underlined.[101]

This does not exclude the view that indications of observance or non-observance of particular rights may have special relevance, such as the right to take part in government, freedom of assembly and association, and the rights of minorities. The rationale of these freedoms is that they underpin and facilitate the exercise of other rights through the collective dimension of their exercise and the element of political challenge they offer to governments. Rights of minorities are a particular barometer of human rights in general; the groups are the inevitable targets and scapegoats for oppressive governments that fail to deliver the minimum of social and economic goods to their peoples. Though no right other than self-determination is the essence of self-determination, the state of such rights may furnish indicators of the peoples' health.[102]

It may also be asserted that political and economic democracy and rights are inseparable. The repeated references to development in the core instruments can be translated into the human right to development which subsumes multiple dimensions of human rights in an integrating concept of human growth. Democratic self-determination can be taken to mandate economic, social and cultural development of peoples. On cultural development, the suggested reading of peoples will act to oppose the construction of artificial homogeneising cultures towards a genuine and ethical concept valuing diverse group contributions. Economic and social dimensions of development demand a building up from deprivation to an existence respecting basic human dignity: as Leopold Senghor once observed, 'human rights begin with breakfast'.[103]

Human rights also function in a limiting manner to rule out conditions or statuses that violate humanitarian principles or, where the State embraces a philosophy of negation, to gauge the scale of the people's defeat.[104] The necessary mutual support between individual and peoples' rights qualifies the 'status' a people may choose. The Copenhagen document of the CSCE Conference on the Human Dimension makes this clear through adaptation of self-determination language in:

> They [the participating States] confirm that they will respect each other's right freely to choose and develop, in accordance with international human rights standards, their political, social, economic and cultural systems.[105]

What is at stake for democratic self-determination is the political or democratic *condition* of the people.

For third generation rights, a methodology of overview is required. The concern with individual rights remains but the language in which the basic concern is expressed is a new language, translatable from the first-order language but able to deploy its own concepts. The relationship between self-determination and human rights humanises the former and lends to the latter a powerful metalanguage to harness the totality of popular aspirations.

FROM THE DECLARATION ON PRINCIPLES TO DEMOCRATIC SELF-DETERMINATION

1 The Declaration on Principles represented a crucial move for self-determination in directing attention to democratic structures, human rights and the limits of territorial integrity. While it contains ambiguities to be expected in consensus texts, it intimates possible directions for self-determination.

2 In terms of a democratic self-determination, the chief weakness of the Declaration lies in a limited concept of representation as opposed to a broader concept of participation. Its approach to a differentiated concept of people and the idea of self-determination as a continuing right is a strength.

3 The democratic aspect of self-determination had been submerged in the texts but is re-emerging. Problems of acceptance revolved around rival conceptions of democracy. The only possible reconciliation is in terms of human rights.

4 The content of human rights has undergone change towards recognition of group rights or the collective dimension of individual rights. General concepts of individual and group participation have also undergone development.

5 Changes in the concept of human rights may impact on self-determination by:

(a) enlarging and democratising our view of the people in more genuinely communitarian directions; in this it contains an embryonic critique of governmental systems based on undifferentiated majority-rule democracy which on a negative reading incorporates the ideology of victor and vanquished within the one State;[106]

(b) assisting in the recognition of new categories of peoples; though so far only indigenous peoples appear to have the capacity to emerge as a new *general* category of people;

(c) affecting our view of the key indicators of self-determination – keeping watch on the treatment of groups, curbing the choice of inappropriate statuses and directing the process of development to incorporate democracy and human rights.

6 Human rights in the full sense is the measure of self-determination which in turn is a language to gauge observance or denial of rights.

I have previously argued that it is better to build individual and group rights than dream unrealistically of a modified self-determination.[107] But change is around us, self-determination renews its vigour, and developments previously identified have matured and prospered in unforeseen ways. The growth of individual and specific group rights proceeds apace, they connect increasingly with peoples' rights, and our readings must take account of this. It is possible to read self-determination as mandating neither secession nor the artificial homogeneity of States but as a potential synthesis of respect and mutual concern between whole societies and their component groups. There is thus a sense in which a people is entitled to exercise a continuing democratic control over governments in the field of human rights, incorporating respect for individual and group dimensions of rights, encouraged but not compelled to resolve difficulties and negotiate the future in a common framework, that could be appropriately termed democratic or internal self-determination. The major ideological reconciliation we are witnessing grants an opportunity to fasten this democratic self-determination into global standards and turn a peoples' right from rhetoric into reality.

NOTES

1 It is therefore confined to colonial situations and expires when the situation is remedied through independence. This is the sense of the Indian declaration on the Covenants on Human Rights: 'With reference to article 1 of the International Covenant on Economic, Social and Cultural Rights [and the Covenant on Civil and Political Rights], . . . the Government of the Republic of India declares that the words "the right of self-determination" appearing in [this article] apply only to the peoples under foreign domination and that these words do not apply to sovereign independent States or to a section of the people or nation – which is the essence of national integrity', *Human Rights, Status of International Instruments*, New York: United Nations, 1987, ST/HR/5, UN Sales No. E.87.XIV.2, 9; CCPR/C/2/Rev.3, 12 May 1992, p.18.

2 This view emerges from the International Meeting of Experts on Further Study of the Concept of the Rights of Peoples, convened by Unesco, Paris, 27–30 November 1989, SHS–89/CONF.602/7. The earlier Unesco involvement in peoples' rights is outlined in paras.7, 8 and 9, and includes the contribution of the Australian National Commission for Unesco, conference papers of which are published in J. Crawford (ed.) *The Rights of Peoples*, Oxford: Clarendon Press, 1988.

3 Unesco Conference, para.19.

4 Ibid., para.24.

5 Ibid., para.27.

6 *The Realization of the Right to Development, Global Consultation on the Right to Development as a Human Right*, New York: United Nations, 1991, HR/PUB/91/2, especially paras.80, 105, 106, 151, 161.

7 This is the primary referent for the formula 'without distinction as to race, creed or colour' found in the Declaration and many other UN resolutions on self-determination and human rights. Of the core instruments on self-determination listed below, the Colonial Declaration uses the phrase in paragraph 5. The South African situation has influenced the law on self-determination, human rights and international criminal law, in all cases towards an elaboration of their anti-racist potential. Elements of its effects are traced in J. Dugard, 'The Influence of Apartheid on the Development of the Law Governing the Protection of Minorities', paper delivered at the workshop *Minorities and Indigenous Peoples in the United Nations System*, Oxford, 1989. The statement delivered by the representative of the United States at the 1992 session of the UN Human Rights Commission summarises much world opinion: 'in the long history of oppression on Earth, few forms of government had been as reprehensible as apartheid, a system that denied persons their

most basic human rights solely because of the colour of their skin. It was a system that was abhorrent to any decent human being and, along with all the other failed experiments of the century that promised justice but delivered repression and suffering, it should be consigned to the dustbin of history', UN Doc. E/CN.4/1992/SR.9, para.1.

8 For a succinct account of these and other groups seeking acts of self-determination, see Minority Rights Group (ed.) *World Directory of Minorities*, London: Longmans, 1990.

9 Summed up in the idea of a 'new world order'. A review of some possibilities for international law in this 'new' era is provided by Doo Kingue, *The Role of the United Nations in the New World Order*, UNITAR, 1991, Sales No. E.91.III.K.CR/33. The representative of The Netherlands to the Human Rights Commission stated that 'the world of 1992 differed from that of ten years earlier. Many dictatorial and totalitarian regimes had given way to democratic governments and there is now an opportunity for people to take the future into their own hands and help to shape the politics affecting them', UN Doc. E/CN.4/1992/SR.44/Add.1, para.50.

10 The growth of ethnic fundamentalism bears out the truth that group identity both includes and excludes. The defence of identity is an absolute necessity and is only now in the process of being properly addressed at the UN and regional levels. Strategies must, however, be found to prevent defence and liberation corrupting themselves into xenophobia and intolerance – see below on the concept of 'the people' and references to recent instruments on minority rights, p.186–9.

11 Useful general accounts of self-determination including democratic 'Wilsonian' aspects are provided in M. Pomerance, *Self-Determination in Law and Practice*, The Hague: Martinus Nijhoff, 1982; and M. Whiteman, *Digest of International Law*, vol.5, Washington: Department of State Publication, 1965.

12 The Wilsonian conception is well described by Pomerance as 'an imprecise amalgam of several strands of thought, some long associated in his mind with the notion of 'self-government', others newly hatched as a result of wartime developments, but all imbued with a general spirit of democracy. Wilson had long held the idea that every people had the right to select its own form of government – an idea that might be termed 'internal self-determination', Pomerance. above n.11, 1.

13 A. Cobban, *The Nation State and National Self-Determination*, London and Glasgow: Collins, 1969, p.63.

14 V.I. Lenin, *The Right of Nations to Self-Determination*, English edition, Moscow, 1947.

15 P. Thornberry, *International Law and the Rights of Minorities*, Oxford: Clarendon Press, 1991.

16 Whiteman, above n.11, p.44.

17 Ibid., p.46.

18 Cited by A. Cassese, 'The Helsinki Declaration and Self-Determination', in T. Buergenthal and J. Hall (eds) *Human Rights, International Law and the Helsinki Accord*, New York: Allanheld, 1977, pp.83–110, 84.

19 R. Falk, 'The Rights of Peoples (In Particular Indigenous Peoples)', in Crawford, above n.2, pp.17–37.

20 Cassese, above n.18.

21 Cf. the reference to 'the CSCE's comprehensive concept of security and stability, which includes human rights, political, military, economic and environmental components', Prague meeting of the CSCE Council, 30–31 January 1992, Summary of Conclusions, para.6.

22 Article 55: 'With a view to the creation of conditions of stability and well-

being which are necessary for peaceful and friendly relations among nations based on respect for the principle of equal rights and self-determination of peoples, the United Nations shall promote . . . (c) universal respect for, and observance of, human rights and fundamental freedoms.'

23 UN General Assembly Official Records (GAOR), 15th session, Supp. 16, 66 (1960); text in I. Brownlie, *Basic Documents on Human Rights*, Oxford: Clarendon Press, 2nd edn, 1981, p.28. The Colonial Declaration was passed by 89 votes to 0, with 9 abstentions: Australia, Belgium, Dominican Republic, France, Portugal, South Africa, Spain, the UK and the USA.

24 The 'milder' Resolution 1541(XV) proposed that self-determination could be achieved through independence, integration with an independent State, or free association with an independent State: UN GAOR, above n.23, p.29.

25 The preamble recalls the Charter's reaffirmation of faith in human rights and links self-determination, human rights and friendly relations. Operative paragraph 1 states baldly that the 'subjection of peoples to alien subjugation, domination and exploitation constitutes a denial of fundamental human rights'; paragraph 7 demands that all States 'shall observe faithfully and strictly the provisions of the Charter of the United Nations, the Universal Declaration of Human Rights and the present Declaration'.

26 For some recent affirmations, see UN Doc. E/CN.4/1992/SR.7, para.1 (Democratic People's Republic of Korea); and ibid., para.38 (Turkey): 'self-determination was a basic rule of international law and an essential prerequisite for the enjoyment of human rights.'

27 Ibid., SR.5, para.12.

28 The text of the General Comment was issued in UN Doc. CCPR/C/21/Add.3 and reproduced in UN GAOR, 39th session, Supp. 40, annex VI, General Comment 12(21) (1984).

29 P. Alston, 'The International Covenant on Economic, Social and Cultural Rights', in *Manual on Human Rights Reporting*, HR/PUB/91/1, New York: United Nations, 1991, p.39 at p.43.

30 See the *Global Consultation*, above n.6, and the UN Declaration on the Right to Development, UN General Assembly Resolution 41/128, UN GAOR, 41st session, Supp. 53, 186 (1986).

31 For an analysis, see Thornberry, above n.15, part IV.

32 Cassese, paper on 'The Right of Self-determination and Non-State Peoples', delivered at the Oxford Conference, above n.7.

33 The open-ended formula expands Resolution 1541, above n.24.

34 'Every State has the duty to promote through joint and separate action universal respect for the observance of human rights and fundamental freedoms in accordance with the Charter.'

35 See above nn.18 and 32.

36 UN Doc. A/AC.125/L.32. See also the text proposed by Czechoslovakia *et al.*, A/AC.125/L.74. One commentator noted that 'a close examination of its text will reward the reader with an affirmation of the applicability of the principle to peoples within existing States and the necessity for governments to represent the governed', R. Rosenstock, 'The Declaration of Principles of International Law' (1971) 65 *A.J.I.L.* 713, 732.

37 The non-recognition of distinct peoples within States must be accounted for in any interpretation of the Declaration. This limiting aspect of the Declaration retains validity for the generality of States.

38 Cassese, above n.18, 88–92; Dugard, above n.7.

39 See for example Article 1(1) of the international Convention on the Elimination of All Forms of Racial Discrimination: 'In this Convention, the term "racial discrimination" shall mean any distinction, exclusion, restriction or

preference based on race, colour, descent, or national or ethnic origin'. For a general review of rather unsteady international terminology, consult W. McKean, *Equality and Discrimination under International Law*, Oxford: Oxford University Press, 1983.

40 McKean, ibid.

41 See Articles 21 and 27 of the Universal Declaration of Human Rights, Article 25 of the Covenant on Civil and Political Rights, Article 15 of the Covenant on Economic, Social and Cultural Rights, Articles 7, 8 and 14 of the Convention on the Elimination of Discrimination against Women, Articles 2, 6, 7, 15, 22 and 23 of the ILO Convention on Indigenous and Tribal Peoples (No. 169) 1989, Articles 1, 2 and 8 of the UN Declaration on the Right to Development, and, among other documents of the CSCE process, paragraphs 32.6 and 35 of the Copenhagen Conference of the Human Dimension 1990. Also H. Steiner, 'Political Participation as a Human Right' (Spring 1988) 1 *Harvard-H.R.Y.* pp.77–134.

42 Religious elements not infrequently serve to constitute important aspects of 'ethnic' or 'racial' identity ; hence the frequent conjunction of religion and ethnic group in international group through texts such as Article 27 of the Covenant on Civil and Political Rights and the Convention on the Prevention and Punishment of the Crime of Genocide.

43 See above n.37. The maxim cited is 'A valuable servant but a dangerous master': P.G. Osborn, *A Concise Law Dictionary*, London: Sweet & Maxwell, 5th edn, 1964, p.131. Preambular paragraph 15 of the Declaration reads: 'Convinced . . . that any attempt aimed at the partial or total disruption of the national unity and territorial integrity of a State or country or at its political independence is incompatible with the purposes and principles of the Charter.'

44 Useful discussions of secession and secession criteria are found in L.C. Buchheit, *Secession : The Legitimacy of Self-Determination*, New Haven, Conn.: Yale University Press, 1978; D. Ronen, *The Quest for Self-Determination*, New Haven, Conn.: Yale University Press, 1979; A. Heraclides, 'Secession, Self-Determination and Non-Intervention: In Quest of a Normative Symbiosis' (1992) 45 *Journal of International Affairs* 399–420. The last-named author draws a sketch of 'four core attributes for a qualified right to secessionist self-determination: 1. A pattern of systematic discrimination or exploitation against a sizable, self-defined minority; 2. The existence of a distinct, self-defined community or society within a State, compactly inhabiting a region, which overwhelmingly supports separatism; 3. A realistic prospect of conflict resolution and peace within and between the new and the old State as a result of the envisaged self-rule or partition; and 4. The rejection of compromise solutions on the part of the central government', pp.410–11. Even such a cautious and careful account of criteria appears as possibility rather than probability in terms of the normative development of general international law.

45 The emergence of Bangladesh is a case in point, though some authors have striven to underline a legal case for the self-determination of the former East Pakistan: International Commission of Jurists, The Events in East Pakistan 1971 Geneva, 1972.

46 For the distinction between a general principle of self-determination and its appearance in internationally recognised rights, see H. Hannum, *Autonomy, Sovereignty, and Self-Determination. The Accommodation of Conflicting Rights*, Philadelphia: University of Pennsylvania Press, 1990, pp.27–49.

47 '[T]he idea of ethnical self-determination or the creation of new nations out of the existing States was rejected categorically [by African States] . . . . The

whole task of national integration and nation-building may require the denial of the right to ethnic self-determination in most territories as they emerge from dependency', Y. Makkonen, *International Law and the New States of Africa: A Study of the International Legal Problems of State Succession in the Newly Independent States of Eastern Africa*, Paris: Unesco, 1983, p.462.

48 P. Thornberry, *Minorities and Human Rights Law* London: Minority Rights Group, 1991. There is little comparison between the panoply of ch. VII Security Council resolutions demanding and facilitating the liberation of Kuwait and the ch. VI action in relation to Kurds represented by Resolution 688. See H. Adelman, 'Humanitarian Intervention: the Case of the Kurds' (1992) 4 *International Journal of Refugee Law* 4.

49 The Conference on Security and Co-operation in Europe has undergone significant expansion since the Final Act of the Helsinki Conference in 1975 in terms of standards, structures and mechanisms. The whole process is still developing, not least in the sphere of human rights. Helpful writings on the process include: A. Bloed, 'Institutional Aspects of the Helsinki Process after the Follow-Up Meeting of Vienna', 1989 *Netherlands I.L.R.*, 342–63; D. McGoldrick, 'Human Rights Developments in the CSCE Process' (1990) 39 *I.C.L.Q.* 923–40; E. Schlager, 'The Procedural Framework of the CSCE: From the Helsinki Consultations to the Paris Charter, 1972–1990' (1991) 12 *Human Rights Law Journal* 221–37.

50 The Statute of the Council of Europe reaffirms in the second paragraph of its preamble the signatory States' 'devotion to the spiritual and moral values which are the common heritage of their peoples and the true source of individual freedom, political liberty and the rule of law, principles which form the basis of all genuine democracy.' Article 3 of the Statute requires that 'every Member . . . must accept the principles of the rule of law and of the enjoyment by all persons within its jurisdiction of human rights and fundamental freedoms.' The protection and promotion of human rights in Europe has been greatly assisted by the European Convention on Human Rights and Fundamental Freedoms, with its attendant institutions of Commission, Court, Committee of Ministers, and Secretary-General of the Council of Europe, and the European Social Charter. See *Manual of the Council of Europe, Structure, Functions and Achievements*, London: Stevens & Sons, 1970. In May 1990, the Committee of Ministers decided to establish the European Commission for Democracy Through Law as a Partial Agreement of the Council of Europe; the Commission's field of action is defined as the guarantees offered by law in the service of democracy, and it will supply opinions on request of the Committee of Ministers, the Parliamentary Assembly of the Council of Europe, the Secretariat General of the same and member States of the Council of Europe. The Commission (the Venice Commission) has already prepared a draft European Convention for the Protection of Minorities, considered below: text of the Convention in CDL (91) 7, 22 February 1991; see also the explanatory report, CDL (91) 8, 11 March 1991.

51 See Article 5 of the 4th Lomé Convention between the Community and ACP countries. Within the framework of the application of the Convention, the concept of democratic adjustment has been elaborated as an inseparable process from economic reforms and development, mitigating the application of harsher concepts of structural adjustment. European Community instruments and institutions have consistently emphasised the links between human rights and democracy. The commitment to human rights is reflected in the Preamble to the Maastricht Treaty of Political Union 1991. See also the Resolution of the European Council and of the Member States Meeting in the Council on Human Rights, Democracy and Development, Brussels, 28 November 1991.

52 See the assessment in T.M. Franck, 'The Emerging Right to Democratic Governance' (1992) 86 *A.J.I.L.* 46–91 ; also Allan Rosas, 'Democracy and Human Rights', in A. Rosas and J. Helgesen (eds) *Human Rights in a Changing East-West Perspective*, London and New York: Pinter Publishers, 1990, pp.17–57.

53 Doc. CAB/LEG/67/3/Rev.5 (1981); (1982) 21 *I.L.M.* 59–68.

54 *Global Consultation*, above n.6. The growth of concern for development and its human rights implications through an extensive range of international instruments is traced in a paper prepared for the UN Centre for Human Rights and the Global Consultation by T. Kunanayakam: 'Annotations to the Declaration on the Right to Development and related United Nations System Instruments, Resolutions and Reports', HR/RD/1990/CONF.1. See also various contributions to agenda item 7 of the 48th Session of the Commission on Human Rights: 'Question of the Realization in all Countries of the Economic, Social and Cultural Rights Contained in the Universal Declaration of Human Rights and in the International Covenant on Economic, Social and Cultural Rights, and Study of the Special Problems which the Developing Countries Face in their Efforts to Achieve these Human Rights'.

55 An excellent general treatment of issues is provided by N. Lerner, *Group Rights and Discrimination in International Law*, Dordrecht: Martinus Nijhoff, 1991.

56 The contribution of NGOs is usefully reviewed in *Bulletin of Human Rights*, vol.90(1), New York: United Nations, 1991, 'II. The Role of Non-governmental Organizations'.

57 (1991) 30 ILM 190.

58 The relationship is very fully set out in the preamble to the Document of the Copenhagen Meeting of the Conference of the Human Dimension 1990 in a manner which captures some of the spirit of the present essay: 'The participating States express their conviction that full respect for human rights and fundamental freedoms and the development of societies based on pluralistic democracy and the rule of law are prerequisites for progress in setting up the lasting order of peace, security, justice and co-operation that they seek to establish in Europe.'

59 In the manner of M. Jules Deschenes, in his elimination of 'non-questions' from the attempt to define 'minority': UN Doc. E/CN.4/Sub.2/1985/31.

60 Declaration of India, above n.1.

61 From Principle VIII of the Declaration on Principles Guiding Relations between Participating States.

62 Fourth Annual Activity Report of the African Commission on Human and Peoples' Rights 1990–1991, Doc. ACHPR/IX/AN/RPT/4, Annex I. According to the Chairman of the African Commission on Human and Peoples' Rights (Mr Badawi), African governments 'were well aware that the protection of human rights was vital to stability and development on the African continent. There could be no development in Africa without respect for human rights and the rule of law and participation by the peoples of Africa in the governing process', UN Doc. E/CN.4/1992/SR.23, para.8.

63 See M. Addo, 'Political Self-Determination within the Context of the African Charter on Human and Peoples' Rights' (1988) 32 *Journal of African Law* 182–93.

64 *Global Consultation*, above n.6.

65 The movements are documented in the annual Human Development Report of the UN Development Programme (UNDP). This and other indicators are analysed by Special Rapporteur Danilo Turk in his second progress report 'Realization of Economic, Social and Cultural Rights', UN Doc. E/CN.4/

Sub.2/1991/17. See also K. Tomasevski, 'Human Rights Indicators: The Right to Food as a Test Case', in P. Alston and K. Tomasevski (eds) *The Right to Food*, The Hague: Martinus Nijhoff, 1984, pp.135–67.

66 UN Doc. E/CN.4/1992/SR.5, para.76.

67 See above n.1.

68 Unesco Experts, above n.2, para.23.

69 Ibid., para.22.

70 Compare the definition of 'minority' in the context of Article 27 of the Covenant on Civil and Political Rights by Special Rapporteur F. Capotorti: 'A group numerically inferior to the rest of the population of a State, in a non-dominant position, whose members – being nationals of the State – possess ethnic, religious or linguistic characteristics differing from those of the rest of the population and show, if only implicitly, a sense of solidarity, directed towards preserving their culture, traditions, religion or language', *Study on the Rights of Persons belonging to Ethnic, Religious and Linguistic Minorities*, UN Sales No. E.91.XIV.2 New York: United Nations, 1991, para.568. Also Deschenes, above n.59.

71 UN Doc. E/CN.4/1992/48.

72 Report of the Working Group on the Rights of Persons Belonging to National, Ethnic, Religious and Linguistic Minorities, UN Doc. E/CN.4/1991/53, para.9.

73 Self-determination 'refers to the right of a majority within a generally accepted political unit to the exercise of power . . . there can be no such thing as self-determination for the Nagas', R. Higgins, *The Development of International Law through the Political Organs of the United Nations*, Oxford: Oxford University Press, 1963, cited by Heraclides, above n.44, p.406.

74 For a recognition of self-determination but with limits on the mode of exercise, see the draft Universal Declaration on the Rights of Indigenous Peoples, below n.81. The representative of Austria suggested to the Commission on Human Rights that 'A distinction between peoples and . . . minorities should be made on a case-by-case basis in the absence of any generally recognized definitions of those concepts', UN Doc. E/CN.4/1992/SR.6, para.35. This is likely to happen anyway, though the development of *general* standards is not assisted by concentration on the *sui generis* case – see n.89 below.

75 P. Thornberry, 'Self-Determination, Minorities, Human Rights: A Review of International Instruments' (1989) 38 *I.C.L.Q*. 867–89.

76 For example, in the Human Rights Committee, the British member, Sir Vincent Evans, stated clearly that in the Covenant(s), 'the reference to 'peoples' meant the whole of the peoples within the independent sovereign State, including minority sections of the population', (1983–84) *Yearbook of the Human Rights Committee*, vol.I, summary record of the 477th meeting, para.68. Some version of a differentiated concept of the people is probably also implicit in the works of those who recognise autonomy as the key concept for internal self-determination: see, generally, Hannum, above n.46.

77 See above nn.49, 50, 55, 58.

78 The condition of the very poor is the particular focus of the ATD (Aide à Toute Detresse) Fourth World Movement, founded in France in 1957: 'Fourth World' was coined after the Fourth Estate of the French Revolution, which comprised the very poorest peoples struggling to be represented in the political changes of the time. ATD Fourth World has consultative status with ECOSOC, Unicef, Unesco, ILO and the Council of Europe.

79 The pluralist theme is perhaps most strongly and insistently conveyed through the ensemble of CSCE instruments.

80 Article 72 of the 1977 Constitution of the USSR was one such constitutional guarantee of secession, applying the principle of free choice to any Union

Republic: *Constitution (Fundamental Law) of the Union of Soviet Socialist Republics*, Moscow: Novosti Press Agency Publishing House, 1977.

81 UN Doc. E/CN.4/Sub.2/1991/40.

82 Indigenous peoples themselves may not be entirely satisfied with the precise formula adopted in the text: see 'On The Record', the paper on the UN's humanitarian efforts – the struggle for indigenous rights and against modern forms of slavery, 30 July 1991, p.1 and 12. For a wide-ranging review of indigenous issues, see R. Stavenhagen, 'Indigenous Peoples' (May 1989) 2 *The Thatched Patio*, No. 3, 1–23 ; and, by the same author, *The Ethnic Question, Conflicts, Development, and Human Rights*, Tokyo: The United Nations University Press, 1990.

83 The draft is at an early stage in the UN processes, and may expect a difficult passage through various stages to and in the General Assembly. On the other hand, the text makes a powerful moral and legal case for indigenous peoples, the general acceptance of which may be promoted by the designation of 1993 as the International Year of the World's Indigenous Peoples and the holding of the World Conference on Human Rights in the same year.

84 Published together with the Agreement on a Comprehensive Political Settlement of the Cambodia Conflict by London HMSO, Cm 1786 (1991) *U.K.T.S.* No. 111.

85 Declaration on the 'Guidelines on the Recognition of New States in Eastern Europe and in the Soviet Union', EC Foreign Affairs Council, 16 December 1991.

86 Part IV, para.7. The Badinter Report on Yugoslavia expressly relies on the *Frontier Lands (Burkino Faso/Mali)* case [1986] I.C.J. Rep. 554.

87 UN General Assembly Resolution 41/128, 4 December 1986, text in Crawford, above n.2, 207–12.

88 See the above analysis which represents a fairly full reading of an admittedly limited text.

89 Heraclides, above n.44. According to the representative of Turkey, his government 'believed that, in States established by two politically equal communities or peoples having the status of corporate political bodies, each community was entitled to determine its own future by exercising its right to self-determination, regardless of its numerical size . . . . It was . . . imperative to take such *sui generis* situations into account', UN Doc. E/CN.4/1992/SR.7, paras.40–1. The unnamed '*sui generis* situation' is undoubtedly that of Cyprus: see the statement of the representative of Cyprus which referred to those who created 'monstrous theories' as to the subjects of self-determination 'and talked of so-called *sui generis* situations, in an attempt to deform both the principle and the right to suit their political expediencies', UN Doc. E/CN.4/1992/SR.5, para.18.

90 UN Doc. E/CN.4/1992/48.

91 For example, paragraph 36 of the Copenhagen Conference of the Human Dimension of the CSCE: 'Every participating State will promote a climate of mutual respect, understanding, co-operation and solidarity among all persons living on its territory, without distinction as to ethnic or national origin or religion, and will encourage the solution of problems through dialogue based on the principles of the rule of law.'

92 'Whereas it is essential, if man is not to be compelled to have recourse, as a last resort, to rebellion against tyranny and oppression, that human rights should be protected by the rule of law', preambular paragraph 3 of the Universal Declaration of Human Rights.

93 Steiner, above n.41. My choice of participation rather than autonomy as the key concept for internal self-determination is partly influenced by the very

negative reception given by many State representatives to 'autonomy' proposals at the December 1992 meeting of the Human Rights Commission's Working Group on Minorities. On the other hand, the draft Declaration on the Rights of Persons Belonging to Minorities readily accepts the participation principle: UN Doc. E/CN.4/1992/48, as do international standards generally.

94 *Yearbook of the Human Rights Committee*, above n.76, SR.515, para.51 (Graefrath) ; ibid., para.48 (Ermacora).

95 Ibid., SR.478, para.17 (Ndiaye).

96 Cited by D. McGoldrick, *The Human Rights Committee*, Oxford: Clarendon Press, 1991, p.263.

97 J.B. Marie,'Relations between Peoples' Rights and Human Rights: Semantic and Methodological Distinctions' (1986) 7 *Human Rights Law Journal* 195, at p.203.

98 B.G. Ramcharan, 'Peoples Rights and Minorities' Rights' (1987) 56 *Nordic Journal of International Law* 9–38, 14, 15.

99 McGoldrick, above n.96, pp.247–68; see, for example, Communication No. 167/1984, *Bernard Ominayak, Chief of the Lubicon Lake Band* v. *Canada*, views of the Human Rights Committee adopted on 26 March 1990, Report of the Human Rights Committee, vol.II, UN GAOR, 45th Session, Supp. No. 40 (A/45/40), pp.1–30.

100 A. Cancado Trindade, paper for the *Global Consultation*, above n.6, HR/RD/1990/CONF.36, 8.

101 Preambular paragraph 3 of the international Covenant on Civil and Political Rights recites that 'the ideal of free human beings enjoying civil and political freedom and freedom from fear and want can only be achieved if conditions are created whereby everyone may enjoy his civil and political rights, as well as his economic, social and cultural rights'. Article 6.2 of the UN Declaration on the Right to Development states forthrightly that 'All human rights and fundamental freedoms are indivisible and interdependent; equal attention and urgent consideration should be given to the implementation, promotion and protection of civil, political, social and cultural rights'.

102 The use of indicators in the assessment of human rights and development currently attracts considerable interest, though it is not without its critics, especially in regard to the content of the 1991 Human Development Report of the UNDP which incorporated for the first time a 'human freedom indicator'. See the remarks by Alston in UN Doc. E/C.12/1991/SR.1, paras.45ff. See also, Turk. None the less, generalised indicators of performance, observance and failure in human rights may provide a valuable input for third-generation peoples' rights as well as other rights. Analogous procedures for mass *violations* of rights are such as those developed by ECOSOC Resolutions 1235(XLII) and 1503(XLVIII). Broad movements in rights and generalising concepts like internal self-determination require narration and communication through appropriate methodologies which go beyond the recording of individual complaints.

103 Cited by J. Hausermann, 'Myths and Realities', in P. Davies (ed.) *Human Rights*, London and New York: Routledge, 1988, p.130.

104 The defeat of human rights in a State does not destroy the standards of rights which continue to function as a critique of States' performance.

105 Paragraph 4.

106 This is clearly an inadequate process for ethnically complex States; hence the need to broaden democratic concepts.

107 Work cited. above n.75.

10 The principle of sovereign equality[1]

Colin Warbrick

INTRODUCTION: SOVEREIGNTY AND EQUALITY

Neither 'sovereignty'[2] nor 'equality'[3] is an idea which is unambiguous or easy to understand. Each has a 'natural' connotation, as in claims that states must be sovereign or that all men are created equal, which make it difficult to prise away the legal meaning of the terms from the powerful political slogans they sometimes represent. Entities must be sovereign to be states. What this means is that one of the criteria of statehood is that the entity must be constitutionally independent.[4] That is not to say they need be omnicompetent in the sense that parliamentary sovereignty is understood in the United Kingdom. Most states submit the exercise of public power to constitutional constraint. Some of those limitations affect the international capacities of the state but they do not bring the international status of the state into question.[5] Constitutional sovereignty is a matter of internal law. International law is relevant only in so far as it requires that the constitutional law of a state should not be exercised contrary to any international obligations of the state, the same as for any other national law.[6] So to act is to exceed the internal sovereignty of the state, the area of activity which is not regulated by international law.[7] It is an area which is constantly mutable, as the international obligations of the state change.[8] It is generally (but not universally) accepted that no sphere of public action may not be subject to international legal regulation, although it may be that the less the business of the state has a direct effect on other states, the greater will be the burden of demonstrating that there are rules of international law which bear on its conduct.[9] The limits of internal sovereignty, then, are set by international law. The external sovereignty of the state is its capacity to engage in international legal relations with other states. In its external aspects 'sovereignty' is an even more misleading term than when it is used in a domestic context. If sovereignty were to mean absolute and unrestrained power, then no system of law could be created to regulate relations between sovereign states, nor indeed to protect the continued personality of any one of them. Sovereignty would be no more than the exercise of effective power and would be contingent wholly on the capacity of a government to continue doing so in the face of whatever internal or external material threats were ranged against its control. An interstate legal system requires that sovereignty be understood in a way that allows states to subject their power to legal obligations, at a minimum obligations which acknowledge the continued right of other states to exist. International law rests on the premise, the hypothesis as Kelsen puts it, that the customary practices of States are capable of generating legal obligations.[10] The right to contribute to the formation of such obligations and the duty to comply with them when they have been created are the equal attribute and responsibility of all states.

Equality is the condition of persons or things being similar or identical or being treated similarly or identically. Entities are equal because they are states: they are not states because they are equal. Given the vast material differences between states in every aspect imaginable – geographical size, population, wealth, resources, military power – equality of states is being used in some constructive sense, the legal identity of the personality of states.[11] States require the same characteristics to claim that status – territory, population, effective and independent government.[12] They have the same capacities in international law. There are other potential legal consequences of equality. Equality may imply an essentially negative obligation on other legal persons not to discriminate between equal persons, that is to say, to serve as a restriction on the exercise of a person's rights and powers. Since material inequality between persons is usually the case, legally equality inevitably has a fictional quality to it. Legal equality may involve positive obligations on the strong, the rich, the able to take action to aid the weak, the poor, the unable, to discriminate favourably towards them. Rules of non-discrimination and obligations of positive discrimination are rules of law.[13] The extent to which they exist in a society of states returns us to the matter of sovereignty.

SOVEREIGNTY, STATES AND THE INTERNATIONAL LEGAL SYSTEM

'The sovereignty and equality of states', Professor Brownlie writes, 'represent the basic constitutional doctrine of the law of nations, which governs a community consisting primarily of states having a uniform personality.'[14] It is a very spare constitutional system that they represent.[15] One might add to them the elementary substantive rules which protect the personality of states, the rules on territorial integrity and non-intervention. These are, perhaps, the international law equivalents of Professor Hart's 'minimum content of natural law' in the domestic context.[16] They are the minimum requirements of an intelligible and useful system of international law but they are rules of law rather than natural prerequisites.

The toleration of the right of states to go to war and the acceptance by the international legal system that the results of war had legal consequences for most of the history of international law are indications that a legal system can operate with rules which leave the personality of some of its subjects contingent on the lawful activities of others.[17]

The capacity to create and to be bound by customary international law is one characteristic of statehood.[18] States can use this capacity to extend their rights and obligations beyond the mere acknowledgement of each other's territorial integrity and political independence. States may, for instance, accept obligations about the protection of diplomats or the treatment of aliens in their territories. However, because they are equal and sovereign, such obligations must be clearly created; they may not be presumed. This is not some forensic device related to the burden of proof but a reflection of the way states are. The words of the Permanent Court remain of importance:

> International law governs relations between independent States. The rules of law binding upon States therefore emanate from their own free will as expressed in conventions or by usages generally accepted as expressing principles of law and established in order to regulate the relations between these co-existing independent communities or with a view to the achievement of common aims. Restrictions upon the independence of States cannot therefore be presumed.[19]

One way in which the *Lotus* test can most easily be satisfied is by relying on a treaty obligation, rather than customary law – the binding force of the treaty coming from a customary rule, the provenance of which is not in doubt.[20]

It is, of course, by using their capacities to enter into new obligations that states have been able to achieve a regime of legal relations beyond the minimum requirements for existence. Co-operation has its material foundation in the needs of all states to engage in relations with other states in trade, investment, communications, transport, the better they are then able to exercise their independent constitutional sovereignty – the exercise of external sovereign power to enter into international obligations may not so much diminish formal constitutional sovereignty as enhance its effective exercise.[21] States have different material capacities to get what they want. Consent rather than direct reciprocity of obligations provides the binding quality of treaties. The result is a wide variety of different sets of treaty rights and duties for states, as wide as there are numbers of states. It is as clearly wrong to speak of the 'equal rights and duties' of states as it is to speak of their material equality. It is the exercise of their equal sovereignties which has resulted in their unequal rights and duties.[22]

EQUALITY OF STATES

In what sense, then, is it possible to refer usefully and accurately to the equality of states? One obvious area is the formal status of states, in what Professor James calls the 'realm of protocol'.[23] If a state is a state, then it is formally equal to all others – entitled to equality in matters of diplomatic precedence, respect for its head of state and other representatives and acknowledgement of the equal weight of its participation in international meetings and conferences. These may seem peripheral matters, of ceremonial significance only, but as a means of removing procedural matters of status from the preliminaries of international negotiations, they have been an important factor in making multilateral diplomacy effective. Very small states have been able to rely on their equal status to influence events. Malta was able to secure decisions favourable to it within the CSCE process by preventing the achievement of consensus on other terms (although its bluff was eventually called).[24] The Holy See made full use of its presence at the UN Conference on Environment and Development (UNCED) in Rio to press for provisions in the final statement on population control congenial to it.[25]

It is sometimes suggested that the rule of the sovereign immunity of states was a further reflection of the formal capacity of states, that the rule that a state could not be made answerable for its conduct in the courts of another state.[26] If this were the basis of the rule (rather than as emanation of the sovereignty of states), it is further confirmation of the legal quality of the principle of equality. The rule of absolute sovereign immunity has been replaced by a pragmatic rule of restricted immunity, reflecting state practice and treaties, that practice a product of the increasing distance between the public functions of the state, to which immunity is still accorded, and the more mundane, commercial, distinctly unceremonial activities in which states have increasingly engaged.[27]

It is difficult to draw on municipal analogies to elucidate the role of equality and non-discrimination in international law because much domestic law on the subject deals with the exercise of public power. The absence of central power in the international system means that there is nothing directly equivalent to discriminatory legislation or administrative decision-making. There is no public authority distributing benefits or allocating licences. Discrimination will be 'private', the result of the action of states in exercising their discretionary powers in favour of this state but against that one. There is no general rule of non-discrimination, although there may be specific ones, for example under a most-favoured national treaty.[28] Another familiar example is the obligation on states not to exercise their power to expropriate foreign property in a way which discriminates between states.[29] It follows from the understanding of sovereignty and the *Lotus* principle that those powers of states which are not subject to legal regulation are free for them to exercise according to their own assessments of their interests. States are free to recognise or not recognise other states, to maintain or not to maintain diplomatic relations with them, to trade or not to trade, to grant aid or not to grant aid. Other discretions, though not wholly immune from legal regulation, are very wide, for instance, the power to confer nationality. These powers are exercised largely according to factual or material considerations rather than legal ones (although there may be legal costs if a state chooses to exercise its discretion in a particular way[30]) but if another state is adversely affected by the decision, it has no grounds for complaint, even if the object of the decision is to do it harm.[31]

If there are few general rules prohibiting discrimination by states, there are even less requiring positive discrimination in favour of the materially disadvantaged states. In moral and political terms, it might be possible to make a case that such rules are not only desirable but essential.[32] If the material position of some states is so diminished that their constitutional sovereignty is of no practical value, the choices that they might want to make being wholly circumscribed by lack of resources or extremes of climate, then the question can be fairly put whether they are really states at all. There are no general rules of law on which states such as these can rely to redress the absence of internal legitimacy or their lack of resources. General international law, with its emphasis on consent and reciprocity, does not demand of states that they act to redress these inequalities. In various maritime boundary cases, arguments have been put to the International Court that a line of demarcation to satisfy the test of 'equitable principles' should take into account the relative distribution of resources between the states on-shore. The open-textured nature of the rule does not exclude a favourable response but the Court has been adamant in denying it.

In the *Libya-Malta* case, the Court said,

> The Court does not . . . consider that the delimitation should be influenced by the relative economic positions of the two States in question, in such a way that the area of continental shelf regarded as appertaining to the less rich of the two States would be somewhat increased in order to compensate for its inferiority in economic resources. Such considerations are totally unrelated to the underlying intention of the applicable rules of international law.[33]

Geographical disadvantage may, however, be a ground to be taken into account in assessing whether a proposed boundary accords with equitable principles. A rare but controversial example of a rule in favour of disadvantaged states is the claim that landlocked states have a right of transit access across the territory of neighbouring states to the sea.[34]

Another aspect of the legal equality of states is the international equivalent to the domestic principle of equality before the law.[35] This is a trite proposition if it means no more than that states are equally entitled to enjoy their rights and obliged to conform to their duties. Because of the infrequency of international litigation, not much more is added by saying that states are equal before international tribunals. Of rather greater practical importance is the equality of states in international organisations though states have no legal right to join international institutions. Once they are in, the significance of equal status is political rather than legal and there are, in any event, many deviations from equality of status. On the other hand the general impact of the rule of equality of states before the law should not be underestimated. It is testimony to their commitment to the international legal regulation of their affairs that states seldom claim not to be bound by a rule of international law (still less not to be bound by international law as a whole).[36] Nor do they lightly admit to having breached international law, even if their attempts to justify their actions sometimes stretch credulity. In the *Hostages* case,[37] Iran gave explanations to justify the detention of the American diplomats which were couched in legal terms. The United States explained its non-appearance before the International Court in the *Nicaragua* case and its subsequent rejection of the judgment on the basis of its legal objections to the exercise of jurisdiction and the merits of the judgment.[38] Again, states explain why they must do what they do not want to do or why they may not do what they do want to do by reference to international legal obligations. The British government has fashioned its responses to adverse judgments of the European Court of Human Rights to take account of the Court's findings, minimally and in a dilatory fashion sometimes, but in compliance none the less.[39] These examples, both complying and not complying, all involve international judicial decisions, which put law compliance in a strong spotlight. They are not typical because another aspect of the legal equality of states is their equal right not to be made subject to third party determination of their disputes without their consent: and they seldom do consent.[40] It is much easier for a state to maintain a stance of legal rectitude where there is no authoritative assessment of its arguments or independent determination of the facts. The more typical case of a dispute between states as to what the law is or what the law requires in the particular circumstances focuses attention once more on the difference between formal and material equality. In cases such as this, it is for a state claiming that its rights have been violated to obtain redress for itself by negotiation and, ultimately, by self-help. All states have an equal formal right to do so.[41] Their material capacities to obtain a remedy are wholly different. Since legitimate self-help embraces non-forcible counter-measures, the differences in economic power and influence of states has a direct bearing on the ability of states to secure the performance of duties owed to them by other states and to resist compromising their positions when the law-breaker is unwilling to comply.[42] States are generally on their own and, certainly where reprisals are contemplated, the rights of third States to involve themselves are limited.[43] Even in the case of collective self-defence, the state under attack has the right only to request assistance, not to demand it.[44]

The result is, in general international law, that states are able to take advantage of their material advantages to influence the content of international law, and furthermore strong states are better equipped to secure compliance with duties owed to them and to resist attempts to make them perform their own obligations. Whatever the formal equality of states, the substantive law is influenced by the material differences between them, even if it does not mirror them exactly.

THE UN CHARTER AND SOVEREIGN EQUALITY

It is nothing new for there to be discrepancies in power between states but the expansion of the international state system through the process of decolonisation brought a new political perspective to bear on these differences. Many of these new states are extremely weak.

Professor Jackson has coined the phrase 'quasi-sovereign' states,[45]

> The ex-colonial states have been internationally enfranchised and possess the same external rights and responsibilities as all other sovereign states: juridical statehood. At the same time, however, many have not yet been authorised and empowered domestically and consequently lack the institutional features of sovereign states as also defined by classical international law. They disclose limited empirical statehood: their populations do not enjoy many of the advantages traditionally associated with independent statehood. Their governments are often deficient in the political will, institutional authority, and organised power to protect human rights or provide socioeconomic welfare. The concrete benefits which have historically justified the undeniable burdens of sovereign statehood are often limited to fairly narrow elites and not yet extended to the citizenry at large whose lives may be scarcely improved by independence or even adversely affected by it. These states are primarily juridical. They are still far from complete, so to speak, and empirical statehood in large measures still remains to be built. I therefore refer to them as 'quasi-states'.

Not only are these states weak but there are many of them. International law is important to them to confirm and protect their formal status and these states have sought to utilise the law to invest it with standards and obligations which will go towards mitigating their vulnerable positions. Their activities in this direction have been channelled through international organisations, particularly the United Nations, where their large numbers give them advantages in the decision-making process. At the level of principle, it is claimed that the idea of sovereign equality has taken on a new dimension under the law of the Charter.

The principle of the sovereign equality of states is one of the foundations of the United Nations Charter. Article 2 reads:

> The Organization and its Members, in pursuit of the purposes stated in Article 1, shall act in accordance with the following principles.
> 1. The Organization is based on the principle of the sovereign equality of all its Members.

And yet the Charter system of collective security represents one of the most significant departures from the principle of equality by elevating the position of the permanent members of the Security Council above the rest of the membership. The concurring votes of the permanent members are required if the Council is to take decisions binding of the whole of the membership for the preservation of international peace and security.[46] In fact, the privileges of the permanent members extend beyond this. Their affirmative votes (or positive participation) are required for the admission of new members[47] and the admission of non-member states to the Statute of the International Court of Justice,[48] for the suspension or expulsion of members,[49] for measures to enforce a judgment of the International Court,[50] for the appointment of the Secretary-General[51] and for the amendment of the Charter.[52] The result is that the permanent members are protected against any decisions uncongenial to themselves while any other member is susceptible to being bound by a decision to which it objects.

The explanation is functional and political. Experience has shown that departure from the unanimity principle, which is a corollary of sovereign equality, is necessary if international institutions are to be effective, particularly if it is envisaged that they should have the capacity to take action directed against a state.[53] Beyond this, if some organisations are to be effective, the active participation of those states with experience and resources is desirable. In the case of the Charter, the enlistment of the political and military power of the permanent members was seen as an essential ingredient of the system of collective security. The political price for the acceptance of this responsibility by the permanent members was their right of veto.[54] For most of the history of the United Nations, the permanent members have shown that they regard as legitimate the right to use the veto to protect their own interests, that its exercise is a sovereign right. There have been only a few occasions when the veto has not been used to prevent binding decisions being reached by the Council. When the Security Council has arrived at valid, binding decisions directed at particular states, these states inevitably reacted by complaining about the political unfairness of the decisions, complaining essentially about the consequences of the departure from the principle of equality.[55]

Some compensation for the ordinary members of the UN was provided for in the voting procedures of the General Assembly and the other collective organs.[56] However, the Charter provides that decisions of the

Assembly are only recommendations. It is an oversimplification to say that General Assembly resolutions have no legal effect[57] but they do not have any uniform legal effect. Aspirations to invest the resolutions with the status of parliamentary legislation enacted on the basis of state majority votes have been unsuccessful.[58] One alternative has been to rely on resolutions as elaborations of the obligations in the Charter itself. So it has been with the General Assembly Resolution 2625 and the principle of sovereign equality.

THE DECLARATION OF PRINCIPLES[59]

General Assembly Resolution 2625 is part of the constitutional law of the UN. It must be read as a whole and with the Charter itself.[60] Its generalities may be reconciled in various ways, territorial integrity being read subject to self-determination, say, and the overriding principle of good faith not to permit the effective reading out of practical effect of the provisions, non-intervention to exclude any concern for self-determination, for instance. Equally, constitutional concepts develop through time. Constitutional law is a process as well as a set of individual rules and decisions. Political expectations do have an impact on the way general provisions will be read. The changes in law and in the political environment since 1970 are profound and have been dramatic.[61] When reading the terms of Resolution 2625, developments in the law resulting from these changes must be taken into account. Resolution 2625, in order to obtain the consensus support in 1970, contains general phrases and studied ambiguities, the actual impact of which were to be worked out in practice. Just as Resolution 2625 was an elaboration and development of the principles in the Charter, so its terms were open to further refinement.

The principal matter of controversy about the principle of sovereign equality was whether it represented the established understanding of the nature of statehood and international law as the legal system that regulated the relations between independent states on the basis of their consent or whether a new idea of a community of states had been instituted by the Charter, in which the promotion and protection of common values, rather than the preservation of individual state ones, was the primary objective of the law.

Writing about the Resolution in 1972, Professor Magarasevic placed as much emphasis on one of the purposes of the UN, 'To develop friendly relations among nations based on respect for the principles of equal rights and self-determination of peoples' as he did on Article 2(1) of the Charter. The references here and elsewhere in the Charter to 'peoples', the link which is established between individual well-being and peaceful relations between States and the resulting competence of the UN and the duties of co-operation of members in Articles 55 and 56 represent 'a new conception of sovereign equality'.[63] This is, he goes on,

> the conception of the equal rights of states, determined generally as equality before international law and equality in rights and duties, is an essential political and legal prerequisite for the maintenance of international peace and stability in international law and international political, economic, social, humanitarian and cultural relations.[64]

Magarasevic was a proponent of further development of Resolution 2625, with the clear expectation that anti-colonial and socialist forces would exercise the predominant influence, so that the ambiguities in the Resolution would be resolved in their favour. His assessment of the possibilities for evolution of Resolution 2625 was accurate but its language is capable of bearing a wide range of meanings, including ones contradictory to his aspirations. Events have not turned out quite as he (or anybody else) imagined they would.[65]

Some of the provisions in the sovereign equality principle in Resolution 2625 reflect other principles in the Resolution: the duties in paragraph 2(c) and (d) are references to the rules guaranteeing the internal sovereignty of states. Paragraph 2(f) replicates the principle of good faith, adding the duty 'to live in peace with other states'. These provisions are reaffirmations of the pre-Charter understandings of sovereignty and equality. While they had been developed by practice under the Charter, they had not been substantially modified by 1970. Paragraph 2(c) was designed to make it clear that no form of political or economic system adopted by the government of a state was a violation of international law. In fact, even by 1970, it was being argued that apartheid was contrary to international law.[66] About the same time, there were the first inklings that gross violations of human rights were proper matters of international concern, even where they went to the central exercise of governmental powers.[67] Generally though, paragraph 2(e) was a strengthening of internal sovereignty.[68]

Reaching a consensus of the principle of sovereign equality was relatively straightforward,[69] the most serious controversy being about the extent the principle protected the right of a state to deal with its natural resources, free from any restraints resulting from their foreign ownership.[70] The most interesting innovation in the statement of the principle is the introduction of the phrase 'States . . . are equal members of the international community'. The traditional concepts of sovereignty and equality were features of an international system of states and that system was largely bilateral in the nature of its legal relationships and served to protect the rights of states themselves, notably each state's right to its independence. The idea of international community implies some notion of common values, not just the several interests of individual states.[71]

Territorial integrity and political independence are of the latter kind –

each state has the same, individual right – but the preservation of international peace and security is a matter of interest to all states, a matter of international concern. The system of collective security established by the Charter is the institution the states have set up to protect this common interest (as well as, if they are simultaneously at risk, the rights of an individual state).[72]

By the process of constitutional development through the practice of the members of the UN and by the elaboration of independent treaty arrangements, it is possible to identify the legal quality of interests which go beyond the concern of a particular state. Most obviously, this is true of the law of human rights where the obligation of a state to observe human rights standards will hardly mean anything at all if other states do not have a legal interest in its behaviour, since, in the typical case, a state will be called upon to carry out its human rights duties with respect to its own population. Human rights practice recognises a distinction between the implementation of human rights standards and their enforcement. For the UN, the enforcement of human rights standards, on the rare occasions action has been taken, has been closely associated with the preservation of international peace and security.[73] Although it has been strongly urged upon them in the academic literature,[74] states have been reluctant to assert or to concede unilateral rights of action to enforce human rights obligations.[75] However, the creation of international institutions and the recognition of the international legal protection of community and individual values has changed the nature of the debate about the assertion of rules of non-discrimination and positive discrimination in international law.

THE INFLUENCE OF INTERNATIONAL INSTITUTIONS

If, in general customary law, it was difficult to find rules either which prohibited a state from discriminating in the exercise of its rights between one state and another or which required a state positively to act in favour of particular state, there is little in Resolution 2625 which clearly takes either case forward. The Resolution can be read as affirming the formal equality and the international sovereignty of states. The differences of opinion were hidden by its general language rather than resolved by it. In the circumstances, developments in the practice of states are important in giving the imprecise language more certain content. The origins of this practice are to be found in the proliferation of international organisations which had begun before 1970. One objective of some organisations was to create legal obligations of non-discrimination.[76] Another was to address (and even redress) some aspects of the substantive inequalities between states.[77] The institutional structures provide the genesis of a public law of international law.

In domestic legal systems, positive discrimination law is part of public law. It requires the identification of beneficiaries and contributors, the establishment of standards of equality – how equal with respect to what rights – the setting up of programmes to deliver the positive benefits and of institutions to supervise the performance of their obligations by those who must contribute to the achievement of the goals. Altruism cannot be assumed; self-enforcement by the weak against the strong is naive. International law is notably deficient in its equivalents to domestic public law. However, the age of international institutions has seen the creation of a variety of devices which serve as something of a substitute. The organisations have engaged in standard-setting and in assistance and co-operative implementation of the agreed standards. Some of this activity is designed to repair the material differences between states though, ironically, this is often sought to be achieved by international organisations whose structures and voting rules constitute departures from the concept of the formal equality of states.[78]

The reasons for providing a preferential status for some states vary. The need to enlist the participation of states likely to have to carry the greatest burden of the organisations' activities in political or in budgetary terms is one justification.[79] Enhanced voting strength, maybe even a veto, protects such states against having unsustainable obligations foisted upon them by a majority of beneficiaries.[80] The participation of states with the greatest interest and expertise in technical matters may be assured by relying on objective criteria as the basis for membership of non-plenary organs.[81] Political acceptability of decisions may be enhanced by representation of geographical areas or political systems of states. Departures from the formal standard of equality are justified on a variety of functional grounds, including some which are designed to repair the inequalities between states. The need to create formal inequality in the cause of material equality is partly a consequence of the requirement that the consent of states is required for the formation of these public law institutions: membership can never be compulsory.[82] A common pattern is for a plenary organ to have wide competence but narrow legal powers of decision while a specialised organ has a narrower competence but stronger powers of decision.

The debates, still unresolved, about the management of the sea-bed beyond the limits of national jurisdiction are a good illustration of this conflict between formal equality and special interest.[83] If no action had been taken, in the early 1970s the resources of the deep sea-bed would have been open equally to exploitation by all states. In fact, the combination of financial investment and technical accomplishments necessary for commercial exploitation was available only to a small number of developed states. Developing countries properly feared that under such a regime what was then believed to be a practically limitless source of profit, would have accrued exclusively to companies from these few states. The first step to pre-empt this was the designation of the resources as the 'common heritage of mankind', establishing some unarticulated community interest in the resources.[84] For the mining states, this interest was no greater than the right of some international body to license claims to exploitation areas, a right to submit claims being open to all states equally, in return for a (not very big) licence fee and (possibly) some share in the profits.[85] For developing countries, the international body was to have powers to administer the entire deep sea-bed area, with extensive governmental powers of taxation and operational supervision. Furthermore, a body was to be established to undertake exploitation on behalf of the community. This body, the Enterprise, was to enjoy preferential rights to enhance its competitiveness with the private mining operators and was to conduct its operations in such a way and to use its profits in such a way that the economics of developing countries enjoyed the overwhelming benefit of its activities.[86] There was furious debate about the composition of the organs of the International Seabed Authority, essentially reflecting the position of the mining states that this was a technical organisation and of the developing states that it was primarily in the business of technological and economic redistribution. The compromise which is Part XI of the UNCLOS treaty was unsatisfactory to several states, including the United States. These states have refused to sign and others have declined to ratify the treaty, which is still not in force.[87] The episode shows that the technical capacity of the international legal system is available to accommodate the structures and standards which would contribute to mitigating the material differences between states; their implementation is dependent upon the orthodox mechanisms of international law-making.[88]

POSITIVE DISCRIMINATION[89]

Most of the activity which has been designed to discriminate positively in favour of certain states has been in the field of international economic law, where the claim is that obligations should be established for developed countries to undertake a variety of actions, granting non-reciprocal trading benefits, providing development funds, securing the transfer of technology – which would contribute to reducing the material differences between states.[90] Neither in aid nor trade did general customary law require developed states to act in the interests of developing countries[91] and, despite a large volume of treaty-making, standard-setting and voluntary programmes, it is difficult to maintain that there are general obligations to provide aid or to allow trade, or duties to maintain a non-discriminatory policy among developing countries if aid programmes are established or trade preferences conceded.[92] It is in this field of international law where one most frequently hears arguments about 'soft' international law[93] and where the most ingenious attempts are encountered to demonstrate the existence of customary law obligations from a variety of materials which do not point unequivocally in favour of such a conclusion.[94] There are, of course, treaty-based exceptions to the general rule. Some, such as the international development organisations, are institutional, where the main obligation on the donor states is in the contribution of funds to organisations with development objectives and where a crucial issue is the power of developing countries to influence the decisions of the organisations.[95] Some are pragmatic, like the UN technical assistance programme. Others are non-reciprocal economic benefits, notably the generalised preference scheme of the GATT.[96] Some of these schemes involve substantial inroads into internal sovereignty as a condition of participation and the contributing states have not been reluctant to seek to attach conditions which go beyond the purely economic field.[97]

The project to create a 'New International Economic Order'[98] founded on the Charter of Economic Rights and Duties of States.[99] as a legal regime of positive discrimination has foundered on two different obstacles. The first is that relying on General Assembly majorities to 'enact' them gives the resolutions no independent legal basis and the content of sovereign equality in Article 2(1) has not evolved to provide a convincing alternative in the Charter itself. The other is that as legal texts, the attempts to preserve internal sovereignty of developing countries while claiming assistance as a matter of right have resulted in provisions the purport of which is difficult to grasp. On the surface, Resolution 3281 may not be significantly different from Resolution 2625, but it did not command the same support[100] and has not had an equivalent effect.[101]

The international development strategy at the interstate and international organisation level has been far from successful.[102] Extra thrust has been sought in the 'Right to Development',[103] which shifts the focus from inter-state relations to human rights. The developed states have placed great emphasis on human rights and they have gradually accepted that political and economic human rights have the same status.[104] To enlist the Western commitment to the promotion of human rights as a source of duties to assist in development has an obvious political advantage to developing countries over the simple assertion of their own rights as states.[105] It is not without its disadvantages either. Human rights are essentially rights which individuals enjoy against their own government. The demand for an international human right to development by developing states will undoubtedly be echoed by groups within the states against their own governments. Furthermore, human rights are matters of international concern, even if the exact susceptibility of a state to interventionary action may be a matter of dispute. This opens up the prospect that donor states will demand rights of supervision of the domestic implementation of the right to development. The claim to positive discrimination in their favour by developing countries brings with it counter-claims which have a significant impact upon their internal sovereignty.[106] Redressing substantive inequality is paid for in differential limitations in internal sovereignty.

The evolution of the human right to development has implications for the structure of international law. It points in the direction of the international legal status of groups and individuals. It holds out the possibility of these groups and individuals enjoying rights in international law, formally against their own state but in reality against their own government.[107] As international legal rights of non-state actors, human rights have the appearance of a more enduring character than the consensual and contingent qualities of orthodox interstate obligations. Unlike the regime for exploiting the resources of the deep sea-bed, where the failure is a failure of state will, an effective understanding of the right to development must still overcome obstacles at the conceptual level.

A NEW WORLD ORDER?

The elaboration of an international law of human rights, including the right to development, might have remained no more than a threat to the sovereignty of states had it not been for the profound political changes in Europe and the Soviet Union after 1988. Until then, the ambiguities of the content of human rights obligations had prevented any general action to protect human rights and had prompted claims by those few states subjected to international scrutiny that they were the victims of unacceptable discrimination, they were the victims of 'double-standards'.[108] Even if there had been a more widely shared understanding of what human rights required of states, the prospects for doing anything about egregious violations by governments were remote. The changes in Eastern Europe, as far-reaching as they had been unanticipated, as swift as they were conclusive, bringing to an end the 'Cold War', were the background against which states reacted to Iraq's invasion of Kuwait in 1990. For a little while at least, statesmen could proclaim and academics could ponder the prospect of a 'new world order', an order which, flatteringly to international lawyers, was to be based on the principles of international law, with mechanisms for the encouragement of observance of the law.[109] In Europe, the Charter of Paris[110] set out a series of criteria for the political legitimacy of states, conditions which were accepted by the new states emerging and re-emerging in the territories of Yugoslavia and the Soviet Union.[111] The insistence on the democratic credentials of governments was, it was argued by Professor Franck, evolving into a general rule of international law.[112] In his view, the rule is closely associated with the effective implementation of the rules against the use of force. He does not conclude that failure to comply with the new standard leads to the illegitimacy of the state but rather that it renders a state under a non-democratic government susceptible to conditional intervention, because of the choice it has made about its political system. This would amount to an inequality between states on the fundamental matter of non-intervention.[113] While there are no direct examples of intervention yet to which one can point,[114] there are instances of states being excluded from international institutions as a response to their internal political arrangements – the credentials of the South African government's representatives were unacceptable to the General Assembly and action against Haiti has been threatened by the OAS after the overthrow of the elected government. A related development was the allied intervention in northern Iraq to protect the Kurds, there because of 'repression' (human rights violations) rather than the denial of a democratic process. UN Security Council Resolution 688 made reference to a threat to international peace and security and called upon Iraq to end the repression, at the same time as acknowledging Iraq's political independence and territorial integrity.[115] But the allied action was not clearly founded upon the Resolution. Instead, it revived the debates about a right of humanitarian intervention. These are singular events yet we find the General Assembly resolutions on electoral processes reiterating the principle of sovereign equality and apparently asserting the priority of the rule of non-intervention over any requirement of electoral accountability.[116] Even if some right of humanitarian intervention is established in international law (and it will be a right and not a duty of other states), the events in the territory of Yugoslavia are an indication of how difficult it will be to give it practical effect.[117]

The Security Council, bolstered by the greater cohesiveness of the permanent members, was charged with supervising the new world order. Whereas it had once been necessary in UN practice to claim that human rights matters were a matter of international concern because their denial threatened international peace and security for them to be considered at all, in the new world order, the Council would be competent to take or to authorise states to take action in response to human rights violations even if the Council had not determined that the situation was a threat to international peace. The ground for the intervention would be humanitarian rather than preserving peace.[118] But this is a formidable power, especially to states which are the object of such decisions. In another context, Libya has asked the International Court to review the finding of the Council that Libya's involvement with international terrorism was a threat to international peace and therefore justified the Council requiring states to impose a variety of economic measures against Libya.[119] The line between the use of the powers of the Security Council to keep the peace and to enforce the law looks hazy in this case. The Council is a political organ and the political enforcement of the law scarcely seems compatible with the formal equality of states before the law. There is unlikely to be a brighter line where action is taken for humanitarian objectives.

Scepticism about the new world order was practically contemporaneous with its promulgation.[120] The confused and limited response of the UN and other organisations to various situations since the invasion of Kuwait, including the obvious difficulties in implementing Resolution 687 against Iraq, are confirmations that the scepticism was not misplaced. Whether the new world order will be a better guarantee of sovereign equality or a partisan threat to it will only be an issue if it becomes an idea of more practical substance.

CONCLUSION

Where do things stand meanwhile? The details of the pre-Charter conception of sovereignty and equality have changed. More and more matters have been removed from the internal sovereignty of states. So removed, they became matters of international concern and a proper subject for action designed to influence a state's behaviour with respect to them. On the other hand, the odd spectacular event to one side, the prospects of unilateral coercive intervention to secure compliance with a state's obligations are remote. Both the setting of standards and their implementation are essentially matters for international co-operation. Co-operation is formally respectful of sovereign equality[121] and, it has been argued, the need for co-operative participation in global or regional regimes enhances the effective external sovereignty of small states.[122] On the other hand co-operation, of itself, does nothing for states seeking to ameliorate their disadvantaged positions. Co-operation here must extend to the obligation-creating level. Indeed, weak states complain that the expansion of international obligations has made them even more vulnerable to external pressure.[123] Strong states must be persuaded that the acceptance of legal obligations is in their interest. The moral claim of the underprivileged state is that the remedial action is necessary to assure at the least the minimum of internal sovereignty, increasingly, it is argued, to allow it to satisfy its human rights obligations to its own population. Not being bound to accede to moral claims, states with the wherewithal to help have extracted conditions, such as a dominant voice in international institutions, such as non-economic conditions for economic aid, such as particular economic solutions to the problem of internal development. They may soon be asking for yet more in matters of arms control and verification and in environmental protection.[124] And still much of the co-operation is at a contingent, bilateral level rather than of an obligatory multilateral form.

For beneficiaries of a positive discrimination regime, the price to pay is in the interference in their internal sovereignty, a matter to which their weakness in any event makes them susceptible. Strong states, already in a better position to secure their interests, demand legal rights to see how the money is being spent. The attempts to fashion a coherent yet practical notion of a human right to development are a clear indication of the difficulty reformers face. The failings of the state system are notorious but only states have the capacity to reform it. They show little inclination to do so. When one looks at internal sovereignty more widely, the appearance of change may be more significant than the reality of the change. When the *Lotus* judgment was given, it was not only theoretically sound but realistic to put the burden on the state asserting that another state was bound by a rule of international law to demonstrate the existence of that rule. It remains of value. Requiring a state to demonstrate its claim that there is a legal basis for the rule on which it relies against another state is an important element in securing voluntary compliance and reducing the friction which results from even successful coercion. The expansion of international law into many areas of activity once wholly within the internal sovereignty of states changes the psychology of the exercise but not its substance. Because so much more is definitely regulated by international law, the assumption is more easily made that a state should explain why something that it has done or not done is not subject to international regulation or why some measure contemplated by another state or by an international organisation is an unwarranted intervention in its affairs.[125] More realistic maybe, more convenient perhaps, more tempting certainly, but wrong. States maintain the right to decide to what obligations they should be subject and resist the imposition of duties on them which they have not clearly assumed. They are willing to assume an increasing range of burdens, to engage in extensive co-operation but on a consensual basis. The sovereign foundation for co-operation is sometimes explicit.[126] International institutions are sensitive to the role of consent as the basis for their activities.[127] The articulation of an agreed set of values commonly shared by states and accepted by them as capable of generating legal obligations is not in prospect.

'Doing something' about situations in other states is a difficult business, even when there is a legal basis for acting. The problems encountered by the United Nations in implementing Resolution 687 against Iraq, the resigned regret among the EC states about the killing and destruction in Bosnia in spite of the pleas by the government for help, the original indifference about the suffering in Somalia in the absence of an effective government are, each in its own way, a testimony to the obstacles to international law enforcement. Every state has an equal right to say it will not get involved in such situations: and they do. That some states behave badly and others will not behave well is a frequent criticism of the international legal system, a practical consequence of statehood (though some would argue a pathological condition)[128] just like equality is a legal consequence. Whatever conclusions should be drawn from such an analysis for the future of an international order, it is clear that states have not been enthusiastic to embrace them yet.[129] If statehood is an enduring arrangement, hope for the future lies in making states better.

The encouragement to be gained from the progression of democratic ideal as an internal condition of statehood is not that failure to achieve it will justify this or that measure against the undemocratic regime. It is the faith or the expectation of the Kantian ideal that democratic states will be 'better' than undemocratic ones – not only less likely to go to war[130] but more likely to agree to help the poor state, to take in refugees, to adopt environmentally protective policies. But they will still be states: international law will not be a higher law but still the law they want and make in the exercise of their sovereign equality: the promise is that democratic states will want and make 'better' law.

In his magisterial review of Resolution 2625, Professor Arangio-Ruiz dismissed the Declaration's enunciation of the principle of sovereign equality as 'too tautological for words'.[131] Perhaps that may be confined to an observation on the drafting for it would be wrong to conclude that it is of no importance. Even its critics concede the foundational quality of sovereign equality.[132] If the principle must be read in the light of other principles in the Declaration, so must they be interpreted to take account of sovereign equality. There is sometimes a temptation to look at sovereignty only from one direction. From its internal aspect the development of international co-operation and the corresponding reduction of domestic jurisdiction might be seen as bringing about some fundamental change in statehood and international society: that the state has become residual rather than foundational. States remain repositories of great power, power which sometimes must be enlisted to implement the objectives of international law.[133] The persistence of the formidable right of external sovereignty as it relates to the generation and implementation of international law serves as a signal that the state still counts.

NOTES

1 The work for this paper was supported by a grant from the University of Durham Research and Initiatives Fund.

2 L. Wildhaber, 'Sovereignty and International Law', in R. St J. Macdonald and D.M. Johnston (eds) *The Structure and Process of International Law*, The Hague: Martinus Nijhoff, 1983, p.425.

3 V. Pechota, 'Equality: Political Justice in an Unjust World', in Macdonald and Johnston, above n.1, p.453.

4 Alan James, *Sovereign Statehood: The Basis of International Society*, London: Allen & Unwin, 1986, pp.22–5. James Crawford, *The Creation of States in International Law*, Oxford: Clarendon Press, 1979, pp.26–7 says that sovereignty is not a criterion of statehood but he uses the term in a different way. Instead, he refers to 'independence' as the 'central criterion' of statehood, ibid, p.48.

5 Consider the debate about the extent of the limitations about the use of the German armed forces abroad, relying on Articles 87(a)(2) and 24 of the Constitution. See Peter Bardehle, 'Germany and Peacekeeping: Constitutional Restrictions as an Excuse for Political Hesitation', paper given at 33rd meeting International Studies Association. Atlanta. 1992.

6 A controversial contemporary example is the claim in the Constitution of Ireland to title to the territory of the Six Counties of Ulster, presently under the sovereignty of the United Kingdom, see *McGimpsey* v. *Ireland* [1988] I.R. 576.

7 This is often referred to as the state's domestic jurisdiction but it gives an incomplete idea of a state's discretionary authority which extends to many areas of international relations, such as recognition and the establishing of diplomatic relations. The term is becoming of even less use as 'domestic' matters do become subject to international law, such as human rights.

8 *Nationality Decrees issued in Tunis and Morocco* (1923) P.C.I.J. Rep. Series B, no.4 (1924); *Liechtenstein* v. *Guatemala (Nottebohm)* [1955] I.C.J. Rep. 4.

9 Ian Brownlie, *Principles of International Law*, Oxford: Clarendon Press, 4th edn, 1990, p.287.

10 Hans Kelsen, *Principles of International Law*, New York: Holt, Rinehardt & Winston, 2nd edn revised and edited by Robert W. Tucker, 1966, p.446.

11 Edwin De Witt Dickinson, *The Equality of States in International Law*, Cambridge, Mass.: 1920; Harvard University Press, Lord McNair, 'Equality in International Law' (1927) 26 *Michigan Law Review* 131.

12 See Crawford, above n.3 pp.31–76; J.D. van der Vyver, 'Statehood in International Law' (1991) 5 *Emory International Law Review* 9.

13 See p.216 below.

14 Above n.8, p.287; also Antonio Cassese, *International Law in a Divided World*, Oxford: Clarendon Press, 1986, pp.129–31.

15 See Hedley Bull, *The Anarchical Society*, London: Macmillan, 1977, p.40–52.

16 H.L.A. Hart, *The Concept of Law*, Oxford: Clarendon Press, 1961, pp.189–95.

17 Ian Brownlie, *International Law and the Use of Force by States* Oxford: Clarendon Press, 1963, ch.2.

18 For debate about the consensual basis of international legal obligations, compare Anthony D'Amato, *The Concept of Custom of International Law*, Ithaca: Cornell University Press, 1971, pp.187–99 and G.J.H. van Hoof, *Rethinking the Sources of International Law*, Deventer: Kluwer, 1983, pp.76–81, 289–291. Reflections of the sovereign right to accept international obligations are found in the rule in favour of the persistent objector to customary law, see J. Charney, 'The Persistent Objector Rule and the Development of Customary International Law' (1985) 56 *B.Y.I.L.* 1 (suggesting that the opportunity is relatively slight), and the rules governing the right to make reservations to multilateral treaties, Vienna Convention on the Law of Treaties 1969, (1980) *U.K.T.S.* No 58, Cmnd 7964, Articles 19–23.

19 *France* v. *Turkey (S S Lotus)* (1927) P.C.I.J. Rep., Series A, No.10, p.19; Crawford, above n.3, p.33.

20 Kelsen, above n.9, p.446.

21 See chs 6, 7 and 8 above.

22 For an explanation of how equal liberty leads to material inequality, see Robert Nozick, *Anarchy, State and Utopia*, Oxford: Basil Blackwell, 1974, p.161–3.

23 A. James, 'The Equality of States: Contemporary Manifestations of an Ancient Doctrine', paper given at 33rd meeting of the International Studies Association, Atlanta 1992.

24 Jan Sizoo and Rudolf Th. Jurrjens, *CSCE Decision-Making: The Madrid Experience*, The Hague: Martinus Nijhoff 1984, pp.58 and 242.

25 *The Times*, 19 May 1992, p.13.

26 *Oppenheim's International Law: A Treatise, Volume 1 – Peace*, London: Longmans, 8th edn, (ed.) H. Lauterpacht 1955, p.264; but now see the more

sceptical view in the 9th edition by Sir Robert Jennings and Sir Arthur Watts, 1992, pp.341–2.

27 International Law Commission, Draft Articles on the Jurisdictional Immunities of States and their Property, (1986-II) *I.L.C. Yearbook* p.8.

28 E. Triggiani, 'Some Thoughts on Most Favoured National Treatment' (1985) 5 *Italian Yearbook of International Law*, 124.

29 Brownlie, above n.8, p.538.

30 Ibid., p.92 pointing out, 'if any entity bears the marks of statehood, other states put themselves at risk legally if they ignore the basic obligations of state relations.'

31 *Case concerning Military and Paramilitary Activities in and against Nicaragua (Merits)* [1986] I.C.J. Rep. 14, pp.69–70, 128.

32 Henry Shue, *Basic Rights: Subsistence, Affluence and Foreign Policy*, Princeton: Princeton University Press, 1980; R.J. Vincent, *Human Rights and International Relations*, Cambridge: Cambridge University Press, 1986.

33 *Continental Shelf (Libya* v. *Malta)* [1985] I.C.J. Rep. 13, 41; also *Continental Shelf (Tunisia* v. *Libya)* [1982] I.C.J. Rep. 18, 77.

34 But even here, such rights are probably found in a treaty or a 'local' custom, see *Right of Passage (Portugal* v. *India)* [1960] I.C.J. Rep. 6.

35 *Corfu Channel (UK* v. *Albania)* [1949] I.C.J. Rep. 35.

36 Louis Henkin, *How Nations Behave; Law and Foreign Policy*, New York: Columbia University Press for the Council on Foreign Relations, 2nd edn, 1979, Chapter 3.

37 *US Diplomatic and Consular Staff in Teheran* [1980] I.C.J. Rep. 3, at pp.18–19.

38 *Case concerning Military and Paramilitary Activities in and against Nicaragua (Jurisdiction and Admissibility)* [1984] I.C.J. Rep. 392; for an analysis of the litigation in terms of state sovereignty and community values, see P.W. Kahn, 'From Nuremberg to the Hague: the United States position in *Nicaragua* v. *United States* and the Development of International Law' (1987) 12 *Yale Journal of International Law* 1.

39 For details, see F. Hampson, 'The United Kingdom before the European Court of Human Rights' (1989) 9 *Yearbook of European Law* 121.

40 See Crawford, above n.3, p.32. Note the setting up of the Secetary-General's Trust Fund to assist States in the settlement of disputes through the International Court of Justice, to provide financial help for states in conducting litigation and implementing judgments, text in (1989) 29 *I.L.M.* 1589.

41 Elisabeth Zoller, *Peacetime Unilateral Remedies: An Analysis of Countermeasures*, Dobbs Ferry, NY: Transnational Publishers, 1984, p.72.

42 The material differences between the powers of New Zealand and France were of central significance in the determination of the *Rainbow Warrior Affairs (New Zealand* v. *France)* 74 I.L.R. 241; 82 I.L.R. 501; J.S. Davidson, 'The *Rainbow Warrior* Arbitration concerning the Treatment of the French Agents Mafart and Prieur' (1991) 40 *I.C.L.Q.* 446.

43 M. Akehurst, 'Reprisals by Third States' (1970) 44 *B.Y.I.L.* D.N. Hutchinson, 'Solidarity and Breaches of Multilateral Treaties' (1988) 59 *B.Y.I.L.* 15.

44 *Nicaragua* case, above n.31.

45 Robert H. Jackson, *Quasi-States: Sovereignty, International Relations and the Third World*, Cambridge: Cambridge University Press, 1990, p.21. This phenomenon was extended once it was accepted that 'mini' or 'micro' entities were indeed states and entitled to sovereign equality, see R. Anand, 'Sovereign Equality of States in International Law' (1986-II) 197 *Hague Recueil des Cours* 9, ch.5.

46 UN Charter, Article 27. On the effect of abstention, see *Namibia Advisory Opinion* [1971] I.C.J. Rep. 22.
47 UN Charter, Article 4.
48 UN Charter, Article 93(2).
49 UN Charter, Articles 5 and 6.
50 UN Charter, Article 94(2).
51 UN Charter, Article 97.
52 UN Charter, Articles 108 and 109(2); also Statute of the International Court of Justice, Article 69.
53 J.L. Brierly, 'The Covenant and the Charter' (1946) 23 *B.Y.I.L.* 83, 87–9.
54 On the origins of the veto, see Leland M. Goodrich, Edvard Hambro and Anne Patricia Simons, *Charter of the United Nations: Commentary and Documents* New York: Columbia University Press, 3rd revised edn, 1969, pp.215–21.
55 South Africa complained about the imposition of an arms embargo against it under Security Council Resolution 418, see P. Vorster and M. Botha, 'Security Council Resolution 418 (1977)', (1978) *South African Yearbook of International Law* 144, and Iraq objected both to the terms and the implementation of resolutions passed after its attack on Kuwait, see *United Nations Monthly Chronicle*, December 1991, pp.4–15.
56 UN Charter, Article 18.
57 B. Sloan, 'General Assembly Resolutions Revisited (Forty Years Later)' (1987) 58 *B.Y.I.L.* 39. See ch.1 above.
58 Ibid., p.142.
59 A. Magarasevic, 'The Sovereign Equality of States', in Milan Sahovic (ed), *Principles of International Law concerning Friendly Relations and Co-operation*, Dobbs Ferry, NY: Oceana, 1972, pp.171–218. Note also, Final Act of the Helsinki Conference on Security and Co-operation in Europe, (1975) 14 *I.L.M.* 1292, principle 1.
60 See ch.1 above. For the need for the same approach to fundamental CSCE principles which bear some similarity to UN General Assembly Resolution 2625, see Douglas Hurd, 'A New System of Security in Europe', speech to Diplomatic and Commonwealth Writers Association, London, 2 June 1992, p.3.
61 In legal terms, the most important change was the modification and now, we must assume, the demise of Soviet international law, see V. Vereschetin and R.A. Mullerson, 'The Primacy of International Law in World Politics', in Anthony Carty and Gennady Danilenko (eds) *Perestroika and International Law*, Edinburgh: Edinburgh University Press, 1990, p.6.
62 UN Charter, Article 1(2).
63 Magarasevic, above n.58, p.187.
64 Ibid., pp.188–9.
65 Even so, his arguments, especially about the capacity of the principle to embrace development obligations have been taken up, see K. Mbaye, 'Article 2, paragraph 1', in Jean-Pierre Cot and Alain Pellet, *La Chartre des Nations Unies*, Paris: Economica, and Bruxelles: Bruylant, 1990, pp.81–96. See also Pechota, above n.2, pp.460, 466.
66 Judge Tanaka, dissenting, *South West Africa case, Second Phase* [1966] I.C.J. Rep. 4, at pp.286–316; *Namibia Advisory Opinion* [1971] I.C.J. Rep. 76.
67 ECOSOC Resolution 1235(XLII) (1967); ECOSOC Resolution 1503(XLVIII) (1970). The pioneering action by the General Assembly was Resolution 3449(XXX) on Chile.
68 See R. Rosenstock, 'The Declaration of Principles of International Law concerning Friendly Relations' (1971) 65 *A.J.I.L.* 713, at p.735.

69 I.M. Sinclair, 'Principles of International Law concerning Friendly Relations and Co-operation Among States', in M.K. Nawaz (ed.) *Essays in International Law in Honour of Krishna Rao*, Leyden: Sijthoff, 1976, p.136.
70 Magarasevic, above n.58, pp.205–10. Magarasevic argued that the right of a state to control its natural resources as an aspect of its sovereignty was so that it could take advantage of the specific provision in Resolution 2625 'freely to choose and develop its political, social, economic and cultural systems'.
71 H. Bull, *The Anarchical Society: a Study of Order in World Politics*, London: Macmillan, 1977, ch.2.
72 United Nations Charter, ch.VII; Oscar Schacter, *International Law in Theory and Practice*, Dordrecht: Martinus Nijhoff, 1991, ch.xvii.
73 For example, Security Council Resolution 221 (Southern Rhodesia); Resolution 688 (Iraq-Kurds).
74 See John Norton Moore (ed.) *Law and Civil War in the Modern World*, Baltimore: Johns Hopkins University Press, 1974, ch.II (R.B. Lillich); Ferando R. Teson, *Humanitarian Intervention: an Inquiry into Law and Morality*, Dobbs Ferry, NY: Transnational Publishers, 1988; and ch.4 above.
75 (UK) Foreign Policy document No.148, paras.II 18 21, quoted in 'United Kingdom Materials on International Law' (1986) *B.Y.I.L.* 618–19. See also, Natalino Ronzitti, *Rescuing Nationals Abroad through Military Coercion and Intervention on Grounds of Humanity*, Dordrecht: Martinus Nijhoff, 1985, pp.89–113.
76 General Agreement on Tariffs and Trade 1947, one of the objectives of which is the 'elimination of discriminatory treatment in international commerce' (Articles 1(2)).
77 United Nations Industrial Development Organisation 1979, one of the objectives of which is the 'promotion and acceleration of industrial development in the developing countries' (Article 1).
78 H. Weinschel, 'The Doctrine of Equality and its Recent Modifications' (1951) 45 *A.J.I.L.* 417; C.W. Jenks, 'Unanimity, the Veto, Weighted Voting, Special and Simple Majorities and Consensus as Modes of Decision in International Organisations', in *Cambridge Essays in International Law: Essays in Honour of Lord McNair*, Stevens: London, 1967, pp.48-63.
79 This is particularly the case for economic institutions where the level of financial contribution of a state is a ready device for fixing voting power, as in the International Monetary Fund, see Kenneth W. Dam, *The Rules of the Game*, Chicago: University of Chicago Press, 1982, ch.5.
80 E. Zoller, 'The "Corporate Will" of the United Nations and the Rights of the Minority' (1987) 81 *A.J.I.L.* 610, at pp.630–4.
81 *IMCO advisory opinion* [1960] I.C.J. Rep. 150.
82 And States may leave international organisations of whose activities they do not approve, see government observations on the First Report from the [Foreign Affairs] Committee, (1989–90) H.C,. 349, about UK membership of Unesco.
83 For an accessible account, Clyde Sanger, *Ordering the Oceans: the Making of the Law of the Sea*, London: Zed Books, 1986, pp.159–93.
84 UN General Assembly Resolution 2574D(XXIV), Moratorium on Exploitation of Resources of the Deep Sea Bed: UN General Assembly Resolution 2749(XXV), Declaration of Principles Governing the Seabed and the Ocean Floor, and the Subsoil thereof, beyond the Limits of National Jurisdiction.
85 For example, United Kingdom Deep Sea Mining (Temporary Provisions) Act 1981, s.9. For references to other national legislation, see D.J. Harris, *Cases and Materials on International Law*, London: Sweet & Maxwell, 4th edn, 1991, p.447.

86 R.P. Anand, *Legal Regime of the Deep Sea Bed and Developing Countries*, Leyden: Martinus Nijhoff, 1976.

87 There are closely parallel debates about Antarctica, see Keith Suter, *Antarctica: Private Property or Public Heritage*? London: Zed Press, 1991, chs11 and 12; R. Lefeber, 'The Exercise of Jurisdiction in the Antarctic Region and the Changing Structure of International Law: the International Community and Common Interests' (1990) 21 *Netherlands Yearbook of International Law* 81.

88 Some examples of unequal regimes can be found outside the context of international organisations, for instance, the Treaty on the Non-Proliferation of Nuclear Weapons, 1968, Article I and Articles II and III.

89 See Pechota, above n.2, pp.475–7; Jackson, above n.44, pp.131–5. Sometimes positive discrimination consists of allowing a beneficiary state to practise otherwise unlawful discrimination, for example, International Covenant on Economic, Social and Cultural Rights, 1966, Article 2(3).

90 Paul de Waart, Paul Peters and Erik Denters (eds), *International Law and Development*, Dordrecht: Martinus Nijhoff 1988; Francis Snyder and Peter Slinn (eds) *International Law of Development: Comparative Perspectives*, Abingdon: Professional Books, 1987.

91 The developed states have resisted the imposition of obligations committing them to devote a fixed percentage of their GNP to foreign aid and assistance.

92 So the 'Lome' system of relations between the EC and developing countries is not open to all developing states but only those the EC chooses to admit to it.

93 S. Zamora, 'Is there a Customary International Economic Law?' (1989) 32 *German Yearbook of International Law* 1; C. Sepulveda, 'Methods of Procedures for the Creation of Legal Norms in the International System of States' (1990) 33 *German Yearbook of International Law* 432.

94 R. Rich, 'The Right to Development as an Emerging Human Right' (1983) 23 *Virginia Journal of International Law* 287; D.M. Trubeck, 'Economic, Social and Cultural Rights in the Third World: Human Rights Law and Human Needs Programs', in Theodor Meron (ed.) *Human Rights in International Law: Legal and Policy Issues, Volume I*, Clarendon Press: Oxford, 1984, p.205.

95 D. Turk, 'Participation of Developing Countries in Decision-making Processes', in de Waart *et al.*, above n.89, pp.341–57.

96 K. Kahn, 'International Law of Development and the Law of GATT', in Snyder and Slinn, above n.89, p.175.

97 'Good Government and the Aid Programme', speech by the Minister for Overseas Development (Mrs Chalker), 25 June 1991 (Overseas Development Administration). The Declaration issued by the Group of Seven at the Munich Summit reiterated that 'good governance and respect for human rights are important criteria in providing economic assistance', 7 July 1992.

98 UN General Assembly Resolution 3201.

99 UN General Assembly Resolution 3281.

100 UN General Assembly Resolution 3281 was passed by 120–6–10. The six states voting against were Belgium, Denmark, Germany, Luxembourg, the UK and the US; the ten states abstaining were Austria, Canada, France, Ireland, Israel, Italy, Japan, the Netherlands, Norway and Spain.

101 See S.K. Chaterjee, 'The Charter of Economic Rights and Duties of States: an Evaluation after Fifteen Years' (1991) 45 *I.C.L.Q.* 669.

102 UN Development Programme, *Human Development Report 1992*, New York: Oxford University Press, 1992.

103 UN General Assembly Resolution 41/128. In its preamble, Resolution 41/

128 refers to practically all the principles in Resolution 2625 except the principle of sovereign equality.

104 UN General Assembly Resolution 32/130.

105 R. Rich, 'The Right to Development: A Right of Peoples?' in James Crawford (ed.) *The Rights of Peoples* Oxford: Clarendon Press, 1988, p.39.

106 P. Slinn, 'Implementation of International Obligations towards Developing States: Equality or Preferential Treatment?' in W.E. Butler (ed.) *Control over Compliance with International Law* Dordrecht: Martinus Nijhoff, 1991, pp.165, 173.

107 For a frank examination of the difficulties of giving practical meaning and effect to the human right to development, see R.L. Barsch, 'The Right to Development as a Human Right: Results of the Global Consultation' (1991) 13 *Human Rights Quarterly* 332.

108 Thomas M. Franck, *Nation against Nation*, New York: Oxford University Press, 1985, pp.231–42.

109 B. Russett and J.S. Sutterlin, 'The UN in a New World Order' (1991) *Foreign Affairs* 69; Concluding Statement of the President of the Security Council, 31 January 1992, SC/5362; Boutros Boutros-Ghali, *An Agenda for Peace: Preventive Diplomacy, Peacemaking and Peace-keeping*, New York: United Nations, 1992.

110 Charter of Paris for a New Europe, 1990, Cmd; 1464.

111 EC Foreign Ministers Declaration on the Guidelines on Recognition of New States in Eastern Europe and the Soviet Union, 16 December 1991.

112 T.M. Franck, 'The Emerging Right to Democratic Governance' (1992) 86 *A.J.I.L.* 46, at pp.90–1.

113 Ibid., p.89. See also L. Damrosch, 'Politics across Borders: Non-intervention and Non-forcible influence over Political Affairs' (1989) 83 *A.J.I.L.* 34–50.

114 The US intervention in Panama would be an example if the explanations given for the action were more distinct, 'Contemporary Practice of the United Sates' (1990) 84 *A.J.I.L.* 545–9. Compare A. Sofaer, 'The Legality of the United States' Action in Panama' (1991) 29 *Columbia Journal of Transnational Law* 218; and D.J. Scheffer, 'Use of Force after the Cold War: Panama, Iraq and the New World Order', in Louis Henkin *et al.*, *Right* v. *Might: International Law and the Use of Force*, New York: Council on Foreign Relations, 2nd edn, 1991, pp.109–72.

115 The Allies claimed no more than that their intervention was 'consistent' with UN Security Council Resolution 688, see H. Adelman, 'Humanitarian Intervention: the Case of the Kurds' (1992) 4 *International Journal of Refugee Law* 4; and C. Warbrick, 'The Invasion of Kuwait by Iraq – Part II' (1991) 40 *I.C.L.Q.* 965, 973.

116 UN General Assembly Resolution 45/150; 45/151.

117 UN Security Council Resolution 770, 13 August 1992.

118 J. Chopra and T.G. Weiss, 'Sovereignty is No Longer Sacrosanct; Codifying Humanitarian Intervention; (1992) 6 *Ethics and International Affairs* 95, at p.114 and referring to UN General Assembly Resolution 46/182, providing for the appointment of a humanitarian aid co-ordinator; M. Bettati, 'UN Droit d'Ingerence?' (1991) 95 *Revue General de Droit International Public* 639.

119 *Libya* v. *United States: Libya* v. *United Kingdom* [1992] I.C.J. Rep. (14 April 1992) (text in (1992) 31 *I.L.M.* 662).

120 S. Hoffman, 'Delusions of World Order' (9 April 1992) *New York Review of Books* 37; B. Urquhart, 'The United Nations in 1992: Problems and Opportunities' (1992) 68 *International Affairs* 311.

121 For example, Manila Declaration on the Peaceful Settlement of Disputes,

UN General Assembly Resolution 37/10; Declaration on the Prevention and Removal of Disputes and Situations which may Threaten International Peace and Security, UN General Assembly Resolution 43/51; Respect for the Principles enshrined in the Charter of the United Nations and international law in the fight against drug abuse and illicit trafficking, UN General Assembly Resolution 45/147; Declaration on Fact-finding by the United Nations in the field of the maintenance of international peace and security, UN General Assembly Resolution 46/59.

122 M.S. Rajan, 'The Sovereign-Nation System, the Non-aligned, and the Democratisation of International Relations' (1991) 28 *International Studies (New Delhi*) 111, at p.123.

123 UN General Assembly Resolution 42/173. See O. Elagab, 'Coercive Economic Measures against Developing Countries' (1992) 41 *I.C.L.Q.* 682.

124 See Statement of Security Council President, above n.108.

125 Brownlie, above n.8, p.288–92.

126 See above n.120.

127 See ch.8 above.

128 Philip Allott, *International Law and International Revolution: Reconceiving the World* (Josephine Onoh Memorial Lecture 1989), Hull: Hull University Press, 1989.

129 M. Koskenniemi, 'The Future of Statehood' (1991) 32 *Harvard International Law Journal* 397. Bull, above n.14.

130 Immanuel Kant, *To Perpetual Peace: A Philosophical Sketch*, 1795, text in Howard Kainz (ed.) *Philosophical Perspectives on Peace*, Basingstoke: Macmillan, 1987, pp. 65–85. R.L. Schuller, 'Domestic Structures and Preventive War: are Democracies more Pacific?' (1992) 44 *World Politics* 235; C.R. Ember *et al.*, 'Peace between Participating Polities: a cross-cultural test of the "Democracies Rarely Fight Each Other" Hypothesis', ibid., p.600. There seems more realistic prospect in proceeding this way than in seeking to democratise the institutions of the international legal system, compare Frank Barnaby (ed.) *Building a More Democratic United Nations*, London: Frank Cass 1991, especially p.223–31.

131 G. Arangio-Ruiz, 'The Normative Role of the General Assembly of the United Nations and the Declaration of Principles of Friendly Relations' (1972-III) 137 *Hague Recueil des Cours* 419, at p.574.

132 Anand, above n.44, p.189.

133 See chs 6 and 7 above.

11 The principle of good faith

Gillian White

THE PRINCIPLE AS RESTATED IN THE DECLARATION: MERELY A STATEMENT OF THE OBVIOUS?

A member of the United States Mission to the UN who was involved in the negotiations which led to the adoption of the Friendly Relations Declaration admitted that it could be argued that the principle of good faith is self-evident, but thought that it was a useful stabilising development to have it 'spelled out to this degree'. He reminds us that the principle is affirmed in Article 2(2) of the UN Charter but that the Declaration had clearly extended it 'to cover the entire structure of international relations'.[1]

It is worth recalling that the reference to good faith in Article 2(2) of the Charter resulted from an amendment to the Dumbarton Oaks Proposals, which had made no mention of good faith. The Colombian proposed amendment received strong support from other States with a civil law system, and delegates in Commission I were reminded of the expression of the principle of good faith in the League Covenant. [2] Initial opposition to the amendment from some delegates, particularly from common law countries, gave way in the face of these arguments. The Panamanian delegate stressed that good faith was 'the chief element of the observance of treaties'.[3]

In discussions of drafts of the Friendly Relations resolution in the Sixth Committee in 1965, Tammes of The Netherlands said that good faith bore two meanings: objectivity in the self-interpretation by States of accepted obligations; and self-restraint by States in application of rules which follow from 'custom and reason'. On the first limb, Tammes urged that States must ascertain the common understanding of those who had taken part in negotiating an international instrument and the expectations raised in other parties by the making of the instrument. On the second limb, he said that good faith had a moral meaning – or no meaning at all – and that it was 'a rule underlying all written rules'.[4] This high moral tone characterised the statement of the Italian representative, Sperduti, who regarded the principle of good faith as 'the foundation of the international legal order'.[5].

A consensus text on the principle was achieved at the 1967 session of the Special Committee on the Friendly Relations resolution and was incorporated without change in the final text of the Declaration.[6] During the debate in the Sixth Committee of the Special Committee's draft it was said that the reference to Charter obligations and their supremacy was no idle repetition of Article 103, but a reaffirmation of the vital importance of the fulfilment of obligations such as that in Article 2(4) of the Charter. Statement of the good faith principle also properly reflected the need for compliance with the international obligations binding on every State, arising from customary or conventional law.[7] However, some limitations on the duty to comply with treaty obligations, formulated in the Declaration as 'the duty to fulfil in good faith its obligations under international agreements valid under the generally recognized principles and rules of international law', were suggested in the Special Committee. Some representatives said that the duty did not apply to 'unequal treaties' but only to treaties freely concluded on a basis of equality. The issue of State succession to treaties by newly independent States was raised. It was argued that reference to 'the generally recognized principles and rules of international law' embodied the principle of free consent and equality of all parties. Other representatives, from Western States, opposed the inclusion of any phrase to the effect that only obligations arising from treaties freely concluded on the basis of equality were binding.

Such language could endanger the stability of treaties, and would prejudice the work of the forthcoming Conference on the Law of Treaties. Only valid obligations were to be honoured in good faith. What was a valid obligation would be considered at that Conference. The International Law Commission would examine, in considering State succession to treaties, whether new States were justified in not accepting that they were bound by 'inherited' treaties regarded by them as manifestly unjust or inequitable. A similar response greeted suggestions that the text should refer to void or voidable treaties, to treaties resulting from coercion of the State or its representative, and to treaties in conflict with *jus cogens*. The good faith principle was confined to valid treaties, and it was for the Conference on the Law of Treaties to deal with conditions for validity.[8]

REPETITION OF THE PRINCIPLE

Before embarking on an examination of post–1970 practice and case law invoking and applying good faith, mention may be made of some public reaffirmations of the principle by States. Both the Vienna Convention on the Law of Treaties (almost contemporaneous with the Friendly Relations Declaration and certainly under negotiation at the same period, in the late 1960s) and the later, 1978 Convention on Succession of States in Respect of Treaties declared in their preambles that the principles of free consent, good faith and *pacta sunt servanda* are universally recognised. The Charter of Economic Rights and Duties of States, 1974[9] declared in its Chapter 1, 'Fundamentals of International Economic Relations', that among the governing principles of economic as well as political relations among States is 'Fulfilment in good faith of international obligations'[10].

In the CSCE forum the Final Stockholm Document on Confidence- and Security-Building Measures and Disarmament in Europe contains a declaration on 'Refraining from the Threat or Use of Force', paragraph 26 of which states: 'They will fulfil in good faith their obligations under international law; they also stress that strict compliance with their commitments within the framework of the CSCE is essential for building confidence and security'.[11] The next paragraph rehearses the supremacy of UN Charter obligations over any conflicting obligation under any other treaty or international agreement – the provision of Article 103 of the Charter affirmed as part of the good faith principle in the Friendly Relations Declaration. [12]

A further example comes from the Geneva Accords on Afghanistan. In his report to the General Assembly in 1988 the Secretary-General referred to their conclusion, observing that this was the first instance of the world's two most powerful States becoming co-guarantors of an agreement negotiated under the auspices of the Secretary-General. He wrote: 'The full implementation of the Accords in good faith by all the signatories will significantly serve the goal of peace in the region and the world'.[13]

In the four-party Agreement on the Interrelationships for the Settlement of the Situation Relating to Afghanistan[14] under which the USSR agreed to withdraw its troops, clause 6 states that it is 'essential that all the obligations deriving from the instruments concluded as component parts of the settlement be strictly fulfilled and that all the provisions of the instruments be completed in good faith'.

Later in the same annual report the Secretary-General stressed the fundamental importance of 'the principle that treaties must be complied with and carried out in good faith', having carefully qualified the application of the principle to treaties 'properly concluded and that have entered into force', echoing the language of the Friendly Relations Declaration.[15]

In the 1991 Agreement on a Comprehensive Political Settlement of the Cambodia Conflict the nineteen signatory States, participants in the Paris Conference on Cambodia, undertook that they 'shall, in good faith and in a spirit of cooperation, resolve through peaceful means any dispute with regard to the implementation of this Agreement.' [16] The signatories also undertook to 'comply in good faith with all obligations undertaken in this Agreement'.[17]

POST-1970 PRACTICE AND CASE LAW ON GOOD FAITH

Most of the examples to be discussed come from the law of treaties, unsurprisingly, since it is in this context that the duty to act in good faith applies most clearly. We begin with the 'pre-contract' situation, by considering the nature of the obligation to negotiate in good faith, frequently affirmed in International Court of Justice judgments of recent years.

Duty to negotiate in good faith

The writer sympathises with Thirlway's questioning whether the addition of the incantation 'in good faith' adds anything to an obligation undertaken by States to negotiate on a particular matter. As he puts it:

> Where an obligation, legal or conventional, is defined by specific words, good faith requires respect not only for the words but also for the spirit; but to negotiate otherwise than in good faith is surely not to negotiate at all.[18]

An example of such an undertaking is Article VI of the Nuclear Non-Proliferation Treaty in which the parties undertake 'to pursue negotiations in good faith on effective measures relating to cessation of the nuclear arms race and to nuclear disarmament'.[19]

The duty seems to consist in an obligation on States so to conduct themselves that their negotiations are meaningful, and there is no genuine (good faith) negotiation if each party, or either one, insists on its position and refuses to compromise on any point.[20] In the *Gulf of Maine* case the court, a Chamber of the ICJ, said that the parties were under a duty to negotiate 'and to do so in good faith, with a genuine intention to achieve a positive result'.[21]

A more extended analysis of the meaning of an undertaking to negotiate and of the effect of the inherent and concomitant obligation to perform the undertaking in good faith was carried out by the Arbitral Tribunal for the Agreement on German External Debts in *Kingdom of Greece* v. *Federal Republic of Germany*.[22] Article 19 of the London Agreement on German External Debts coupled with paragraph 11 of its Annexe I comprised an undertaking by the parties to negotiate their dispute, *in casu* relating to claims of Greece arising out of the Mixed Graeco-German Arbitral Tribunal's determination of World War I claims against Germany. The provisions constituted a *pactum de negotiando*, as distinct from a *pactum de contrahendo*.[23] It meant, said the Tribunal

> that both sides would make an effort, in good faith, to bring about a mutually satisfactory solution by way of a compromise, even if that meant the relinquishment of strongly held positions earlier taken. It

> implies a willingness for the purpose of negotiation to abandon earlier positions and to meet the other side part way.

As a matter of interpretation of the provisions the Tribunal held that they 'require the parties to negotiate, bargain, and in good faith attempt to reach a result acceptable to both parties and thus bring an end to this long drawn out controversy'. Such a positive result was necessarily more desirable in international relations than in relations between individuals given 'the infinitely higher stakes' involved. The need for peaceful solution of differences between States is so essential to the well-being of the community of nations that 'when disputants have reached a point of signifying their agreement to negotiate an outstanding dispute, the subsequent negotiations normally ought to lead to a satisfactory and equitable result.'[24]

It should be noted that the Tribunal expressly declared its interpretation to be in accordance with the general rule in Article 31 of the Convention on the Law of Treaties, which requires a treaty to be interpreted in good faith in accordance with the ordinary meaning of its terms in their context and in light of the treaty's object and purpose.

O'Connor observed that some civil law systems, including the French, have developed rules of good faith in the area of pre-contractual negotiations. International law may employ specific rules derived from good faith, for instance, estoppel, and apply these to negotiations for a treaty, but O'Connor contended that there was scope for more generalised application of the principle of good faith in the sometimes complex and protracted negotiating process.[25] The present writer remains sceptical as to whether there is indeed much scope for further elaboration. International courts have applied good faith in the context of a duty to negotiate and have spelled out the content of the principle in this context.

Validity of treaties. Breach of internal law. Practice and good faith

The validity of an agreement by exchange of letters in 1960 between France and Portugal, fixing the maritime boundaries between Guinea-Bissau and Senegal, was disputed between the two African States in the *Case Concerning the Arbitral Award of 31 July 1989.*[26] The Agreement was not published in the Portuguese official journal nor in the then province of Guinea, and for this and other reasons Guinea-Bissau submitted that it was void. Applying customary international law as it stood in 1960 and not Article 46 of the Convention on the Law of Treaties, the Tribunal noted the absence of judicial or arbitral precedents for a treaty being declared void because one of the contracting States had violated its own law in concluding it. The Tribunal considered that its decision must be governed by the principle of good faith: 'That principle was undoubtedly the rule observed by States in 1960 with regard to the conclusion of international agreements'.[27]

Hence, the question whether a treaty had been concluded in conformity with a State's internal law had to be examined in the light of that law as actually interpreted and applied by the State's organs, including its courts and administrative organs. Scrutiny of the contemporary practice of the President and National Assembly of Portugal in relation to international agreements showed that some significant agreements, including the UN Charter, had not been submitted for the Assembly's approval. The 1960 Agreement had been signed by Dr Salazar, then undisputed head of the Portuguese government. If account were taken of these factors 'it may be concluded that the French government had good reason to believe in all good faith that the treaty which had been signed was valid'.[28]

Good faith in the interpretation of treaties

We come now to one of the most fruitful fields for the operation of the principle of good faith.

What does it involve?

Mann posed the question, what is meant by good faith in Article 31 of the Vienna Convention on the Law of Treaties, and what is added to the process of interpretation by the reference to good faith?[29] Part of the answer lies in the history of treaty negotiating and drafting, at any rate, among European sovereigns. Schwarzenberger's research showed that for centuries rules on good faith were included in express treaty clauses which stipulated that the treaty was to be 'observed, applied and interpreted in good faith, without malice, fraudulent intent or circumvention (*absque omni dolo et fraude* or *absque ulla fictione*)'.[30] The canonist lawyers mainly responsible for treaty drafting in the medieval period inserted clauses stating that the treaty should be *bona fidei negotia* – to be kept in good faith. With the passage of time, sovereign rulers became accustomed to treating with each other on the basis of law, and so it became taken for granted that bad faith was incompatible with the performance of legal obligations of any kind.[31] The old clauses dropped out of the text of the treaties themselves but lingered on in instruments of ratification.[32] Schwarzenberger considered that such transposition indicated that the rule embodied in those clauses had developed 'into a general practice accepted as law or, in other words, a rule of customary international law'. Further, the observance of treaty obligations in good faith imports considerations of equity in the sense of *jus aequum* into the legal relations created by the treaty. The parties formulate their mutual rights and obligations as relative, rather than strict or absolute rights, while being free to stipulate strictly if that is their mutual wish. He summarised the historical development which culminated in Article 2(2) of the UN Charter as follows:

> The typical intention of the parties is that these [relative] rights should be equitably interpreted, that is, in a spirit of good faith, common sense and reasonableness. Thus, good faith in this context is no longer restricted to what it meant primarily in the earliest phase of the evolution of the law of treaties – *bona fides*, as distinct from *mala fides* – but means emphasis on *jus aequum*, as distinct from *jus strictum.*[33]

In a classic exposition of the principle of good faith as applied in the interpretation of treaties, Judges Sir Hersch Lauterpacht, Wellington Koo and Sir Percy Spender said: 'It is consistent with enlightened practice to apply the test of reasonableness to the interpretation of international instruments – a test which follows from the ever present duty of States to act in good faith.'[34] They went on to stress that the test of reasonableness must itself be applied reasonably, and not by reference to extreme or exaggerated contingencies; or to 'examples bordering on absurdity'. For instance, if a State invokes a treaty provision some twelve years from the date of its entry into force, it would be contrary to the test of reasonableness to defeat its claim on the ground that it would be quite unreasonable for the State to invoke that treaty after, say, one hundred years.[35] It seems clear, also, that the instruction in Article 31 of the Vienna Convention that a treaty must be interpreted in good faith reflects the notion of effective interpretation. The ILC did not formulate this notion separately, considering that as a matter of existing law it was incorporated sufficiently in the rule of interpretation in good faith in accordance with the ordinary meaning.[36] The ILC stated:

> When a treaty is open to two interpretations one of which does and the other does not enable the treaty to have appropriate effects, good faith and the objects and purpose of the treaty demand that the former interpretation should be adopted.[37]

The Commission also recalled that the principle of interpretation in good faith 'flows directly from the rule *pacta sunt servanda*' restated in Article 26 of the Vienna Convention.[38]

Whose good faith?

A moment's reflection on the historical development and the contemporary understanding of the rule that treaties are to be interpreted in good faith answers the question posed above. The parties to a treaty must themselves act in good faith and the spirit of reasonableness when invoking the treaty, making or resisting claims based upon its provisions. So equally must any third party interpreter, such as a court, municipal or international, or arbitral tribunal.

If the original parties to the treaty have been succeeded by new States when an issue of interpretation falls to be determined, the good faith of both predecessor and successor States parties is in point for a tribunal seeking to interpret the provision by reference to any subsequent agreement between the parties regarding its interpretation or application. An instructive example is provided by the judgment of the Court of Arbitration in the *Guinea–Guinea-Bissau Maritime Delimitation* case.[39] If, however, the Court has recourse to preparatory work, it must be the good faith of the original parties which governs, together with the Court's own adherence to this principle in the performance of the interpretative task.

It is, of course, entirely possible for a treaty text to be interpreted in good faith by opposing litigants and for two quite different meanings to be produced. In the *Guinea–Guinea-Bissau Maritime Delimitation* case the Court noted that the two States, accepting the rule for interpretation in Article 31 of the Vienna Convention, had reached differing conclusions as to the meaning of the final paragraph of Article I of the Franco-Portuguese Boundary Convention of 1886:

> the interpretations presented . . . with sufficient reasons for an international tribunal not to judge them to be anything but an expression of their complete good faith, resulted in diverging final conclusions.[40]

Guinea submitted that the Convention established a general maritime boundary between the possessions of France and Portugal in West Africa, while Guinea-Bissau argued the contrary, concluding that the line defined in that paragraph merely designated which islands belonged to Portugal. The Court undertook a careful examination of the text, the object and purpose of the Convention, the parties' subsequent practice, and their prior intentions, as indicated by the preparatory work. It held that the Convention did not determine the maritime boundary between the French and Portuguese possessions.[41]

Good faith taken for granted

Any binding international agreement, that is, any agreement by which the parties intended to create legal obligations and whose language is sufficiently specific to give effect to such intention, must be interpreted and performed in good faith. As has been well observed, the autointerpretation by the parties of their own treaty obligations does not empty the agreement of its obligatory character.

> Even if the parties are given the competence to decide for themselves the existence and extent of their respective obligations, it is stated, the agreement can be authoritative, since the parties will then be under an obligation to exercise their power in good faith, and the issue

whether it was so exercised or not would be amenable to third party determination.[42]

An example concerned provisions in the 1961 Single Convention on Narcotic Drugs and the 1971 Convention on Psychotropic Substances that any such drugs or substances in illegal traffic 'shall be liable to seizure and confiscation'. Did these provisions prohibit parties from using the law enforcement technique of 'controlled delivery', namely, permitting passage through the territory of one or more States of consignments of illicit drugs under surveillance but without interfering with the shipment? Enforcement agencies are able to track such shipments from origin to destination. The technique had not been perfected in 1971. Did the Convention require immediate seizure and confiscation, or merely impose on parties the duty to authorise seizure, leaving them a degree of discretion in deciding how to exercise such authority?

The UN Secretariat's legal opinion was that controlled delivery constitutes a legitimate exercise of the discretion which the Conventions left to the parties. After quoting the general rule of interpretation from Article 31(1) of the Vienna Convention the opinion continued: 'The good faith interpretation of the Conventions under consideration here is self-evident and we need not concern ourselves with this aspect of the problem'. The conclusion was reached on the basis of ordinary meaning and in light of the Convention's object and purpose.[43].

In the *La Bretagne* arbitration of 1985 between Canada and France the Arbitral Tribunal observed that the parties might have determined more precisely the beneficiaries of Article 4 of their 1972 Agreement on access to and regulation of fishing in the Gulf of St Lawrence. The provision referred to trawlers registered in the French territories of Saint-Pierre and Miquelon, with no requirements as to crewing, or the origin of the capital of ship-owning or fishing companies operating such trawlers. Moreover, the Tribunal said that it could not disregard the circumstances in which Article 4 was discussed during the negotiation of the Agreement, in view of Canada's expressed concern to avoid French metropolitan trawlers disguised as locals, or even trawlers with foreign crews but registered in those territories, taking advantage of any privilege Canada might be willing to concede, but concede only in favour of authentic Saint-Pierre vessels.[44] Such concern, the Tribunal noted, 'came up against France's refusal to modify the provision that she herself had proposed'. It therefore concluded that the registration of trawlers, effected in conformity with French legislation,

> was considered by the Parties, together with the principle of good faith which is of necessity a principal factor in the performance of treaties, as affording a sufficient guarantee against any risk of the French Party exercising its rights abusively.[45]

Good faith in the performance of treaties

The presence or absence of good faith in one party to an agreement in respect of its performance of obligations thereunder emerged as probably the central issue in the *Rainbow Warrior* arbitration, which determined whether France had duly fulfilled its obligations under the original agreement with New Zealand following the destruction of that vessel by French government agents. The 1990 *Rainbow Warrior* arbitration concerned the repatriation to France of the two agents who had pleaded guilty in New Zealand to manslaughter and criminal damage and were subsequently released into French custody to spend three years on a French military base on Hao island in the Pacific. New Zealand argued that the crucial clause in the 1986 agreement between the two States, implementing the Secretary-General's mediatory ruling,[46], carried subsidiary obligations to act in good faith. The clause stated: 'They [Major Alain Mafart and Captain Dominique Prieur] will be prohibited from leaving the island for any reason, except with the mutual consent of the two Governments.' New Zealand submitted that this mutual consent provision carried three subsidiary obligations to act in good faith:

1 to give full and timely information about circumstances in which consent was to be sought;
2 not to impede New Zealand's efforts to verify this information; and
3 to give the New Zealand Government reasonable opportunity to reach an informed decision.[47]

In the case of Major Mafart's illness on Hao, New Zealand submitted that France had breached all these obligations, and in Captain Prieur's case New Zealand's consent had not been sought on either the ground of her pregnancy or of her father's serious, indeed fatal, illness, but France had presented New Zealand with a *fait accompli*. France did not deny that the provisions of the 1986 Agreement 'have not been literally honoured' since the officers' return to mainland France was not preceded by New Zealand's formal consent, and they had not remained on the island for the agreed three-year period. But, in its submission, France had not committed internationally wrongful acts because 'circumstances of extreme urgency' were involved.[48] France apparently did not contest the proposition that the parties were obliged to act in good faith in implementing the mutual consent clause.

The Arbitration Tribunal ruled that among the three conditions which would be required to justify France's conduct in both cases was 'the existence of a good faith effort to try to obtain the consent of New Zealand in terms of the 1986 Agreement.'[49] By 2 votes to 1, the initial evacuation of Mafart was not wrongful, albeit carried out without New Zealand's consent, since subsequent examination showed that he needed medical treatment not available in Hao. Sir Kenneth Keith, dissenting, held that the French authorities did not give New Zealand appropriate opportunity to consider in good faith the request for consent to the evacuation and to make a decision before the proposed departure from Hao. France had not established the need to act in apparent breach of its treaty obligations. There was no sufficient urgency: 'France was in a position to facilitate a proper medical assessment by New Zealand in the performance by New Zealand of its good faith obligations under the agreement. It did not meet its obligations in that respect'.[50]

In Captain Prieur's case the Tribunal was unanimous. France had committed a material breach of the Agreement by not endeavouring in good faith to secure the consent of New Zealand to her immediate repatriation.[51] During the oral proceedings New Zealand produced the text of an interview given by the French prime minister at the relevant time, which indicated that Captain Prieur's removal to France had taken place 'against the backdrop of French presidential elections in which the Prime Minister was a candidate'. Declining to enter into any search for the French government's motives, the Tribunal merely observed that during the day of 5 May 1988, France did not seek New Zealand's approval for Captain Prieur's sudden departure, and that accordingly her return to Paris was a violation of the 1986 Agreement.[52]

The obligation to perform treaty commitments in good faith applies equally to situations in which the provision falls to be carried out by the State itself, as in the *Rainbow Warrior* case, and to those in which the provisions are implemented by its nationals.[53] An example of the latter type is the 1972 Agreement between Canada and France on access to and regulation of fishing in the Gulf of St Lawrence. A double limit was set to the fishing effort of French trawlers registered in Saint-Pierre and Miquelon. The number of such vessels allowed to fish in the Gulf was limited to ten, and they were not to exceed 50 metres in length. The dispute concerned Canada's claim to be entitled to prohibit filleting of fish at sea in the Gulf. Canada feared that the fleets registered in Saint-Pierre and Miquelon would replace those being phased out in the metropolitan French fleet, with the result that the Gulf would be overfished. However, the Tribunal held that a prohibition on filleting at sea could be ordered and enforced only if Canada could prove that such filleting would inevitably lead to overfishing or exceed the quotas set by Canadian authorities. This occurrence was unlikely for the reason, *inter alia*, that

> Irrespective of the storage capacity of a filleting trawler operating in the Gulf, any over-fishing on the part of that trawler would have to be treated as a breach of good faith involving the liability on the part of France which, as a Party to the 1972 Agreement, has a duty to ensure that its nationals scrupulously respect the international commitments it has entered into on their behalf.[54]

This consideration was reached in the light of a declaration by the French agent in the oral proceedings that French factory trawlers, filleting or not, would not take one kilogram of cod beyond the authorised quota. The Canadian member of the Tribunal, dissenting, observed that if the guarantees in the Award, including the one summarised above, did not succeed in preventing the return 'in force' of French factory freezer trawlers to the Gulf, Canada might be justified in invoking a fundamental change of circumstances in regard to those at the time of conclusion of the Agreement.[55]

Where a treaty is silent on some aspect of the matters with which it deals, the obligation to implement it in good faith can create the basis for a supplementary clause to fill the gap. For example, the Algiers Declarations which settled the Iranian-US hostages crisis in January 1981[56] contain no express provision on the satisfaction or enforcement of any awards of the Iran-US Claims Tribunal in favour of Iran or Iranian nationals. The Security Account established as part of the overall settlement is available only to satisfy awards in favour of US claimants. But Article IV(1) of the Claims Settlement Declaration provides that all decisions and awards of the Tribunal are final and binding. In *Iran* v. *US, Case A/21* the Tribunal noted that awards against named US nationals did not bind the US government to pay the Iranian party, who was free to seek enforcement through municipal court proceedings.[57] But the US was obliged to implement the Algiers Declarations in good faith, meaning 'to provide some procedure or mechanism whereby enforcement may be obtained within its national jurisdiction, and to ensure that the successful Party has access thereto'. If no such procedure existed, it would have to be established by legislation or other means, and it 'must be available on a basis at least as favourable as that allowed to parties who seek recognition or enforcement of foreign arbitral awards'.[58]

One should caution against the notion that a State claiming that its treaty partner is in breach of some provision of their treaty must prove bad faith on that State's part before it can be said to have established violation of the obligation. Evidence of bad faith might serve to prove aggravated breach, to borrow an expression from English common law, but it is certainly not a prerequisite of establishing breach as such. In the *Namibia Advisory Opinion* the ICJ rejected the contention that before it could be established that South Africa was in breach of its obligations under the Mandate it would be necessary to prove that South Africa was not acting in good faith in exercising its legislative or administrative powers.[59]

Good faith and treaties not in force

Article 38(1)(a) of its Statute requires the ICJ to apply treaties 'establishing rules expressly recognised by the contesting States'. The provision refers to 'a source of mutual obligations of the parties'.[60] If both, or all, litigating States have ratified a particular multilateral treaty which has not entered into force by the time of the litigation, the treaty's provisions ought to be applied by virtue of this mutual commitment principle. At least one Judge of the ICJ, sitting as an arbitrator, considered good faith to be the rationale for this commitment. In contrast to the bold assertion by the majority in the *Guinea-Bissau–Senegal* arbitration[61] that the 1982 Law of the Sea Convention 'does not apply in this case because it has not yet entered into force' Bedjaoui, in his dissent, argued persuasively for its applicability to the arbitrating States 'as a body of rules accepted by them' because they had both ratified the Convention. It could not apply as a body of treaty law, but

> the act of ratification of the Convention by each of the two Parties means that each of them is prepared to apply it to any other party which accepts to do the same. Ratification represents a final and definitive commitment which, in all good faith, makes it incumbent upon the two States to consider themselves bound with respect to each other by the Convention.[62]

Reciprocal application of a treaty not in force between States which have ratified it, should be carefully distinguished from the obligation imposed by Article 18 of the Vienna Convention on the Law of Treaties upon States which have signed a treaty subject to ratification but not ratified it, or have consented to be bound by a treaty (by ratification or other means) which has not entered into force. The obligation is not to *apply* the treaty *vis-à-vis* other States in the same position, but rather the minimal obligation to refrain from acts which would defeat the object and purpose of the treaty. However, the two obligations have a common root, the duty to act in good faith. Bedjaoui takes this to be the governing principle, in the passage quoted, as does Sinclair in his discussion of Article 18 which he regards as 'an expression of what is an autonomous obligation imposed upon States by virtue of the principle of good faith, quite independently of the treaty'.[63]

TREATY OBLIGATIONS CONFLICTING WITH THE UN CHARTER ARTICLE 103 AND THE FRIENDLY RELATIONS TEXT

The fourth paragraph of the good faith section of the Friendly Relations Declaration echoes, but does not repeat verbatim, Article 103 of the UN Charter. The Declaration states:

> Where obligations arising under international agreements are in conflict with the obligations of Members of the United Nations under the Charter of the United Nations, the obligations under the Charter shall prevail.

Since 1970 there has been one celebrated instance of States invoking

Article 103, namely, Cyprus, represented by the Greek Cypriot government, and Greece, in relation to the 1960 Cyprus Treaty of Guarantee and the Turkish military intervention in Cyprus in 1974. The Cypriot and Greek governments claimed that Turkey's action violated Articles 2(1) and 2(4) of the Charter, and that, to the extent to which the Treaty of Guarantee authorised forcible action it was void under Article 103. In the Guarantee Treaty the guarantor States, Greece, Turkey and the United Kingdom, undertake to consult together on any measures necessary to ensure observance of the Treaty (which governed the bi-communal independence Constitution of Cyprus) in the event of a breach of its provisions. Article IV goes on to provide that if concerted action by those States is not possible, each guarantor 'reserves the right to take action with the sole aim of re-establishing the state of affairs created by the present Treaty'.[64] However, Necatigl has demonstrated convincingly that the Cypriot and Greek argument is unfounded.[65] Article 103 may be read as restricted to cases in which the conflicting obligations are those of the same State, e.g. State A's Charter obligation to impose economic sanctions against State B might be inconsistent with A's treaty obligations to trade with B. Article 103 applies and A's Charter obligations prevail over its treaty obligations to B. But Article 103 cannot apply to the Cyprus situation, since the alleged conflict is between Turkey's obligations under the Charter and *Cyprus's* obligation to respect *Turkey's rights* under the Treaty of Guarantee. While this interpretation of Article 103 is consistent with its ordinary meaning [66], the different phrasing of this part of the good faith principle in the Friendly Relations Declaration might at first sight support the Cypriot and Greek argument. The Declaration is more loosely worded, referring to 'obligations arising under international agreements' being in conflict with 'the obligations of Members of the UN under the Charter'. But it remains the case that the conflict is one between Turkey's obligations under the Charter and its *right* to take action under the Treaty of Guarantee. This is not a clash of obligations. The Cypriot and Greek argument requires one to interpret the Declaration's formulation as follows:

> Where [the obligations of Cyprus to respect Turkey's rights under the Treaty of Guarantee] are in conflict with the obligations of [Turkey] under the Charter of the UN, [Turkey's] obligations under the Charter shall prevail.

Quite apart from the strained nature of such a reading, the General Part of the Friendly Relations Declaration provides, *ex abundanti cautela*, that nothing in the Declaration is to be construed as prejudicing in any manner the provisions of the Charter. Article 103 prevails over the paraphrase of it in the Declaration.

Necatigl also noted that neither the Security Council nor the General Assembly has declared the Treaty of Guarantee void, even though the issue has been raised frequently in both organs; and in any event Article 103 does not invalidate a treaty with provisions in conflict with the Charter. The treaty is valid and remains in force subject to the condition that members must give priority to their Charter obligations. The Friendly Relations formulation is to the same effect.

GOOD FAITH AND ABUSE OF RIGHTS

Without devoting too much space to what may seem to be an academic debate on the existence and scope of the doctrine of abuse of rights in international law, there is undoubtedly a vital thread connecting this doctrine, or rule, and the principle of good faith, or rather its obverse, bad faith. In his pioneering study Cheng treats the theory of abuse of rights as 'merely an application of this principle [good faith] to the exercise of rights'.[67] Taylor formulated the following proposition, based on an extensive review of international case law:

> A State or person acts in bad faith where it abuses its rights – by pursuing an improper purpose, taking account of an irrelevant factor, or acting unreasonably – and does so knowing that it is abusing its rights.[68]

He submits that knowledge is the crucial element, and it is this which has led to the judicial reluctance to find that a State or person has acted in bad faith. 'Internationally, good faith is presumed and a State is entitled to rely on the word of another State'.[69]

Fitzmaurice based the doctrine upon a duty to exercise rights in good faith. His formulation, derived from the jurisprudence of the ICJ, including dicta from separate or dissenting opinions, is as follows:

> The essence of the doctrine is that although a State may have a strict right to act in a particular way, it must not exercise this right in such a manner as to constitute an abuse of it; it must exercise its rights in good faith and with a sense of responsibility; it must have *bona fide* reasons for what it does, and not act arbitrarily or capriciously.[70]

Good faith and abuse of rights have now been linked in a treaty provision, Article 300 of the Law of the Sea Convention, not yet in force but which many States have now ratified. The article is headed 'Good faith and abuse of rights' and provides:

> States Parties shall fulfil in good faith the obligations assumed under this Convention and shall exercise the rights, jurisdiction and freedoms recognized in this Convention in a manner which would not constitute an abuse of rights.[71]

GOOD FAITH AND GENERAL ASSEMBLY RESOLUTIONS

It is the abuse of rights application of good faith which has come to the fore in the continuing debate on the legal effects of General Assembly resolutions. The duty to consider in good faith recommendations contained in such resolutions is founded upon the obligations of co-operation assumed by Members in Articles 1(3), 2(5) and 56 of the Charter. When these obligations to co-operate in good faith are ignored to the point of becoming an abuse of right, a breach of duty to act in good faith emerges.[72]

More than thirty years ago, Judge Sir Hersch Lauterpacht argued that in some circumstances there arose a duty not merely to consider the recommendation in good faith but to act upon it. Not to do so, to continue to disregard successive General Assembly resolutions in the same sense addressed to a particular State, is for that State to act at its peril. The State may be taken to have crossed 'the imperceptible line between impropriety and illegality, between the exercise of a legal right to disregard the recommendation, and the abuse of that right'.[73] Commenting on this celebrated passage, Fitzmaurice reminds us that logically, a cumulation of non-binding recommendations cannot convert such resolutions into sources of legal obligation. But the wisdom, as distinct from the legality, of the 'target' State's continued rejection of the General Assembly's recommendations repeated by a quasi-unanimity or large majority of States 'which, for the purposes of the argument, it must be assumed are themselves acting responsibly and in all dispassionate good faith (for if not, *cadit quaestio*)' constitutes evidence, although not proof, of a lack of good faith on the part of the addressee State. Action not in good faith is a breach of a general international law obligation, even if it is a breach which is hard to establish and whose consequences may be uncertain.[74]

Good faith enters into the process of weighing various factors to determine the legal effects, if any, of particular General Assembly resolutions. A resolution can have no legal, and minimal practical, effect if it lacks credibility, and in this regard resolutions adopted by consensus can score well. If followed by all members in good faith, the consensus procedure gives opportunity for credible results.

> The majority is prepared to forego its preponderant voting advantage in order to reach a result which is generally satisfactory. Good faith requires, however, that all members make a genuine effort to achieve reasonable results, and that once a consensus is reached it be respected by all sides.[75]

ALLEGATIONS OF BAD FAITH

Allegations of bad faith on the part of States have been made on occasions before municipal courts. Such a court would be reluctant to hold that a friendly foreign State had acted in bad faith, and would require the clearest evidence before so finding. The Swiss Federal Tribunal was asked to hold that Italy should not be allowed to invoke State immunity in proceedings by a private party seeking the return of certain historic stone tablets. The tablets had been handed over to Italy by the Swiss authorities to be evidence in criminal proceedings, pursuant to a request under the European Convention on Mutual Assistance in Criminal Matters. The argument ran that to allow Italy to invoke immunity would be contrary to good faith since, by Article 6(2) of the Convention, Italy was bound to return the tablets to Switzerland. The request for assistance was part of an 'astute manoeuvre' intended to allow Italy to reverse roles and become the defendant instead of the claimant. The court found no facts to support such a conclusion, and in any event Article 6(2) required evidence handed over to be returned 'as soon as possible', a vague expression. It was not clear whether the criminal proceedings had ended. Even if the tablets were at present in a museum 'it could not be concluded irrefutably that Italy was refusing to return them'.[76] For these and other reasons, the court could not accept that Italy had usurped the role of defendant by recourse to procedures which were contrary to good faith.[77]

From such relatively low-key issues, we turn now to the arena of high politics involving matters crucial to States' security and defence.

GOOD FAITH IN ARMS CONTROL AND DISARMAMENT. VERIFICATION OF COMPLIANCE

As so often, Schwarzenberger has drawn attention to the significance of verification provisions as a necessary earnest of good faith performance of treaty obligations in sensitive areas:

> It is significant that the draftsmen of the United Nations Charter still considered it advisable to incorporate in the seven Principles embodied in article 2 the duty of members to fulfil in good faith their obligations under the Charter. Even more pointedly, the parties to the SALT II Treaty between the United States and the Soviet Union considered it necessary to guard expressly against each other's bad faith and circumvention of their mutual obligations.[78]

Some of the relevant provisions of the SALT II Treaty, concluded in 1979[79] are those which conferred more responsibilities on the Standing Consultative Commission (SCC) established in connection with the SALT I group of treaties in 1972.[80] The Commission is a forum for ongoing dialogue between the two Parties, to which each side can submit any issue within the competence of the SCC to determine. The SCC meetings are private but commentators have gleaned that it has proved valuable and that Soviet attitudes in the SCC have been positive.[81]

Article XVI of SALT II provides that within the SCC framework the parties will, *inter alia*:

> (a) Consider questions concerning compliance with the obligations assumed and related situations which may be considered ambiguous;
> (b) Provide on a voluntary basis such information as either party considers necessary to assure confidence in compliance with the obligations assumed;
> (c) Consider questions involving unintended interference with national technical means of verification, and questions involving unintended impeding of verification by national technical means of compliance with the provisions of this Treaty.

Since the early 1960s 'national technical means' have enabled States parties to arms control agreements or agreements limiting nuclear testing to verify the other parties' compliance with their treaty undertakings by methods under the control of the verifying State, requiring no co-operation from any other State. The means include satellites, seismological stations, radar and other radioelectronic installations.[83] SALT II relied solely on national technical means for monitoring and verification.[83]

Limitations of space preclude any attempt here to review the development of techniques of verification and of the drafting formulas to give effect to consensual acceptance of their use in particular arms control agreements.[84] Issues of interpretation, in which good faith supposedly controls parties' claims, have offered States the opportunity to circumvent inconvenient restrictions on the development or deployment of weapons systems, and gave rise in the mid–1980s to sharp exchanges between the United States and the former Soviet Union.[85] Again, an evaluation of this specialised area of the practice of these two States lies beyond the scope of the present chapter. But international lawyers should be aware of these episodes which dramatically illustrate the operative significance of the presence or absence of mutual trust, or, in other words, of the belief or lack of it in the other party's basic good faith.[86]

An example in the arms control area but involving many States, not simply the United States and the former USSR, is the 1971 Biological Weapons Convention[87] which originally lacked any provisions for verification and control.[88] Article V requires parties to consult and co-operate in solving any problem which might arise in the application of the Convention, and Article VI provides that any party which 'finds' that any other party is in breach of its Convention obligations may lodge a complaint with the UN Security Council. Each party undertakes to co-operate in carrying out any investigation which the Security Council may initiate. Any such action by the Council would be subject to the veto, which could be used equally by China, a non-party.[89] Some limited measures of exchange of information and publication of results of relevant biological research were 'agreed' by the States parties participating in the Second Review Conference in 1986. The Final Declaration of the Conference[90] refers in the preamble to its purpose, namely, assuring that the Convention provisions are being realised, and contains a declaration by the participants of 'their continued dedication to its principles and objectives and their legal obligations under international law to implement and *strictly* comply with its provisions'.[91]

Forms and modalities for these exchanges of information were to be finalised in an *ad hoc* meeting of scientific and technical experts in spring 1987. A Third Review Conference, scheduled for autumn 1991, was to consider whether further actions were called for to create 'further co-operative measures in the context of Article V, or *legally binding improvements* to the Convention, or a combination of both'.[92] This language clearly signals the non-binding status of the exchange of information etc. clauses in the Final Declaration, a status determined by their inclusion in a conference declaration rather than in a formal revision of the Convention, which would be subject to ratification by States parties.[93]

In the background to these developments at the 1986 Review Conference lay a change of position by the former USSR, which had long opposed any modification or addition to the Biological Weapons Convention.[94] The USSR formally proposed the adoption of an additional protocol to the Convention to strengthen (arguably, to create) a system of verification of compliance. Parties at the Review Conference welcomed this change, but decided not to consider whether legally binding improvements should be introduced until the 1991 Review Conference. It was deemed appropriate to await the conclusion of a Chemical Weapons Convention and only in the light of its verification provisions to consider what supplementary formal obligations were needed for the Biological Convention.[95] Meanwhile, as noted, parties believed that compliance procedures could be strengthened 'within the framework of the original text of the Biological Weapons Convention through informal, voluntary undertakings'.[96]

What we see here is a combination of treaty obligations, to be performed strictly, and informal undertakings moving towards a system of verification and made possible by a change of policy on the part of one important State party, giving rise to a possible reliance by all on the good faith compliance of the other parties. Goldblat observed that it was generally acknowledged at the Review Conference that verification procedures were needed 'not only to provide confidence that the terms of the Convention were adhered to, but also to provide those whose compliance might be called into question with the means of proving their innocence'. He added that the agreed confidence-building measures, exchange of information and so forth, might be useful in removing suspicion of breaches 'if, in fact, the governments honour the commitments expressed in the Final Declaration'.[97]

As for chemical weapons, there is no general convention yet in force prohibiting their development, production or stockpiling and requiring their destruction.[98] The Security Council in its 1987 resolution calling for a cease-fire in the Iran-Iraq war deplored the *use* of chemical weapons contrary to the 1925 Geneva Protocol.[99]

The failure by Iraq to implement its disclosure and disarmament obligations under Security Council Resolution 687 of 3 April 1991, adopted on the termination of hostilities in the Gulf War and accepted by Iraq on 6 April 1991, was condemned by a unanimous Council in Resolution 707 on 15 August 1991. These obligations related to chemical, biological and nuclear weapons and to ballistic missiles with a range greater than 150 km. In the preamble to Resolution 687 the Security Council expressly encouraged the forthcoming Review Conference of the Biological Weapons Convention 'to reinforce the authority, efficiency and universal scope of the Convention' and stressed the importance of an early conclusion of a chemical weapons (prohibition) convention.

Resolution 687 as a whole is replete with detail in the paragraphs requiring Iraq to disarm and not to acquire or develop nuclear weapons or weapons-usable material. It provided for a Special Commission to carry out on-site inspections of Iraq's biological, chemical and missile capabilities, and to receive and destroy, or supervise the destruction of, all such weapons and capabilities. On-site inspection of Iraq's nuclear capabilities was the responsibility of the International Atomic Energy Agency. Subsequent press and media reports have revealed the obstacles and difficulties which these missions encountered. Iraq's good faith was conspicuous by its absence, and was not indeed presumed, as would normally be the case. The Security Council in the preamble to resolution 687 *reaffirmed* 'the need to be assured of Iraq's peaceful intentions in the light of its unlawful invasion and occupation of Kuwait'.[100] Resolution 687 embodied verification and control procedures as part of the conditions for a cease-fire between Iraq and Kuwait and the member States cooperating with Kuwait. Iraq's acceptance of Resolution 687 was a precondition for the formal cease-fire becoming effective.[101]

Finally, to bring this section up to date so far as possible, mention may be made of the Strategic Arms Reduction Treaty (START) signed by President Bush and the then Soviet President Gorbachev on 31 July 1991. It is not yet ratified, nor has a text been published. The head of the US Delegation to the negotiations has written of the verification provisions of the START:

> The reductions and limitations of the Treaty will be conducted under the terms of highly intrusive verification procedures. The START Treaty builds on the three years of experience from the INF Treaty

> with inspections by each side of virtually every significant strategic installation of the other side. All told, the START Treaty includes 12 different types of inspections plus continuous monitoring at the facilities in each country that produce mobile ICBMs or their first stages.
>
> The Treaty also creates an extensive system of over 80 separate notifications – each side being required to tell the other about new missile systems as well as about movements, operations, and eliminations of the forces subject to the Treaty – to increase the understanding each side has of the other's intentions and actions.[102]

There is to be exchange of magnetic tapes of missile flight test data (telemetry) following such tests by either side. Such an agreement, said Brooks, the US Delegation head, would have been impossible during any other time in the history of US-Soviet relations. The 'new era of co-operation' had made it possible, and with START 'we will be able to further dispel mistrust'[103]. Paradoxically, but understandably in view of this past history, the emergence of co-operative relations is manifested by treaties containing very detailed and intrusive verification provisions. Good faith may be growing in these new relations between the Superpowers, but good faith alone is too weak a reed to bear the weight of the need to be assured that the other party will comply fully and strictly with its disarmament obligations.

IN CONCLUSION

As Virally has put it, good faith is in many respects the basic postulate of the international legal order. Such a principle is essential to a non-formalistic order, which allows the most room for the creation and performance of law by the will of those who are subject to it, and which lacks a system of enforcement independent of their will. International law, as well as many national systems, have borrowed the principle of good faith from the ethical realm and turned it into a juridical principle of considerable value.[104]

NOTES

1 R. Rosenstock (1971) 65 *A.J.I.L.* 713 at p.734.
2 League members agreed to carry out 'in full good faith' any award or decision that might be rendered in any dispute between them. Article 94(1) of the UN Charter omits reference to good faith.
3 UNCIO Docs, vol.6, pp.71–8 and 332–3.
4 UN General Assembly 6th Committee, 20th session, 874th meeting, para. 12, 12 November 1965.
5 Ibid., 881st meeting, para.33, 23 November 1965.
6 UN GAOR 22nd session, Annexes, Agenda item 87, Doc. A/6799, Report of the Special Committee on Principles of International Law, para.285.
7 *Repertory of Practice of UN Organs*, Supp. No. 4, vol.II, p.370, para.41.

8 See UN Doc. A/6799, Report of the Special Committee, paras.236–300. See in particular paras.264–84, Compliance with obligations arising out of treaties and other sources of international law.

9 UN General Assembly Resolution 3281(XXIX).

10 CERDS does not define 'international obligations'. Cf. para.8 of UN General Assembly Resolution 1803(XVII) on Permanent Sovereignty over Natural Resources which begins: 'Foreign investment agreements freely entered into *by, or between*, sovereign States shall be observed in good faith' (emphasis added). See the arbitral award in *Revere Copper* v. *OPIC* [1978], 56 I.L.R. Rep. 258, at p.271 on assurances given in good faith to aliens as an inducement to making investments affected adversely by subsequent host State action contrary to the initial investment agreement.

11 Text in (1987) 26 I.L.M. 190. 'They' are the CSCE participating States which then numbered 35, including the former USSR and the two Germanies.

12 See further p.242 below.

13 UN GAOR, 43rd session, Supp. No. 1, A/43/1. Text of the Accords in (1988) 27 *I.L.M.* 577: the US-USSR Declaration of International Guarantee is at p.584.

14 27 (1988) *I.L.M.* 587. The parties are Afghanistan, Pakistan, the USA and the USSR.

15 See UN Doc. A/43/1, p.8.

16 Article 25; text in (1992) 31 *I.L.M.* 174 at p.187.

17 Article 28(1).

18 'The Law and Procedure of the ICJ, 1960–1989', in (1989) 60 *B.Y.I.L.*, at p.25.

19 In the 1986 Review Conference of the Biological Weapons Convention the participating States parties reaffirmed their obligations under Article IX to continue negotiations in good faith towards 'an early agreement' on effective measures for the prohibition of the development, production and stockpiling of chemical weapons and for their destruction. A multilateral convention has now been signed. See p.248 above. A bilateral Agreement banning chemical weapons was concluded by the USA and the former USSR in 1990 which refers in its preamble to the need for a multilateral convention. Text in (1990) 29 *I.L.M.* 932.

20 See the *North Sea Continental Shelf* [1969] I.C.J. Rep. 3, para.85(a); the *Continental Shelf (Tunisia/Libya) Interpretation of Judgment*, [1985] ICJ Rep. 229; Judge Gros, Diss. Op. in *Continental Shelf (Tunisia/Libya)* case, [1982] I.C.J. Rep. at pp.144–5; *Aegean Sea Continental Shelf* case, [1978] I.C.J. Rep., paras.106, 108.

21 [1984] I.C.J. Rep., at pp.292, 299.

22 (1972), 47 I.L.R. 418.

23 Such a *pactum* is created only when parties have already undertaken a legal obligation to conclude an agreement. See Lord McNair, *Law of Treaties*, Oxford: Oxford University Press, 1961, p.27 *et seq*. For example, Article. 9 of the Protocol on Prohibitions or Restrictions on the Use of Mines, Booby-Traps and Other Devices, annexed to the UN Convention on Prohibitions or Restrictions of Use of Certain Conventional Weapons, 1980. The article provides: 'After the cessation of active hostilities, the parties shall endeavour to reach agreement . . . on the provision of information and technical and material assistance . . . necessary to remove or otherwise render ineffective minefields, mines and booby-traps placed in position during the conflict.' Contrast the *pactum de negotiando* in Article IX of the Bacteriological (Biological) and Toxic Weapons Convention of 1972, referred to in n.19 above.

24 These principles were repeated in summary in paragraph 4 of the operative

part of the decision in which the Tribunal stated the broad principles that should guide the negotiations: 47 I.L.R. 462.

25 J.F. O'Connor, *Good Faith in International Law*, Aldershot: Dartmouth, 1991, p.111.

26 Arbitral Tribunal (1989), 83 I.L.R. 1.

27 Para.55 at p.33.

28 Para.59 at p.34.

29 F.A. Mann, 'The Commercial Law of Nations as Reflected by Cmnd. 1 to 10,000' (1989) 60 *B.Y.I.L.* 359, at p.434.

30 'International Jus Cogens' in G. Schwarzenberger, *International Law and Order*, London: Stevens, 1971, p.27, at p.34.

31 Ibid.

32 G. Schwarzenberger, 'The Fundamental Principles of International Law' (1958-I) 87 *Hague Recueil des Cours* 195, at p.300.

33 In 'Myths and Realities of Treaty Interpretation' in (1971) *International Law and Order* 110 at p.118. See also the review of Gentili's views on the principle of good faith in O'Connor, above n.25, pp.49–53.

34 Joint Op. in *Aerial Incident Case* (*Israel* v. *Bulgaria*) [1959] ICJ Rep., 188.

35 See also McNair, above n.23, p.465: a party would not be acting in good faith if it put forward an interpretation which the negotiators knew did not represent the intention of the parties.

36 I. Brownlie, *Principles of International Law*, Oxford: Clarendon Press, 4th edn. 1990 p.631, citing *I.L.C. Yearbook 1966*, vol.2, p.219, para.6. See also I. Sinclair, *The Vienna Convention on the Law of Treaties*, Manchester: Manchester University Press, 2nd edn, 1984, at p.118), differing from D. P. O'Connell's view of Article 31 in *International Law*, London: Stevens, 1970, p.255.

37 *I.L.C. Yearbook 1966*, above n.36. For a robust use of this principle of effectiveness, see the Joint Diss. Op. in the *Young Loan Arbitration* (1980) 59 I.L.R. 494 at pp.569–71. These arbitrators accepted the view that the references to 'good faith' and 'object and purpose' in Article 31 of the Vienna Convention subsume the principle of effectiveness. The Tribunal's application of the object and purpose criterion lacks any reference to good faith or effectiveness: see pp.540–41, 549–50.

38 *I.L.C. Yearbook 1966*, vol.2, p.221.

39 (1983) 77 I.L.R. 636, at pp.666–8.

40 Ibid., at p.661.

41 Ibid., pp.669–74.

42 B.S. Murty, *The International Law of Diplomacy*, Dordrecht: Martinus Nijhoff, p.574, citing J. E. S. Fawcett, 'The Legal Character of International Agreements' (1953) 30 *B.Y.I.L.* 381, at p.391.

43 *UN Juridical Yearbook, 1979*, p.174.

44 (1990) 82 I.L.R. 591, at pp.613–14.

45 Ibid., p.614.

46 See *Rainbow Warrior*, (1987) 74 ILR 241 at pp.256 and 274.

47 (1990) 82 I.L.R. 499, at p.543.

48 Ibid., p.547.

49 Ibid., p.555.

50 Ibid., p.583.

51 Ibid., pp.560–3.

52 Ibid., p.563.

53 The European Court of Justice said in 104/81 *HZA Mainz* v. *Kupferberg & Cie KG* [1982] E.C.R. 3641 at pp.3663–4: 'according to the general rules of international law there must be bona fide performance of every agreement'.

54 *La Bretagne Arbitration* (1985), 82 I.L.R. 591, at p.637.
55 Ibid. p.670.
56 (1981) 20 I.L.M. 224.
57 (1987) 14 Iran-U.S. C.T.R. 324, *Request for Interpretation by the Full Tribunal of the Algiers Declarations with respect to Whether the US is Obligated to Satisfy Promptly Any Award of this Tribunal Rendered in Favour of Iran against Nationals of the US*.
58 Ibid., pp.330–331.
59 [1971] I.C.J. Rep., 17, at paras. 128–31; 49 I.L.R. 2, at pp.46–7.
60 Brownlie, above n.36, p.3.
61 *Case Concerning the Arbitral Award of 31 July 1989*, 83 I.L.R. 1 at p.43.
62 Ibid., p.86.
63 Sinclair, above n.36, p.86.
64 Cmnd. 1093 (1960).
65 Z. Necatigl, *The Cyprus Question and the Turkish Position in International Law*, Oxford: Oxford University Press, 1988, pp.119–20.
66 Brownlie, above n.36, p.625 puts a wider and, it is submitted unjustifiable interpretation on Article 103: that it is an example of a treaty providing expressly 'that it is to prevail over subsequent incompatible treaties'. Article 103 is drafted carefully in terms of conflicting *obligations* of Members under the Charter and *their* obligations under any other treaty.
67 Bin Cheng, *General Principles of Law as Applied by International Courts and Tribunals* London, Stevens, 1953, at p.121.
68 'The Content of the Rule Against Abuse of Rights in International Law', (1972–73) 46 *B.Y.I.L.* 323, at p.333.
69 Ibid., p.334 citing *Lake Lanoux* case, 24 I.L.R. 101, at p.126.
70 *The Law and Procedure of the International Court of Justice*, Cambridge: Grotius, 1986, vol.I, p.12. See also ibid., p.183, and vol.II, pp.609–10, drawing on later cases.
71 The obligation in Article 18 of the Vienna Convention on the Law of Treaties not to defeat the object and purpose of a treaty prior to its entry into force is treated by Taylor, above, n.68 p.335, under the heading 'Unratified Treaties and Bad Faith'; he points out that Article 18 is a wider prohibition, not limited to cases of bad faith. See also Sinclair's view, at above n.63.
72 See Blaine Sloan, 'General Assembly Resolutions Revisited' (1987) 58 *B.Y.I.L.* 39, at p.121.
73 Sep. Op. *S.W. Africa Voting Procedure* case, [1955] I.C.J. Rep. 1955, pp.118–20.
74 In 'Hersch Lauterpacht – The Scholar as Judge, II' (1962) 38 *B.Y.I.L.* 1, reprinted in *The Law and Procedure of the International Court of Justice*, above vol. II, n.70, p.713.
75 Sloan. above n.70, p.138.
76 *Italian State* v. *X* (1985) 82 I.L.R. 24, at p.28.
77 Ibid., p.29.
78 In 'The Conceptual Apparatus of International Law' in R.St.J. Macdonald and D.M. Johnston, (eds) *The Structure and Process of International Law*, The Hague: Martinus Nijhoff, 1986, p. 685, at pp.686–87.
79 Text in (1979) 18 *I.L.M.* 1112.
80 See J. Dahlitz, *Nuclear Arms Control*, London: George Allen & Unwin, 1983, p.150.
81 See M. Sheehan, *Arms Control, Theory and Practice*, Oxford: Basil Blackwell, 1986, p. 139 and A. Carter, *Success and Failure in Arms Control Negotiations*, Oxford: Oxford University Press, 1989, Chaps. 5 and 6.
82 It is generally agreed that verification can be subdivided in terms of methods

employed into three broad categories: 1) traditional intelligence (diplomatic techniques; scrutiny of published material; espionage); 2) national technical means; and 3) on-site-inspection. See M. Sheehan, above n.81, p.132 for five subdivisions of on-site-inspection, ranging from prepositioned cameras or seismic devices to unlimited inspection visits in defined zones.

83 See helpful review of SALT II by S. Lunn and J. Seabright in *SIPRI Yearbook 1983*, at pp.65–66.

84 Refer to the works by Carter, Dahlitz and Sheehan cited in nn.80 and 81 above, and literature cited by these authors. See also the annual *SIPRI Yearbooks, World Armaments and Disarmament* for detailed reports on new agreements and on allegations of breach of existing agreements with expert, neutral evaluations of such allegations. The 1983 and 1987 *Yearbooks* have numerous examples of such allegations.

85 On the US re-interpretation of the ABM Treaty, which formed part of the SALT I group of treaties, see C. Bertram, in *SIPRI Yearbook, 1987*, at pp.334–6, and L. Freedman, in *The Independent*, 18 February 1987. Statements and documents from both parties are reprinted in (1987) 26 *I.L.M.* 282. The ABM Treaty text is at (1972) 11 *I.L.M.* 784. See also reply in the House of Lords by a minister giving the UK government's view, that 'as a non-party, we have no locus to interpret it': HL Debs., vol.508, col.496, 24 May 1989; UKMIL 1989, in (1989) 60 *B.Y.I.L.*, at 640.

86 The INF Treaty, USA-USSR, on the Elimination of their Intermediate-Range and Shorter-Range Missiles, text in (1988) 27 *I.L.M.* 84, contains elaborate memoranda and protocols on the exchange of data, procedures for the elimination of the missile systems and on-site inspections – the first time that these two States have agreed to such inspections. Inspections of the elimination of missiles and systems in third countries were agreed by the countries concerned in agreements concluded shortly before the INF Treaty itself. See the 'Basing Country Agreements' between the USA and Belgium, F.R.G. of Germany, Italy, the Netherlands and the UK in (1988) 27 *I.L.M.* 58, and Exchanges of Notes between the GDR and the USA at ibid. p.73. Similar Notes were exchanged between the USSR and the five US Allied Basing Countries. Verification as such was not a matter of dispute between the USA and the USSR in negotiating the INF Treaty. Both sides agreed on the need for on-site inspections. See the account in Carter, above n.81, pp.215–17, 225.

87 Convention on the Prohibition of the Development, Production and Stockpiling of Bacteriological (Biological) and Toxin Weapons and their Destruction, entered into force 26 March 1975, text in (1972) 11 *I.L.M.* 313.

88 See criticism by Alva Myrdal, *The Game of Disarmament*, Manchester: Manchester University Press, 1977, pp.273–4.

89 The other four permanent members of the Security Council are parties to this Convention.

90 See Final Declaration of 26 September 1986, adopted by consensus, in (1987) 26 *I.L.M.* 197.

91 Emphasis added. Possibly the affirmation of the *jus strictum* character of the Convention explains the absence of any reference to performance of the parties' obligations 'in good faith', which could have been interpreted as a statement that the Convention constitutes *jus aequum*. See Schwarzenberger, above n.32. The Final Declaration, in its text relating to Article V of the Convention, speaks of 'encouraging strict observance of the provisions subscribed to'.

92 Emphasis added. Final Declaration at Article XII, (1989) 26 *I.L.M.* 199.

93 See D.H.N. Johnson, 'Conclusions of International Conferences' (1959) 35 *B.Y.I.L.* 1.

94 For example, in 1982 the USSR voted against a General Assembly resolution, Resolution 37/98 C, recommending a special conference to be held to create a flexible, objective and non-discriminatory procedure to deal with issues of compliance.

95 For a thorough review and critique of the draft Chemical Weapons Convention published in the 1986 report of the Conference on Disarmament, CD Doc. CD/727, see J. Goldblat in *SIPRI Yearbook 1987*, at pp.383–7. A convergence of views had emerged by the end of 1986 that confidence in any such treaty should be maintained by routine inspection, and that any party must be entitled to have confidence that any suspicions of non-compliance which it voiced would be promptly investigated by agreed procedures. Press reports in January 1993 recorded the signing by more than 120 States of a Chemical Weapons Convention which, assuming its entry into force, should lead to the verified destruction of all chemical weapons on a universal basis. The text provides for extensive and intrusive verifications of suspect sites with only 5 days' notice – the so-called 'challenge inspections'. See, for example, the *Independent*, 13 and 14 January 1993.

96 J. Goldblat, 'The review of the Biological Weapons Convention' (1987) *SIPRI Yearbook* 409, at p.411.

97 Ibid., p.414.

98 The USA and the USSR concluded a bilateral Agreement on the Destruction and Non-Production of Chemical Weapons in 1990, text in (1990) 29 *I.L.M.* 932. For inspection and verification provisions see Articles V and VI, and the earlier Memorandum of Understanding in (1989) 28 *I.L.M.* 1438. Other bilateral agreements concluded at the same time were Verification Protocols to the 'Threshold' Nuclear Test Ban Treaty, (1990) 29 *I.L.M.* 969, and to the Treaty on Underground Nuclear Explosions for Peaceful Purposes, ibid. 1025.

99 Resolution 598, 20 July 1987, see (1987) 26 *I.L.M.* 1479 and Iran's response, para.15, ibid., p.1483. For the UN specialist team's report of March 1986 on allegations by Iran that Iraq had used chemical weapons see S/17911. The allegations were well-founded. See (1987) *SIPRI Yearbook* 388. For earlier allegations see UN Security Council Official Reports Supp. 1984 (July-Sept.) pp.10–11, 26–27.

100 The text of Resolution 687 is at (1991) 30 *I.L.M.* 847.

101 See paragraph 33. Iraq's acceptance was notified to the Secretary-General and the Security Council on 6 April 1991.

102 Ambassador Brooks,'The Strategic Arms Reduction Treaty: reducing the risk of war', in (October 1991) 39 *NATO Review*, No. 5, pp.8–9.

103 Ibid.

104 M. Virally, review essay of E. Zoller, *La Bonne Foi en Droit International Public* (1977) in (1983) 77 *A.J.I.L.* 130, at pp.132, 133.

Appendix

Declaration on Principles of International Law concerning Friendly Relations and Co-operation among States in accordance with the Charter of the United Nations[1]

PREAMBLE

THE GENERAL ASSEMBLY

Reaffirming in the terms of the Charter that the maintenance of international peace and security and the development of friendly relations and co-operation between nations are among the fundamental purposes of the United Nations.

Recalling that the peoples of the United Nations are determined to practise tolerance and live together in peace with one another as good neighbours.

Bearing in mind the importance of maintaining and strengthening international peace founded upon freedom, equality, justice and respect for fundamental human rights and of developing friendly relations among nations irrespective of their political, economic and social systems or the levels of their development.

Bearing in mind also the paramount importance of the Charter of the United Nations in the promotion of the law among nations.

Considering that the faithful observance of the principles of international law concerning friendly relations and co-operation among States, and fulfilment in good faith of the obligations assumed by States, in accordance with the Charter, is of the greatest importance for the maintenance of international peace and security, and for the implementation of the other purposes of the United Nations.

Noting that the great political, economic and social changes and scientific progress which have taken place in the world since the adoption of the Charter of the United Nations give increased importance to these principles and to the need for their more effective application in the conduct of States wherever carried on.

Recalling the established principle that outer space, including the Moon and other celestial bodies, is not subject to national appropriation by claim of sovereignty by means of use or occupation or by any other means, and mindful of the fact that consideration is being given in the

United Nations to the question of establishing other appropriate provisions similarly inspired.

Convinced that the strict observance by States of the obligation not to intervene in the affairs of any other State is an essential condition to ensure that nations live together in peace with one another since the practice of any form of intervention not only violates the spirit and letter of the Charter of the United Nations but also leads to the creation of situations which threaten peace and security.

Recalling the duty of States in their international relations from military, political, economic or any other form of coercion aimed against the political independence or territorial integrity of any State.

Considering it essential that all States shall refrain in their international relations from the threat or use of force against the territorial integrity or political independence of any State, or in any other manner inconsistent with the purposes of the United Nations.

Considering it equally essential that all States shall settle their international disputes by peaceful means in accordance with the Charter.

Reaffirming in accordance with the Charter, the basic importance of sovereign equality and stressing that the purposes the United Nations can be implemented only if States enjoy sovereign equality and comply fully with the requirements of this principle in their international relations.

Convinced that the subjection of peoples to alien subjugation, domination and exploitation constitutes a major obstacle to the promotion of international peace and security.

Convinced that the principle of equal rights and self-determination of peoples constitutes a significant contribution to the contemporary international law, and that its effective application is of paramount importance for the promotion of friendly relations among States, based on respect for the principle of sovereign equality.

Convinced in consequence that any attempt aimed at the partial or total disruption of the national unity and territorial integrity of a State or country or at its political independence is incompatible with the purposes and principles of the Charter.

Considering the provisions of the Charter as a whole and taking into account the role of relevant resolutions adopted by the competent organs of the United Nations relating to the content of the principles.

Considering that the progressive development and codification of the following principles:

(a) The principle that States shall refrain in their international relations from the threat or use of force against the territorial integrity or political independence of any State, or in any other manner inconsistent with the purposes of the United Nations.
(b) The principle that States shall settle their international disputes by

peaceful means in such a manner that international peace and security and justice are not endangered.

(c) The duty not to intervene in matters within the domestic jurisdiction of any State, in accordance with the Charter.

(d) The duty of States to co-operate with one another in accordance with the Charter.

(e) The principle of equal rights and self-determination of peoples.

(f) The principle of sovereign equality of States.

(g) The principle that States shall fulfil in good faith the obligations assumed by them in accordance with the Charter, so as to secure their more effective application within the international community would promote the realization of the purposes of the United Nations.

Having considered the principles of international law relating to friendly relations and co-operation among States.

1. *Solemnly proclaims* the following principles:

The principle that States shall refrain in their international relations from the threat or use of force against the territorial integrity or political independence of any State, or in any other manner inconsistent with the purposes of the United Nations.

Every State has the duty to refrain in its international relations from the threat or use of force against the territorial integrity or political independence of any State, or in any other manner inconsistent with the purposes of the United Nations. Such a threat or use of force constitutes a violation of international law and the Charter of the United Nations and shall never be employed as a means of settling international issues.

A war of aggression constitutes a crime against the peace, for which there is responsibility under international law.

In accordance with the purposes and principles of the United Nations, States have the duty to refrain from propaganda for wars of aggression.

Every State has the duty to refrain from the threat or use of force to violate the existing international boundaries of another State or as a means of solving international disputes, including territorial disputes and problems concerning frontiers of States.

Every State likewise has the duty to refrain from the threat or use of force to violate international lines of demarcation, such as armistice lines, established by or pursuant to an international agreement to which it is a party or which it is otherwise bound to respect. Nothing in the foregoing shall be construed as prejudicing the positions of the parties concerned with regard to the status and effects of such lines under their special régimes or as affecting their temporary character.

States have a duty to refrain from acts of reprisal involving the use of force.

Every State has the duty to refrain from any forcible action which deprives peoples referred to in the elaboration of the principle of equal rights and self-determination of their right to self-determination and freedom and independence.

Every State has the duty to refrain from organizing or encouraging the organization of irregular forces or armed bands, including mercenaries, for incursion into the territory of another State.

Every State has the duty to refrain from organizing, instigating, assisting or participating in acts of civil strife or terrorist acts in another State or acquiesing in organized activities within its territory directed towards the commission of such acts, when the acts referred to in the present paragraph involve a threat or use of force.

The territory of a State shall not be the object of military occupation resulting from the use of force in contravention of the provisions of the Charter. The territory of a State shall not be the object of acquisition by another State resulting from the threat or use of force. No territorial acquisition resulting from the threat or use of force shall be recognized as legal. Nothing in the foregoing shall be construed as affecting:

(a) Provisions of the Charter or any international agreement prior to the Charter régime and valid under international law: or
(b) The powers of the Security Council under the Charter.

All States shall pursue in good faith negotiations for the early conclusion of a universal treaty on general and complete disarmament under effective international control and strive to adopt appropriate measures to reduce international tensions and strengthen confidence among States.

All States shall comply in good faith with their obligations under the generally recognized principles and rules of international law with respect to the maintenance of international peace and security, and shall endeavour to make the United Nations security system based upon the Charter more effective.

Nothing in the foregoing paragraphs shall be construed as enlarging or diminishing in any way the scope of the provisions of the Charter concerning cases in which the use of force is lawful.

The principle that States shall settle their international disputes by peaceful means in such a manner that international peace and security and justice are not endangered.

Every State shall settle its international disputes with other States by peaceful means, in such a manner that international peace and security, and justice, are not endangered.

States shall accordingly seek early and just settlement of their international disputes by negotiation, inquiry, mediation, conciliation, arbitration, judicial settlement, resort to regional agencies or arrangements or other peaceful means of their choice. In seeking such a settlement the parties shall agree upon such peaceful means as may be appropriate to the circumstances and nature of the dispute.

The parties to a dispute have the duty, in the event of failure to reach a solution by any one of the above peaceful means, to continue to seek a settlement of the dispute by other peaceful means agreed upon by them.

States parties to an international dispute, as well as other States, shall refrain from any action which may aggravate the situation so as to endanger the maintenance of international peace and security, and shall act in accordance with the purposes and principles of the United Nations.

International disputes shall be settled on the basis of the sovereign equality of States and in accordance with the principle of free choice of means. Recourse to, or acceptance of, a settlement procedure freely agreed to by States with regard to existing or future disputes to which they are parties shall not be regarded as incompatible with sovereign equality.

Nothing in the foregoing paragraphs prejudices or derogates from the applicable provisions of the Charter, in particular those relating to the pacific settlement of international disputes.

The principle concerning the duty not to intervene in matters within the domestic jurisdiction of any State, in accordance with the Charter

No State or group of States has the right to intervene, directly or indirectly, for any reason whatever, in the internal or external affairs of any other State. Consequently, armed intervention and all other forms of interference or attempted threats against the personality of the State or against its political, economic and cultural elements, are in violation of international law.

No State may use or encourage the use of economic, political or any other type of measures to coerce another State in order to obtain from it the subordination of the exercise of its sovereign rights and to secure from it advantages of any kind. Also, no State shall organize, assist, foment, finance, incite or tolerate subversive, terrorist or armed activities directed towards the violent overthrow of the régime of another State, or interfere in civil strife in another State.

The use of force to deprive peoples of their national identity constitutes a violation of their inalienable rights and of the principle of non-intervention.

Every State has an inalienable right to choose its political, economic, social and cultural systems, without interference in any form by another State.

Nothing in the foregoing paragraphs shall be construed as affecting the relevant provisions of the Charter relating to the maintenance of international peace and security.

The duty of States to co-operate with one another in accordance with the Charter

States have the duty to co-operate with one another, irrespective of the differences in their political, economic and social systems, in the various spheres of international relations, in order to maintain international peace and security and to promote international economic stability and progress, the general welfare of nations and international co-operation free from discrimination based on such differences.

To this end:

(a) States shall co-operate with other States in the maintenance of international peace and security;
(b) States shall co-operate in the promotion of universal respect for and observance of human rights and fundamental freedoms for all, and in the elimination of all forms of racial discrimination and all forms of religious intolerance;
(c) States shall conduct their international relations in the economic, social, cultural, technical and trade fields in accordance with the principles of sovereign equality and non-intervention;
(d) States Members of the United Nations have the duty to take joint and separate action in co-operation with the United Nations in accordance with the relevant provisions of the Charter.

States should co-operate in the economic, social and cultural fields as well as in the field of science and technology and for the promotion of international cultural and educational progress. States should co-operate in the promotion of economic growth throughout the world, especially that of the developing countries.

The principle of equal rights and self-determination of peoples

By virtue of the principle of equal rights and self-determination of peoples enshrined in the Charter, all peoples have the right freely to determine, without external interference, their political status and to pursue their economic, social and cultural development, and every State has the duty to respect this right in accordance with the provisions of the Charter.

Every State has the duty to promote, through joint and separate action, the realization of the principle of equal rights and self-determination of peoples, in accordance with the provisions of the Charter, and to render assistance to the United Nations in carrying out the responsibilities entrusted to it by the Charter regarding the implementation of the principle in order:

(a) To promote friendly relations and co-operate among States; and
(b) To bring a speedy end to colonialism, having due regard to the freely expressed will of the peoples concerned:

and bearing in mind that subjection of peoples to alien subjugation, domination and exploitation constitutes a violation of the principle, as well as a denial of fundamental human rights, and is contrary to the Charter of the United Nations.

Every State has the duty to promote through joint and separate action universal respect for and observance of human rights and fundamental freedoms in accordance with the Charter.

The establishment of a sovereign and independent State, the free association or integration with an independent State or the emergence into any other political status freely determined by a people constitute modes of implementing the right of self-determination by that people.

Every State has the duty to refrain from any forcible action which deprives peoples referred to above in the elaboration of the present principle for their right to self-determination and freedom and independence. In their actions against and resistance to such forcible action in pursuit of the exercise of their right to self-determination, such peoples are entitled to seek and to receive support in accordance with the purposes and principles of the Charter of the United Nations.

The territory of a colony or other non-self-governing territory has, under the Charter of the United Nations, a status separate and distinct from the territory of the State administering it; and such separate and distinct status under the Charter shall exist until the people of the colony or non-self-governing territory have exercised their right of self-determination in accordance with the Charter, and particularly its purposes and principles.

Nothing in the foregoing paragraphs shall be construed as authorizing or encouraging any action which would dismember or impair, totally or in part, the territorial integrity or political unity of sovereign and independent States conducting themselves in compliance with the principle of equal rights and self-determination of peoples as described above and thus possessed of a government representing the whole people belonging to the territory without distinction as to race, creed or colour.

Every State shall refrain from any action aimed at the partial or total disruption of the national unity and territorial integrity of any other State or country.

The principle of sovereign equality of States

All States enjoy sovereign equality. They have equal rights and duties and are equal members of the international community, notwithstanding differences of an economic, social, political or other nature.

In particular, sovereign equality includes the following elements:

(a) States are juridically equal.
(b) Each State enjoys the rights inherent in full sovereignty;
(c) Each State has the duty to respect the personality of other States;
(d) The territorial integrity and political independence of the State are inviolable;
(e) Each State has the right freely to choose and develop its political, social, economic and cultural systems;
(f) Each State has the duty to comply fully and in good faith with its international obligations and to live in peace with other States.

The principle that States shall fulfil in good faith the obligations assumed by them in accordance with the Charter

Every State has the duty to fulfil in good faith the obligations assumed by it in accordance with the Charter of the United Nations.

Every State has the duty to fulfil in good faith its obligations under the generally recognized principles and rules of international law.

Every State has the duty to fulfil in good faith its obligations under international agreements valid under the generally recognized principles and rules of international law.

Where obligations arising under international agreements are in conflict with the obligations of Members of the United Nations under the Charter of the United Nations, the obligations under the Charter shall prevail.

General part.

2. *Declares* that:

In their interpretation and application the above principles are interrelated and each principle should be construed in the context of the other principles.

Nothing in this Declaration shall be construed as prejudicing in any manner the provisions of the Charter or the rights and duties of Member States under the Charter or the rights of peoples under the Charter taking into account the elaboration of these rights in this Declaration,

3. *Declares further* that:

The principles of the Charter which are embodied in this Declaration constitute basic principles of international law, and consequently appeals to all States to be guided by these principles in their international conduct and to develop their mutual relations on the basis of their strict observance.

NOTE

1 *UN General Assembly Resolution 2625(XXV), 24 October 1970. UN GAOR 25th session, Supp. No. 28, 121. UN Doc. A/8028 (1971).*

Index

abuse of rights 244
Achille Lauro 142
Afghanistan (1980) 34, 40, 70–1, 163, 232
African Charter on Human Rights 104
Air Services case (1978) 63
American Convention on Human Rights 104
Anglo–French Continental Shelf case (1977) 63
arbitration 50, 54–6
asylum 150

Bangladesh (1971) 71, 74
Beagle Channel case (1977) 55
Brezhnev doctrine 70
BP v Libya (1973) 63

Calvo clauses 79
Chernobyl (1986) 120, 124
Chile (1973) 71
  human rights 97, 113
Cobden, R. 77–8, 84
Cold War 1, 28
conciliation 50, 52–3
Congo (1960, 1964) 71, 74
Council of Europe 147, 184
CSCE 39, 60–1, 104–5, 120, 184, 185, 188, 190, 193, 207, 223
  see also Paris Charter
Cuba (1961) 71
Cyprus (1974, 1978) 71
Czechoslovakia (1968) 70

development 217
diplomatic law 2
disarmament 233, 246–50
domestic jurisdiction 68, 72–3, 86
Dominican Republic (1965) 71
Drago doctrine 79

economic blockade and coercion 39, 40
Egypt (1956) 71
Eichmann case (1961) 140, 155, 157
Elliott case (1949) 155
environmental law 28, 39, 120–36
European Community 58, 104, 150, 151, 184, 189
European Convention on Human Rights 104
European Court of Human Rights 57–8
extradition 139, 146–9
  aut dedere aut judicare 143, 146–9
  political offence 139, 148–9

Falklands/Malvinas conflict 39, 71
force 33–48
  see also: International Court of Justice, *Nicaragua* case; self-defence
Friendly Relations Declaration
  drafting 1–4, 36
  evaluation 5–9

genocide 9, 145, 189
good faith 204–9, 213
Grenada (1983) 44, 71
Guatemala (1952) 71
Guinea/Guinea Bissau case (1985) 63 237
Guinea Bissau/Senegal case (1989) 234, 242, 253

Hague Conventions (1899 and 1907) 52

Helsinki Final Act (1975) 29, 42, 90, 91, 105, 117–18
see also CSCE
Hobbes 75
human rights 28, 85–119, 150, 191, 193, 213, 214, 217
see also Universal Declaration on Human Rights
humanitarian intervention 39
Hungary, Soviet invasion (1956) 70
HZA Mainz v. Kupferberg 252

indigenous peoples 95–6, 112, 188–9, 190
see also self-determination
inquiry 50, 52
Inter-American Court of Human Rights 57–8
International Court of Justice:
ICJ cases
Aegean Sea Continental Shelf (1978) 50, 57, 251
Aerial Incident (1959) 252
Barcelona Traction (1970) 106
Corfu Channel (1949) 70, 82, 91, 224
Diplomatic Hostages (1980) 57, 59, 62, 64, 209, 224
Elettronica Sicula (1989) 64
Fisheries Jurisdiction (1974) 50, 57, 62, 122
Frontier Dispute (1986) 64, 202
Gulf of Maine (1984) 63, 233
Haya de la Torre (1951) 82
Headquarters Agreement (1988) 62
IMCO (1960) 226
Interhandel (1959) 82
Libya/Malta (1985) 208, 224
Lockerbie (1992) 80–1, 152, 159, 228
Namibia (1971) 18, 225, 241
Nicaragua (1984) 20, 21, 27, 56, 209, 224
Nicaragua (1986) 20–8, 31, 32, 33, 41–3, 57, 59, 61, 70, 71, 91–4, 111, 159
Nicaragua/Honduras (1988) 61, 62
North Sea Continental Shelf (1969) 20, 22, 62, 251
Norwegian Loans (1956) 82
Nottebohm (1955) 223
Peace Treaties (1950) 109
Right of Passage (1960) 224
South West Africa (1966) 119, 224, 225, 253
Tunisia/Libya Continental Shelf (1985) 62, 224, 251
PCIJ cases
Lotus (1927) 145, 206, 207, 221
Nationality Decrees (1923) 82, 86, 109, 223
chambers 57
'Optional clause' 20, 26–7, 55–6, 63

International Labour Organization 188
intervention *see* non-intervention
Iran–Iraq conflict 163, 249
Iran v US A/21 case 241, 253
Iran–US Claims Tribunal 55
Iraq, human rights 107
UN action (1991) 80, 163, 184, 218, 249
Israel, human rights 97, 114
Italian State v. X case (1985) 246, 253

Jan Mayen commission (1980) 52, 63
jus cogens 7

Kampuchea (1978) 71
Kelly and Macfarlane case 155
Kingdom of Greece v. F.R. Germany case 233
Kuwait v AMINOIL (1982) 63

La Bretagne case (1986) 63, 238, 253
Lac Lanoux case (1957) 122, 124, 128, 132
law of the sea *see* sea
Law of the Sea Convention, 1982 51, 53–4, 57, 123, 125, 126
League of Nations 72, 141, 160, 230
Lebanon (1985, 1982) 71, 74
Liberia (1990) 71
Littlejohn case 155

Maldives (1988) 74
Manila Declaration on Peaceful Settlement 33, 40
mediation 50, 52
Mill, J. S. 77, 79
minorities 177, 180, 182, 187, 189, 192
see also self-determination
Monroe Doctrine 71, 82–83

negotiation 50–2, 122
Non-Aligned Movement 35
non-intervention 32, 39, 40, 66–84, 85–119, 137, 140, 141, 186, 218

Northern Iraq–Kurds 163, 165, 168, 184, 219

offences against mankind 40, 46
opinio juris 9–27, 31, 41–2, 105
Organization of African Unity 58, 184–5
Organization of American States 58, 147

Panama (1989) 44, 71
Paris Charter for a New Europe (1990) 61, 184, 218
  see also CSCE
peaceful co-existence 2, 3, 29
Permanent Court of International Justice *see* International Court of Justice
pollution *see* environmental law

Rainbow Warrior case (1986) 60, 63, 224, 239, 240, 252

Savakar case 140
Scott case 140
sea, law of the 2, 22, 122
Secretary-General of the UN 162–4, 211, 222
self-defence 25–6, 38–9, 41
self-determination 7, 8, 25, 28, 39, 68, 96, 175–203, 212
Somalia (1977) 71, 74
  UN action (1992) 80, 81
soft law 11, 12, 24, 123
South Africa, human rights 97
Sovereignty 6, 204–29
Sri Lanka (1987) 71, 74
State responsibility 40, 41, 46, 106, 152, 209, 231

Taba case (Egypt/Israel) (1988) 63
territorial integrity 140–1, 189, 212, 213
  see also UN Charter article 2(4)
terrorism 137–59
Third World views
  'new' international law 2, 28
TOPCO v Libya (1977) 63
treaties, law of 18–19

Uganda (1976, 1978) 71, 74
UNCED (1992) 121
UNEP 121, 123
United Nations
  G.A. Resolutions, legal force 8–28, 36, 42–3
  Human Rights Commission 96–101, 104, 106
  Human Rights Committee 101–3, 116
  Security Council 140, 152–3, 160, 164, 168, 211, 219, 247, 249
  Sixth Committee 2, 34, 36
  Special Committee on Principles 4, 5, 25, 28, 38
  World Conference on Human Rights (1993) 91, 107

Universal Declaration of Human Rights 12, 101
uti possidetis 79

Vattel, E. de 75–7

Wolff, C. 75, 83

Yugoslavia, UN action (1992) 80–1

Zaire (1978) 71